D0875763

Literary History and the Challenge of Philology

The Legacy of Erich Auerbach

Figurae:

READING MEDIEVAL CULTURE

Literary History and the Challenge of Philology

The Legacy of Erich Auerbach

Edited by Seth Lerer

Stanford University Press, Stanford, California, 1996

Stanford University Press
Stanford, California
© 1996 by the Board of Trustees of the
Leland Stanford Junior University
Printed in the United States of America

CIP data appear at the end of the book

Stanford University Press publications are distributed exclusively
by Stanford University Press within the United States, Canada, Mexico,
and Central America; they are distributed exclusively
by Cambridge University Press throughout the rest of the world.

Acknowledgments

Support for the original conference at which these papers were offered was provided by the Departments of English and Comparative Literature and the Humanities Center of Stanford University. As organizer of the conference and as editor of this volume, I have the pleasure of thanking the Chairs of those departments, Martin Evans, Ronald Rebholz, Hans-Ulrich Gumbrecht; the Associate Director of the Humanities Center, Charles Junkerman; and the Associate Dean of Humanities and Sciences, Susan A. Stephens, for securing funding and encouraging this project. I am grateful, too, to R. Howard Bloch, Hayden White, John Bender, Herbert Lindenberger, and Gene Suarez for much welcome advice on the planning and organization of the conference; to Nancy Lerer for advice on matters of style and translation; to Kevin Brownlee for welcoming this collection into the Figurae series at Stanford University Press; to the Press's referees and to its Literature Editor, Helen Tartar, for rigorous yet supportive criticism; and to the contributors and participants at the conference for helping to make it such a memorable occasion.

S. L.

Contents

Contributors

KEVIN BROWNLEE is Professor of French at the University of Pennsylvania and the author of *Poetic Identity in Guillaume de Machaut*. His most recent editorial projects include, with Sylvia Huot, *Rethinking the Romance of the Rose* (Pennsylvania, 1992), and with Marina Brownlee and Stephen G. Nichols, *The New Medievalism* (Johns Hopkins, 1992).

LUIZ COSTA-LIMA is Professor of Theory of Literature and Comparative Literature at the Universidade do Estado do Rio de Janeiro. His most recent book in English is *The Dark Side of Reason: Fictionality and Power* (Stanford, 1992).

SUZANNE FLEISCHMAN is Professor of French at the University of California, Berkeley. Among her many publications on historical linguistics and sociolinguistics is *Tense and Narrativity: From Medieval Performance to Modern Fiction* (Texas, 1990).

JESSE M. GELLRICH is Professor of English at Louisiana State University and the author of *The Idea of the Book in the Middle Ages* (Cornell, 1985), and *Discourse and Dominion in the Fourteenth Century* (Princeton, 1995).

GEOFFREY GREEN is Professor of English at San Francisco State University. He has published on Freud, Nabokov, and Pynchon, and is the author of *Literary Criticism and the Structures of History: Erich Auerbach and Leo Spitzer* (Nebraska, 1982).

HANS ULRICH GUMBRECHT is the Albert Guérard Professor of Literature and former Chair of the Comparative Literature Department at Stanford University. A collection of his essays has recently appeared as *Making Sense in Life and Literature* (Minnesota, 1992), and his *Eine Geschichte der spanischen Literatur* will soon appear in an English translation from Stanford.

THOMAS R. HART has recently retired from the Department of Comparative Literature at the University of Oregon, where he edited the journal *Comparative Literature*. A student of Erich Auerbach's, he dedicated his recent *Cervantes and Ariosto* (Princeton, 1989) to his former teacher.

CARL LANDAUER is a lawyer and independent scholar living in San Francisco. He has published articles on modern German intellectual history, on Victorian culture, and on Ernst Robert Curtius and Erich Auerbach.

SETH LERER is Professor of English at Stanford University. His most recent book is *Chaucer and His Readers* (Princeton, 1993).

HERBERT LINDENBERGER is the Avalon Professor of the Humanities and Professor of English and Comparative Literature at Stanford University. He has published books on Wordsworth, historical drama, and opera, as well as the recent collection of essays *The History in Literature: On Value, Genre, Institutions* (Columbia, 1990).

STEPHEN G. NICHOLS is the James M. Beall Professor of French at the Johns Hopkins University. In addition to editing many collaborative volumes and the special January 1990 issue of *Speculum* devoted to the "New Philology," he is the author of *Romanesque Signs* (Yale, 1993).

BRIAN STOCK is Professor in the Centre for Comparative Literary Studies at the University of Toronto. The author of *Implications of Literacy* (Princeton, 1993) and other studies of medieval intellectual culture, he has recently completed a book on St. Augustine and the history of reading.

CLAUS UHLIG is Professor in the Institut für Anglistik und Amerikanistik at Philipps-Universität, Marburg. The author of books on courtly satire, Chaucer, and American literature, he has also published *Theorie der Literarhistorie* (Heidelberg, 1982).

HAYDEN WHITE has recently retired as Professor in the Program in the History of Consciousness at the University of California, Santa Cruz. Best known for his groundbreaking studies *Metahistory* (Johns Hopkins, 1973) and *Tropics of Discourse* (Johns Hopkins, 1978), he has also published *The Content and the Form* (Johns Hopkins, 1987).

Literary History and
the Challenge of Philology

The Legacy of Erich Auerbach

Seth Lerer

Introduction

Now the difference between legend and history is in most cases easily perceived by a reasonably experienced reader. It is a difficult matter, requiring careful historical and philological training, to distinguish the true from the synthetic or the biased in a historical presentation; but it is easy to separate the historical from the legendary in general. . . . To write history is so difficult that most historians are forced to make concessions to the technique of legend.

Philology is the set of activities that concern themselves systematically with human language, and in particular with works of art composed in language. . . . The need to constitute authentic texts manifests itself typically when a society becomes conscious of having achieved a high level of civilization, and desires to preserve from the ravages of time the works that constitute its spiritual patrimony.

Readers of Erich Auerbach's *Mimesis* will remember the first of these epigraphs as a moment in which history and legend fuse to mark the making of his book.[1] The famous story of Odysseus's scar has just been recollected, with its close attention to the detail of its characters and setting; and the story of the sacrifice of Isaac has been retold as a foil for the Homeric style, where the narratives of the Old Testament give us but little of the setting and the motivations of its actors. Auerbach, in his opening chapter, has been distinguishing between the legendary flavor of Homer and the historical feel of the Elohist, when he announces that such a distinction "can be easily perceived by a reasonably experienced reader." But what may not be so apparent, and what stands in the ellipses of my epigraph, is the history behind

the making of *Mimesis* itself, and the ways in which that history has
been transformed—by Auerbach, by later readers, and by the institutions of professional literary study—into a legend of the writer in exile,
remembering the texts and contexts of a past. What interrupts the
reading of Odysseus's scar, and what interrupts Auerbach's own career,
is "the history which we ourselves are witnessing": "Anyone who, for
example, evaluates the behavior of individual men and groups of men
at the time of the rise of National Socialism in Germany, or the behavior of individual people and states before and during the last war,
will feel how difficult it is to represent historical themes in general, and
how unfit they are for legend."[2] With the complexity of motives, the
bluntness of propaganda, and the ambiguities of political discourse, a
simple understanding of these public events becomes nearly unimagin-
able. No "careful historical and philological training" can distinguish
true from false, *das Wahre vom Gefälschten*, in these matters. "To write
history," he concludes, "is so difficult that most historians are forced to
make concessions to the technique of legend."

It is such moments in *Mimesis* that contribute to our understanding of the legacy of Erich Auerbach and help construct his place in
histories of criticism.[3] They separate him poignantly from his contemporaries, Leo Spitzer and Ernst Robert Curtius. All three are often
grouped together as the great exponents of a German philological tradition; yet, Spitzer is today largely remembered for his impassioned
if idiosyncratic teaching at Johns Hopkins and his acute application
of techniques of *explication de texte* to medieval and Renaissance works,
while Curtius remains, except to specialists in *Romanistik*, the distant
compiler of the *topoi* that fill *European Literature and the Latin Middle
Ages*.[4] It is the personal, the self-reflective, in Auerbach that late-
twentieth-century readers treasure, as if what marked the *magisterium*
of his work was the very suffering that brought him from Marburg, to
Istanbul, to Pennsylvania State, and finally to Yale where he died as
Sterling Professor of Romance Languages in 1957.[5]

The second epigraph is probably less well known to us. As the
opening sentences to an introductory handbook of Romance philology, a handbook written originally for the Turkish students of Auerbach's exile, they seem, at first glance, to articulate the verities of a
tradition rather than the idioms of an individual.[6] Their definition of
philology, the importance that they place on textual criticism, and

their loose associations between method and cultural understanding would have been familiar to most any European student at midcentury. With over a hundred years of institutional history behind them, Auerbach's opening lines affirm the centrality of philological investigation to recovering the character of "high civilization" and its origins.[7] They call to mind such affirmations of the "social value" of philology as those of Friedrich Diez in 1821 ("that the serious study of literature reveals utterly characteristic directions and tendencies in the mind of man");[8] of Charles Aubertin in 1874 ("L'histoire des origines de la langue est l'histoire même des origines de la nation");[9] and of the many late-nineteenth- and early-twentieth-century French and German attempts to locate the search for national identity in the curricula of language study.[10]

These opening texts, written most likely in the space of the same year, stand as the two poles of Auerbach's career and may introduce a reassessment of his project as a whole and of his reputation in the academic study of both medieval and modern literature. Both center on the techniques of recovery; both juxtapose a potentially destructive time against the endurance of culture; and both valorize the power of the philological-historical to distinguish true from false, the originary from the secondary, the authentic from the ersatz. They stimulate our efforts to separate out the historical from the legendary in the scholar's work and may become, for such a purpose, subjects of textual inquiry themselves. Much recent work has focused on the national origins and ideological consequences of the development of philology: on the tensions between French and German Romanists from the 1820's to World War I, on the agendas of post–World War II American New Criticism and the German revival of the *Grundriß* project, and on the changing status of medieval studies in the canons of professional training.[11] Some gestures have been made toward situating Auerbach in these various constellations, largely drawing on the more explicitly theoretical of his writings (the opening chapter of the early *Dante als Dichter des irdischen Welt* [1929] and the late essays "Philologie der Weltliteratur" [1952] and "Epilegomena zu *Mimesis*" [1953]).[12]

Relatively little has been made, however, of Auerbach's more subtle and complex adjudications between literary history and philology, and it is the goal of this volume of collected essays to redress somewhat this critical imbalance and, ideally, to provoke a reassessment of Auerbach's

place in the intellectual inheritance of the academy. The title of this
volume attends not to the balance between the two poles of Auerbach's
career, nor to an idealized synthesis constructed for him by later historians of criticism, but to the tensions between literary history and philology. The challenge of philology thus represents a twofold feature of
this tension. First, the discipline of philology as Auerbach conceived
it—the systematic investigation of human language, coupled with the
editorial restoration of those literary monuments that testify to the
historical development of individual vernaculars and the societies that
spoke them—poses a challenge to the study of style and genre that had
shaped the trajectory of *Literaturgeschichte*. As he had put it in "Philology
and Weltliteratur": "The inner history of the last thousand years is the
history of mankind achieving self-expression: this is what philology, a
historical discipline, treats."[13] Here, the challenge of philology is, in
some sense, a challenge to the philologist. The tensions in this view
lie in the space between "inner history" and "self-expression," in other
words, between the spiritual and social growth that marked the path
of western cultural experience and the literary and linguistic forms deployed to articulate, celebrate, or critique such a growth. Between the
representation of reality in literature and the chronicling of reality in
lived experience lies the domain of Auerbach's historical philologist.
     Second, the challenge of philology is the disciplinary challenge of a
craft. Historical linguistics, textual criticism, stylistic analysis—all are,
to put it coarsely, hard to do, and Auerbach returns again and again
to the need for training and the difficulties of deploying philological
knowledge with skill and subtlety. Whether in parsing out the clotted
lines of Einhard's Latin *Life of Charlemagne*[14] or unfolding the layers
of colloquial and literary diction that wrap up the tone and tenor of a
simple phrase of Dante's,[15] Auerbach displays in a highly self-conscious
manner the resources of his philological training to do nothing less
than cultural history. And yet, at moments such as these, Auerbach
is also concerned with perceiving these earlier authors as philologists
themselves: as writers acutely aware of language change and linguistic variety. The shifts among the diachronic and the synchronic—the
subject of professional linguistics since the nineteenth century—are
themselves subjects for writers from late antiquity through the early
modern period. Indeed, what defines periodicity for Auerbach at times
seems to be this consciousness of diachronic change and synchronic

variety. It separates the writers of the Late Antique from those of classical Rome; it makes of Dante the great vernacularist of medieval poetry; and, in a strikingly prescient assessment in the final chapter of *Mimesis*, it makes Virginia Woolf the paradigm of modernist self-consciousness.[16]

From such a viewpoint, Auerbach's notion of the historicity of philological inquiry may shift our understanding of the shape of his career and of the academic legacy his work bequeathed. The sense of Auerbach as the discerner of the "sermo humilis" in western Christian literature, as the discoverer and codifier of "figura" as the central mode of medieval literary discourse — this is the primary force of appreciation in the modern academy.[17] Literary realism, especially in earlier texts, is thus located at the nexus of the humble and the sublime. What I am suggesting, however, and what several of the essays in this collection have sought to argue, is that Auerbach's sense of the tensions in the history of literature is as much linguistic as stylistic: that, instead of seeking that synthesis between sermo humilis and sublimis as the keystone of the western cultural experience, we might productively find its tensions in the radical shifts of spoken dialects and the ossifications of literary forms that mark so much of western literature. The fissures noted in the final essay of *Literary Language and Its Public*, entitled "The Western Public and Its Language," show us a Europe on the cusp of classical and medieval, a Europe in which "a time had dawned and would long endure when the leading classes of society possessed neither education nor books nor even a language in which they could have expressed a culture rooted in their actual living conditions."[18]

It would, no doubt, be a great oversimplification to aver that Auerbach's preoccupations with a literary Europe in decline — with the politics of literary language and the language of literary politics — reflect his own experiences as a Jew in 1930's Germany, as an academic exile in Turkey, and, later, an intellectual émigré in America. And yet the question must arise, not just for the historian of literary criticism but for the practitioner of contemporary scholarship, of just what the relationship might be between Auerbach's philologically imagined literary history and the politically fractured world of mid-twentieth-century Europe, or between Auerbach's own life and work and those of academics at the close of the twentieth century. The legacy of Erich Auerbach, the subtitle of this collection, may thus be sought in a variety of places: in the critical reception of his writings, in the example of his career, in the inspiration of his choice of subjects, or in the reaction against his approaches and beliefs.

The vision painted of Auerbach in the legends of the European and American academy is of a scholar almost willfully detached from social activism. The various interpretations advocated for the origins of Auerbach's projects—their Hegelianism, their Viconianism, their commitments to a humanist philology—are in their own way curiously removed from the history of German university life between the World Wars.[19] And, to a certain extent, the criticisms of *Mimesis*'s reception in America after the war and of its embrace by the formalist New Critics, hinge on the criticism of the work itself: its lack of a self-conscious methodology, its apparent garbling of the theoretical and the historical.[20] This apprehension of the book is due largely to its first reviews by German and American readers. As Paul Bové has argued, the original reviews in American journals were by German émigrés who, apparently unfamiliar with Auerbach's work on Dante and figuralism, considered *Mimesis* an idiosyncratic collection of essays without guiding principles of method or of style.[21] The historical moment of its making, and its thematic and ideological consequences for the book were lost on early readers, who saw Auerbach's exile more as impediment than challenge to his project.[22] To Helmut Hatzfeld, who wrote the first American review in 1949, "the book was doomed to remain eclectic because of the working conditions of the author in Istanbul."[23] And to the audiences who heard him in the first Princeton Seminar in Literary Criticism (later to be called the Gauss Seminars) in the fall of 1949, Auerbach's personal experience was almost cinematically heroic. "A Jew, an *émigré* from Germany, for years homeless, putting his big book together in Istanbul without benefit of the great libraries he longed for, Auerbach had faced with his flesh and blood the reality of evil force; the extremity of Pascal's thought [the subject of the first seminar] answered, for him, an extremity of experience."[24]

These two sides to the book's early reception—the one flat, the other romantic—share nonetheless a predilection for effacing the political subtext to Auerbach's reflections. The Turkish exile is externalized, made either a problem in research or a badge of honor, yet nowhere relocated in the critic's narratives.[25] This depoliticizing of *Mimesis* is in the interest of the institutions of postwar academic criticism, and the emphases on sensitivity and belletrism in the early reviews do not indicate simply a misunderstanding on the part of Auerbach's contemporaries. They represent a conscious strategy to efface the disturbing political and personal themes of the book, and indeed, of Auerbach's career as a whole: to make it safe for the reader in the study, the student in the library, the connoisseur in that literary gallery where we may all breathe, in the words of one early reviewer, that "humane atmosphere" of intellectual comfort.[26] And in spite of the rigorous, ideological critiques of Paul Bové and Timothy Bahti,[27] the idealism of these early reviewers still informs contemporary understandings of the Auerbachian legacy. Jan Ziolkowski's foreword to the paperback republication of *Literary Language and Its Public* explains "the enduring relevance of Auerbach's criticism" as a function of "its own almost Balzacian integrity." What Ziolkowski sees as the "constancy of Auerbach in his self-understanding and in his lifelong engagement with European literature" offers an "indeed attractive" antidote to the "self-definitions of the professors" of "our days," and the "dizzying rapidity" of critical fashion: "the literary historian or critic of the day before yesterday became the deconstructionist or Marxist critic yesterday, only to become the cultural critic, New Philologist, or New Historicist today—and who would venture to wager how many ephemeral self-designations tomorrow holds in store?"[28]

The timeliness of Auerbach may, indeed, rest in his enduring alternative to a contemporary ephemerality. Yet such endurance is itself mixed with the critical anxieties of *Mimesis*'s own project. As Michael Holquist has discerned it, the exilic quality of Auerbach's work resonates with many of our own postmodern occupations with the act of writing as dialectic of exile and return. And Holquist furthermore suggests that, far from standing as a monument to a discarded Eurocentric criticism, *Mimesis* may itself "be perceived as a foundational document" of the recent turn to "cultural criticism."[29] Indeed, the very emphases on homelessness, on borderlands, and on the shifting status of the subject that defines the current culturalist turn may be discerned in Auerbach's own autobiographical subtext. The last moments of *Mimesis* end, he writes, "naturally with the last moments of its subject"—a subject that is both the West and the critic. Far from articulating a self-defined constancy, Holquist's Auerbach is the "great singer of diversity, [a] subtle opponent of all homogenizing forces."[30]

A century after his birth and fifty years after the composition of *Mimesis*, Auerbach still stands as a touchstone for contemporary academic debates on the place of historical criticism in the construction of literary history, on the relations between intellectual activity and political action, and on the function of the critic in recording—or effecting—social change. More than an occasion to review past accomplishments or revel in the nostalgias of prewar Marburg or postwar New Haven, the papers offered in this volume seek to reassess Auerbach's work and his example for the modern academic. Their genesis lay in a conference at Stanford University held in October 1992, and while they do not represent a consensus of opinion or a uniformity of school or approach, they all share the recognition of the timeliness of such a reassessment.

For Hans-Ulrich Gumbrecht, such a timeliness is itself the subject of Auerbach's professional career. Drawing on newly recovered documents from the Marburg State Archives, and dovetailing this archival research with a profound understanding of the political condition of the German intellectual, Gumbrecht helps the modern reader recover the centrality of both the "earthly" and the "everyday" that had formed the controlling interests of his scholarly life, from his early *Dane als Dichter des irdischen Welt*, to the concerns with *dargestellte Wirklichkeit* in *Mimesis*. Gumbrecht's essay thus opens this volume, not simply, then, to limn the biographical contours of Auerbach's existence but to urge us to historicize his critical practice in distinctively archival ways.

Historicizing Auerbach has, as its consequence, a new inquiry into Auerbach's historicism, in particular his sense of literary history. Claus Uhlig's essay reaffirms the origins of Auerbach's sense of history in Vico and Dante. Teasing out the tensions between the antitheoretical stance of Auerbach's writings and the profoundly theoretical challenges of Viconian history, Uhlig seeks to unmask the "hidden" theory behind the sweep of *Mimesis* and *Literary Language and Its Public*. By contrast, Luiz Costa-Lima's contribution historicizes the idea of literary history itself, tracing the legacy of eighteenth- and nineteenth-century inquiries into the nature of historical change and literary representation in order to discern Auerbach's "historical perspectivism." Auerbach, in Costa-Lima's reading, becomes less Balzacian than Flaubertian: a figure living out his historical predicament as an aesthetic condition.

The following two sets of papers seek to bring these theoretical concerns with literary history to bear on some of the specific techniques Auerbach deployed to understand relations between language and society, literature and belief. In the first set, Suzanne Fleischman, Stephen G. Nichols, and I inspect a particular example of his technique. Focusing on Auerbach the textual critic and historical philologist, these papers seek to understand the role of both in constructing the idea of the vernacular in Old French texts. They seek to reassess Auerbach's own treatise on philological practice, the *Introduction aux études de la philologie romane*, together with one of his most elaborate and explicit demonstrations of editorial method, the "Adam and Eve" chapter of *Mimesis*, in the contexts of modern sociolinguistics (Fleischman), 1940's fears of collaboration (Lerer), and the current ideological critiques of textual criticism (Nichols). In the second set, a pair of meditations on what may be Auerbach's most familiar bequeathal to historical criticism—the notion of "figura"—Hayden White and Jesse Gellrich seek to understand the genealogy and legacy of Auerbach's preoccupations with this term. In the process, they not only interrogate Auerbach's own historical practice (by questioning, for example, the precise sources for his terminology), but also refigure the conception of figura as a trope of modernism.

Refiguring these relations between the medieval and the modern may provoke new inquiries into Auerbach's notions of literary periodization and the relations between shifts in style and discourse and shifts in cultural self-definition. The Late Antique and the late medieval are, for Auerbach as well as for more recent intellectual historians, the moments that not only emblematize the problem of periodicity itself but also compel the construction of new canons of literariness to incorporate the products of those times. The essays of Brian Stock and Kevin Brownlee take these two periods, respectively, not just to reexamine Auerbach's conception of historical change, but to take from the suggestions of *Mimesis* and *Literary Language and Its Public* and define anew the contours of the "late" in literary history. Their essays illustrate, as well, the legacy of Auerbach's choices, and they may thus be appreciated as new contributions to the study of those periods that *Mimesis* and *Literary Language* helped to canonize.

The contributions of Stock and Brownlee—as well as those of Fleishman and Nichols—suggest some of the ways in which the legacy of Auerbach as a philologist and literary historian may shape our own contemporary practice of these disciplines. This volume's concluding group of essays charts the various social, intellectual, and institutional environments in which that legacy was passed to American critics. Lindenberger, Green, Landauer, and Hart—drawing both on ideological critiques and personal experiences—chronicle the vicissitudes of Auerbach's *Nachleben*, showing, in effect, that the nature of the Auerbachian project may be as much constructed by his readers as developed by its author. This closing set of essays on *Rezeptionsgeschichte* historicizes the current reader and, in so doing, helps us to understand the legacy of Erich Auerbach not just as literary historian or historical philologist but as an example for current academic practice.

To return to Auerbach's work in the last decade of the twentieth century is to rephrase its maxims about history and legend.

Let the reader think of the history which we ourselves are witnessing; anyone who, for example, evaluates the behavior of individual men and groups of men at the time of the rise of National Socialism in Germany, or the behavior of individual peoples and states before and during the last war, will feel how difficult it is to represent historical themes in general, and how unfit they are for legend; the historical comprises a great number of contradictory motives in each individual. . . . To write history is so difficult that most historians are forced to make concessions to the technique of legend.

One may say today that to live historically is so difficult that most of us are forced to make concessions to the narratives of literature. This tension between the distance of past literary works and the immanence of present social life may speak directly to current debates on academic humanism and on the place of an archival historical criticism in the university curriculum. As this volume may illustrate, a career in scholarship—whether Auerbach's or our own—is one of continual renegotiations of the scholar's pact with the past and of his or her responsibilities to a politically charged present.

Part I

The Everyday and History

Hans Ulrich Gumbrecht

"Pathos of the Earthly Progress": Erich Auerbach's Everydays

This portrait of the great philologist Erich Auerbach[1] will be based on the contrast between two meanings of the concept "everydayness." Facing a surprising scarcity of documents and testimonies (which may well reflect an intention of Auerbach),[2] I will try to describe the particular style and attitude that shaped his everyday life. Such biographical components of my essay, however, will appear in conjunction with a concept of "everydayness" that played a crucial role in western intellectual history during the early decades of the twentieth century. Everydayness became an epistemological issue during the 1890's as a substitute for the philosophical notion of "truth"; it contributed to the emergence of "sociology" as an academic discipline, and it certainly had an impact on what was to become Erich Auerbach's predominant research interest, "the serious representation of everyday reality in literature."[3] As a legitimation for focusing on such a correspondence between Auerbach's life and his work, I can refer to a short remark from the introduction to his last book, Literary Language and Its Public in the Late Antiquity and in the Middle Ages.[4] *There, in uncharacteristically strong terms, Auerbach expresses his disagreement with the habit of contemporary New Criticism to disregard the author's biography in the interpretation of literary texts. "What we understand and love in a work," he writes, "is the existence of a human being as a possibility for our own being." Very much in this sense (and very much, thus, from the perspective of an intellectual concern that has become historical for us), it is the "existential meaning"[5] of the topic "serious representation of everyday reality" for Erich Auerbach that I will seek to approach from the angle of a "mutual clarifica-*

tion" ("wechselseitige Erhellung," as the Germanist Oskar Walzel used to say in the 1920's) between his life and his work.

Auerbach's Dismissal

On September 23, 1935, Erich Auerbach wrote a letter from Rome, where he had spent a late summer vacation, to Walter Benjamin in Paris. Auerbach and Benjamin, who were both born in 1892, had probably known each other since the early 1920's,[6] but they remained distant enough to maintain the formal *Sie* in their short exchange of letters. The impulse for the renewal of this contact, as Auerbach explicitly mentions, came with the publication of an excerpt from Benjamin's *Berliner Kindheit um Neunzehnhundert* in the *Neue Zürcher Zeitung* (Saturday, September 21, 1935),[7] which Auerbach's wife Marie had first discovered and, in the specific political climate of that time, read with strong emotions. Erich Auerbach's letter itself leaves no doubt about how much he was aware, by the summer of 1935, that sooner or later he would have to leave his position as a professor of Romance philology at the University of Marburg and share the fate of emigration with Benjamin:

We are healthy; I am still in office, but I make very little use of my status. My junior colleague [*Privatdozent*] Werner Krauss is teaching the main lecture course and the seminar, and he is also holding the examinations; he turns out to be a big success on every level. It is more than questionable whether I will be able to offer any courses at all during the winter semester; nevertheless, it is possible; it is impossible, however, to give you an idea of the strangeness of my situation.[8]

While enumerating details about the everyday academic life in Marburg that could hardly interest Benjamin, Auerbach, throughout his letter, writes from the perspective of an outside observer. His mild irony recalls the tone in some nineteenth-century novels, and it appears much more enigmatic to us than the "strangeness of the situation" described. This peculiar tone was probably an inevitable ingredient of a personal style that strictly avoided any dramatic expressions and complaints.

As he had correctly expected, Auerbach would never teach the three courses announced in the Marburg *Vorlesungsverzeichnis* for the winter semester 1935–36 (ironically, the first Marburg *Vorlesungsverzeichnis* printed in Gothic letters) as "History, Methods, and Instruments of Romance Philology," "Giambattista Vico," and "Colloquium on the Dogmatic Content of Selected Romance Texts."[9] On October 16, 1935, immediately before the beginning of the teaching period, the long-expected letter of dismissal by the *Universitätskurator* Ernst von Hülsen[10] was sent to Auerbach's private address at Friedrichstrasse 3:

After our conversation held yesterday and your confirmation in regard to the decree of the National and Prussian Minister of Science, Schools, and Popular Education of October 14, 1935 . . . , concerning those Jewish civil servants with two racially full-Jewish grandparents, I release you in the name of the above-mentioned Minister from all your duties previously fulfilled at the University of Marburg. This decree is effective immediately.[11]

The procedural accuracy of this document cannot conceal the time pressure under which the legal authorities were operating. They must have been obsessed with the intention not to begin the academic year 1935–36 with any active participation by Jewish professors. Only one day after the publication of the relevant decree at the Ministry in Berlin, Auerbach was cited before the provost, and on the following day he received the official letter of dismissal. The subsequent document announcing Auerbach's forced retirement from the status of a German civil servant (with a handwritten addition explaining the incompatibility between this status and the loss of German citizenship for Jews since November 14, 1935) was written on December 23, 1935, and effective as of January 1, 1936. Some of the Jewish professors, however, especially World War veterans such as Auerbach, would receive a pension whose exact amount was yet to be determined. According to the German academic tradition, closure of this procedure was reached when, on January 23, 1936, the Berlin Ministry gave permission to the University of Marburg to replace Auerbach. By the same standards, however, it was highly irregular that this permission contained a clause urging the Marburg authorities to give specific attention to Professor Schürr from the University of Graz (who probably was a member of the National Socialist Party, and who indeed would soon receive and accept the respective offer).[12]

The Italian vacation during which Auerbach resumed his contact with Benjamin seems to have marked an important change in his evaluation of the life conditions under the Third Reich. In a letter to Benjamin which bears the date of October 6 and was mailed from

Florence, his mild irony interferes with a harsh perspective of self-criticism:

Concerning Marburg, I could tell endless anecdotes, but it is impossible to write them down—and this not only has to do with external reasons. All over, there was not much wisdom required . . . , only a certain amount of composure (which was not always easily available). Besides, there was more foolishness than wisdom. At Marburg, I am living among people who are not of our origin, and whose conditions are very different—but who, nevertheless, think exactly as we do. This is wonderful, but it implies a temptation for foolishness; the temptation consists in the illusion that there is a ground to build upon—although individual opinions (however numerous they may be) simply do not count. Only this voyage liberated me from my error.[13]

Auerbach's reference to his "foolishness" was an allusion to academic (and perhaps even social) normality that came out of an ideal working situation at Marburg. Although he was yet far from being acknowledged as a nationally (or internationally) outstanding literary critic, and although the 1920's as the greatest intellectual moment of his university's *Philosophische Fakultät* had ended before Auerbach's appointment, he was surrounded by a small group of seemingly outstanding students and by a number of interesting and, by any contemporary German standards, liberal colleagues. But what Auerbach considered to be the best aspect of his situation was the collaboration with Werner Krauss, who had been recommended to him by Karl Vossler, the then-undisputed leader of *Romanische Philologie*.[14] Having finished a doctoral dissertation on Spanish medieval literature at the University of Munich in 1929, Krauss came to Marburg in 1931, where, with strong (moral rather than intellectual) support from Auerbach, he reached the status of *Privatdozent* in 1932.[15] While, according to the German university tradition, it can be considered normal that Krauss was not appointed to become Auerbach's successor after the latter's emigration in 1935, several initiatives to offer professorial positions to Krauss at other German universities failed due to his eccentric character—which National-Socialist scholars were reading, correctly from their perspective, as a symptom of his lack of political reliability.[16] In August 1940 Krauss was drafted by the Wehrmacht as an interpreter for the analysis of Spanish press reports. He worked in Berlin, where the Gestapo arrested him as a member of the resistance-organization Rote Kapelle on November 24, 1942, ironically only four months after his appointment to the rank of *Ausserordentlicher Professor* at Marburg. He was sentenced to death in January 1943 by a jury whose chair was an SS officer.[17] Krauss's survival was due to one of the most unbelievable rescue missions undertaken on behalf of potential victims of the Third Reich. Seemingly at the initiative of his friend, the philosopher Hans Georg Gadamer (who by 1943 had become a professor at Leipzig), a number of colleagues from the University of Marburg[18] argued for an appeal of Krauss's death-sentence, presenting his eccentric behavior as evidence of a schizophrenic condition. Among other "clinical symptoms" it was mentioned, in this context, that Krauss had been conceived following a deep crisis in his parents' marriage and that, during his Marburg years, the daily shaving had regularly left traces of blood on his face. Without ever having met Krauss, Professor Kretschmer, the director of the Psychiatric Clinic at Marburg who was highly respected by the Nazi authorities,[19] confirmed the pertinence of these "observations."[20] A retrial was opened on December 30, 1943, and in September 1944 Krauss's death sentence was reduced to five years of jail. After the end of the war Werner Krauss came back to Marburg where the permission to return to his former academic position was issued only after a lengthy bureaucratic procedure.[21] As no initiative was taken to appoint him to a full professorship, and, more important, as he became increasingly pessimistic about the political future in the western "zones" of Germany, he accepted an offer to become full professor at Leipzig in 1947. Twenty-nine years later Werner Krauss died in East Berlin. He had become the founder of the only school of Marxist literary historians in "his" country whose research remains important even from a post-1989 perspective. Until Auerbach's death in 1957, Krauss stayed in contact with the mentor of his early Marburg years.

Auerbach's Composure

"Composure," the attitude that Auerbach had emphasized as a necessary but not always easily available state of mind in his second Italian letter to Benjamin, had been an important concept in Heidegger's *Existentialphilosophie* since the publication of *Being and Time* in 1927. There, it appeared as related to the central capacity of "authentic existence" to face death "with open eyes" as the inevitable fate of human existence. Much more than for Werner Krauss in his struggles with the

vicissitudes of German history, this attitude became indeed a leitmotiv
for Erich Auerbach's life. Proud of his Prussian education, he made
every possible effort to maintain behavior of perfect normality under
the National Socialist regime and to fulfill the most absurd duties imposed upon Jewish civil servants (*Beamte*) after January 30, 1933. Sometimes these duties did not even formally exist, as was the case during
the spring break of 1934 when Auerbach formally asked the *Rektor* of
his University for the permission to spend some days of vacation in
"Rapallo, perhaps also in Florence." [22] Only a few months later, on
September 19, 1934, he swore the "German civil servants' oath of allegiance" to Adolf Hitler. The fact that the month of August which
was printed as the anticipated date on the official form of confirmation for this procedure was substituted by a handwritten "Sept." could
suggest that Auerbach had tried to postpone the ceremony as long
as possible. When, through an organization specializing in negotiating university positions outside of Germany for German academics,[23]
Auerbach received an offer from Istanbul in the summer of 1936, he
submitted a translation of his new contract to the University of Marburg and to the Ministry in Berlin and did not leave the country before
receiving the official permission allowing him to take residence up in
Turkey. Despite the increasingly life-threatening situation he and his
family faced in Germany, and despite considerable time pressure from
his prospective employer in Istanbul, Auerbach successfully negotiated
the possibility of returning after 1941 to what he continued to consider
his "fatherland." His then still unbroken belief in the legality of the
German institutions appears in the authorization of a Berlin lawyer[24]
to represent him in still open financial requisitions.

Quite literally, however, Auerbach's file as a *Beamter* at the University of Marburg was still far from being closed after his departure to
Istanbul. Several inquiries from the local tax office make it clear that
at least some German authorities felt uncomfortable about his having
obtained the permission to return. A far more dramatic express letter from the Minister of Science, Education, and Public Instruction
reached the Marburg provost on November 24, 1936:

I just received information indicating that the professional activity of Professor Dr. Auerbach abroad may be in conflict with German politico-cultural
interests, because Professor Auerbach is judged negatively from a political
perspective. . . . I therefore request an accelerated complementary report

concerning the facts on which your approval was based. A comment of the Party representative for the Marburg faculty [*Führer der Dozentenschaft*] has to be added.

Despite the provost's favorable (and strangely formal) answer to this inquiry, the party representative Düring[25] wrote the following comment to the minister:

According to my observations, Professor Auerbach used to maintain an attitude of extreme political reservation during his employment at Marburg. This notwithstanding, he has always been against National Socialism in his convictions. One cannot expect that he will further the interests of the Third Reich abroad in any significant way. Rather, I hold it to be inappropriate to let Jews travel abroad as representatives of German scholarship because, from a long-term perspective, this will inevitably have pernicious effects.

A final document confirming the impression that Auerbach's emigration had not marked the end of his interactions with the authorities of the National Socialist state is a report on his activities in Turkey established by the German Consulate General and dated January 4, 1941. Astonishingly, it was motivated by Auerbach's request to extend the permission of his residence abroad. In its tone, this report appears inconclusive[26]—and it produced a strangely inconclusive bureaucratic decision. "For reasons of principle," the Minister did not extend the permission for Auerbach's residency in Istanbul, but he neither obliged him to return to Germany. Even the financial situation of the (former?) civil servant remained unresolved.[27]

Auerbach's Fascination

It has often been said—and it is certainly true—that the reading of Vico, which stood at the beginning of Auerbach's career as a humanist and accompanied him through the later stages of his life,[28] was a decisive formative experience. From Vico came the conviction that everything created by humans—and only things created by humans—could be objects of interpretation and understanding. From Vico Auerbach had learned how historical understanding needs to find an appropriate perspective for each period in time. Because of the philosophical position in which such perspectivism is grounded, it excludes belief in general laws of historical change as well as in transhistorical struc-

tures of human life. At the same time, historical perspectivism relies on
"philological truth" as *certum* in opposition to a more ambitious concept of "philosophical truth" as *verum*.[29] Finally, one might even argue
that Vico's work inspired Auerbach's interpretation of his own time as
one where European culture in its traditional form and meaning had
reached a stage of exhaustion.[30]

But this conception of history and this method of historical interpretation, in spite of all their complexity, do not explain why, among
an infinite number of possible topics and questions, the "serious representation of everyday reality" almost exclusively occupied Auerbach's
attention throughout his career. In addition, even if we take this thematic selection for granted, the question remains how everyday reality
relates to concepts such as "fate," "drama," or "tragedy" that Auerbach constantly used when he moved from the level of strictly textual
analysis to more philosophical (and not always very original) reflections
about human existence.[31] The answer to these questions establishes a
link between Auerbach's own everyday life and his fascination with the
concept of everyday reality, between his biography and his work. For
in order to bear the inevitability of fate and the tragedies of everyday
reality, *composure* is required. In other words, composure as a style of
behavior was just the other side of that world experience which the historical environment imposed upon Auerbach and whose illustrations
he sought in the European literary tradition. The most complete account of this conceptual configuration can be found in his book *Dante,
Poet of the Secular World*, which Auerbach published in 1929 and which,
during the same year, he submitted as a *Habilitationsschrift* to the University of Marburg.[32] Its motto, printed in Greek and Latin characters on
the first page, is Heraclitus's maxim "A man's character is his fate."[33]
This opening announces the main perspective in Auerbach's reading
of the *Divina Commedia*. For him Dante was the first European poet
who had painted characters in their individuality. Auerbach's concept
of individuality, however, emphasized the "earthly" aspects of human
life—probably because he shared the intellectual concern, typical of
the 1920's,[34] of defining "authenticity" as a unity of body and spirit:
"Ever since its beginnings in Greece, European literature has possessed the insight that a man is an indivisible unity of body (appearance
and physical strength) and spirit (reason and will), and that his individual fate follows that unity, which like a magnet attracts the acts and
sufferings appropriate to it."[35]

With "fate" and "authenticity" shaping the notion of "individuality" developed in *Dante, Poet of the Secular World*, Auerbach's most important interpretive innovation lay in the hypothesis that the *Divina Commedia* unfolded two further implications of individuality, "namely, the idea . . . that individual destiny is not meaningless, but . . . necessarily tragic and significant, and that the whole world context is revealed in it."[36] Individuality, however, comes into play not only *as fate* and as the origin of tragedy. At the same time individuality *as form* is presented as that principle that alone can maintain and even assert itself against tragedy. Through this very aspect, according to Auerbach, tragic individuality in Dante can be distinguished from the representation of human personality in the classical Greek tragedies:

That struggle, which stands out most clearly in Sophocles, is such that those who enter into it lose a part of their individual nature; they are so caught up in their extreme plight, so carried away by the final struggle, that nothing remains of their personality but their age, sex, position in life, and the most general traits of their temperament; their actions, their words and gestures are wholly governed by the dramatic situation, that is, by the tactical requirements of their struggle.[37]

But while it is comparatively easy to analyze how this particular philosophical configuration emerged in Auerbach's work under the impact of his contemporary intellectual environment,[38] the biographical documents do not explain the decision, crucial for his career, to submit the Dante book as *Habilitationsschrift* to the University of Marburg.

On September 26, 1929, the Prussian Minister for Science, Art, and Popular Education transferred the *Bibliotheksrat* Erich Auerbach from his position at the Prussian State Library in Berlin, where he had been working since 1923, to the Marburg University Library. A purely bureaucratic maneuver that allowed Auerbach to begin his career as an academic teacher at Marburg without losing his status as civil servant,[39] this procedure became another trial for his composure. Three weeks before the ministry's decision became effective, the Marburg provost had sent a letter to the director of the Prussian State Library inquiring whether Auerbach's economic situation would justify the plan to let him teach without any remuneration. Clarifying that Auerbach's salary was supposed to come from his new employment at the Marburg Library, the negative answer from Berlin ended with the following paragraph: "We do not have any precise information concerning

Dr. Auerbach's private sources of income. Seemingly, he enjoyed a privileged financial situation in the past, but I believe that he suffered considerable losses during the inflation." Only half a year later, in March 1930, Auerbach had to return 253.71 Reichsmark (about half of what was then his monthly salary) to the ministry, for an overpayment received in 1927. He fulfilled this obligation in two installments — which indirectly seems to confirm the State Library's opinion about his financial situation.[40]

Such administrative problems (and their solutions) indicate that the initiative for Auerbach's transfer came from the ministry in Berlin rather than from the University of Marburg. This interpretation casts some doubt on the widespread assumption that his recruitment into the academic world was a master plan designed by Leo Spitzer, who then held the chair of Romance philology at Marburg. In contrast to all the complicated bureaucratic transactions, however, Auerbach had passed the preceding academic ritual of his *Habilitation* during the summer semester of 1929 as smoothly as any external candidate. Among the reports written by the senior faculty members, there was but one slightly negative remark, which itself appears to have been quite typical of the German politico-intellectual climate around 1930: the Anglicist Deutschbein observed that in a passage of Auerbach's Dante book "the misleading expression 'Germanic *barbarians*' should be deleted in any scholarly treatise." In addition, we may assume that the Latinist Lommatzsch (who simply expressed his agreement with the generally positive judgment of his colleagues) was not especially happy with the prospect of having Auerbach among his colleagues. As a former professor at the University of Greifswald, Lommatzsch had given Auerbach the lowest possible grade (*rite*) on his Ph.D. exam in 1921. More important — and more surprising — than such details, however, is the fact that Leo Spitzer's extremely laudatory and, by contemporary standards, very long report on *Dante, Poet of the Secular World* did not dedicate a single word to Auerbach's intellectually central concern with the serious representation of individuality and everyday tragedy. With a clarity that makes any interpretation superfluous, the initial paragraph of Spitzer's text shows that, while he was somehow aware of the contrast between Auerbach's professional style and his own, he could not help reading the younger colleague's book as an intervention within a scholarly debate. Nothing was more remote from the academic image that Auerbach began to cultivate during those years than such an attitude, but nothing, on the other hand, was more characteristic of Spitzer's own professional identity:

Uninterrupted by any polemical remarks, the smoothly balanced, elegant tone of Auerbach's Dante book could make the reader forget that the author pursues an extremely polemical goal in his rigorous critique of B. Croce and K. Vossler, two leading contemporary Dante scholars. He fights Croce's intention of separating the poetic beauties of the *Commedia* (as the only aspect that has remained meaningful for us) from the system of medieval knowledge displayed in Dante's text. . . . And he also fights Vossler's opinion according to which Dante thematizes less the earthly world or the celestial world in his poem than his own life and personality.

While Spitzer's description of the differences between Auerbach's reading of the *Commedia* and the interpretations by Croce and Vossler was certainly adequate, he overestimated by far Auerbach's willingness as an intellectual to engage in polemical debates—and he was therefore blind to the latter's "existential" concern. This complex incompatibility between Spitzer's critical and personal temperament and his own did not escape Auerbach's attention. Having obtained the *Habilitation* for Romance philology on July 13, 1929, and after his first concrete experience in academic teaching during the winter semester 1929–30, Auerbach wrote a long retrospective on the initial stage of his university career in a letter to his friend Ludwig Binswanger, a student of French literature who did not hold an academic position.[41] Emphasizing that he considered his impression as yet far from definitive, and mentioning a generally friendly reception on the "positive side" of his experience, Auerbach continued with what he called the "comedy of Spitzer and the students"—and also the "problematic side, to say the least" of his account:

Spitzer is the son of a Viennese Jew and an opera singer. He is full of activity and tactlessness, he has very lively ideas and not even a shadow of culture and true critical spirit, he is very cordial, very malicious, very presumptuous, very insecure, very emotional, he is open-hearted beyond belief, and a born comedian. He is incapable of sitting still for a moment, he must always work, dance, love, move, and set others into motion. In general, I like him fine, and I can learn a lot from him. But he does not have the slightest idea of what I am like; both in his admiration and his critique he always fails, and our friendship is a tissue of misunderstandings. At the same time, he believes it to be his right and his mission to educate me. You should see him. The face of a comedian, always ahead, a long and baroque nose, with his curls beginning to turn grey, always on the street with a coat that is too short. And this man loves the students, is wooing for their sympathy, gives them his whole heart, and relies on their judgment.

Regardless whether this caricature does justice to Spitzer,[42] it accounts for Auerbach's need to define his own identity against the presence of a figure who, only five years his senior, had long before emerged as the child prodigy of their common profession. Nothing was more opposed to an ideal of composure and to a tragical sentiment of everyday life than Auerbach's image of Spitzer, and it is therefore not surprising that, next to Spitzer, he felt "like a little grey eminence."[43]

When Auerbach wrote his letter to Binswanger in March 1930, he was probably not yet aware that Spitzer had accepted an offer from the University of Cologne during those very weeks. As early as April 26, 1930, Auerbach was officially charged with replacing Spitzer for the summer semester and, seemingly without any search,[44] he was appointed full professor for Romance philology by the University of Marburg on October 28, 1930. But Spitzer's intellectual and institutional absence did not free Auerbach's mind from Spitzer's haunting presence. One of Auerbach's first publications as an *Ordinarius* was a review of Spitzer's *Romanische Stil- und Literaturstudien* in which, with the gesture of a true grey eminence, he complained about the tension between Spitzer's eminent talent and his lack of maturity:

Sometimes it appears as if he [Spitzer] wanted to beat the work of art with his own imitating words. And what words does he often use! This master of style criticism has not yet found his own style, and meanwhile he compensates for this lack with poorly chosen models. Often we find phrases that remind us of outdated journalistic fashions, and it is not without pride that Sp. uses the favorite words of the literary authors of 1918. Therefore, we can only occasionally and randomly agree with him, and the admiration and sympathy caused by every page of his book is tempered with the regret that such a vast and exact knowledge, such an almost unprecedented talent, and such a passionate mind can lack so much interior reflection and cultivation.[45]

These harsh words by the newly appointed professor were published in 1932 — and, as if to continue their puzzling play of mutual provocations, Spitzer invited Auerbach to Cologne for a lecture during the same year. Auerbach replied with yet another gesture in the style of an *éminence grise* when he wrote the following sentence into the guest book of the Cologne institute: "Our object is not the lore of Being and Culture, but rather '*that* Rome whence Christ is Roman.'" [46] Taking distance from the high-flying philosophical and pedagogical discourses of his time, these words show how Auerbach became increasingly secure in his role "as member, sufferer, and unbeliever" of western culture, and as "the bookish, textual self-teacher, the expounder of difficult texts, the surviving member of a great culture, the sensitive receptor of ideological crosswinds, the deliverer of himself." [47]

In the preface to his book *Deutscher Geist in Gefahr*, Spitzer's and Auerbach's colleague Ernst Robert Curtius had given a bleak description of the political scenery in Germany at the turn of the year 1931–32: "Everybody in Germany feels that the year we are entering will be a year of great decisions. . . . Germany is trembling in convulsions, and we have but *one* hope left: our situation must improve because it cannot get any worse." [48] While Curtius was passionately pleading for the renewal of a somehow vague humanism against the threat of an anti-intellectualism which he attributed, without any distinction, to fascists and bolsheviks,[49] Auerbach described to Binswanger the "enchanting journeys to the Neckar- and Main-valley, and to Italy" which he had undertaken during the year 1932 with his family in their Ford convertible. He seemed to be in a strangely optimistic mood: "I don't find our days so deeply entrenched in marasmus, I think that life is coming back from many directions; of course I am no longer really a part of it, but neither do I bother." [50] Composure had given Auerbach a distance from the tragic of everyday life, and it provided the calm of privacy. But it also came at the price of political short-sightedness.

Auerbach's Environment

Erich Auerbach's fascination with everyday reality was part of an important epistemological shift within western culture whose beginnings go back to the late nineteenth century.[51] The search for absolute truth, which had become a political program during the age of Enlightenment, was progressively given up and replaced by the more pragmatic concern with "everydayness" and "reality" as that which was a necessary—and sufficient—ground for action and interaction.

This substitution generated such manifold reactions and so many different cultural consequences that in a historical retrospective of the decades after 1900, the German poet Gottfried Benn spoke of "reality" as "Europe's demonic concept."[52]

Paradoxically, however, the loss of truth as a guarantee for the possibility of cognitive and existential certainty led to a transfer of certain functions and expectations from the truth concept to the new concepts of reality as its substitutes. With a strong anti-intellectual affect, Martin Heidegger based the ontology he unfolded in *Being and Time* on "average everydayness."[53] Likewise, the notion of "life-world" emerged as a ground for practical orientation in Edmund Husserl's reaction to the "Crisis of European Science," which set the agenda for the final stage of his work.[54] On the other hand, the increasingly complex reality concept became a criterion that made possible the critique of certain contemporary phenomena as characterized by "a lack of substance"—and therefore "unreal." A typical example is Oswald Spengler's analysis of the medium of money in the final chapters of his *Decline of the West*, first published in 1918:

The dictature of money marches on, tending to its material peak, in the Faustian civilization as in every other. And now something happens that is intelligible only to one who has penetrated to the essence of money. If it were anything tangible, then its existence could be forever—but, as it is a form of thought, *it fades out as soon as it has thought its economic world to finality*, and has no more material upon which to feed.[55]

More than any specific political or economic conditions of the early twentieth century (and certainly more than any philosophical arguments), the experience of the above-described shift from a truth-based to a reality-based epistemology *as a loss* or *as a decline* probably caused its frequent coupling with utterly pessimistic views of human existence. Such configurations were recurrent on every level of intellectual quality—from Martin Heidegger's insistence on the necessity of facing death as the defining condition of human life and Miguel de Unamuno's internationally influential (but conceptually poor) essays on *El sentimiento trágico de la vida* and *La agonía del Cristianismo* from 1912 and 1926.

Finally, such feelings of loss and decline, of tragedy and emptiness, motivated a growing desire for compensation, a need to find a new ground, or to oppose something "substantial" to this "existential void." With firsthand realities appearing as desubstantiated, such compensations were not readily available—and this situation explains the concern of the intellectual movement called the "Conservative Revolution"[56] with such singular tasks as the re-creation of Nature or the reinvention of Myth.[57] Even re-created Nature or reinvented Myth, however, did not bring back the security and the concreteness of a given ground, and therefore *concreteness of form* as an aesthetic achievement became a site of intellectual and artistic convergence. For some of the historical protagonists, as for Auerbach's colleague Karl Vossler, this reaction turned into a concern with the elegance of their behavior.[58] In the work of Ernst Robert Curtius it led to the identification of culture with a repertoire of rhetorical figures inherited from classical antiquity. Heidegger's ideal of "authentic existence" was motivated not by ethical arguments but rather by the implicitly aesthetic contrast between authenticity and the anonymous "They" (*das Man*). The evocation of this context makes us understand that Auerbach's personal composure and his fascination with the representation of individual character emerged out of a historically specific perspective on human existence, a perspective that gave existential value to the dimension of form.

Auerbach's Progress

For Germans of Auerbach's generation, the final examination before graduating from high school, the so-called *Abitur*, marked one of the most important biographical thresholds.[59] In the lives of many outstanding scholars a brilliantly passed *Abitur* figures as the debut of an unusual intellectual career. Erich Auerbach's *Abitur* at Berlin's prestigious Französisches Gymnasium during the fall of 1911, in contrast, could at best have been the introduction to a narrative of "late vocation." The evaluations he received from his teachers did not show the slightest signs of enthusiasm: "Indolent by nature and shunning any continuous intellectual effort, this gifted student was mostly superficial and inadequate in the fulfillment of his duties."[60] For a young man from a well-to-do family of merchants—especially for a young man who had not yet shown any specific talents or inclinations—the most normal decision was to study the law, as Erich Auerbach did at the universities of Berlin, Freiburg, Munich, and Heidelberg after 1911.[61] But his receipt, in July 1913, of a doctoral degree in law at the University of Heidelberg after less than two years of studies was certainly unusual, even by early twentieth-century standards.[62] In his first dissertation Auerbach discusses different ways of dealing with the problem of coperpetration, and this topic established a relationship between his intellectual beginnings and the central fascination of his work as a literary historian. Combining a component of guilt with a component of innocence, the role of the coperpetrator contains in its very structure a potential for tragedy. Although it is difficult to discover any inclination toward a specific dogmatic solution to this problem, Auerbach obviously relished inventing everyday examples of coperpetration and pointing to paradigmatic cases from the tradition of European literature. The following quotation is one of many passages where he shifts from a more abstract argument to a demonstration *"in modo concreto"* (as he frequently describes his own discourse):

In this context, we have to insist that the distinction between persons with free determination and persons without free determination is quite unsatisfying. Even if one postulates the possibility of free determination, it cannot be denied that there are cases in which a person has spiritual power over another person . . . , and in which any possibility of free determination is excluded for the person who finds himself or herself under somebody else's influence. We find many examples for this situation in everyday life. (2) Whether such a situation is actually given must be decided in each concrete case. [Text of footnote (2):] Examples are Don Quijote and Sancho Pansa; Adelheid's impact on Wieslingen and Franz; Kätchen von Heilbronn; Savonarola. As we see, most of these cases have to do with erotic fascination or religious ecstasy. Until recently, the legal practice underestimated the importance of such cases.[63]

The literary culture displayed in his legal dissertation makes plausible the smooth transition toward literary studies that Auerbach described many years later in his curriculum vitae for the Marburg *Habilitation*:

Already as a student of law I dedicated my main interest to the fields of philosophy, art history, and Romance literatures, and I undertook long voyages abroad; in the last year before the war, I transferred to the School of Humanities and began my studies of Romance philology with Professor Morf at Berlin. At the beginning of the war, I became a soldier and served from December 1914 until April 1918. . . . After recovering from a heavy injury,[64] I returned to my study of philology toward the end of 1918.

Auerbach wrote a second dissertation, and received his Ph.D.—with the second-best grade *valde laudabile*—in June 1921 at the University of Greifswald where his Berlin advisor Eberhard Lommatzsch[65] had been appointed full professor some months earlier. In the Greifswald thesis Auerbach focused on literary techniques in early Renaissance novellas from Italy and France. While this topic may seem unrelated to the problem of coperpetration with which he had dealt in the legal dissertation, he found a perspective from which it was possible to continue his reflection on the everyday tragic. The context of literary history allowed Auerbach to formulate, for the first time, his favorite paradox according to which the thematization of the everyday tragic was excluded by conventions inherent in the genre of tragedy itself. In exchange, he postulated a historical relationship between the everyday tragic and the form of literary prose:

Whereas entire nations speak in tragedies and epic poems confronting themselves with God and the human fate (so that, beyond any specific time and place, the soul is moved in its depth), it is the social world that constitutes the topic of the novella. Therefore this genre has worldness in general (i.e., that which we call culture) for its object; it does not investigate being, or search for a ground, or an essence, but rather focuses on that which is concrete and valid.[66]

Beginning in the early 1920's, the dominant tonality in Auerbach's life also began to shift from the style of a highly privileged young man to a growing involvement with those rituals of normality and everydayness that had long fascinated him in the works of literature. In 1922 he passed the *Staatsexamen* which qualified him to become a high school teacher of French and Italian. But instead of pursuing this career, Auerbach entered the service of a librarian at the Prussian State Library in October 1923. On February 27 of the same year, he had married Marie Mankiewitz, the daughter of a renowned lawyer,[67] and on November 30, 1923, their son Clemens was born. Probably the foundation of a family in the economic climate of postwar inflation caused Auerbach to choose the secure professional position of a librarian. Still, his ability to afford a leave of absence from his position "during most of the year 1925" to write a number of scholarly articles in Italy and France suggests that not only economic reasons had determined his choice of the normality of existence as a civil servant. This life form must also have attracted Auerbach as an existential (if not as an aesthetic) principle — no less than the literary topic of everydayness.

During those years Auerbach elaborated the complex configuration of the concepts of everydayness, fate, and tragedy in relation to individuality and authenticity that so perfectly reflected the contemporary intellectual environment in Germany, and that was to inform the reading of the *Divina Commedia* in his Dante book of 1929. The 1926 edition of the journal *Germanisch-Romanische Monatsschrift* contains an essay by Auerbach on "Racine and the Passions" which develops the thesis that Racine's characters do not "possess a sphere of everyday life," that "they are but empty vessels of autonomous passions and vital instincts."[68] In a scholarly article published the same year by the prestigious *Deutsche Vierteljahrsschrift für Literaturwissenschaft und Geistesgeschichte*, Auerbach argued for a reevaluation of the autobiographical prose of Paul-Louis Courier, a widely forgotten author of the French Restoration, emphasizing Courier's "sensuous talent" for the representation of fate and "the meaning of tragedy."[69] Only a year later and in the same journal, he presented Saint Francis of Assisi as a historical character who incarnates that type of the individual for which the 1920's had cast a new meaning of "authenticity:" "Saint Francis of Assisi became a poetic character in Vico's sense of the word because he entirely became a visible expression of his own being." As Saint Francis's "most personal side" Auerbach admired "the warm and drastic power of his expression which seems to penetrate into the body of things and to open them from inside."[70] Although it was already obvious at this early stage in Auerbach's career that he had the temperament of a literary historian rather than that of a critic of contemporary literature, he reacted, as did so many other German intellectuals,[71] to the publication of Marcel Proust's novel *A la recherche du temps perdu*, which marked one of the cultural sensations of that decade. Typically, however, Auerbach was not primarily interested in the world-creating function of memory but praised Proust for his representation of "the earthly world" as an "unknown, unexplored, mysteriously composed substance." In the remarkable concluding sentence of his Proust essay, which describes the *Recherche* as "the true epic of the soul," Auerbach brought together, probably for the first time, all the different aspects of his fascination with the literary presentation of everyday reality:

This chronicle of interior life flows in a quiet epic rhythm because it is but re-membering and introspection. It is the true epic of the soul, the truth proper which entangles the reader in a sweet and long dream. He suffers much in this dream, but he can also enjoy release and consolation. It is the authen-tic, quietly flowing, always depressing and always exhilarating pathos of the earthly progress.[72]

The phrase of the "always depressing and always exhilarating pathos of the earthly progress" both foreshadows the central argument of *Dante, Poet of the Secular World* and also may well be the most condensed and the most pregnant formula for a constitutive ambiguity in the practical existentialism that had become the leitmotiv of Auerbach's personal identity and on whose literary representations his work increasingly concentrated. In Auerbach's eyes fate as concrete everyday life was always depressing. But he also experienced everyday life as always ele-vating and exhilarating because it implied the obligation to oppose the forms of composure and authentic individuality to the suffering which it caused. This may have been why Auerbach, instead of trying to es-cape his contemporary world, eagerly exposed himself to the fate of its challenges and trials.

Auerbach's Legacy

Undoubtedly the years between 1911 and 1929 were the formative period in Erich Auerbach's life. Seen from this perspective, the books and essays that he published during his career as a professor of litera-ture appear as an epilogue or, more poetically speaking, as a harvest. I therefore do not believe that his passionate and distanced view of European culture emerged during his exile in Istanbul or even after his emigration to the United States in 1947. At most, the experience of expatriation that the National Socialist regime had inflicted upon him gave Auerbach the opportunity to become fully aware of his distanced and sometimes melancholic perspective on western culture as a culture that had entered its final stage. It may also have helped him under-stand how eccentricity could strengthen that form of individuality with which he sought to resist daily sufferings. In 1946 — and seemingly with support from the political authorities in the then "Soviet-occupied zone" of Germany — Auerbach's former assistant Werner Krauss tried

to interest him in accepting a professorship at the Humboldt University
in Berlin. Although Krauss could assure him that such a move would
only imply the expectation of a "basically positive disposition"—not
that of an intellectual or political commitment—toward socialism or
communism, Auerbach's reply shows that he had accepted by then the
distance and eccentricity imposed upon him as *his* mode of existence:

> In so far as you describe it, your request attracts me. But is this really my
> place? I am, after all, a typical liberal. If anything, the very situation which the
> circumstances offered to me has but strengthened this inclination. Here I am
> enjoying the great liberty of *ne pas conclure*. More than in any other situation, it
> was possible for me to remain free of any commitment. It is exactly this atti-
> tude of somebody who does not belong to any place, and who is essentially a
> stranger without the possibility of being assimilated, which is expected from
> me. In contrast, where you want me to go, a "positive basic disposition" is
> required.[73]

Although (as we now can say: typically enough) Auerbach never theo-
rized the strong and increasingly deliberate convergence between his
life and his work, one may speculate that their oscillation contains the
reason for both his colleagues' admiration and their inability to follow him as the "head" of a "critical school." Either his students did
not share the intellectual and historical experience of the time between
1910 and 1930, or it brought them, as was the case with Werner Krauss,
to different existential decisions. In the present generation of critics
and historians of literature, we have become much more skeptical—
perhaps too skeptical—regarding any form of relationship between
literary texts and our everyday lives. The intellectual style of deconstruction might be the only contemporary exception, but the one *existential value* that it attributes to the reading of literature is the bleak
insight into the impossibility of any stable meaning and, with it, into
the illusory character of any *existential orientation*.

On the other hand, in the absence of a circumscribed "theoretical
position" or "method," what constitutes the (mostly hidden) fascination that we connect with Auerbach's name today is the *figure of emplotment* that shaped his life and his literary readings. Even those who
would feel embarrassed to use his very concepts may finally not be so
far from Auerbach's experience that individuality as fate emerges out
of the inevitably tragic sphere of everyday life, and that this condition

obliges us to invent our identity as a form.[74] At the same time, since this figure of existential emplotment came out of a situation that was not exclusively Auerbach's, it can contribute to our historical understanding of what looks like a strange form of tolerance (and sometimes even of complicity) among many Jewish—or simply dissenting—intellectuals towards the Third Reich. They appeared almost eager to undergo the rituals of humiliation and torture with which National Socialism persecuted them, perhaps because these rituals provided the obligation to invent themselves as individuals.

To a certain degree, this may also have been the case of Ernst Robert Curtius, Auerbach's greatest antagonist among the literary historians of their generation. Without Jewish family relations and without any compromising political contacts, Curtius could afford to stay in Germany, although the distance that he kept from the Nationalist Socialist state was notorious. Curtius's and Auerbach's reactions to the postwar situation, however, diverged significantly. In a conversation with an American journalist during the fall of 1945, Curtius explained why he had not left Germany after 1933. While he seemed to accept a national responsibility for the war (without dedicating a single word to the Holocaust), he loudly complained about the behavior of the American forces of occupation. Here are two passages from Stephen Spender's dialogue with Curtius:

Since 1933, I have often wondered why C- didn't leave Germany. I think really the reason was a passion for continuity, a rootedness in his environment which made him almost immovable. He had modeled his life in the idea of that Goethe who boasted that during the Napoleonic struggle he had been like a mighty cliff towering above and indifferent to the waters raging hundreds of feet beneath him. If he always detested the Nazis he also had little sympathy for the Left, and the movement to leave Germany was for the most part a Leftwards one. Above all, he may have felt that it was his duty as a non-political figure, to stay in Germany, in order to be an example before the young people of the continuity of a wiser and greater German tradition. In spite of everything, he was very German.

The C-'s had many complaints about the Occupation. What struck me in conversation with them and with other intelligent Germans was the undiscriminating nature of those complaints. Some of the things complained about, though distressing, seemed inevitably the result of losing a war. For example, when Bonn University was occupied (Bonn was first occupied by the Americans), an American soldier was observed in the library tearing all those books which had been rescued from the fire, and which were laid on a table, out of their bindings, and then hacking at them with a bayonet. On being approached by a Professor, he explained his conduct by saying: "I hate everything German." This story was circulated in University circle as an example of American barbarity. To my mind, it illustrates nothing except the stupidity inevitably attendant on war.[75]

In contrast to Curtius, who tried to find consolation in playing with highly abstract stereotypes and by thus maintaining a belief in the superiority of the same European culture out of which fascism had grown, the letters that Auerbach wrote to Werner Krauss in Marburg between 1945 and 1947 were exclusively concerned with everyday life under postwar conditions. He wanted to know about the fate of innumerable colleagues and former students, he worried over Krauss's severely affected health, and he tried to help him by sending Turkish cigarettes, Swiss food, and American medicaments (through the mediation of his son Clemens, who had meanwhile become a student at Harvard). On June 22, 1946, Auerbach went so far as to express his embarrassment because, given the economic situation in Istanbul, the sale of family possessions did not yield enough money for all the concrete help he wanted to offer: "Here, those who profited from the war are undergoing a deep crisis these days. I am therefore encountering some difficulty in selling my grand piano—however badly I need the money. But these are worries of a very bourgeois kind. After all, we are enjoying a very good life here."[76] Such words explain what Erich Auerbach had in mind when, in the last sentence of his article "Philologie der Weltliteratur," published in 1952, he described himself as "someone who wants to achieve authentic love for the world."[77] They even make us understand the attitude behind the uncanny—if not irresponsible— generosity with which he hoped, during the last years of his life that "the Germans would lose their guilt complex."[78]

Auerbach's spiritual generosity was certainly not matched by any material generosity from the bureaucracy of the Federal Republic of Germany where, after 1945, he again pursued his claim to a pension. The most recent document in the Auerbach file at the Hessisches Staatsarchiv in Marburg is a letter from the *Hessische Kultusminister* to Marie Auerbach. On the basis of a complicated argument, this letter denies her claim to receive any retroactive payments for the time after her husband's death on October 13, 1957. Ironically, the main reason for this decision seems to have been that, due to Erich Auerbach's tenacious legal resistance, his status as a German civil servant had never been definitively revoked.

Claus Uhlig

Auerbach's "Hidden"(?) Theory of History

~~~~~~

Whether visible in the foreground or hidden in the background, our assumptions about the nature of history are always with us and inform our speech and writing. But seeing that, despite all its supposed cycles of recurrence or lines of development, not to mention its vertical coordinates as opposed to these two horizontal ones, really only one thing can safely be said about history, namely, "that it happens,"[1] it might be wisest after all to take our views of history's course—yet another metaphor!—as deriving just as much from our psychological or existential as from our intellectual needs.[2] Erich Auerbach's whole career as a Romance scholar, it seems to me, bears this out.

As Ernst Robert Curtius once remarked, the life of the mind is organized by "systems of affinity"[3]—a remark well suited further to introduce a treatment of Auerbach from the vantage point of the centennial, as witness particularly the two lodestars of his entire work and thought, Vico and Dante (in that chronological order).[4] In view of the known fact that Auerbach himself always favored and recommended a concrete "point of departure" (*Ansatz*) as against abstract or speculative approaches to a subject, I shall, in heeding this advice, focus precisely on Vico and Dante in what follows, thus hoping to uncover some of the theoretical axioms which, perhaps from an aesthetic temperament's congenital aversion to conceptualizations,[5] he chose rather to keep in the background.

I

Vico provided Auerbach with his first scholarly inspiration, and, on the evidence of altogether thirteen publications devoted to the Neapolitan philosopher, it was to last to the end of his life.[6] According to his own testimony, Auerbach owes to the *Scienza nuova* (final edition 1744) insights into the theory of historical knowledge as well as the difference between philosophy and philology.[7] To start with the first issue, Vico's anti-Cartesian epistemology paves the way for Auerbach's personal (i.e., aesthetic) version of historicism in that it grounds knowledge in the identity of the knower with the known.[8] This principle of *verum ipsum factum*, when applied to history, means that man can know what he himself has made, the world of mankind, *il mondo delle nazioni*, as opposed to the physical world, *il mondo della natura*, created by God and therefore known only to God. Of course here the problem of Divine Providence, interfering as it does with the notion of man-made history, arises,[9] but for the moment we must concentrate on the fact that Vico by this theory had established the right of the historical sciences, whereby all possible forms of past human life and thought, when viewed from any given present, can be said to be accessible in the potentialities of the human mind, *dentro le modificazioni della nostra medesima mente umana*. Thus we should be able to re-evoke—or "re-enact," as Collingwood, who via Croce also stems from Vico, would put it[10]— human history from our own mind.[11]

It is clear that Vico's theory of historical knowledge already amounts to a foundation of historicism as we have known it ever since the second half of the eighteenth century. "The nature of things (human institutions)," Vico holds in the *Scienza nuova* (par. 147), "signifies only that they came into being at certain times and under certain circumstances"—a justification of historical "relativism" or "perspectivism," as Auerbach prefers to call it.[12] And as such we also find it in one of the few openly theoretical passages of *Mimesis*, where its author exhorts us to realize "that epochs and societies are not to be judged in terms of a pattern concept of what is desirable absolutely speaking but rather in every case in terms of their own premises."[13] When Vico, however, further states that historical nature is subject to law (his theory of cycles, i.e., the idea of *corso* and *ricorso*, the eternal recurrence of the same events within his *storia ideale eterna*), then Auerbach dissociates himself from his master,[14] for he is just as mistrustful of historical determinism as Karl R. Popper in his attack on the whole intellectual trend under discussion.[15] Latter-day historicist that he is, Auerbach for his part stresses the "incomparability of historical phenomena" and wishes to "appreciate the vital unity of individual epochs, so that each epoch appears as a whole whose character is reflected in each of its manifestations."[16] Yet it is precisely here that we must part company with Auerbach, since his Vichian, or rather post-Vichian, aesthetic historicism sounds too good to be true. In other words, more recent theoreticians of history have drawn our attention to the fact that the historical universe tends to show nonhomogeneous structures and that simultaneous events may at times be intrinsically asynchronous.[17]

The second great lesson Auerbach assumes to have learned from Vico is directly related to his historicist perspectivism and his dislike of "abstract and general forms of cognition," as voiced in the same passage of *Mimesis*, that is, the difference between philosophy and philology. Refusing to identify truth, the *verum*, with certainty, the *certum*, as Descartes does, Vico assigns the realm of the former to philosophy, occupying itself with thought's conformity to the reality of objects as created by the eternal reason of God, whereas the latter, certainty, is relegated to the human sphere, for which philology is held responsible, investigating what the various peoples regarded as beyond doubt at each cultural stage (Vico's three stages of human history from the age of the gods via that of the heroes to that of men).[18] Still, in Vico the opposition between philosophy and philology is not an absolute one, and it is exactly history that is held to function as a link between the two realms of knowledge. For if one aspect or another of the divine *verum* is always actualized in every stage of history, then it is the duty of philology to seek out its traces by studying the various *certa* knowable to man both individually and in their systematic cohesion. Interested in the systematic or universal aspect of history, although working his way up by induction from the analysis of particulars, Vico thus is a philological philosopher or philosophic philologist—surely Auerbach's own scholarly ideal in view of his aspiration to a kind of "synthetic historical philology."[19]

But how to realize this dream in the teeth of theoretical reticence or abstinence? In this connection a word on Auerbach's own reflections on philological method is in order. More than once, albeit once only in

Mimesis,[20] he has warned, in discussing his *Ansatz*, against starting from generalities and urged the approach to a given phenomenon through particulars. If one holds with Vico—and Auerbach constantly does this in his *explication de texte*—that every historical epoch has its characteristic unity (a question-begging assumption, as we saw), every text, as part of this epochal whole, must provide at least a partial view on the basis of which a synthesis or a more systematic account should be possible. Turned the other way round, the whole, for being in the part, can only be approached through this very part, in aspects and nuances, for instance, of an author's worldview or style. That is why Auerbach emphasizes the necessity of concreteness for an *Ansatz*, which as a rule ought to originate in "specific questions."[21] This endeavor, by the way, unites him with Leo Spitzer. Spitzer, however, always concerned himself with an exact understanding of the individuality of texts, while the author of *Mimesis*, even if by intellectual formation likewise rooted in philology and stylistics, after his close readings of texts deliberately tends, in true Vichian manner, to branch out into totalizing visions of historical processes.[22]

Now, the terms Auerbach uses in his methodological self-reflection make clear that although he does not openly say so, he is wrestling with the most vexing problem of hermeneutics, namely, the circle of understanding, as it manifests itself in any historical inquiry. No matter which particular theory of hermeneutics one has in mind, the circle generally describes how, in the process of understanding and interpretation, part and whole are necessarily related in a circular way, not to mention later developments in hermeneutic philosophy on the part of Martin Heidegger and Hans-Georg Gadamer that further take into account the historicity of understanding itself and thus ground interpretation in human existence.[23] Doubtless familiar with the problem of hermeneutics as it had evolved in the tradition of German *Geistesgeschichte*, Auerbach nevertheless refrains from discussing it in technical terms. In defending his method of procedure in *Mimesis* he even writes that he would ideally have liked to avoid all generalities and to content himself with a suggestive account of particulars.[24] While thereby again warding off the danger of falling victim to ready-made clichés or modern abstract categories of classification such as "romanticism" or "classicism," and keeping the "question" he wishes to address to a text steadily in focus, he cannot avoid that we, after a quarter of a century of hermeneutical debates, wonder why this "question" itself is never put into question. Relying too much on the explanatory power of the "concrete universal" and his seemingly unfailing aesthetic intuition,[25] he reveals at the same time a surprising limitation in his theoretical self-awareness which, although not so conspicuous in his scholarly practice, might well hide, as some of his critics believe, ideological motifs of thought unacknowledged even to his own consciousness.[26] Be that as it may (and veneration of the man and his work do not permit the present writer to go that far), the pitfalls of what René Wellek, speaking of Auerbach's "historical perspectivism" and concomitant "relativism," once called "his antitheoretical central theory"[27] might have become clear by now. At any rate, Auerbach himself was soon to realize that a Vichian type of historicism—in that respect his theoretical introduction to *Literary Language and Its Public* conveys only half the truth—was not enough, especially when, in an equally lifelong pursuit, it became incumbent on him to study Dante in depth.

II

Auerbach's first and only book devoted to a single author is the publication *Dante als Dichter der irdischen Welt*, which came out in 1929 and brought him the appointment to the chair of Romance philology at the University of Marburg. Reading this early study with the hindsight derived from his much later *Mimesis: Dargestellte Wirklichkeit in der abendländischen Literatur* (1946), it is surprising to see that an almost obsessive tenacity of purpose imbued the great scholar's entire career.[28] For already in 1929 the literary representation of reality is his central theme. Contrary to his later theoretical persuasions, he is not yet afraid of sweeping generalizations when, in the first chapter of that book, he offers, much in the manner of Vico, a broad historical survey over the "idea and fate of man in literature." In the course of this exposition, classical antiquity is said, in the wake of Plato, merely to imitate appearances, or rather only those images of the real to be found in man's own mind, whereas Christianity was to change all this dramatically by subjecting the idea to the cruel injustice of a terrestrial event, thereby in the end investing the real with a new and above all concrete spiritual dignity; hence the possibility for literary representation to treat the sublime and the familiar in the same breath, especially since biblical narrative hallowed such a procedure with its authority.[29] Vast as this thesis may be (and the exceptions taken to it by professional classical scholars need not concern us right now),[30] Auerbach put it to good use in his first sustained reading of the *Divine Comedy*, although his interpretations, despite their manifold adumbrations of *Mimesis*, remained for the time being on a descriptive level only.

Consequently, in order to deepen his preliminary observations on Dante, he had to buttress them with a theory that would account for the astonishing reality, the unity of body and spirit so characteristic of the inhabitants of Dante's other world. The long and famous essay on "Figura" (1939) was the result of this search for a theoretical key. Figural or typological interpretation, according to this essay expounding the time-honored methods of biblical exegesis, is a way of connecting two events or persons in historical time, whereby the first of the two signifies both itself and also the second, while the second, the *antitype* to the preceding *type*, fulfills the first, much as a prophecy can be said to be fulfilled by a later happening. What Auerbach is at pains to stress is that this exegetical technique differs radically from the usual habits of thought that take for granted historical sequence, i.e., a continuous development in chronological and horizontal succession, whereas typological interpretation, by combining two events causally and chronologically remote from each other in time but having a meaning common to both, operates along a vertical line. In its worldview the ultimate goal of human history is known, because it has been revealed to mankind in the Scriptures, and by the same token the Old Testament, no longer conceived to be the law and the individual history of the Jewish people alone, becomes a series of prefigurations of Christ, of his Incarnation and Passion as told in the New Testament. Yet despite this vertical structure of history referring everything to a providential design, it is important to note, as Auerbach further emphasizes, that neither the prefiguring nor the prefigured event or person loses its literal and historical reality through its typological interrelation.[31]

Now, in this method of interpretation Auerbach found the key not yet available to him in the book on Dante of 1929. When he made a renewed attempt to penetrate the mystery of the *Divine Comedy* in the eighth chapter of *Mimesis*, he pointed—as, by the way, in many subsequent contributions to Dante studies[32]—to more than one instance of the poet's reliance on the typological system thanks to which his figures, vertically related to both their former historical existence and their divinely ordained present situation, can be understood as fulfilling, in practical "omnitemporality," their ultimate reality.[33] Let it suffice for the moment to remain on this general level of exposition—especially since it may be taken for granted that the chapter on "Farinata and Cavalcante" is one of the points of culmination in *Mimesis*—in order to ponder some of the theoretical or, if I may hark back to my introduction, psychological as well as existential implications of the method under discussion. For why is it necessary, in the study of literary texts, to subject all the material of human history, both sacred and profane, to the typological mode of thought and to operate with the concept of figura—certainly a universalizing concept, if ever there was one—with such intensity?

Paul J. Korshin has distinguished among "conventional" typology, principally dealing with biblical situations, "applied" typology, commonly used for literary and by extension also for political purposes, and "abstracted" typology, totally dedicated to the symbolic properties of all things.[34] Auerbach's "Figura," chiming in with a resurgence of interest in typology during the 1930's, can in the light of Korshin's classification now clearly be seen as the literary application of a hermeneutic technique to a central medieval text, and that not only for critical but presumably also for political reasons.[35] For the primitive Christians, let us remember, typology as a system of exegesis was employed to elucidate historical relationships between the Old Testament and the New as well as the overall perplexities of recent political history; and because temporal power was in heathen hands, past and present history, through the interplay of *type* and *antitype* (or vice versa), quite necessarily became reshaped into a future-directed history, thus giving it a meaning and a point.[36] In a similar vein, Dante appropriated history—and "appropriation" is used deliberately here for being a concept of hermeneutics which entails the notion that the meaning of an event or a text is what the interpreter finds to be relevant to his own interests[37]—above all Roman history, conceived along patristic lines as leading up to Christian universal history and following the plan of Divine Providence, to voice his political ideas and to subject, with a confidence precisely due to the coherent view of history he had inherited, the inhabitants of his other world to their often severe penalties according to the principle of *contrapasso*.[38] Likewise Auerbach, given the known political circumstances of his own situation in place and time, must have felt both the intellectual and the emotional need to stem the tide of barbarity and, at least in writing, to oppose himself to what might well have appeared to him as yet another Vichian *ricorso*. At least Geoffrey Green, in his reading of "Figura," makes a case for such an understanding of Auerbach's adherence to a theory of history based on the typological system and functioning as a guarantee of Judeo-Christian continuity.[39] For in fact a theory of history it is; and in view of the passionate way in which Auerbach has written about it time and again, there is no doubt that it had become, unlike Vico's cyclicity in this respect, *his* theory of history. In this connection one could perhaps further suggest that *figura* and typology in Auerbach's life fulfilled the same function as the famous *topoi* of classical rhetoric for Curtius in his vision of historical continuity presented by *Europäische Literatur und lateinisches Mittelalter* (1948), and that especially when considering the dedication of both scholars to the idea of European cultural unity.

Yet unity and continuity are precarious constructs even at the best of times. To be more precise, it is above all Auerbach's notion of "omnitemporality," despite its heuristic value in interpreting the *Divine Comedy*, that creates a theoretical problem here. The concept was devised to point up the transcendental fulfillment of a historical and concrete figure's earthly existence in an eternally present beyond— a situation which at the same time constitutes this figure's ultimate reality. By making this vertical relationship possible at any moment of time in history—provided, that is to say, one does not lack Christian belief in the first place—the panchronistic concept in question tends to destroy history as a process and to reduce its subjects to the level of mere existence. Mingling the realms of profane and sacred history, Dante, not unlike God Himself, may well be able to pass judgment on all history,[40] but when Auerbach, centuries later, with evident sympathy shares this view of the world, he, as an earthly human being who certainly does not occupy the seat of umpire Providence, appears to be much closer to the tenets of an unhistorical existentialism than to those of a theoretically sound historicism.[41] And seeing that this statement of a paradox, stemming from one-sided premises in historical theory on Auerbach's part, sounds very much like what René Wellek once criticized as the "special realism" of *Mimesis*,[42] it is high time now to turn to

Auerbach's "representation of reality in Western literature" as narrated in that momentous work.

III

Auerbach's scholarly desire not only to give an account of but also to account for the concrete nature of Dante's presentation of reality provided one of the driving forces behind the project of *Mimesis*. In accordance with his own methodological postulate for well-defined points of departure, he begins *Mimesis* with the ancient conception of the three levels of style, asking all the selected texts about their relationship to it.[43] The elevated style of the Homeric poems, in the historical perspective thus adopted by Auerbach, can be shown to reflect the static hierarchy of a feudal society, whereas among the nomadic peoples of the Old Testament the sublime and the tragic descend, so to speak, on the social ladder and merge stylistically with the domestic concerns of everyday life.[44] The mixture of styles subsequent to this move is then continued in the New Testament, especially in the story of Christ's Incarnation and Passion. Thereby what formerly was low and undignified now becomes rehabilitated and amenable to literary treatment; and following up this sublation of the classical separation of styles through analyzing a number of texts from late antiquity and the Middle Ages, Auerbach is in a position to disclose some of the influences of Christianity on the development of literary expression. The Christian convergence of humility and sublimity, resulting in that mixture of styles which is basic to Auerbach's whole conception of realism, finally culminates in the *Divine Comedy*, which he characterizes as deriving its poetic power from the said mixture of styles on the one hand, and the figural conception of reality already discussed on the other.[45]

Yet while "Figura," as we saw earlier on, had already paved the way for Auerbach's renewed reading of the *Divine Comedy*, a full theoretical grounding of the interpretation advanced in terms of stylistics was still outstanding by 1946, despite the article "Sacrae Scripturae sermo humilis" of 1941,[46] only briefly touched upon in *Mimesis*. It came some time later, in the United States, with "Sermo Humilis" (1952), Auerbach's other major contribution to historical semantics and as important as "Figura" for his whole way of thinking. Taking his cue from Augustine's reflections on this lowest of the three styles of discourse according to ancient rhetoric, Auerbach works out how, owing to the impact of Christianity, Cicero's system of stylistic differentiation loses its relevance and is gradually replaced by Augustine's radical modification of ancient rhetorical doctrine. Given that the Christian mode of expression is not literary but existential, Auerbach makes the resulting stylistic implications explicit. The style of the Bible is "lowly," that is, "humilis," which also denotes the Christian virtue of humility, the purpose of this humility of style being to make the Scriptures available to all. Their subject matter, however, is sublime, treating as they do of the holiest mysteries for Christians. It is in these or similar terms that Auerbach, again with empathy, describes the decisive change in the history of style that was to reach its poetic climax in the early fourteenth century: "The greatest document of this Christian sublimity," Auerbach writes, "is Dante's *Divine Comedy*."[47] No doubt this view of things was bound to spring from an interest in those elements of the *Comedy* that were "low," that is, horrible, ugly, grotesque, and vulgar; elements that embodied the temporal and worldly and that, through abolishing the traditional separation of styles into sublime, intermediate, and lowly, had to be integrated into the sublime to reach into Dante's transcendental world, without, however, losing their concrete reality. This is the point of Auerbach's full interpretation of the *Divine Comedy*, and it is at the same time the essence of his concept of realism.

   To be sure, such a notion carries conviction within a Christo-centric universe, but serious doubts arise the moment when, in later phases of literary history, it is applied to texts which are on the whole worldly in character. Thus, for instance, Montaigne's self-description as a constantly changing human being in the essay "Du repentir" (III, ii), as analyzed in chapter 12 of *Mimesis* (significantly entitled with the existentialist caption "L'humaine condition," taken from Montaigne's text), might still conform to Auerbach's reading, in which it is said, with the help of other passages culled from the *Essais* for support, to be rooted in the creaturality of Christian anthropology.[48] Yet, much later, as Auerbach proceeds to the French novelists of the nineteenth century, his wide-ranging extrapolations from the textual material, indebted as they are not so much to his method of close reading as to his scholarly "foreknowledge" in *Geistesgeschichte*, seem to be a weak echo of the humble-sublime rhetoric of Christianity or, conversely, ultimately rooted rather in relativistic, if not positivistic, modes of thought.[49]

This comes clearly to the fore in the most explicit definition of modern realism to be found in *Mimesis*: "The serious treatment of everyday reality, the rise of more extensive and socially inferior human groups to the position of subject matter for problematic-existential representation, on the one hand; on the other, the embedding of random persons and events in the general course of contemporary history, the fluid historical background—these, we believe, are the foundations of modern realism."[50]

It is neither necessary nor timely now to rehearse all the arguments brought forward against Auerbach's very special as well as highly partial concept of realism in the course of his great book's critical reception, particularly since more often than not his critics had their own ideological axes to grind. To some, "the repeated stylistic embodiments of man's existential struggles" throughout history, the kind of "existentialism embedded in historical relativism," as traced and evidenced in *Mimesis*,[51] are too sociological in purport, and that to the detriment of a given artwork's aesthetic structure;[52] to others again, writing from quite a specific social, if not downright Marxist, point of view, Auerbach, predictably, is not sociological enough,[53] while more or less neutral or balanced accounts of *Mimesis*, comparing its author to advantage with Georg Lukács, for example, have remained few and far between.[54] Be that as it may, the dust once raised by these controversies has settled meanwhile, so that we are better able to concentrate on Auerbach's bent of mind, his *forma mentis*, as the humanists would have said. And in doing this, we might perceive that it is deeply antihierarchical, not to say thoroughly democratic at bottom. For how else can we understand that, in "Sermo Humilis" and throughout *Mimesis*, he privileges what is humble and low? Why, in other words, does he stress, in his version of Christianity, the Incarnation and the Passion of Christ rather than the triumph of the Resurrection, if not in order to bring across those existential and creatural elements of the Scriptures that serve his subconscious theoretical ends in working out the rise of European realism from a biblical rhetoric conceived in humble-sublime terms?[55] What is more, in emphasizing Christian creaturality over Christian spirituality (we may here also think of the opposition between, say, Montaigne and Pascal, not to mention medieval anxiety as opposed to baroque or classical joy in the face of God), he really operates only with partial aspects of the truth, as it must even appear to a Christian believer. Yet agnostics, too, might feel tempted to object to seeing man in his history reduced to mere existence, nay, the latter being extolled over and above the spirit. Pursuing this point yet further, it is possible to line these observations up with Auerbach's anticlassical bias, conspicuous as it is in *Mimesis*. Ultimately fostered by Vico's anti-Cartesianism, it is a formation of the mind directed against any predominance of norms and prescriptions in the sphere of culture. As is well known and explained by Auerbach himself, historicism, his own avowed creed, took its root exactly here, in a reaction against French classicism and its theories which based poetry on imitation of models, educated taste, and well-defined rules.[56] Now, in placing more value on instinct, imagination, and intuition than on reason and reflection, the early historicists seem to me, if I were to categorize their predilections, to come very close to what Auerbach later, when working within the framework of Christianity, conceived in terms of creaturality and existence. And if Vico held that man can know man in history on account of the common humanity of mankind, then this axiom is tantamount to asserting that man knows man because he is man, history not being necessary anymore in the process. As was suggested already in discussing the concept of "omnitemporality," pondering the issues raised by Auerbach's unconscious theorizing will thus in the end lead to a destruction of the very concept of history itself, principally differentiated as it is and must remain from that of mere existence. Pondering any problem long enough, let me add, is of course bound to annihilate reasonable solutions for good; so it would be better to stop this train of thought here. All that needed highlighting, however, was the danger lurking in a lack of full theoretical self-awareness, plus a post-Vichian confusion of one realm of discourse with another, namely, in the present case, philology with philosophy. For the typological system of exegesis, expounded philologically in "Figura," actually contains a philosophy of history, scarcely hiding its will to power over time; likewise "Sermo humilis," equally investigated by means of philology, strives, in analogous philosophical manner, to foist a view of the world on us we might be able to understand but not be willing to share.

IV

To conclude, no matter what one says in criticism (and affection as well as admiration should not preclude criticism, surely), Auerbach's legacy as available to us in his writings will abide. Here and there, glancing at scholarly publications that have come one's way at random (Auerbach's own method of procedure, by the way, if we are to believe his confession in *Mimesis*), we can trace marks of his influence. Above all the famous first chapter of *Mimesis*, contrasting the two types of style used to represent reality in the *Odyssey* on the one hand and *Genesis* on the other, seems to have found favor with students of both biblical narrative in general and biblical history in particular, although they have of course deemed it necessary to elaborate upon his otherwise uncontested notion of the Bible's cryptic conciseness that kept the existential dilemma broached "in the background."[57] As was forseeable, also the mode of figural or typological interpretation that Auerbach adopted, in conjunction with Christian rhetoric, with such success in his reading of the *Divine Comedy*, has radiated into other spheres of medieval literature, and that with regard not only to practical textual exegesis but also to principal discussions of that period's historical understanding by modern scholars.[58] Likewise, his brilliant chapter on Montaigne in *Mimesis* will never lose its luster, I think, while the pages devoted to novelists of later epochs, especially those on Proust, Joyce, and Virginia Woolf, could fade with time, because the inner reality these modern authors try to capture through language is no longer methodically accessible to Auerbach's heuristic instruments.

Still, given that on the whole any critical assessment of past scholarly achievement reveals at least as much about its own moment of origin as about the work under consideration, critical responses of Auerbach should not be overestimated. Thus comments still close to him in terms of chronology, while neutral at best, mildly complain of his "radical relativism, uninformed by a certain belief in the eventual relevance of the historic patterns discovered upon a plane of absolute truth,"[59] which clearly amounts to demanding the impossible. A decade later, "deconstruction" is already in the air, constructing a system for *Mimesis* first, only to destroy it a while later by charging its author, said to pose as a simple observer of the textual phenomena he treats, with "situating himself within the empiricist philosophical tradition."[60] And as for actualizing attempts, construing a relationship, that is to say, between the central thesis of *Mimesis* and Bakhtin's fashionable concept of the *chronotope*,[61] Auerbach does not need them, since he can even now hold his own in critical discourse. More than anything else, his Vichian ideal of a "synthetic historical philology aspiring to encompass the cultural destinies of Europe"[62] is more timely than ever; only that today, as Auerbach, to judge from his magisterial late essay "Philologie der Weltliteratur" (1952), was among the first to recognize, the center of gravity must shift away from Europe to take in the whole world.[63]

Finally, the synthesizing activity envisaged by Auerbach will remain a viable proposition, it appears to me, provided one keeps the two areas of interest involved, namely, philology and philosophy, strictly demarcated from each other in any initial act of analysis, postponing the moment of their interaction until one has evolved mediating notions that then will have to be "foregrounded" in order to avoid possible strictures on account of ideological subterfuge. Auerbach's lifelong adherence to what Harold Bloom, in a different cultural context, has called "text-centeredness"[64] should still be of great help in this process, notwithstanding his equally protracted antitheoretical stance. Even so, I hope to have brought out both the theoretical and historical implications of his two most important contributions to literary scholarship and intellectual history, "Figura" and "Sermo Humilis." Hiding as they do to all intents and purposes Auerbach's personal assumptions about the course of history, they could almost be compared to the two side panels of an altarpiece, flanking the central picture which is *Mimesis*. Whether agnostic himself or not,[65] Auerbach always saw in the Scriptures more than just material for the historical study of literature. That is perhaps why history and existence for him coalesced into one. Ultimately, the textual milieu he was most conversant with (apart from Vico and Dante of course), namely, late antiquity and patristic literature, provided his spiritual home, wherever he lived and worked.

Luiz Costa-Lima

Auerbach and Literary History

How does Auerbach relate to the tradition of literary history? To answer this question, we must identify five traits in nineteenth-century literary history: (a) the assumption that the passage of time is identical with progress; (b) the loss of the absolute prestige that mathematics had enjoyed since the Renaissance; (c) the inference that positive — that is, nonspeculative, nonmetaphysical, not purely rational — thinking presupposes that there are no interruptions or gaps between the species of entities; (d) the perfect fit, made possible by the idea of representation, between the creative individual, national history, and the general history of civilized nations; (e) the individual as the primary center, his quintessence being genius.

A few comments are in order. The item (a) finds its most complete expression in evolutionism. This desideratum may be scientistic or it may be identified with a more "spiritual" yearning, so that literary periods are taken as indicators of progress being diffused through human society. Item (b), which in turn implies less emphasis on the conceptual, focuses more on experiments or the mere cataloging of facts than on the regulated ordering of ideas. Hence the proliferation of literary histories like Sismondi's, in which the author is content to present series of names of authors, dates, and influences, arranged diachronically and according to nationality. The safest way to ensure that one's work was sound was to adopt descriptive neutrality. As to (c), it is important to observe that this belief underlay the preference for causal description. It is not necessary to comment on items (d) and (e). Instead, let me try to answer the question: What were the uses of the sort of literary history I have described?

It might seem strange to say that literary historians seemed to be more concerned with determining what writers *represented* than with asking historically what literature was considered to be in the period under study, or what specified the literary situation, or what procedures it was made up of. Could it be that, just as biologists do not necessarily have any empathy with the beings they investigate, literary historians left out whatever interest they might have in the literary object? Though Gervinus's statement, "Aesthetic judgements on objects do not concern me, I am neither a poet nor a lover of belles lettres,"[1] may be representative of his peers, it would be arbitrary to infer from it that literary history was programmatically anaesthetic.[2] In any case, what is most interesting about this observation is not that it confirms this anaesthesia, but that it was not in opposition to any aestheticizing tendency. Though potentially anaesthetic, literary history was no less aestheticizing for that. As Hayden White observes, apropos of the canon of nineteenth-century historiography in general:

> For this tradition, whatever "confusion" is displayed by the historical record is only a surface phenomenon. . . . If this confusion is not reducible to the kind of order that a science of laws might impose upon it, it can still be dispelled by historians endowed with the proper kind of understanding. And when this understanding is subjected to analysis, it is always revealed to be of an essentially aesthetic nature.[3]

Aestheticness depended on the special configuration of a particular object, a literary work, only to the extent that it arose from the fact that the work, as a *historical object*, made it possible to "prove" the existence of the great chain that made up the world.[4] This was so because aestheticization, promoted by historiography, provided a *religious* sort of satisfaction that did not require belief in any God. Further, this *lay religiousness* served the interests of the state, for it affirmed itself through celebration of the degree of civilization reached by societies, as reflected in their respective literatures. In this sense, as David Lloyd demonstrates, literary history had a political mission, justifying, in the case of Matthew Arnold and Samuel Ferguson, British domain over the Irish, which was supposedly beneficial to both the ruler and the ruled.[5]

   These are the questions I believe should be considered in an examination of the work of Erich Auerbach in literary history. Strictly speaking, Auerbach wrote only two theoretical essays: the "Epilegomena" to

Mimesis and the "Introduction: Aim and Method" to his posthumous *Literary Language and Its Public in Late Antiquity and in the Middle Ages*. But in his case it is the very distinction between theoretical and analytical essays that does not hold. Consequently, it is not material that we lack, but rather, to quote from *Mimesis*'s epigraph, "world enough and time."

To return to the five traits discussed above, it would be ridiculous even to pose the question whether Auerbach's work had anything to do with an evolutionist tendency. Instead, it would be more profitable to consider (b). Here it must be admitted that in Auerbach the conceptual mode is not particularly valued. The justification for this distaste appears in "Epilegomena": In the history of the spirit (*Gestesgeschichte*) there is no identity or strict obedience to laws (*Gesetzlichkeit*); here synthesizing abstract concepts falsify or destroy phenomena. Thus ordering should proceed so as to let phenomena unfold themselves freely.[6]

Auerbach sees this rejection of *abstraktzusamenfassende Begriffe* as fundamentally important to allow concrete approaches to effect a "historical perspectivism" ("Epilegomena," p. 16). But on close examination, it is clear that this passage contains more than just negatives. For how could perspectivism be achieved unless the position of the observer were kept constant, so as to establish a viewpoint? Is the observer in question simply the author—that is, the analyst? The passage goes on to clarify: "If it had been possible, I would have avoided all general terms and instead suggested ideas to the reader by the mere presentation of a sequence of passages" ("Epilegomena," p. 17).

In other words, if in the human sciences (*Geistesgeschichte*) concepts cannot be justified from above, because they are not related to laws that might subsume particular cases, they are displaced to their lowest point: that at which generalization has the sole function of helping to provide the historical placement and the respect of the particularity of each text. We might then say that the subject of Auerbach's historical perspectivism is not as much the analyst as the language.

This inference is borne out when we juxtapose the sentence quoted above to the passage in which Auerbach analyzes Flaubert. Concerning the impersonality of the scenes in *Madame Bovary*, he writes, "We hear the writer speak; but he expresses no opinion and makes no comment. His role is limited to selecting the events and translating them into language, and this is done in the conviction that every event, if one is able to express it purely and completely, interprets itself and the persons involved far better and more completely than any opinion or judgement appended to it could do."[7] Thus the difference between the critic-historian and the novelist is that the latter can trust language completely, while the former, even if innerly resisting, must resort to the generalizing function of the concept.

When we come to (c), once again the profound difference between Auerbach's work and the Enlightenment paradigm is made plain. As we have seen, the assumption of the "great chain of being" led to the operational prevalence of the mechanism of causality. In both historiography in general and literary history in particular, this prevalence presupposed the determination of a chain of causes from which a *necessary* constellation of effects derived; the chain was founded on a social—or rather, socionational—situation, and the constellation included author and work. We shall see shortly how Auerbach's practice diverges from this approach.

As to (d) and (e), Auerbach's position is characterized less by divergence than by subtlety, which in turn already follows from what he had elaborated as he positioned himself in relation to (b) and (c).

Let us now turn to Auerbach's interpretive practice. The crucial issue here is made up of the elements "causal explanation," "role of language," and "author's role as historical critic." The first decisive document is given by the opening chapter of *Mimesis*. As is well known, in this text Auerbach contrasts the Greek experience, represented by Homer, and the Hebrew experience, illustrated by a passage from the Old Testament. Since this is a familiar text, it is not necessary to do more than quote a passage that may be taken as its synthesis: "In the mimetic art of antiquity, the instability of fortune almost always appears as a fate which strikes from without and affects only a limited area, not as fate which results from the inner process of the real, historical world" (*Mimesis*, p. 29).

The episodes of Odysseus's recognition by his nurse and Isaac's sacrifice represent two radically distinct *modes of presentation*. In the Greek example, everything is made explicit in the text. The narrator may even delay the action in order to explain in detail an accident—in the example, Odysseus's scar. In the Hebrew text, in contrast, the series of initial questions, culminating in the question why Jehovah orders Abraham to sacrifice his innocent son, are left unanswered. But the

examples are not juxtaposed so that the analyst may then affirm or inti-
mate his preference for either of the two modes. If in the Homeric
poems man's image is simpler and less problematic, its greater complexity in the biblical text is counterbalanced by its tyrannical claim
to truth: "The Bible's claim to truth is not only far more urgent than
Homer's, it is tyrannical—it excludes all other claims" (*Mimesis*, p. 14).
Curiously, this passage coincides with Kafka's much earlier remark on
the subject, which Auerbach could not possibly have known.[8] However, what in Kafka leads to the predicament of nonchoice, in Auerbach—a completely assimilated Jew—points to a solution, where the
idea of *figura*, grounded in Hegel, is crystallized. But before examining it, let us ask in what sense the example we have chosen belies the
mechanism of historical causality. The answer is quite simple: Auerbach does not attempt to submit the difference between the two modes
of presentation to a causal explanation. Rather, he suggests that the
Hebrew mode is autonomous, not dependent, and it may be inferred
that the same is true of the Greek: "The concept of God held by the
Jews is less a cause than a symptom of their manner of comprehending
and representing things" (*Mimesis*, p. 8).

Thus the *Geistesgeschichte* does not explain cause-and-effect relationships. In it, modes of presentation—assuming differentiated ways of
constructing a narrative, independent of any sociohistorical causative
mechanisms—are seen as able to articulate themselves and adjust to
conditioning social factors. To consider them under this second aspect from the outset is in fact to distort them somehow, though to go
no further than the first aspect—that is, independence from sociohistorical mechanisms—would be no less a distortion. Both practices are
well known in the intellectual history of the last few centuries: the first
is sociologism, the second is idealism. The opening pages of *Mimesis*, then, are the start of an alternative path. What might such a path
be like?

As originally expounded, it leads to the notion that the two modes
of presentation adapted to the separation of styles, the elevated—
tragedy and epic—and the low—comedy and farce. That is: as they
find their way into the sociohistorical atmosphere of European history,
the two modes interpenetrate. But their differences do not cancel each
other out; to say so would be to compromise the effectiveness of the
modes of presentation. We need go no further than the chapter I have

been discussing to see that such a conclusion would be a misreading of Auerbach. Toward the end of the discussion of Odysseus's scar, the author observes that "with the more profound historicity and the more profound social activity of the Old Testament text, there is connected yet another important distinction from Homer: namely, that a different conception of the elevated style and of the sublime is to be found here." But he also underscores the contrasting ways domestic realism is handled in the two modes: "Domestic realism, the representation of daily life, remains in Homer in the peaceful realm of the idyllic, whereas, from the very first, in the Old Testament stories, the sublime, tragic, and problematic take shape precisely in the domestic and commonplace" (*Mimesis*, p. 22). That is: western history is no melting pot in which everything blurs into an indistinct mass. On the contrary, even if Christianity has merged the two heritages and been carried by the same sociohistorical current as they, differences still remain.

Whereas the primacy of causality in nineteenth-century historiography—and, indeed, in mainstream twentieth-century history—eliminates the sublime, as Hayden White notes, because only a desublimized history could seem to be ruled by laws, in Auerbach the modes of presentation that were seminal for the West are animated on the one hand by the principle of beauty (the Homeric model) and on the other by the principle of the sublime (the Hebrew model). Auerbach confronts them precisely because he believes he can find in western thought the way to separate them while keeping both. Here the influence of Hegel's thought seems to have been decisive.

The association between Auerbach's treatment of the notion of *figura* and Hegel's concept of *Aufhebung* is well known. Rather than focus on the affinity between the two, let us attempt a closer understanding of *figura*.

The concept implies both the prefiguration of something yet to come and the historical preservation of the figuring and figured terms: "*Figura* is something real and historical which announces something else that is also real and historical."[9] Stressing the importance of this notion in early Christian thinkers and the role it plays in the articulation between the Old Testament and the New, Auerbach constantly reiterates the preservation of the historicity between the terms compared.[10] He also adds that it is because this interpretive trend predominates over the spiritualistic, intellectualized, and abstracting one that the idea of *figura*, though quite close to that of allegory, is not to be confused with it: "Since in figural interpretation one thing stands for another, since one thing represents and signifies the other, figural interpretation is 'allegorical' in the widest sense. But it differs from most of the allegorical forms known to us by the historicity both of the sign and what it signifies" (*Scenes*, p. 54).

Here we touch on a crucial point. Clearly Auerbach does not simply behave as a scholar who feels he has finished his task once his idea is expressed; it is obvious that this category means much to him because it secularizes and historicizes a principle that had originally served religious exegesis only. Further, it may be that he undertakes its analysis because it offers him both an alternative to the sort of factualistic history he had been trained in, as a philologist, and an operational principle that, together with the *Stiltrennung*, would allow him to write an *inner history*—not just an accidental and external one—of literature. This question cannot be asserted with any certainty. But the long passage below reveals his position, in an ironic, indirect way:

History, with all its concrete force, remains forever a figure, cloaked and needful of interpretation. In this light the history of no epoch ever has the practical self-sufficiency which, from the standpoint both of primitive man and of modern science, resides in the accomplished fact; all history, rather, remains open and questionable, points to something still concealed, and the tentativeness of events in the figural interpretations is fundamentally different from the tentativeness of events in the modern view of historical development. In the modern view, the provisional event is treated as a step in an unbroken horizontal process; in the figural system the interpretation is always sought from above; events are considered not in their unbroken relation to one another, but torn apart, individually, each in relation to something other that is promised and not yet present. Whereas in the modern view the event is always self-sufficient and secure, while the interpretation is fundamentally incomplete, in the figural interpretation the fact is subordinated to an interpretation which is fully secured to begin with: the event is enacted according to an ideal model which is a prototype situated in the future and thus far only promised. (*Scenes*, pp. 58–59)

Dante, because he actualizes this figurativeness, is for Auerbach the *diletto* poet par excellence. True, one may read as neutral praise the passage in which he resumes the thesis of his first book, *Dante als Dichter der irdischen Welt* (1929): "For Dante the literal meaning or historical reality of a figure stands in no contradiction to its profounder meaning, but precisely 'figures' it; the historical reality is not annulled, but confirmed and fulfilled by the deeper meaning" (*Scenes*, p. 73). But we prefer to see Dante as the very epitome of the ideal for the critic-historian. With no such qualifications and much more straight-forwardly, Timothy Bahti writes: "Thus, a history of literary secular-ization is a figural writing of history, a *literary* history with the accent on the adjective—an *allegory* of history as its own literalization."[11]

To round off my argument, I will add that to Auerbach the literary dynamics of the West assumes that the separation of styles is slowly corroded by their fusion. While Christianity paved the way for this corrosion to the extent that the Christian principle of equality of all men prevailed over the differentiated treatment of nobles and common people, ironically it was actually achieved outside the scope of Chris-tianity, in nineteenth-century French realism. The crucial texts here are the chapter on Flaubert in *Mimesis* and Auerbach's later essay on Baudelaire, "Baudelaires 'Fleurs du mal' und das Erhabene" (1951). In both cases the transgression of *Stiltrennung* is emphasized. The conse-quent *Stilvermischung* is actualized by the elevated treatment of a prosaic subject. (The mixture of styles, I might note in passing, achieves what the separation of styles had not been able to do: the breakdown of the separation between the Greek and the Hebrew modes of presentation.) The congruency of the two passages is clear:

The serious treatment of everyday reality, the rise of more extensive and socially inferior human groups to the position of subject matter for problematic-existential representation, on one hand; on the other, the em-bedding of random persons and events in the general course of contemporary history, the fluid historical background—these, we believe, are the founda-tions of modern realism. (*Mimesis*, p. 491)

[Baudelaire] was the first to treat matters as sublime which seemed by nature unsuited to such treatment. The "spleen" of our poem is hopeless despair; it cannot be reduced to concrete causes or remedied in any way. A vulgarian would ridicule it; a moralist or a physician would suggest ways of curing it. But with Baudelaire their efforts would have been vain. (*Scenes*, p. 208)

However, the effect of this fusion reaches far beyond the literary sphere. For all the admiration he felt for the French realists—"The great French novelists are of fundamental significance for the fundamental issue of *Mimesis*; my admiration for them is great" (*Epilegomena*, p. 14)[12] — Auerbach realized that there was something unexpected in them. Once again the comparison between the two essays is highly revealing:

> What is true of these two [i.e., Emma and Charles] applies to almost all the other characters in the novel; each of the many mediocre people who act in it has his own world of mediocre and silly stupidity, a world of illusions, habits, instincts, and slogans; each is alone, none can understand another, or help another to insight; there is no common world of men. . . . But what the world would really be, the world of the "intelligent," Flaubert never tells us; in his book the world consists of pure stupidity. (*Mimesis*, p. 489)

> But what then of the hope? How can nothingness be a new sun that will bring flowers to unfolding? I know no answer. There is none to be found in *Les Fleurs du mal*. (*Scenes*, p. 223)

Much to his merit, Bahti, relating the essay on Dante to the one on Flaubert, observes that the latter is the culmination of the *figura* contained in the former, and in this Auerbach's conception of history is revealed: " 'History' is literally the past, figuratively its meaning as the history that is thought and written. And this history . . . must always reduce history as an ontological object into a dead letter, so that it might be 'meaningful,' the literal sign for an allegorical meaning."[13] And Bahti did not fail to notice the irony in the promise contained in Dante: "This, then, is the fulfillment of Dante's promise of the history of Western realism: representation without reality or so much as the possibility of life; truth as falsehood and nothingness; characters lacking both fulfillment *and* prefiguration of 'their own proper reality' except in their figural fulfillment as signifying letters."[14]

Indeed, we may say that both Flaubert and Auerbach, although for different reasons, were aware that they were living a moment of predicament: "Are we far from the return of universal listlessness, the belief in the end of the world, the expectation of a Messiah? But, since the theological basis is missing, what will provide the basis for this enthusiasm that is unaware of itself?"[15] As to Auerbach, since it would be impossible to find a passage as explicit as this, it is necessary to take a more roundabout route. The advantage is that this method may throw light on the possible limits of his critical and historical vision.

In 1975, David Carroll published a devastating critique of *Mimesis*, showing that for all the author's suspicion of the effectiveness of concepts, there was a theoretical conception underlying his work. If concepts seem to him to *verfälschen oder zerstören die Phaenomene* (falsify or destroy phenomena), it is precisely because, Carroll argued, there is something independent from them "which makes the real predictable and comprehensible." This something, he then added, presupposed "the living, feeling subject," originator of the "relationship with the real," in which "nothing precedes or determines the relationship." In other words, "the self is the concept which guarantees the integrity of the present."[16]

Carroll's deconstruction was no doubt exemplary. However, less than twenty years later it already begins to seem dated. Not that it is unfair or that the point it raises no longer seems crucial. Why, then, do *Mimesis* and the rest of Auerbach's small output remain alive, even though founded on the same epistemological fallacy? In order to answer this question, let us return to the predicament I mentioned above.

It was because he believed in the constancy of the self, its independence from explanatory constructions, and its power to correct conceptual or ideological distortions that Auerbach had a particular view of mimesis. Schematically, this view presupposes (a) a subject that is potentially a corrector of falsifying views; and (b) "a profound trust in the truthfulness of language," as he wrote apropos of Flaubert. Mimesis was the precipitate of these two assumptions, manifesting itself as the correct and adequate representation of what free eyes were able to see. I should now like to add that the predicament that Auerbach identified in the mid-nineteenth century, specifically incarnated in Flaubert's parody of the fullness promised by the *figura* in Dante, may be better understood if we consider Auerbach's analysis of *Madame Bovary* in *Mimesis*: more precisely, his interpretation of *discours indirect libre* (free indirect style). To Auerbach, its use by Flaubert implied that the novelist left out his own comments, potentially enlightening for the reader, trusting the capacity for enlightenment contained in "the truthfulness of language." "Every event, if one is able to express it purely and completely, interprets itself and the persons involved in it far better and more completely than any opinion or judgement appended to it could do" (*Mimesis*, p. 486).

Today we tend to feel that the interpretation of the procedure achieved much less than it could. As Dominick LaCapra observed, the free indirect style "involves a dialogue not only between self and objec-

tified other but one within the self—a dialogue entailing a high degree
of uncertainty and doubt."[17] That is why the reader cannot be oriented
by the narrator. Further, throughout the work the boundaries between
individual voices remain fuzzy. Is *Madame Bovary* a critique of French
society—postrevolutionary, post-Napoleonic, Restoration, bourgeois,
once again imperial? Of course it is. But in the name of what is this
society criticized? Now, as long as language lacks confidence in its
complete truthfulness—or rather, as long as language no longer en-
lightens the subject, freeing it from prejudices and distortions—how
can mimesis be seen as a faithful homologue, an adequate representation of reality? Might the answer be that mimesis is rather a potential
event and that, in the strong sense of the term (that in which an event is
distinguished from a mere occurrence), it is an incidence that cannot be
explained by a previously constituted structure? In contrast with what
has been legitimated by an old tradition, mimesis as an event—that is,
in its moments of maximum activation—is not homology, and thus
not similarity with something previously constituted, but rather the
production of difference. Thus Flaubert's feeling of being in a predicament
was necessary for conditions to allow a reconsideration of mimesis.
These conditions, however, were not actualized by Auerbach because
he, like the rest of the generation that grew up before World War II, remained committed to the valuation of the individual subject and to the
Hegelian legacy of *representation*. We should then be aware of this limit
so that we can fruitfully return to his starting point. In doing so, we
may well ask: How can his Greek and Hebrew modes of presentation
be seen—since they are not to be explained in terms of determination
or causality—if not as seminal events?

Auerbach remains precious to us—and even this adjective is insufficient to convey his real worth—in spite of the deconstruction of his
humanistic aporia because he is one of the few who allow us to conceive literature in an alternative way. For reasons of limitation of space,
I shall do no more than observe that this alternative way allows us to
look at mimesis without the anathema that we are used to attaching to
it, and refashions its own mode of operation. Mimesis, then—let me
repeat—is not a homologue, not *Vorstellung*, but a disruptive event, a
producer of difference that affects the way we understand the world.

Translated by Paulo Henriques Brito

Part II

Philology, Language, and History

Stephen G. Nichols

Philology in Auerbach's Drama of (Literary) History

I got to know Erich Auerbach rather intimately about three or four years after his death in 1957. Our acquaintance grew over the space of a year or so by virtue of my visiting his apartment once a week—I think on Tuesday afternoons, but I can't be certain. Punctually at two, I would ring the bell and Marie Auerbach, his widow, would answer the door, carefully dressed as though it were her "afternoon to receive" in Berlin, or Marburg, or Istanbul. We would spend the next several hours sorting through Auerbach's papers and notes, each one seeming to recall a special occasion whose background and significance Mrs. Auerbach would gloss with reminiscences of university politics and intellectual quarrels from Weimar Germany (she did not much care to discuss their years in Istanbul).

There would be letters from Erwin Panofsky, from Thomas Mann, from Catholic prelates; the latter especially delighted her since it seemed at once droll and ironic that Roman Catholic churchmen would consult a Jewish refugee on abstruse matters of Christian theology or history. We found letters from a pantheon of the major scholarly fig-ures of the 1940's and 1950's—but none from Ernst Robert Curtius, despite intellectual affinities and relationship to that extraordinary Ro-manist, Karl Vossler (1872–1949), who created a school of German sty-listics to which, in their several ways, Auerbach, Curtius, and Spitzer each subscribed. Mrs. Auerbach considered Curtius with contempt, an opportunist who, as she saw it, usurped the prestige in Germany her husband should have had and who became a medievalist by appropriating at least the spirit if not the letter of her husband's ideas.

Perhaps because we spoke French primarily, a language she handled easily whereas my spoken German was rudimentary to nonexistent, I had the sense of being transported on those afternoons into another world, a world of European intellectual life as lived in Germany before the Third Reich. This was a world, it seemed, where ideas were mediated not by abstract theories, but by the individuals who espoused them and by the friends and colleagues who debated them in long, handwritten letters.

Auerbach did not seem to possess many manuscripts of his scholarship; we never found that last unpublished article or note that I fantasized our turning up late on a winter's afternoon just before our ritual coffee. In my imagination it would have been unfinished and Mrs. Auerbach would naturally ask me to complete and publish it — *The Yale Review? The Kenyon Review?* In the way of oneiric musings, I never contemplated the problem of language. Would I have translated it into English first? But there was nothing.

What he had left were offprints carefully labeled *Handexemplar* and filled with notes in the margins, between lines, sometimes with interleaved pages of writing. These he obviously intended to republish as reworked articles. Others he would label emphatically: *Nicht wiederzuveröffentlichen!* It appeared that he spent a good deal of time reviewing his publications, less in order to modify the theoretical or methodological postulates than to argue particular points more subtly or, more often, to bring in new supporting examples.

These sessions would always conclude in the same way. Mrs. Auerbach would make coffee and serve a cake or pastry she had baked that morning. We then talked of their life in Germany and the trials they had been through subsequently. She still harbored shock from the trauma of moving to the U.S. thinking they had at last found a refuge at Penn State only to discover they would have to leave after several years because a routine physical by the university's insurance company turned up a preexisting heart problem and Auerbach could not be insured.

Panofsky gave them temporary refuge at the Institute for Advanced Study in Princeton, but then as now the institute did not view literature as serious scholarship worthy of permanent representation on its faculty. Happily, Henri Peyre found them and immediately offered Auerbach his American apotheosis first as professor of French and Romance Philology, then as Sterling Professor at Yale. Mrs. Auerbach's account of those uncertain years always resonated pride that they had lived so rather than accept the offer of a chair in West Germany proposed after the war. Never would they have agreed to live in the land that had cast them out, but which nevertheless still formed the stuff of her memories and her lifestyle. They were proud to have become American citizens, she said, in a ceremony whose details she recounted to me more than once. And so our conversation would go. At 5 or 5:30, I would leave the old world of Auerbach's *Nachlaß* and Marie Auerbach's memories to return to Yale and my dissertation.

Thirty years later, it is difficult to imagine what a magical work *Mimesis* seemed to us in the 1950's. Some of that excitement is conveyed in the blurbs by Alfred Kazin, Delmore Schwartz, and René Wellek that may still be read on the back of the Princeton University Press paperback edition. Unquestionably, a good part of its appeal came from the conception of historical philology that Auerbach developed for *Mimesis*.

This was the first major study to appear after World War II that attempted to examine key texts from western literature to demonstrate concretely how they constructed themselves in their respective contexts as lively examples of authentic discourse, the kind of speech people used in real life. What seemed amazing, however, was Auerbach's further assertion, relentlessly argued in each chapter, that historical specificity, the sense of a given period, might be gleaned from studying discourse in this way. Auerbach had translated Giambattista Vico's *The New Science* into German in 1924,[1] but few could have anticipated how he would realize the potential of Vico's conception of poetic wisdom—the idea that one might represent the history of a period dialectically through its discourse, as Auerbach himself said in his posthumous *Literary Language and Its Public in Late Latin Antiquity and in the Middle Ages*.[2]

Indeed, Auerbach construed Vico as equating philology with history[3] since the multiple dimensions of culture—for example, thought; oral, written, and visual expression; law; religion; and economics— all may be found "in the same basic conditions [*Bedingungen*]: specifically in a given cultural moment of human society taken as a whole."

Philology opened the door to history because the interdependence of modes of cultural expression was such that insight into any one social configuration at a particular moment of its development provided the key to understanding all the other configurations at the same stage.[4]

At a moment when formalism held sway, these were radical thoughts. They unsettled the system of genres and the generally accepted sense of the appropriate separation of intellectual disciplines, for example, literature *and* history, philosophy *and* literature, where the "and" was a boundary marker more than a conjunction. René Wellek, for example, while recognizing the genius of *Mimesis*, deplored the relativism of its approach, describing Auerbach's refusal to respect boundaries as "an extremely dangerous conception of criticism and scholarship."[5]

Without, I think, fully appreciating Auerbach's admittedly weak theorizing of Vichian philological anthropology, Wellek decries the rejection of a recognizable critical system in favor of "philology," charging that Auerbach relies overly much on creative intuition and contextual definition, rather than conceptualization, and thereby fails to observe generic boundaries, mixing literary genres with nonliterary texts from "histories, chronicles, memoirs, essays, personal letters, and critical manifestoes." As a result, he constantly and consciously "oversteps the limits of literature as fiction."[6]

Because he could not admit the efficacy of philological anthropology for analyzing the way discourse broadly conceived can reveal significant cultural movements, Wellek found problematic Auerbach's linking of existence and history. These two categories should, he argues, be kept separate because they "combine two contradictory conceptions of realism," one that is existential and one, historicist—one deriving from Kierkegaard, the other from Hegel, whom Kierkegaard detested and against whose influence his work was intended as a protest and a corrective.[7]

Wellek finally grows impatient with Auerbach's insistence on clinging to the term "philology" because it obscures his real vocation as a literary historian and critic. From Wellek's perspective, Auerbach would better account for his method if he abandoned "philology" in favor of more precise terminology. Wellek was at least consistent in his impatience, having already written the obituary of philology in the mid-1940's in chapter 4 of his and Austin Warren's *Theory of Literature*.[8] Wellek and Auerbach personally debated these issues in New Haven during the 1950's. In the methodological reflection that introduces *Literary Language and Its Public*, "Über Absicht und Methode," Auerbach struck back at Wellek's charges point by point (but without mentioning his friend by name).

Vico's idea of philology, he says, places it opposite philosophy. Philology inquires into the laws and limits of specific historical periods, seeking to determine what the people in those periods hold for true. Philology deals with the historical mode of life and mutations of a period; this is the *Wirklichkeit*, the reality or realism Auerbach seeks. And it is paradoxically via this anthropological turn that philology connects with philosophy which in Vico's schema deals with metaphysical truth, *Wahrheit*. But as this truth can only be known— at least conceptually—through the whole course of history, which it is philology's task to elucidate, philology and philosophy ultimately converge. For history and metaphysics, reality and truth finally deal only with us: "One can thus . . . just as well talk about a philology as a philosophy. It is a question, in this philological philosophy or this philosophical philology, only of one thing, humans on planet earth."[9]

Ironically, while Auerbach was defending his conception of philology against the attacks of René Wellek and other literary critics, he was being equally assailed from within the fortress of philology itself. Text editors and textual critics were appalled at the anthropological turn Auerbach's version of philology had taken. To make philology a key to history, to equate it with philosophy, seemed to some a threat to the disciplinary boundaries that confined philology narrowly to establishing texts, to editing them, and to studying historical languages.

We see this attitude strongly stated in 1953 by a Dutch philologist named Joseph Engels, for whom the work of Auerbach, Curtius, and Spitzer belonged in the realm of aesthetics and literary criticism rather than to philology.[10] Precisely because Auerbach and Curtius called themselves philologists, Engels, like Wellek, felt that the term had become too broad and should be abolished. I would argue that the popular success of *Mimesis*, on the one hand, and its mode of cutting through and across disciplinary boundaries to show that language could be the key to a sociology of textual study, on the other, stimulated the critique of philology from both the textual critics and the literary critics. In Auerbach's hands, philology had become an unstable element capable of undercutting formalist dogma of all kinds.

Engels's response to this threat was typical of a good many philologists of the period. He urged adherence to the new discipline of linguistics, citing with approval the Danish linguist Otto Jespersen's rejection of philology as the historical study of the culture of a nation having little or nothing to do with the scientific study of language. The appeal of Jespersen for Engels seems to have been the focus on language as the tangible element, the "hard" substance at the center of the various components of a Romance philology increasingly difficult to pin down in any way that seemed practical. Salvation, or at least logic, lay for Engels in reformulating philology to move it closer to a Jespersen-like linguistics.

Engels wanted linguistic philology to deal only with aspects of communication in literary texts. As soon as language "begins to be the expression of an artistic thought,"[11] it becomes a vehicle for literary aesthetics (*"le beau littéraire"*); "to apply the term 'philology' here would only serve to create confusion and misunderstanding."[12] In other words, Engels effectively rules the study of literature out of bounds to philology, since literary texts will simply serve as tokens or "informants" providing examples of language to be studied from a purely linguistic viewpoint.

In effect, Engels divorces representation from the reality of its contextualization, its historical situation, since it is only in the context of the literary setting that a given expression can have its full meaning. *"Songe"* and *"mensonge"* in the *Romance of the Rose* of Guillaume de Lorris, for instance, have very different meanings from what we find in other "informant texts." The lexical register of thirteenth-century Old French would be the poorer were one to divorce these terms from their rhetorical context, and that is precisely one of Auerbach's main contentions. In the name of maintaining a narrow disciplinary focus, Engels sought to discriminate within literary language between aesthetics and communication, the latter being conceived as a monodimensional element, whose putative content he never defines.[13]

Neither Engels nor Wellek could admit the significance of Auerbach's attempt to synthesize representation and reality, *Darstellung* and *Wirklichkeit*. It would be two decades before Brian Stock, in a prescient article in *New Literary History*, demonstrated the consequences of Auerbach's philological anthropology.[14] He did so by showing how Auerbach had succeeded in achieving "the difficult union of representation and reality, the goal after which in different ways better philosophers like Cassirer and Lukács had vainly striven" (p. 232).

Auerbach achieved this synthesis by finding the universal in the particular, in this case the concrete phenomenon of a historically grounded language, in whatever source he could turn up. In other words, he situated "his empirical analyses in a comparative framework explicitly designed to facilitate interpretation" (ibid.). As Stock noted, the universal element Auerbach sought in his textual informants, "das Allgemeines," resided neither in laws nor in categories of classification" (p. 531), which is one reason scholars like Engels and Wellek who were committed to such disciplinary laws and categories reacted as they did to the approach.

His success in isolating this universal element and in capturing the "dialectical relationship between representation and reality" lay in Auerbach's appropriation of the concept *Ausformung*, beautifully characterized by Stock as akin to "medieval Latin *ornatus*, amplification, which would capture the Platonic and Wölfflinesque flavor of a term that hovers delicately between literary style and the linearity of the plastic arts" (p. 532). In Auerbach's own terms, this sensuous amplification of phenomena (*sinnlicher Ausformung der Erscheinungen*) seeks "to represent phenomena in a fully externalized form, visible and palpable in all their parts, and completely fixed in their spatial and temporal relations."[15]

Pursuing the implications of *Ausformung* leads to a recognition that philology has the potential for offering a picture, an image of an age through its material manifestations, such as documents, architectual monuments, almost any surviving artifact that can be connected to a textually grounded program of representation. Since these documents can be shown to encapsulate a dialectic between representation and reality, they may be seen to form a dynamic image, a performance or theatricalization of the dialectic that makes that particular moment in time and space different from others.

This means nothing less than a theory of cognition that is at once performative and visual, but also participatory, since it engages those who would recover the traces of earlier periods. "Re-evocation" is the term Auerbach uses for this participatory process of experiencing *Aus-formung* through critical study of historical documents, as he says in "Vico and Aesthetic Historicism":

> The second point is Vico's theory of cognition. The entire development of human history, as made by men, is potentially contained in the human mind, and may therefore, by a process of research and re-evocation, be understood by men. The re-evocation is not only analytic; it has to be synthetic, as an understanding of every historical stage as an integral whole, of its genius . . . a genius pervading all human activities and expressions of the period concerned.[16]

In the few pages remaining, I would like to examine the workings of the concept of *Ausformung* with its attendant theoretical consequences for chapter 7 of *Mimesis*, "Adam and Eve," the first of the four chapters in *Mimesis* that Auerbach devotes to dramatic works. In many ways "Adam and Eve" deals with the most universal as well as the most temporally idiosyncratic of dramas.

Whereas the other plays, by Shakespeare, Molière, and Schiller, remain at least nominally accessible today without special training, *Le Jeu d'Adam*, an anonymous twelfth-century Latin–Old French liturgical drama, remains something of a mystery even for philologists. At the same time, as a dramatization of a foundational event for western culture, the book of Genesis from the Hebrew Bible, its subject matter is known to people who have never read Shakespeare's *Henry IV Part 2*, Molière's *Tartuffe*, or Schiller's *Luise Millerin*.

It may well be the very centrality of the subject matter of the *Jeu d'Adam* that underlies the difficulty that Auerbach experiences with the material in this chapter. Chapter 7 ought to be a prime showcase for *Ausformung* and the dialectic between representation and reality in the twelfth century. In many ways, it does illustrate Auerbach's fluency with the dissimilar idioms of Latin theology and vernacular imaginative literature. It begins for example with a lively discussion of the *Jeu d'Adam* (ca. 1150–75), the first vernacular liturgical drama to be represented outside the Church and away from a purely liturgical context. It then reprises the theme of "sermo humilis," the humble style of expression introduced in chapter 3. Auerbach illustrates the difference between the high and the low style in contrasting passages from Bernard of Clairvaux (twelfth century) and Saint Francis of Assisi (thirteenth century) in order to demonstrate the realism of *sermo humilis* and its historical specificity. He concludes with an analysis of a passage from a Passion poem in dialogue form by Jacopone da Todi (b. 1230), a thirteenth-century mystic and poet of the period immediately before Dante. The dialogue Auerbach analyzes in Jacapone da Todi's poem focuses on the Virgin Mary at the moment she learns that her son has been condemned to die.

Always a more subtle reader of texts than E. R. Curtius and possessed of a command of the Church Fathers and their high medieval avatars like Bernard of Clairvaux or Saint Francis, Auerbach also had a fine sense of their vision, a sensitivity to their writing that makes them come alive under his pen. In chapter 7, however, this fluency leads him to weave an image of the period reminiscent of a diptych or triptych, an altarpiece recounting the salvation history on which so much of medieval civilization was focused.

Adam and Eve in this chapter do not simply refer to the Latin–Old French *Jeu d'Adam*, or *Ordo representationcis Ade* (to give it its more accurate designation), but to the whole Christian Salvation cycle that the *Ordo* implies. In effect, the chapter utilizes the structure of the *Ordo* to give an updated version of the Salvation cycle woven out of authentic medieval works that substitute for the biblical material of the *Ordo*. The latter has a three-part structure which (although unfinished) allows us to recognize that it was meant to demonstrate the link from the Fall and its dire consequences for human history to Christ's redemption of that historical event. The three remaining sections of the *Ordo* are the story of Adam and Eve, the story of the repetition of their sin by Cain and Abel, and a procession of the prophets who announce the ultimate arrival of a Messiah.

The purpose of placing the *Ordo* at the beginning of the chapter (and of naming it "Adam and Eve") gains piquancy from the realization that it must represent the conception of *figura* that Auerbach had worked out in the 1930's. From this perspective Adam and Eve prefigure Christ and Mary, showing the necessity for the Christian transit. Just as figural interpretation makes the Old Testament a metaphoric gloss on the New, so Auerbach structures his Adam and Eve chapter to show medieval works as a figural fulfillment of Scripture.

Viewed from this perspective, the *Jeu d'Adam* becomes a paradigm for medieval symbolic expression. Adam and Eve reenact the Fall; the selections chosen from Saint Bernard and Saint Francis illustrate examples of life in the fallen world and the way these Christian prophets explain it by referring forward to the coming of Salvation; and, finally, the Passion poem by Jacopone da Todi plunges us into the midst of a reenactment—in the "modern" vernacular—of the coming of the new Eve and the Second Adam. The chapter thus begins with EVA and closes with AVE. It is a brilliant and subtle *Ausformung* of *figura* and *sermo humilis*, the two principles by which Auerbach transformed medieval studies generally and Dante studies in particular.

If one turns away from *Mimesis*, however, and back to the text of the *Ordo representationis Ade*, the foundational work for the chapter, one encounters a certain disjunction between the text and the account Auerbach gives of it. It appears that philology, as opposed to philosophy, did not play as prominent a role in the *Ausformung* of the chapter as it should have done. Either that, or else Auerbach's definition of philology did not extend to close attention to manuscripts. It matters very much as it happens because Auerbach predicates his account of the *Jeu d'Adam*, so crucial for setting up the chapter's typology, not simply on a close reading of the play, but also on a critical textual reading: in short, an old-fashioned philology. Yet he seems not to see that the issue is not the language of the *Ordo* simply, but the *Ausformung* of that language: its elaboration and representation in the specific time and space of the unique manuscript that has transmitted it to us. I take that manuscript space to be both image and performative discourse.

As it happens, the single manuscript in which the *Ordo* has come down to us, MS Tours 927, has been the theater for a textual drama in which Auerbach's chapter plays an interesting and not altogether flattering role, at least as it reflects on his philological rigor. There is a major discrepancy between the reading of the manuscript in lines 280–87 and the version Auerbach provides of it, the version on which he builds his argument.[17] To my knowledge, no one has noticed that even though he was writing in the early 1940's, he used a German edition published in 1891 which had undergone revision in two subsequent editions by 1928 (see my Appendix at the end of this essay for a fuller exposition of the textual questions discussed). In Marburg, where he first taught the *Ordo*, Auerbach did have access to a later French edition, or at least the manuscript reading on which it was based (and which became standard in subsequent editions, including the third edition of the text he accepts). Not only did he not use the French edition, he argues strongly against it, even though it revised the *Ordo*'s textual history to conform more with the evidence provided by the manuscript.

Just to make sure we understand the issues: Auerbach rejects the version that conforms more closely to the historical evidence, imperfect though it may be, and defends the most modern of the versions, one that even imposed a modern metrical schema on the work. More curious still, the version Auerbach insistently defends had been repudiated by its own editor more than thirty years before Auerbach wrote.[18]

Why would he have made so conscious a departure from historical evidence? Almost certainly on the Vichian grounds of historical aestheticism. As he understood, alone among the commentators on the play, the discourse attributions in this rapid-fire exchange between Adam and Eve radically alter the image by which we conceive of each character, but especially Eve. A good deal of low-level misogyny, both medieval and modern, underlies the shifting discourse attributions to Eve in this passage. Auerbach's own condescension is patent:

It is evident that Etienne [against whose interpretation Auerbach is arguing] conceives of Eve as an extremely skillful and diplomatic person, whose object is to soothe Adam and make him forget the tempter Satan against whom he is prejudiced. . . . Eve in fact is clumsy, very clumsy, even though her clumsiness is not hard to understand. For without the Devil's special help she is but a weak—though curious and hence sinful—creature, far inferior to her husband and easily guided by him. That is how God created her from Adam's rib.[19]

This is not Auerbach speaking for himself, but Auerbach giving the aesthetic-historicist version of a twelfth-century Eve. He needs this image because it is precisely this female anthropology that Mary, the New Eve, will rectify, thereby transforming EVA to AVE. His editorial interventionism in the text of the *Ordo* seeks to establish and defend the figural symmetry of the Eve/Virgin Mary couplet not in the name of demonstrating the ethical lapse of Eve in the *Ordo*, nor in order to condemn her ill-starred participation in what Luiz Costa-Lima has called "the eternal struggle between reason and the passions and prejudices."[20] Instead, we have an early example of how Auerbach uses Vico's aesthetic historicism to postulate a higher image of medieval culture. Eve offers an example of *Vorstellung* or meta-history by incarnating the Vichian concept of folk genius.[21]

Had he paid more attention to the *Ausformung* offered by the visual text, that is, the manuscript text of the *Ordo*, he might have perceived a reason for the confusion of discourse attribution at precisely the moment that Eve begins to find her own voice. MS Tours 927 shows us something important at this point, when the scribe betrays uncertainty as to the appropriate discourse attributions in this passage in which something unexpected and quite revolutionary occurs before his and our own eyes, as it were. Eve upsets the symmetry of the seigneur-vassal relationship that dominates the prior dialogues between the *figura* and Adam, Diabolus and Adam, and even Diabolus and Eve. Eve exhibits a new attitude and willful rationality by interrogating the prohibitions Adam accepts so unquestioningly.

Heretofore, the issue of the forbidden fruit has been one of knowledge, sa*ver*. But Eve alters this radically by a question that she alone asks: what taste, sa*vor*, has the fruit (ll. 252, 296, 303–5). With one deft question, she intrudes the body, and with it sensuality and desire. Her play on *saver/savor* structures her speeches at three decisive moments leading to Adam's action, that is, his submission to Eve's will in eating the fruit.

Action, *actio*, was the classical definition given to drama. Eve engenders the *actio* and thus the drama of the *Ordo* by unbalancing her *homo erectus*. The principles of disequilibrium and asymmetry that she introduces into the Latin–Old French drama come directly from the jeu d'esprit *saver/savor* by which she introduces the mind/body problem into what used to be Adam's Paradise. This may not be the *sermo humilis* or the *figura* Auerbach had in mind, but it *is* what philology, when challenged, can offer to literary history.

Appendix:
Note on Auerbach's Textual Philology

Here is the text of the passage of the *Jeu d'Adam* that Auerbach finds so crucial for his presentation of Eve as representative of a medieval historical folk genius, following the notion of aesthetic historicism he develops from his reading of Vico. The text given by Auerbach in *Mimesis*, chapter 7, appears on the left, while on the right, the transcription from the unique MS Tours 927. Auerbach's version comes from Karl Grass's 1891 edition.

We know that Auerbach taught a seminar on the *Jeu d'Adam* in 1934 in Marburg. Marburg must have had Grass's two later editions (1907, 1928), each different from the 1891 version (which Grass ultimately repudiated).

Auerbach, *Mimesis*		Ms 927, Bibliothèque de Tours	
ADAM:	Ne creire ja le traïtor! [l. 280]	A.	Ne creire ia le traitor.
	Il est traïtre, bien le sai.		Il est traitre. E. Bien le sai.
EVA:	Et tu comment?	A.	E tu comment. E. Car jo lai oi.
A:	Car l'esaiai!		De co quen chat me del ueer.
E:	De ço que chalt me del veer?	[A.]	Il te fera changer sauer.
	Il te fera changer saver.	E.	Nel fra pas car nel crerai.
A:	Nel fera pas, car nel crerai		De nule ŗien tant que la sai.
	De nule rien tant que l'asai.	A.	Nel laisser mais venir sor toi.
	Nel laisser mais venir sor toi.		

The first edition (of three) of Karl Grass's German edition—*Das Adamsspiel, anglonormannisches Gedicht des XII. Jahrhunderts,* mit einem Anhang, ed. Karl Grass, Romanische Bibliothek, 6 (Halle a. S., 1891)—is the only one of the six complete editions since Luzerche's *editio princeps* (Tours, 1854) to have all of the following forms:

L. 281: *Il est traïtre, bien le sai* [Grass, 1891 (but NOT in 1907 or 1928, the second and third editions); Studer, 1918].

L. 282: *Car l'esaiai* [Grass, 1891 (but NOT in 1907 or 1928)]. Studer and Grass use discourse reassignments as per the *Mimesis* version.

L. 283: *qu'en chalt* [Grass, 1891; Studer, 1918]. The *Mimesis* version is closest to Grass, 1891, of all the editions extant in Auerbach's lifetime.

(Aebischer's 1963 edition, chez Droz, is the only one to use the exact form Auerbach has, interestingly enough.)

L. 285: *Il te fera* [Grass, 1891].

One must conclude that Auerbach used the first German edition of Karl Grass from 1891 (not the *Zweite verbesserte Auflage*, 1907, nor the *Dritte verbesserte Auflage*, 1928). This is in itself interesting, since Grass's second edition appeared well before Auerbach began his medieval studies, as Hans Ulrich Gumbrecht demonstrates. Grass's first edition was generally viewed as flawed for reasons summed up by Paul Studer in his edition of 1918:

Based on a careful collation of the Tours MS. (by the late W. Foerster), this edition shows a distinct improvement on its predecessors; but, as Suchier and Tobler have clearly shown in their reviews, it cannot in any sense be considered final. Grass attempted to make such emendations as the context or the metre rendered imperative, taking for granted that the verses should scan according to the canons of standard French prosody.[22]

We know that Auerbach had S. Etienne's 1922 article, "Note sur les vers 279–287 du *Jeu d'Adam*," and would certainly have had access to Henri Chamard's 1925 edition[23] at Marburg, though he does not follow it for the reasons he explains.

It is interesting to note that Grass, in his 1928 edition, did heed Etienne's article, as did Paul Aebischer in his 1963 edition. One would imagine that Auerbach would certainly have felt compelled to comment on Grass's third edition of 1928, as he comments on Chamard's, if he had consulted it. One must also conclude that he had no knowledge of, nor apparent interest in, MS Tours 927, aside from what he could glean from descriptions in Etienne's article. There is a good description in Luzerche, but nothing suggests he consulted this either.

That Auerbach made no effort to review this section upon his arrival in the United States when he again had access to decent libraries merits reflection. His general inattentiveness to textual questions, in the technical sense of the term, suggests a philological perspective, as Luiz Costa-Lima argues, more fixed on the "historical horizon" than on critical textual studies. The best text for Auerbach was the one that most accurately could convey an image of the medieval imagination that was most exciting, most satisfying to modern sensibilities. He showed, in Michel de Certeau's terms, that "History is probably our myth. It combines what can be thought, the 'thinkable,' and the origin, in conformity with the way in which a society can understand its own working."[24]

Seth Lerer

Philology and Collaboration: The Case of Adam and Eve

I had to dispense with almost all periodicals, with almost all
the more recent investigations, and in some cases with reliable
critical editions of my texts.

— Auerbach, *Mimesis*

The seventh chapter of *Mimesis* begins, unlike those that have preceded
it, neither with a problem in the history of literary style nor with an
exemplary passage in the shifting sensibilities that mark the antique
from the classical and the classical from the medieval. "Adam and Eve"
begins by trying to establish a text. The opening quotation for that
chapter—the dialogue in which Adam and Eve first quarrel, then debate, then fall—comes from a play "extant in a single manuscript."[1]
Of the little that survives of the vernacular, liturgically oriented drama,
the *Mystère d'Adam* is "one of the oldest specimens" (p. 146). Unique
and originary, marking the starting point both of a distinctive genre
and of a vernacular literary history, the play's text stands here at the
opening of "Adam and Eve" in ways far different from the quotations
that begin *Mimesis*'s other chapters. It appears not as some randomly
selected, exemplary section of a larger work; nor is it one of those "few
passages" that, in the phrasing of the book's close, "can be made to
yield more, and more decisive, information about [authors] and their
times than would a systematic and chronological treatment of their
lives and works" (p. 548). This is a passage carefully selected for its
individualities and not its commonplaces. It tells a story of a set of
firsts: the first human communication, first sin, first desire, and first
text of a tradition that articulates the sublime in colloquial form. It
is a story of a loss; yet, in the larger context of *Mimesis*, it provides

the occasion for recovery. This passage from the *Mystère d'Adam* enables Auerbach to deploy those few resources of *Zeitschriften* and *Untersuchungen* in his Turkish exile. It enables him to use the techniques of philology to re-create "reliable critical editions" of his texts and, in the process, to restore methodological control over the study of the European Middle Ages.

"Adam and Eve" has often formed the core of modern discussions on the history of medieval drama and the nature of vernacular expression in the tense juxtapositions of Church and populace that mark the plateaus of the so-called twelfth-century Renaissance. Indeed, the very canonicity of the *Mystère*, or as it now is known, the *Jeu d'Adam*, is largely due to its discussion in *Mimesis* and, in turn, its sanctioning within the literary history constructed for it by the book.[2] And yet, for all its influence, the major point of Auerbach's interpretation — one hinging on a reconstruction of the text and the rejection of an editor's emendation — has been elided in most critical discussions. The gap between Auerbach's role as literary historian and textual critic widens here, as we inspect the rhetorical and ideological fissures of his argument. What I propose here is that "Adam and Eve" reenacts the very techniques of figural interpretation that Auerbach developed for the study of medieval literature. By reading Auerbach's own writing allegorically or figurally, I hope to make visible the powerful, political subtext behind his quarrel with a French editor and his reinterpretation of the quarrel between a French Eve and Adam. "Adam and Eve" has many purposes: an education in the arts of scholarly edition, an allegory of collaboration, a plea for the constructive ends of national philology. By reading Auerbach rhetorically, and by setting such a reading against another, contemporary essay on collaboration (Jean-Paul Sartre's "Qu'est-ce qu'un collaborateur?"), I hope to expose a facet of the unique history that made *Mimesis*, as Auerbach put it, the work of "a certain man at a certain time." That history, I suggest, is to be found not just in the explicit self-references that charge this volume with its poignancy, but in the figurations of its philological interpretations and its allegories of power.

Because the *Mystère d'Adam* and its manuscript encompass the discussion of first things, Auerbach seems anxious from the start to find its correct and originary form. Textual and literary criticism intertwine themselves here as in no other chapter of *Mimesis*, for the crux of Auer-bach's interpretation turns on the correct edition of the manuscript. Adam and Eve speak in what Auerbach defines as the familiar idioms of French life. The first man "calls his wife to account as a French farmer or burgher might have done when, upon returning home, he saw something he did not like," while the first woman responds with "the sort of question which has been asked a thousand times in similar situations by naive, impetuous people who are governed by their in-stincts: 'How do you know?'" (p. 147). The correct assignment of the dialogue is central to Auerbach's reading, not so much because it gov-erns the play's action as because it helps articulate its characters. The opening paragraphs of the chapter have, in fact, already sketched out the broad contours of those characters: Adam, good, noble, a repre-sentative of the French citizenry; Eve, intuitive, childish, even clumsy in her wiles. The text of the *Mystère*—garbled by medieval scribe and confused by modern editor—must be brought into line with the es-sentials of these characters, their idiom, their motivations, and their sensibilities.

In his *Introduction aux études de la philologie romane*, Auerbach sets out the methods of the editor, delineating the procedures for establishing a text beset by problems in transmission:

As for lacunae and passages that are irreparably corrupt, he [the editor] can try to reconstruct the text by making conjectures, that is, by forming his own hypothesis about the original form of the passage in question; of course, he must indicate, in this case, that he is making his own reconstruction of the text, and he must also record the conjectures, if there are any, that others have made about the same passage. One sees that the critical edition is, in general, easier to do if there exist few manuscripts or only a single manuscript; in this last case, one only has to have it published, with scrupulous accuracy, and to record any conjectures, if there should be any.[3]

This moment in the *Mystère d'Adam* offers a test case for this advice. The manuscript is, as Auerbach states, "somewhat confused" (p. 148), "ein wenig in Unordnung" (p. 145). His goal will be to restore "the original form of the passage in question," a task seemingly easy when faced with this "single manuscript." But there is little that is easy about the editing of this text. The distribution of these lines has been con-fused by one S. Etienne who, in a note published in *Romania* in 1922, proposed a new reading of the lines:[4]

ADAM: Ne creire ja le traïtor!
      Il est traïtre, bien le sai.
EVA: Et tu comment?
A: Car l'esaiai!
E: De ço que chalt me del veer?
      Il te fera changer saver.
A: Nel fera pas, car nel crerai
      De nule rien tant que l'asai.
      Nel laisser mais . . .
    (ll. 280–87, Auerbach's edition)

ADAM: Ne creire ja le traitor!
      Il est traitre.
EVA: Bien le sai.
ADAM: E tu comment?
EVA: Car l'asaiai!
      De ço que chalt me del veer?
ADAM: Il te ferra changer saver.
EVA: Nel fera pas, car nel crerai
      De nule rien tant que l'asai.
ADAM: Nel laisser mais . . .
    (ll. 280–87, Etienne's edition)

This is, to Auerbach, clearly no "proper reconstruction of a text" but a complete misunderstanding; from a manuscript only "somewhat confused," Etienne constructs a reading now "completely confused" ("völlig durcheinandergemischt"). The problem with the manuscript lay in the assignation of the parts, signaled by the scribe with a capital *A* and *E* for the respective speakers. Now, in Etienne's note, this particular passage "ont embarrassé la critique." It is "très curieux," presenting a problem in what Etienne calls the psychological continuity of the speakers.[5] What seems clear to him is that the scribe has mangled the assignment of the lines, shifting radically the tone of Adam and Eve. Etienne's goal, therefore, is to rescue the text from its copyist's mistakes; in Auerbach's terms, defined in the first page of the *Introduction aux études de la philologie romane*, "to preserve them not only from oblivion, but also from the changes, mutilations, and additions that necessarily result from popular consumption or the negligence of copyists."[6]

For Auerbach, however, there is no "negligence of copyists" in the text of the *Mystère d'Adam*. Rather, it is Etienne who misconstrues both the characters and the themes of the drama. Eve, in Etienne's edition, is far too knowing for Auerbach, far too skillful and self-assured. The emendation presents a dynamic of seduction and control, where the Serpent's intercession simply augments Eve's advance. To Auerbach, though, it is the Serpent who masterminds the Fall. Eve is clumsy (*ungeschikt*), "for without the Devil's special help she is but a weak— though curious and hence sinful—creature, far inferior to her husband and easily guided by him" (p. 149). Adam, the good French citizen ("ein braver Mann, ein französischer Bürger oder Bauer," p. 147), must be approached "where he is weak," must be confused into compliance. After the Devil's intercession, Eve can take control; only after taking counsel from the Serpent can she master the situation.

> The Devil has taught her how to get the better of her man; he has showed her where her strength is greater than his: in unconsidered action, in her lack of any innate moral sense, so that she transgresses the restriction with the foolhardiness of a child as soon as the man loses his hold [*sa discipline*] upon her. (pp. 150–51)

Eve's character, for Auerbach, remains stable, even though her actions shift in form and direction. Before and after her encounter with the Serpent she is childish, impetuous. Her earlier question was akin to that of "kindlichen, sprunghaften, instinktgebundenen Menschen"; here she has the "Tollkühnheit des Unmündigen," the rashness of the underaged. By contrast, Adam is always adult, always the head of the household. His fall, in these terms, is the fall of the grown-up trapped by games of the child. The pathos of his situation lies in this vision of a "poor confused, uprooted Adam" with whom Eve plays (*spielt*). She eats, as if to goad him into playing—"und dann ist es geschehen," and then all is over and the game is won (Eng., p. 151; Ger., p. 148).

   Auerbach offers this analysis as a case study of the way in which the Christian drama of redemption gives voice to sublime ideas in simple form. The juxtaposings of the learned and the popular, the Latin and the Old French, illustrate how vernacular literary experience becomes the vehicle for moral truth. The profundity of the Fall resounds in a scene of "everyday reality," a dialogue "in simple, low style." Its pathos and its power look back to those moments in the *sermo humilis* of Augustine while they anticipate the Tuscan idioms of Dante. The possibilities for figural interpretation—here as in nearly all the medieval texts Auerbach handles—lie precisely in this nexus of the high and low. God, the *figura* of the *Mystère d'Adam*, is both judge and savior, legal officer and spiritual father. He embodies the capacity of medieval literature to use historical or biblical personae to prefigure spiritual forms while holding both distinct as historical "realities." The simple surfaces of medieval Christian drama simultaneously shadow and reveal the underlying patterns of Creation, Incarnation, Passion, and Last Judgment that define what Auerbach identifies as "the very truth of the figural structure of universal history" (p. 158).

The everyday and real is thus an essential element of medieval Christian art and especially of the Christian drama. In contrast to the feudal literature of the courtly romance, which leads away from the reality of the life of its class into a world of heroic fable and adventure [*Sage und . . . Abenteuer*], here there is a movement in the opposite direction, from distant legend and its figural interpretation into everyday contemporary reality [*aus der fernen Legende und ihrer figürlichen Ausdeutung in die alltäglich-zeitgenössische Wirklichkeit hinein*]. (Eng., p. 159; Ger., p. 155)

But what precisely is this everyday contemporary reality for Auerbach? As he reminds us at the close of *Mimesis*, it is a scholar's life without the tools of scholarship: the journals, studies, and editions of the philological profession. As he announces at the opening, it is an exile's life without a nation, a moment when political and military action so challenges relations between truth and falsehood that "most historians are forced to make concessions to the technique of legend" (*Konzessionen an die Sagentechnik zu machen*).

These similarities of phrasing blur the line between the philological and the political. Read in tandem, they point towards the construction of a scholarly *figura* of their own, a recognition that debates on the establishment of texts may adumbrate the arguments of nations. The high and low are not just styles of literature but styles of scholarship as well. The place of the sublime in the colloquial becomes an issue not just for the story of the Fall but for the narrative of its edition. To paraphrase the reading of the drama, we might say that "Adam and Eve" moves from distant readings and their scholarly interpretations into the language of everyday contemporary reality.

Throughout the chapter, technical analyses are couched in the colloquial expressions of feeling. Arrestingly informal, the conversational gambit that opens the discussion of the play disarms the reader: "Now let us examine" (p. 147). But we are really asked, in Auerbach's *Betrachten wir nun* (p. 144), to reflect and meditate, to move in that realm of impression and response that early German reviewers of *Mimesis* found characteristic of its *Feingefühl*, its almost belletristic sensitivity.[7] Auerbach asks us to share his imagination of the everyday. The ordinariness of his French Adam is translated into language full of idiom and commonplace. Eve's question, we are told, is asked a thousand times. We are, in his translations and his paraphrases, on familiar turf here, much as we are in Auerbach's own analysis. "I find this impossible" (p. 148; "Mir scheint es unmöglich," p. 145), he rejoins to Etienne's emendation. Exclamations, rhetorical questions, appeals to common sense — these are the argumentative devices of this scholar. "I know from experience": this might as well be Auerbach's as well as Adam's line. Indeed, it might as well be that of the reader of *Mimesis*, for what the scholar is relying on here is not so much a refined ability with ancient languages as simple clearheaded observation. Experience is what is at the heart of "Adam and Eve," an experience of how people react, of how men speak to women, and of how the stories from the past can resonate with present lives. Eve is, after the serpent's tuition, "Herrin der Lage" (p. 147), idiomatically master of the situation. She is "to use the language of sport . . . in great form" (p. 150; "wie man in der Sportsprache sagt, in großer Form," p. 148), and as she plays (*spielt*) with her confused husband we can see the transformation not only of the Fall into a game but of the discipline of textual edition into sportsmanship.

For it is Auerbach himself who is *in großer Form* here, Auerbach who deploys all the cliches of *his* everyday reality to offer up a *sermo humilis* of philological control whose simple, low style may conceal the subtleties of criticism. The quarrel with Etienne replays the quarrel of his Eve and Adam: a quarrel about what we know, about the control of *sa discipline*, about what might be thought of as the spiritual patrimony of high civilization. There is an allegory to the philological. Textual recovery becomes a kind of restitution, and these pages in *Mimesis* work out, in practical form, the directives of the *Introduction aux études de la philologie romane*. Philology saves texts "not only from oblivion, but from the changes, mutilations, and additions that necessarily result from popular consumption or the negligence of copyists." The emendation of

Etienne, and its acceptance and reprinting in the published text of
Henri Chamard, presents a fallen text to Auerbach. Its misassignments
of the dialogue place Eve over her husband, rewrite in effect the challenge of serpentine guile in the subversions of the first couple. Eve may
play here, may be in the fine form of the competitor, may be the master
of the situation; yet, it must remain for Auerbach to show *his* form, to
reaffirm the competitive edge of textual criticism to become the master
of the interpretive situation. Auerbach, in short, replays a competition
between French and German critics and philologists charged with the
politics of the academy.

The story of Romance philology is a distinctively German story, for
the discipline arose "in a period in which German intellectuals were ac-
customed to taking the French to task as effete [*Welsche*]."[8] The origins
of *Romanistik* worked in tandem with the origins of European nation-
states, and a good deal of the institutional support for literary studies
hinged on the recovery of a cultural patrimony for the emerging political entities. The character of literature and the character of a people
came to stand as elements in an equation whose solution was a national
identity conceived through educational structures. Philology, to paraphrase von Clausewitz, became a form of politics by other means;
indeed, it could become a form of war by other means. The French responses to the "German science" often couched themselves in military
terms. Léon Gautier could write of his defeated countrymen in 1870:
"We find before us a nation which makes war scientifically. . . . For
the Prussian fights in the same way he criticizes a text, with the same
precision and method."[9] And in 1913, Henri Massis could complain:
"there is a clear, logical link between our system of classical studies and
the capitulation of Metz, as, of course, between the methodology of
German universities and the invasion of Paris."[10] The rise of chairs of
literature in France, the establishment of journals dedicated to medieval culture (*Romania* being among the first), all contributed to what
Gaston Paris could think of as a medieval literature emanating from
French soil: *plantes indigènes.*[11]

What was Auerbach to make of all this? He had been compelled, as
a Jew, to leave his appointment at Marburg, the very university town
where, Gautier had complained nearly seventy years before, "there
were more Germans working on the chanson de geste than were
French scholars in all of France."[12] For Auerbach, the anxieties of exile

go beyond the mere lament for journals, up-to-date investigations, and reliable editions. They embrace something of the taint of having been a part of the ongoing war with France and French philology. The quarrel with Etienne, thus on the surface, seems to recapitulate these national philology wars, seems to revile the scholar in *Romania* for constructing an interpretation of the *Mystère d'Adam* that is *Welsche*, even feminized in its imagining of a controlled and controlling Eve. But only on the surface. Rather than reinvest in the rhetoric of military conquest, Auerbach recasts his quarrel with philology, and in turn his reading of the play, as a story of collaboration. In reading his analysis of Eve, we find not the "invasion of Paris" but the infiltration of the French countryside. We find her assault on her husband—called, almost pathetically now, "ein braver Mann, ein französischer Burger oder Bauer"—worked not by the machinery of all-out war but in the machinations of betrayal.

Eve's claims, in her discussion with her husband, always rely on appeals to the here and now. She wishes for their betterment, speaks of experience in its most commonplace terms, and queries Adam on his understanding of the hard facts of life. Hers is the language of betrayal, and much of Auerbach's discussion hinges on Eve's failure to appreciate the line between her realistic questioning and her real betrayal. *Verrat, Verräter,* and *verraten*: these are the words that predominate in Auerbach's German. For Adam himself, the idiom is always that of being led astray: *verführen* is the operational verb, as Satan becomes the *Verführer* of the cause. The heart of Auerbach's objection to Etienne's reading is that Eve cannot be the "extremely skillful and diplomatic person" generated by his emendation. Diplomacy is far from Auerbach's concerns here. Eve's discussions with the serpent, and her temptation of Adam, do not go on in the realm of skill or political savvy. They transpire in the worlds of instinct, of impression, and of a blithe unawareness of the historical (if not the spiritual) consequences of her acts.

The picture of the Fall drawn here fits neatly in the terms of another, exiled essayist of collaboration. In his "Qu'est-ce qu'un collaborateur?" (published first in New York in August 1945), Jean-Paul Sartre defines the logic of collaboration as the logic of realism.[13] Sartre's paradigmatic collaborator succumbs to the "tentations de la defait," the temptations not just of defeat but of defeatism. What he identifies as the "réalisme" of collaborationist thought devolves to a sense of the *fait accompli*, a sense that what is about to happen has already happened. Realism, he writes, is the "denial of the universal and of the law" ("Réalisme, refus de l'universel et de la loi," p. 60). It signals a confusion between judgment and experience. Instead of judging facts in the light of the law, the realist collaborator judges the law in the light of facts. He evidences an odd sort of passivity; indeed, he is not necessarily a *he* at all. There is a certain "fémininité" about collaboration, not simply a docility in the face of facts but a participation in the subversion of natural laws and hierarchies. Femininity might be thought of here as a figure for the *fait accompli* itself, and this is precisely how Auerbach defines the serpent's swaying of Eve in her Edenic collaboration. His counsel to the woman "upsets the order of things established by God, . . . makes the woman the man's master, and so leads both to ruin" (*Mimesis*, p. 149). He continues: "The serpent accomplishes this by advising Eve to break off the theoretical discussion [of sin and treason] and to confront Adam with a wholly unexpected *fait accompli*." Adam's knowledge of the law, his sense of right inextricably now a part of his condition as a good Frenchman, finds its subversions in the claims of Eve. "Manjue, Adam," eat, Adam, she implores, until she eats the fruit herself "and it is all over."

Auerbach tells the story of the Fall as the figural narrative of collaboration for specific pedagogical as well as political goals. It is not so much that he wishes to condemn Eve as much as that he wants to save Adam. Again and again, the "character" of Adam is affirmed as good, as noble, and as French. This sense of character is what bridges the political and the philological. Etienne's misunderstanding of the characters of the *Mystère* now may be seen as standing for that larger misinterpretation of the French themselves and of the national characters of all the European peoples. What is "völlig durcheinandergemischt," completely confused, is the notion of responsibility in the face of political challenge. How do we evaluate, as Auerbach had put it in "Odysseus's Scar," "the behavior of individual men and groups of men at the time of the rise of National Socialism in Germany" (*Mimesis*, p. 19)? To whom do we assign blame? What is the relationship between the national character and the individuals who live and act within, and sometimes for, those nations?

Such questions find their answers in the course of Auerbach's whole chapter, a sequence of brief assessments and long quotations designed to illustrate the humble and sublime in the religious literatures of the thirteenth century. From the *Mystère d'Adam*, we traverse the works of Bernard of Clairvaux, Saint Francis of Assisi, and a range of early French and Italian dramas. Unlike the other chapters of *Mimesis*, in which ancillary texts appear as foils for the declared subject—the Old Testament to Homer, Proust to Virginia Woolf—here, we seem to lose sight of the focus. The reader moves through a variety of European Latin and vernacular texts, from anonymous plays in unique manuscripts to named, canonical authors writing at their most authoritative. What remains a constant in this panoply is the editor. Each text, no matter how exemplary or marginal, receives its full citation. Editors are acknowledged: Förster-Koschwitz, Ferdinand Brunot, H. Böhmer, P. Eduardus Alenconiensis, E. Monaci. The volumes build, each with its comprehensive title of the past half century of learning: *Übungsbuch*, *Histoire*, *Analekten*, *Crestomazia*. German, French, Latin, and Italian stand side by side, as Auerbach re-creates on these pages the European resources he had abandoned. Now, in this chapter and only in this chapter, do we get the range of *Zeitschriften*, *Untersuchungen*, and *zuverlässige-kritische Ausgabe* whose loss he had lamented at *Mimesis*'s end.

"Adam and Eve" recites a literary history not in the narratives of the textbook but in the selections of the anthology. It compiles a chrestomathy in miniature, a selection whose illustrative texts may complement the story told in the *Introduction aux études de la philologie romane*. As in that work, the *telos* of "Adam and Eve" is the restoration of a "patrimoine spirituel" for high civilization, or as he puts it in the final paragraph of the chapter, "the character of the people" (*Mimesis*, p. 173; "das Charakter des Volkes," p. 168). "Adam and Eve" thus answers questions about national character and individual motivation not by meditating on politics but by doing philology. By offering a miniature anthology of European texts, it recovers and sets out in clear order a moral conscience for a medieval and a modern Europe. By locating the "Charakter des Volkes" in the idioms of the vernacular, it illustrates the power of philology to find the ethic that inheres in nations. And, finally, by couching this discussion in the old debates between the national philologies, it realigns relations between literary origins and political types. Auerbach does more than seek to reclaim Romance philology from the French; he seeks to reclaim it from the Germans. He seeks a politically pacifist philology, one that restores the possibilities of language study and literary criticism to a humanist agenda. He is not depoliticizing scholarship, as later critics hoped to do. Rather, he re-politicizes it. The allegory of collaboration behind the *Mystère d'Adam* and its interpretation, by the chapter's end, takes as its moral the belief in the inherent goodness of the European peoples. We need not blame the good French like Adam, only the childish, instinct-governed, im-petuous French like Eve, who would succumb to the temptations of a satanic *Verführer*.

"Sed inimici hominis domestici eius," but a man's enemies are the men of his own house. These are Bernard of Clairvaux's words, quoted in this chapter as a guide against "the prickings of temptation" (p. 163). And when Saint Francis of Assisi speaks, he gives voice to the very theme and method of the whole of Auerbach's enterprise. Develop-ing the observation that the bulk of the saint's sentences, in one of his letters to Brother Leo, all begin with *et*, Auerbach notes (speaking as much, perhaps, for himself as for Francis): "But the person who writes these hurried lines is obviously so inspired by his theme, it fills him so completely, and the desire to communicate himself and to be understood is so overwhelming, that parataxis becomes a weapon of eloquence [*zu einer Waffe der Beredsamkeit wird*]" (Eng., p. 166; Ger., p. 162). "Adam and Eve" may well be seen as something of an armory of those weapons of eloquence, an education in the powers of phi-lology both to read and to write figurally. It teaches us that the political occasions of linguistic study can, in themselves, come to be the sub-ject of scholarly erudition. It teaches, too, that allegory may become a mode of writing far more "historical" than history itself, for to find the historical resonance of "Adam and Eve"—to discern its political subtext—we need to read the chapter allegorically, as if it were itself a text in need of figural interpretation.

Writing a decade later in the "Epilegomena zu *Mimesis*," published as a response to the early reviews of the volume, Auerbach set out not just to quarrel with his critics but to rehistoricize the making of his book.[14] This essay, which opens the 1953 volume of *Romanische For-schungen*, offers an occasion to respond to queries about individual in-terpretations by catching up on current scholarship. Yet, in the course of his responses to reviewers and the extended rejoinder to Curtius's essay on the three styles, published in *Romanische Forschungen* in 1952, Auerbach grows more personal. He reminds the readers of the period in Istanbul (p. 5), recalls his youthful training in Germany (p. 15), and at the close explicitly addresses the historical and biographical moment in which the book took shape: "*Mimesis* is quite consciously a book that a certain man, in a certain situation, wrote at the beginning of the 1940's." [15] A certain man, at a certain time, in a certain "situation" (*Lage*)—this is the closing key to understanding *Mimesis*, to reading its *figurae* of the person and the present. Auerbach's phrasing takes us back to the chapter on Adam and Eve, where Eve herself, "Herrin der Lage," overthrows the order of her God and man, and it reminds us, too, of Auerbach's quarrel with Etienne over who will be the master of the editorial situation.

It would be rewarding to close by naming Auerbach the winner in that quarrel and by showing that, in spite of all the manglings of *Mimesis* in the early reviews and the later appropriation of Auerbach himself into the canons of literary studies, his editorial decisions on the *Mystère d'Adam* stood up to professional approval. But apparently, they do not. The critical edition of the play by Paul Aebischer, published in the Textes Littéraires Français series, accepts without question Etienne's distribution of the lines between Adam and Eve.[16] And while the diplomatic edition of Leif Sletsjöe, published with a facing-page facsimile of the manuscript, does not print the text of the speeches as Etienne edits them, it does state in a note to line 283 that Adam probably should speak this line and that the *A* used by the scribe to signal the speaker has probably been lost from the margin of the manuscript.[17] Sletsjöe and Aebischer both cite Etienne approvingly, and while their spellings of the individual words of the text may differ from the earlier scholar's, they both confirm an ordering of speeches first suggested on the pages of *Romania* in 1922. So powerful has been this editorial tradition that, in a recent American anthology of medieval drama edited by David Bevington, Etienne's version appears without question. And yet, so powerful is Auerbach's example for the institutions of American medieval studies, that Bevington can quote his interpretation of the play as received wisdom.[18]

This fissure in a classroom anthology, perhaps more precisely than the record of the histories of scholarship, shows the paradox of the place of Auerbach's *Mimesis* in the institutions of medieval studies. On the one hand, it accepts the critical interpretation, treasures its appreciation of the humble and the everyday in the articulations of the sublime in order to breathe fully in that atmosphere of humanistic scholarship. On the other hand, it rejects—or, better yet, ignores—the textual interpretation, bypasses the very heart of Auerbach's display of philological erudition that enables him to recover the character of European peoples and to write their literary history. One can only speculate on why Etienne's interpretation succeeds while Auerbach's fails, though such speculation might well say something about the French control of a national textual legacy and its authoritative impact on later, American students. Such speculation, too, might take us back to the very style of Auerbach's chapter and to the paradoxes of *Mimesis* itself. The colloquialism of the presentation in "Adam and Eve" shifts scholarly attention away from the details of his editorial technique and towards the sensitivities of belletrism. Ironically, it may be Auerbach himself who seems to lack the precision of method he demanded in the *Introduction aux études de la philologie romane*. The paradoxes of *Mimesis* lie in the tensions between the scholarly and the colloquial, between the learned techniques of *Geisteswissenschaft* and the felt experience of *Feingefühl*, between the historical and the legendary as Auerbach defined them. "Again and again, I have the purpose of writing history."[19] This widely quoted passage has been used throughout much recent scholarship on Auerbach to emphasize the theory of historical understanding that grounds even his most affective of readings. But, as I have suggested here, we might do well to find his purpose not in writing *Geschichte* but in writing *Sage*, and to recall, as he asks us, that in times such as those in which he wrote *Mimesis*, "most historians are forced to make concessions to the technique of legend."

Suzanne Fleischman

Medieval Vernaculars and the Myth of Monoglossia: A Conspiracy of Linguistics and Philology

Erich Auerbach died in 1957. That same year saw the publication of Noam Chomsky's *Syntactic Structures*, the book that inaugurated a revolution in the field of linguistics that would alter its course in directions Auerbach could not have foreseen, notwithstanding his keen interest in linguistics as one of the "auxiliary sciences" crucial to the enterprise of philology.

In the opening section of his *Introduction aux études de la philologie romane*, a pedagogical manual written in 1943 while Auerbach was in Turkey and published in 1949, in French,[1] Auerbach defines philology as "the set of activities that concern themselves systematically with human language, and in particular with works of art composed in language." Acknowledging that this definition makes of philology a rather broad discipline, encompassing a range of scholarly activities, Auerbach goes on to observe that, of its various constituent activities, the philological activity par excellence—*la forme pour ainsi dire classique*—and the one still viewed by many scholars as "the most noble and the most authentic" is the critical editing of texts.[2]

This statement, let us recall, was made in 1943. And although the ideology of tolerance for diversity that so dominates the humanities today might well discourage us from making such overtly evaluative pronouncements about the relative position of our scholarly activities on "the great map of knowledge" (notably vis-à-vis those of our misguided colleagues), nonetheless, history seems to have upheld Auerbach's assertion about the centrality of textual criticism to the philological enterprise; so much so, in fact, that for many in the humanities today, philology *is* textual criticism.

The need to constitute authentic texts, Auerbach explains, "manifests itself typically when a society becomes conscious of having achieved a high level of civilization, and desires to preserve from the ravages of time the works that constitute its spiritual patrimony; to preserve them not only from oblivion but also from *the changes, mutilations, and additions that necessarily result from popular consumption or the negligence of copyists*" (my emphasis; in the spirit of Auerbach's statement, I have not presumed to edit his language for political correctness!).[3]

Auerbach goes on to point out to his intended readership of neophyte philologists that the establishment of authentic texts is not an activity that can be carried out in a vacuum; rather, it must rely on the collaboration of other branches of philology, and often, he concedes, on "auxiliary sciences" that are not, strictly speaking, philological. The texts philologists are concerned with, he notes, are typically *older* texts, written either in a dead language or in a (more or less) archaic form of a living language. I subsume both of these *états de langue* under the heading of "text languages," this label reflecting the fact that, unlike living languages, text languages have a data corpus that is finite by virtue of the fact that it is based exclusively on surviving *texts*.[4] Auerbach acknowledges that in order simply to *understand* the language of older texts, editors must have recourse to studies on grammar and to research in linguistics.[5]

This brings me to a convenient point at which to articulate my agenda for this essay. The observations I propose to offer in the pages that follow do not so much concern Auerbach himself as they do an aspect of his legacy (the broad topic around which the conference that gave rise to this book was organized). As the title of the essay suggests, what is of interest to me here is the collaboration of philology with linguistics, specifically as it relates to the construction of historical grammars.

As noted above, Auerbach explicitly acknowledged this collaboration. He acknowledged, moreover, that it is a two-way street: while text editors rely on linguists and grammarians to elucidate conundrums in the language of older texts, edited texts in turn provide the crucial *data* on which historical grammars are based. Auerbach takes the second part of the claim even further, arguing that older texts provided the data that enabled nineteenth-century scholars to formulate hypotheses not only about the evolution of individual languages but about language change as a general historical process as well.[6]

The term "historical grammar" is commonly used to refer to two quite different approaches to language study: one has as its goal a diachronic analysis of the changes a language has undergone over the course of its history; the goal of the other is to produce synchronic linguistic descriptions of text languages. My primary concern here is with the second of these approaches, and the text language I will focus on to make my case is Old French. What I propose to demonstrate, within the limitations of this essay, is how the methodologies of linguistics and philology, and the ideologies of language that underwrite them, have conspired, albeit unwittingly, to produce descriptions of the language of Old French texts that are in large measure grammatical fictions. Though my discussion will concentrate on Old French, the issues I will be raising can be extrapolated *mutatis mutandis* to other medieval vernaculars and philological traditions.

It was in conjunction with its claim to the status of a science, in the later decades of the nineteenth century, that linguistics endeavored to emancipate itself both from pedagogical grammar and from subservience to the ends of philology. Philology, as Auerbach reminds us, is interested in linguistic facts solely as a key to understanding the literary monuments of earlier ages. But the new "science" of linguistics insisted that language be studied for its own sake, for intellectual interests of its own, and for no ulterior purpose.

In order to establish itself as a science, linguistics first had to constitute for itself an object of study that was stable and homogeneous. Like a butterfly that must be immobilized so that its morphology can be studied under a microscope, so too the heterogeneous raw material of language activity needed to be disciplined in order to render it stable enough for scientific scrutiny.

Now, the language of all speech communities contains a not insignificant measure of variation; yet variation inevitably poses difficulties for any attempt to systematize language. Therein lies the rub for descriptive linguistics, now and in its various historical avatars. In a powerful indictment of mainstream linguistics and the ideological foundation on which it rests, Roy Harris articulates the dilemma thus:

> The variability which confronts the inquirer appears to be such as to make it questionable to what extent any elements of linguistic behavior are consistent enough or delimitable enough to be describable. . . . On what basis is it possible to disengage from the incessant variability of language any clearly defined object of analysis at all? This is the basic problem for a science of language.[7]

As Harris's statement suggests, the scientificity of linguistics, which is still taken comfortably for granted in most quarters today, is founded on an illusory object: a stable, unitary, monolithic entity that has no existence in the reality of actual language activity, but rather is a construct of linguistic practices, an object of our own fabrication. Harris refers to this as "the myth of monoglossia." In a similar vein, Jean-Claude Milner, in a probing critique of linguistic praxis entitled *Introduction à une science du langage*, insists that modern linguistics distinguishes itself methodologically from "truly scientific disciplines" by taking on an obligation no empirical science would ever assume: to reject any material for description that it has not itself constructed, either axiomatically—in formalist versions—or via observation—in empiricist versions.[8] Or as Tony Crowley puts it in a recent essay provocatively entitled "That Obscure Object of Desire: A Science of Language": the object of linguistics which Ferdinand de Saussure discovered is "twice removed from the reality of language," having been "united by the repression of *heteroglossia*, and [then] . . . reified as a stable 'thing' of the world."[9]

In short, the essential task mainstream linguistics has set for itself has been to describe the language of *an ideal speaker-hearer in a homogeneous speech community*. This particular formulation of the doctrine, to which I will return, is Chomsky's; however, the crucial point—that *linguistics must idealize its object in order to describe it*—harks back through the structuralist paradigms to Saussure.

Now, then, if the "myth of monoglossia" has provided an important piece of the ideological underlayment of modern linguistics, or at least of mainstream linguistics in its so-called autonomous variety, what does this have to do with philology?[10]

As stated above, nineteenth-century linguistics, in order to achieve a respectable academic status as a "science," needed to constitute for itself an object of study that was stable, regular, and homogeneous. From this perspective, the language of Old French texts, to the eyes of the positivistic scholars who undertook to describe it, appeared to be characterized by a fundamental and unsettling heterogeneity. To begin with, there was the ever-present textual variation among manuscripts; add to this an unstable, haphazard orthography and the variability of the linguistic forms themselves: inconsistant use of case-marking; a proliferation of suffixes, often seemingly interchangeable; widespread apophony in verb roots; multiple paradigms for individual tenses; a seemingly chaotic freedom of word order; and an overwhelming diversity of syntactic constructions. I could go on. Philology's response to this disconcerting heteroglossia was not to seek out "a method to the madness" but to dissolve it, to repress or ignore the ubiquitous variation that so characterizes the language of Old French texts.

In a provocative (provocational?) essay tracing the history of philology in France, Bernard Cerquiglini distinguishes three periods in the evolution of textual criticism in the French tradition.[11] In the earliest period, manuscript variation was tolerated, the primary agenda being simply to publish the texts and make the data available. The second period, dominated by the figure of Gaston Paris, favored collating the various manuscripts of a text into a "perfect" critical edition whose language was, in a word, a phantom, a homogenized composite idiom with little basis in the empirical reality of the constituent texts — the philological analogue of that hero of mainstream linguistics, the ideal speaker-hearer. The prevailing methodology of the third period of French philology, associated with Joseph Bédier, involved selecting the best manuscript and editing *it*, ignoring the data provided by other manuscripts or relegating the variants atomistically to critical notes.[12] While Cerquiglini prefers Bédier's approach to that of Gaston Paris, neither method, he insists, makes adequate provision for *variation* — at once the essence of medieval textuality and the nemesis of philology.

The "native speakers" of a text language are the manuscripts. Yet the heteroglossia of a text language like Old French goes beyond that of living languages in ways that bear on how we conceive of — and write grammars for — text languages. To begin with, the language of a medieval manuscript is already a hybrid, reflecting not the idiolect of an individual language user but the language of an author/composer—which may not even have been his native dialect (see below)—filtered through one or more textual copies and subject to greater or lesser modification in the process. Accordingly, it is likely to be dialectally heterogeneous and will presumably contain genre-specific features as well.

Confronted with variation on so many levels, how have grammarians proceeded in their attempts to describe the language of Old French texts? The prefaces to Old French grammars are instructive in this regard. All acknowledge the diversity—orthographic, morphological, and notably dialectal—but then proceed to seek out, as Robert-Léon Wagner put it, "the underlying system that transcends dialectal variation," "the unity of what was felt by speakers in the Middle Ages to be a homogeneous system."[13]

I would point out here, parenthetically, that texts—particularly from the twelfth and thirteenth centuries—known to have originated in identifiable regions have come down to us in forms in which the dialect of origin manifests itself only superficially and typically in combination with features of other dialects. This state of affairs led scholars of the last century to hypothesize that if the linguistic forms of a text were mixed, then the text must have been composed originally in a borderland between two dialects. This view, which led inevitably to the "discovery" that *all* Old French texts must have been written in borderlands, has since been abandoned.[14]

An alternative explanation put forth to account for the dialectal hybridization of the language of Old French texts is that this language represents a conventional, supradialectal *écriture*—for which Louis Remacle coined the term *scripta*—that all writers in the *langue d'oïl*, irrespective of origin, allegedly made use of.[15] Though the *scripta* theory has come to be widely accepted, and by now has found its way into most language histories and manuals of Old French,[16] it has recently been challenged by a group of Dutch researchers who have carried out extensive quantitative analysis of orthographic and morphological variables documented in charters and literary texts from the entire *langue d'oïl* area.[17] Their findings have led them to reject the idea of a supraregional written norm in northern French, at least prior to the fourteenth century.

Closing the parentheses and returning to the testimony of the grammarians, we come across the following statement in the Preface to William Kibler's *Introduction to Old French*: "Out of the diversity of Old French we can identify a period (c. 1100–1285) and a dialect (Francien)[18] that, more than any others, *typify 'Old French' and constitute the basis of a grammar of the language.*"[19] To cite one last example, the "myth of monoglossia" that provides the underpinning for so many paradigms of modern linguistics asserts itself transparently in the title of a recent methodological essay on Old French, "The Linguistics of Older Languages and the Systematization of Their Data"—this in the face of data that at every level seem to resist systematization.[20] As Cerquiglini states it, "l'écriture médiévale ne produit pas des variantes, elle est variance"—medieval writing does not *produce* variants; variation is the name of the game![21] And if variation can provide the cornerstone for a renascent philology, as Cerquiglini proposes in his essay, might it not also, *a fortiori*, provide a more solid foundation for grammatical descriptions of Old French?

~~~~~

The "ideal speaker-hearer" of autonomous linguistics is said to be "a member of a completely homogeneous speech community, who knows its language perfectly, and is unaffected by such grammatically irrelevant considerations as memory limitations, distractions, shifts of attention and interest, and errors (random or characteristic) in applying his knowledge of the language in actual performance."[22] *Mutatis mutandis*, medieval philologists have long held similar views—sometimes acknowledged but more often unconscious—about the authors of Old French texts, ascribing the disconcerting variation and "errors" of the manuscripts—the very same lapses referred to in Chomsky's quote—to the negligence, defective linguistic knowledge, or mechanical copying methods of scribes.

Elaborating on his dictum that "toute copie est un déclin"—every copy gets a little worse—Cerquiglini writes:

The essential "inferiority of the copy," one of the founding notions of philology, rests on the assumption of a pristine, flawless original: authors are not entitled to lapses. The assumption of a flawless original likewise underlies the doctrine of language pejoration: incorrect usage, impreciseness, not to mention variation, are not phenomena attributable to authors. But given that all medieval manuscripts are copies, all manuscripts are therefore, by definition, faulty and disparate reproductions—given the negligence of scribes and the diversity of their interventions—of blemish-free originals, whose language once bore the invariant, homogeneous imprimatur of a writer of talent. *As for historical grammar, it has, in its myopia, shown itself to be a discipline that is eminently suspicious, seeking out, beneath the flawed readings offered up by the manuscripts, the homogeneous linguistic system that the original ostensibly sought to deliver.*[23]

Underlying this belief in the inferiority of the scribe's language is a long-standing and pervasive ideology of language that equates "change" with "decay" and seeks a return to an erstwhile state of imagined linguistic plenitude, of consummate regularity now lost. Language change as decay—the linguistic analogue of the topos of the *exordium*.[24] The force of this ideology—which underwrites all normative approaches to language!—is strikingly manifest in the methodology of textual criticism, for example, in editors' preference for the *lectio difficilior*.[25] This ideology is also deeply embedded in the *metalanguage* textual critics use to talk about their praxis: terms like "declensional solecisms," "orthographic anomalies," "corrupt readings," "*loci desperati*." The term "textual criticism" itself, as Eugène Vinaver observed, implies a fundamental mistrust of texts; it assumes (not incorrectly) that in any copied text errors are inevitable, and that the editor's main function is to correct them and to restore order in language.[26]

This brings me to the paradigm example of what is alluded to in the title of this essay: how grammatical fictions have come to be perpetuated through curious—and often unwitting—collaborations between linguistics and philology.

It has been variously pointed out that Gaston Paris, the venerable patriarch of French philology, systematically regularized the case-marking (what traditional grammars, especially those that follow European grammatical nomenclature, refer to as "declension") in his 1872 edition of the *Life of St. Alexis* to conform to his belief about how the case system was supposed to have operated in the eleventh century.[27] Now, Paris's edition, and others of the same text-critical orientation, have figured prominently in constituting the data base for grammars of Old French, to which later editors in turn appeal as the authority on matters of language. Indeed, every grammar of Old French informs us that the medieval vernacular had a two-case system, nominative and oblique (*cas sujet* and *cas régime* in French), the radically reduced legacy of Latin's more abundant case-marking system.

So here we have a paradigm example of the reciprocity that has long existed between textual criticism and historical grammar, a reciprocity which Auerbach saw as essential to the enterprise of philology. Yet a careful scrutiny of the manuscript data has led various scholars, independently, to the conclusion that by the twelfth century, and probably even earlier, case was an anachronistic grammatical fiction with no foundation in the reality of Old French texts, or at best a largely empty redundancy, easily dispensed with (and just as easily overgeneralized to no effect). As for the morphology—or what remained of it (a single marker −*s*)—insofar as it was functional at all, it appears to have been doing other work in the language.

Opening a brief parenthesis, let me point out that natural languages tend to be reasonably efficient, well-functioning "economies" that make better use of available resources than do their controlled counterparts in government. *A fortiori* in the "service sector," which in language is the grammar. Thus, if in a language morphology is present that is not—or not always—being used for its designated (or original) grammatical function, it will generally be pressed into service to do other work in the language. In other words, morphology is a resource that tends not to be wasted: either it gets recycled or, over time, is discarded. This is a simplified—and, obviously, metaphorical—explanation for a number of diachronic developments that have taken place in grammar, certain of which I discuss elsewhere.[28] I invoke the economy principle here in regard to the final −*s* that appears on certain Old French nouns and their modifiers: to the extent that this morphological marker was operative at all in the twelfth century, it may have been doing work in the language other than marking case.[29]

Yet Old French grammars have stubbornly resisted acknowledging the loss of case from the grammatical legacy bequeathed by Latin.[30] Like other challenges to received ideas about Old French grammar and textuality, the "revisionist" view of case has had little if any impact on subsequent grammatical descriptions (see above, n. 16). Seeking to maintain the illusion that this portion of the grammatical inheritance survived into Old French, historical grammarians have explained away discrepancies between the grammars they produce and the testimony of the texts as "declension errors."

The example of Gaston Paris and the Old French case system cited above is striking as an illustration of the unconscious conspiracies through which grammars of text languages come to be constructed on a foundation part fact, part nostalgic longing—for older, more perfect taxonomies, and for monoglossia.[31] Underlying editors' emendations of many so-called corrupt readings is an unarticulated—and no doubt unconscious—desire for the stability and regularity that come with *institutionalized written language*, but which the developing textual vernacular of medieval France fails to deliver.[32]

Philological thinking about the practice of emendation has, of course, evolved since the time of Gaston Paris, now favoring less rather than more editorial intervention. Still, text-critical methodology routinely sanctions some measure of regularization, notably of spelling. Observing, for example, that scribes tended to avoid writing the letter *e* twice in a row, Alfred Foulet and Mary Blakely Speer advise: "*it is the editor's duty* to insert the missing third *e* in feminine past participles of verbs like *creer*."[33] A subtle slippage here through which the philologist's desire for standardization, for felicitous, monoglossic textuality, converts from a linguistic desideratum to a *moral* imperative. We encounter similarly "injunctive" statements about emendation from other authorities on textual criticism. Thus, Eugène Vinaver writes: "'Impossible' readings are those which can be shown to result from scribal errors; such readings *it is our duty* to correct." Christopher Kleinhenz cautions similarly: "If there exists an obvious corruption or lacuna in the text . . . then *the editor is duty bound* to correct it through *emendatio*."[34]

Language, as Freud tells us, is never innocent; the statements cited above, which appear to be representative of current thinking among textual critics, reveal the extent to which philology has subtly—and presumably unconsciously—converted our *desire* for regularity and homogeneity in language, for monoglossia, into a moral imperative of rigorous scholarship. Text-critical praxis is still informed by the belief—no longer explicitly acknowledged, but nonetheless present as a tacit agenda—that the published text should reflect the verbal activity of "the most skilled users of the language."[35] Historical grammars, likewise, have on occasion yielded to the temptation to describe not documented usage but, rather, "how a medieval cleric *ought to have* expressed himself."[36] What is this practice if not a post-hoc application, to a language no longer spoken, of the venerable French doctrine of *bon usage?* — a doctrine which, since its advent in the seventeenth century, has prescriptively controlled the natural economy of the French language to a degree unparalleled among languages of the world.[37]

Another striking example of covert normativity posing as linguistic description can be seen in grammarians' unanimous choice of the Francian dialect (associated with the region in and around Paris) as the standard for Old French. Interestingly, not a single Old French text offers a *pure* specimen of Francian; moreover, the scarcity of texts localizable to the Paris region would seem to pose a serious challenge to its privileged status. But there is more to this story.

The term "Francian" was unknown before the end of the nineteenth century when Gaston Paris, operating under the "nominalist imperative,"[38] invented it as a label for the language of the Ile-de-France. Paris's term corresponded to no historical reality in medieval France, not even a province (as did the names of other dialects, such as Norman, Picard, or Burgundian); the Ile-de-France, as an administrative entity, only came into being in the sixteenth century.

In a suggestive essay entitled "Le Francien (1815–1914): La Linguistique au service de la patrie," Gabriel Bergounioux makes a compelling case for viewing the post-hoc invention of Francian — *qua* putative ancestor of what would eventually become standard French — as part of an inventive rewriting of linguistic history designed to buttress the nationalist ideology of the dominant classes during the period of the Third Republic. This ideology sought to reclaim France's prestige as a nation-state (notably after the debacle of the Franco-Prussian War), with Paris its natural capital, and standard (Parisian) French its naturally selected idiom.[39] Without explicitly stigmatizing the local dialects and patois — what is standard French, after all, if not "un patois qui a réussi"?[40] — nineteenth-century philologists justified excluding them from the history of the language through appeal to the preeminence, historical as well as literary, of the Parisian standard and through anachronistic projection of this ideology of the standard back to the Middle Ages.[41] This involved finding a medieval vernacular capable of occupying the privileged position of historical forebear of The French Language, which for many in France had come to stand for — as it still does — French national identity, French culture, and France's position in the world.[42] Logically, the chosen candidate should be the most highly valued of the dialects of the *langue d'oïl*, the one associated with the social, economic, and religious center of France,[43] and—not insignificantly—one less tainted by Germanic influence than Burgundian, Picard, or Norman—in short, the vernacular of the Ile-de-France. Thus, philologists defended Francian with the same passionate conviction with which the Republicans, in 1870, defended Paris.[44]

The consequence of this choice of Francian as the medieval standard is that grammars of Old French are based in large measure on what is ultimately a linguistic construct, a grammarians' fiction. Confronted with the question: whose language is being delivered in grammars claiming to "describe the linguistic facts" of Old French texts?, the honest response must be: no one's. What, then has been the contribution of mainstream linguistics to French philology? It has primarily taken the form of linguistic descriptions of Old French and histories of the French language—the two avatars of historical grammar—that are to greater or lesser degrees at odds with the reality of the texts, where the name of the game is clearly variation.

What I have set out to do here is to shed some new—and admittedly provocative—light on a disciplinary collaboration which Erich Auerbach, writing in the 1940's, saw as essential—and eminently salutary—to the enterprise of philology, albeit a collaboration whose ideological underpinnings have for decades remained largely unexamined. What linguistics held out to philology at the end of the nineteenth century was a methodology for systematizing, reifying, and in the process, I have argued, *denaturing* its object of study in the name of a "scientific" approach to linguistic description. Granted, the problem of "idealization" in linguistic description, that is, the degree to which linguists ignore aspects of the variability of their data, is a highly complex issue, the ramifications of which transcend the bounds of this essay. However, the following statement from Lodge's *French: From Dialect to Standard*, unique among histories of French in its emphasis on variation and its incorporation of sociolinguistic concerns, articulates a stance on this issue with which I find myself in agreement:

If general statements are to be made about linguistic evolution, then some degree of idealisation is inevitable. However, traditional histories [of French] have tended to evacuate too many variable elements from the data they have wanted to consider, insufficiently aware perhaps that *language change has its very roots in language variation.* (p. 9, my emphasis)

But let me not end this discussion on an overly pessimistic note. Even in the current age of postmodernism, with destabilizing decon-structions assailing us from all sides, we still yearn for happy endings. And occasionally light does shine through at the end of interdisci-plinary tunnels. Sociolinguistics, notably the "variationist" paradigm associated with the work of William Labov,[45] represents an increasingly important current in linguistics today and one that poses a serious challenge to the mainstream doctrine of "the ideal speaker-hearer in a homogeneous speech community."

A philological analogue of variationist sociolinguistics is to be found in Cerquiglini's proposal to reconstitute textual criticism on a new foundation of *variation.* This proposal, eloquently set forth in *Eloge de la variante,* evolved out of a growing discomfort with traditional phi-lology's attempts to repress—or ignore—the ever-present heteroglos-sia that constitutes the essence of medieval vernaculars, a discomfort which, *mutatis mutandis,* echoes that of a number of linguistic theorists today, several of whose views are cited above. I should point out that Cerquiglini makes no reference in the *Eloge* to research in sociolinguis-tics; but the theoretical and methodological affinities are there. So once again we see benefits to be derived from a collaboration between lin-guistics and philology, a new collaboration to which Erich Auerbach, though he probably could not have foreseen the form it would take, would likely have given his blessing.

Part III

Figural History, Historical Figures

Jesse M. Gellrich

Figura, Allegory, and the Question of History

The strangeness of the medieval view of reality has prevented modern scholars from distinguishing between figuration and allegory.

—Auerbach, "Figura"

Although Auerbach set forth his argument for distinguishing *figura* from allegory in 1938, subsequent criticism has not maintained the separation as rigorously as he conceived it. I presume he would have regretted this development, since he expressed disapproval of allegorical style and allegorical interpretation on various other occasions, most notably as late as 1952 when he reiterated the original argument without modification.[1] His claim, we may recall, is that *figura* is an instance of what he would later call *Ansatzpunkt*, a point of departure providing insight into very large literary or cultural movements — in this case the separation between classical and Christian forms and attitudes.[2] The history of the word *figura* charts this development, from Greek literature where it signifies the form or shape of representations in language and visual art, to the "figures of speech" and levels of style in Roman oratory, and finally to the radically new uses it assumed among Christian authors. Concerned primarily with the last development, Auerbach holds that writers of the patristic and medieval centuries used *figura* to signify the relation between two equally real persons, events, or circumstances, the first of which is a prefiguration of the second; but "neither the prefiguring nor the prefigured event lose[s] [its] literal and historical reality by [its] figurative meaning." Allegory, for Auerbach, is another matter entirely, since one of the terms in the relation "does not belong to human history; it is an abstraction or a sign."[3]

Acknowledging the fact that *allegoria* is prominent in medieval exegesis, Auerbach nonetheless insists that *figura* is the dominant mode, and that it displaces allegory as a category for the Christian interpretation of the Bible and the physical universe. Yet we must note that when he turns to explaining the Scriptural foundation of the "figural method" for "the Church Fathers" and subsequent exegetes, his references to the Greek terms for interpretation do not always take account of their rendering in Jerome's translation.[4] And thus the question of the "influence" of *figura* is not squared off against the use of other key Latin terms, and one of them is *allegoria*. For instance, Jerome translates Paul's use of *typoi* in I Corinthians 10.6 with *figurae* to characterize the Hebrews in the desert as "figures" of later Christian society: "Haec autem in figura facta sunt nostri."[5] The same kind of "figural method," says Auerbach, is to be found in Galatians 4.21–31, where Paul explains the story in Genesis of Abraham's two sons, one by Hagar the Slave and the other by Sarah the free woman, through Isaiah 54.1: the women are the two covenants; they betoken the division between the old law and the new, bondage and grace, Jerusalem on earth and Jerusalem in heaven. But the word *figura* is not used in the Vulgate version of this passage; rather, Paul's comment on his own interpretational method in Galatians 4.24 is rendered, "quae sunt per allegoriam dicta" (which things are said by an allegory). Though Auerbach is presumably attending to the Greek text, he occasionally refers to the Latin, since he is documenting the foundations for the influence of a Latin word on subsequent commentary. And thus it is pertinent to observe that his emphasis on *figura* is sometimes made at the expense of other terms which Jerome, for one, selected in order to render the so-called figural method—not only *allegoria*, but also *umbra* (Col. 2.17), *similitudo* (Rom. 5.14), and *velamen* (II Cor. 3.14). In this connection, it is also relevant to point out that the word *figura* in Jerome's translation of Paul's interpretations can only be documented in I Corinthians 7.31, 10.6–11, and Hebrews 1.3.

Why, then, does Auerbach insist on such a firm demarcation between *figura* and allegory? The question is urged not only by the Scriptural references, but even more so by the fact that *allegoria* eventually became the conventional category in medieval exegesis for describing the prefiguring characteristics of the Old Testament that Auerbach reserves for *figura*.[6] Since he did not address these questions in particular, we will not have his thoughts on the matter. But the questions deserve scrutiny, since they suggest precisely the kind of conflict Auerbach himself would probe as a possible *Ansatzpunkt*. If the opposition of figure and allegory is such a point of departure, then what is the larger problem to which it provides access? To begin an answer, we may follow a lead from the 1938 essay. There Auerbach is concerned predominantly with the Christian departure from classical uses of *figura* in rhetoric and oratory, but he also discusses the distinction from allegory, which he represents as a Greek literary form and an Eastern influence fundamentally incompatible with the historical interests of Western exegesis. Tertullian and Augustine are to be separated from Origen and Philo of Alexandria, insofar as the Greek writers compose an allegorization that devalues the relevance of the historical record by rendering the entire Old Testament as a mere shadow show of moral concepts and future happenings.[7]

For Auerbach the consequence of Alexandrian influence was that "not only texts and events, but also natural phenomena, stars, animals, stones, were stripped of their concrete reality and interpreted allegorically or on occasion somewhat figurally." He calls this approach "the spiritualist-ethical-allegorical method," and he notes that it continued into the Middle Ages, but "it is very different from figural interpretation. . . . There is something scholarly, indirect, even abstruse about it" ("Figura," p. 55). If we consider this evaluation in the context of later medieval formulations about exegetical method, we must acknowledge that it is partial to understanding *figura* as a mode distinct from Hellenistic literary forms and attitudes.

For instance, in *Allegoriae quaedam sacrae scripturae*, Isidore discusses the relation of Adam and Christ from I Corinthians 15.45: "The first man Adam was made into a living soul: the last Adam into a quickening spirit." Concerning the first half of the verse from Genesis 2.7, Isidore explains: "Adam figuram gestavit Christi" (Adam brought forth the figure of Christ), and then he remarks immediately, "Haec allegoria est Apostoli" (This is the allegory of the Apostle).[8] The same substitution of *allegoria* for *figura* is to be found in Aquinas's definition of the "allegorical sense" of Sacred Scripture: "Therefore, as the things that are of the Old Law signify those that are of the New Law, there is the allegorical sense [sensus allegoricus]."⁹ This reading is exactly what Auerbach insists on calling the "figural" sense. And finally, from a different realm of commentary, we may note Bersuire's entry in *Repertorium morale*, which lists *figura* as "the exterior image or form" of the "mystical understanding [mysticam intelligentiam]." Here we have exactly what Auerbach reserves for the "allegorical" sense.¹⁰

These are representative illustrations of what became a commonplace substitution of one literary mode for the other, a practice already authorized by Paul, as Isidore demonstrates. Auerbach's qualification of "allegory," therefore, needs to be read in the context of his statements against Hellenistic influences on representation. His remarks suggest that he is less bothered by the reference of the mode to metaphysical ideas and moral categories than by what he understands as its disregard of the concrete, historical reality of the people and events in Old and New Testament narrative. In one of his last essays, Auerbach claimed, "my purpose is always to write history."¹¹ In the early stages of his career, his configuration of the opposition between figure and allegory is an expression of that interest. And in this case, the conflict reveals that he associates the historicity of recorded events with the prefiguring stories about the Hebrews in the Bible. Hebraic narratives have historicity, as he uses the term, and they are in danger of evaporating into mere "signs" by the allegorizing intention of Hellenic forms of thought. In other words, the preference for *figura* and the disapproval of allegory are recto and verso of a single attitude, an inclination to conserve the specific contribution of the Hebrews to the New Testament and to the contour of history that exfoliated from it in the Western Middle Ages.

Let me recall, however, that the 1938 essay does not propose the historicism of interpretation through a close reading of stylistic qualities of narrative in the Hebrew documents. Rather, Auerbach discusses historical implications with reference to *figura*, which is the result, as he puts it, of "the Christian break with Judaism" ("Figura," p. 56). Nevertheless, the style of Hebrew narrative has a definite place in Auerbach's historicism, and he links it to *figura* in his subsequent work, principally the study of Western realism in *Mimesis*. The first chapter of the book sets forth his well-known claim for historicity in the Hebraic style by contrasting Old Testament narrative with the Hellenic style of the Homeric poems. In this essay, Auerbach does not expand upon the distinction between allegory and figure drawn in his earlier work. But the opposition he argues for these two literary forms, it seems to me, is clarified significantly by the Hebraic-Hellenic tension explored in *Mimesis*.[12] Two initial points encourage such an approach: first, his defense of the historical basis of the Christian form is linked back to his argument for the unique difference of Hebraic style; second, the opposition to Hellenic style points suggestively toward his argument against allegory as a Hellenizing form that threatens to efface the individuality and realism of Hebraic narrative. In short, *Mimesis* suggests that the distinction between allegory and figure may depend less on the putative "historicity" of literary form than on Auerbach's searching interest in the persistence of Hebrew influence against forces that would compromise or occlude it from Western representations of reality.

If the essay and book realize such an interest, we would do well to pause over how much of it was motivated by philological inquiry alone.[13] When we consider, for instance, Auerbach's own personal circumstances during the mid-1930's, it becomes apparent that he had no little cause for taking such an interest in the past. While researching the essay and book, his position as a professor (*ordinarius*) in the University of Marburg was becoming increasingly tenuous, until October 16, 1935, when he was dismissed by the Nazis from all duties and responsibilities, including teaching. After taking refuge the next year in Istanbul, Auerbach finished drafting the essay on *figura* from notes gathered before he had left Germany and from research undertaken in Turkey.[14] He then turned to the chapters of *Mimesis*, which were written with very few resource materials and virtually no periodical literature, although notes compiled at Marburg may have been used in some of the chapters (such as the seventh, on the *Mystère d'Adam*).[15] It is difficult to explain and impossible to prove a direct connection between his personal situation and the philological subjects he was embarked upon during these years. That his outlook could have been anything other than "pessimistic" seems unlikely.[16] But it is also possible to gather quite a different sense of Auerbach's response to the uncertainty of his personal circumstances during the period of his approaching banishment from Germany and the subsequent twelve years he spent as a foreigner teaching at the State University in Istanbul. His personal correspondence, professional documents, and publications suggest an extraordinary complexity, perhaps even an "air of irony," about his own situation.[17] For instance, we may sense something of this typical attitude toward uncertainty in a letter Auerbach wrote to Walter Benjamin about the days immediately prior to his dismissal from the University. Auerbach writes that it is unlikely he will offer courses in the coming term, but nonetheless it is possible; "it is impossible," he goes on, "to express the strangeness [*Seltsamkeit*] of my circumstance."[18]

In his philological projects, perhaps the most poignant note of personal uncertainty appears in the closing sentences of *Mimesis*, where Auerbach first acknowledges the paucity of research materials available to him while composing the book and then expresses the hope that his work will find a readership, specifically his "friends of former years, if they are still alive."[19] This note, perhaps, is a minor one, but it makes a telling connection. The disappearance of his friends would include, of course, those Jews who like Auerbach, his wife, and his son were lucky enough to flee Nazi Germany, as well as those who were not. Their disappearance is briefly brought into alignment with the absence of the essential textual means of access to history and to keeping it alive for posterity. In his final sentence Auerbach completes the connection when he offers his book, in a most medieval gesture, as a source for "bringing together again those whose love for our western history has serenely persevered" (*Mimesis*, p. 492). But his gesture is more than medieval nostalgia. To forestall the disappearance of the historical record, Auerbach offers his own record, and if it does not contain the story of the impending disappearance of Jews from Europe, his project nonetheless bears witness to it in the philological story about the tension in Western realism created by the opposition of Hebraic style to the forms that would occlude it from history.

His principal argument in the first chapter, to repeat, is not only that the narratives of the Pentateuch are different from Homer, but also that Hebraic style is "historical." Homer, as Auerbach puts it, "knows no background"; his style leaves "nothing which it mentions half in darkness and unexternalized"; the "basic impulse" of this style is "to represent phenomena in a fully externalized form, visible and palpable in all their parts, and completely fixed in their spatial and temporal relations"; everything "takes place in the foreground—that is, in a local and temporal present which is absolute" (*Mimesis*, pp. 2, 3, 4). In contrast, the style of representative passages in Genesis or Kings provides only so much of the detail as is necessary for the narrative, "all else [is] left in obscurity"; decisive points are mentioned, but they are not explained; "time and place are undefined and call for interpretation; thoughts and feelings remain unexpressed"; and "the whole, permeated with the most unrelieved suspense . . . remains mysterious and 'fraught with background.' " Biblical figures, therefore, are individual, whereas the heroes of Homer are typical. Nestor, Agamemnon, and Achilles "appear to be of an age fixed from the very first." "But what a road, what a fate, lie between Jacob who cheated his father out of his blessing and the old man whose favorite son has been torn to pieces by a wild beast—between David the harp player, persecuted by his lord's jealousy, and the old king . . . whom Abgishag the Shunnamite warmed in his bed, and he knew her not!" The Old Testament creates contested, eventful situations in which "men are differentiated into full individuality" and are given a "personal history." The result is that "Homer remains within the legendary with all his material, whereas the material of the Old Testament comes closer and closer to history as the narrative proceeds" (*Mimesis*, pp. 9, 14, 15).

I cite these distinctions from *Mimesis* in order to focus on the alignment between the historical claim Auerbach would make for Hebraic narrative and the nature of historical experience he would assume in general for other periods. That he intends such an alignment, extending even to the experience of history in his own contemporary moment, is made explicit in the first chapter of *Mimesis* itself when he refines further the distinction between the "legendary" and the "historical." Legend, he says, "exists for itself, contains nothing but itself." It portends no "secret second meaning," and thus it "cannot be interpreted" (*Mimesis*, p. 11). Because it arranges its material "in a simple and straightforward way," legend "detaches itself from its contemporary historical context." And we may note this factor, says Auerbach in a telling illustration, from the legends of the martyrs, in which "a stiff-necked and fanatical persecutor stands over against an equally stiff-necked and fanatical victim." The example is an extension of a pattern of images of persecution Auerbach calls upon in the chapter to argue his case for historical difference. In this instance, he cites the much more complicated situation of Christian persecution in Pliny's letter to Trajan, which he points out is totally "unfit for legend." But even that example, he continues, is relatively simple. By comparison, "let

the reader think of the history which we are ourselves witnessing; anyone who, for example, evaluates the behavior of individual men and
groups of men at the time of the rise of National Socialism in Germany . . . will feel how difficult it is to represent historical themes in
general, and how unfit they are for legend; the historical comprises a
great number of contradictory motives in each individual, a hesitation
and ambiguous groping" (*Mimesis*, p. 16).

However Auerbach may have been led to this characterization of
historical experience as a philologist of Abraham's sacrifice in Genesis
22, he is indicating that he has also been led to it as a Jew living in
Nazi Germany during the persecution and sacrifice of his people. In
the Biblical text, he has argued, we find the quintessential break with
the legendary, specifically because the record is so unspecific about
why Isaac must be sacrificed, what the boy understands, and how his
father feels about the matter. The hesitation and ambiguous groping
of Abraham are rendered unmistakably by what is left unsaid. "The
journey is like a silent progress through the indeterminate and the
contingent, a holding of the breath, a process which has no present,
which is inserted, like a blank duration, between what has passed and
what lies ahead." The experience of contradictory motives that distinguishes the encounter with contemporary history becomes the center
of focus in the ancient text: from one slender appositive, "Take Isaac,
thine only son, whom thou lovest," Auerbach construes the "terror"
of Abraham's response, which is all the more ambiguous since God is
looking on fully aware of it. The point is that the entire "history of the
Jews," as Auerbach uses the phrase, hangs in the balance of Abraham's
action; and yet not an iota of its consequences for history is rendered
explicitly in the account: the result is that an "overwhelming suspense"
takes over the narrative "to rob us of our emotional freedom" (*Mimesis*,
pp. 7, 8).

Persecution, sacrifice, suspense, bondage—these are not in themselves the stuff of history writing, since they are hardly exclusive to Biblical narratives. But Auerbach's claim is that the experience of historical
reality is distinguished by the unique representation of such factors in
the Hebraic style, and that Abraham's sacrifice is not unlike the groping and suspense of individuals and groups in modern-day Germany
or Turkey. In view of such an alignment, Auerbach's anachronistic reference to "the Jews" for a people who had yet to inhabit "Judah" or

know themselves as "Judahites" appears to be more than simple coincidence. Be that as it may, much more telling is the alignment Auerbach suggests between Abraham's testing and the bondage of the reader or listener's response. He maintains that here we encounter the refining experience of "the individual." Homer, of course, also has individuals; but they are typical and predictable; something about them remains fixed from the first; their grandeur and generality "bewitch the senses." But the Biblical figures remain ultimately unknown in the sources of their responsibility or their failures; their deeds are represented much more boldly within a claim to truth, the absolute truth of historical events. And yet because they leave so much unexpressed, they call for interpretation, which they received from Paul and the church fathers who read them as "a succession of figures prognosticating the appearance of Christ." The individual, in short, is both complete in itself and everchanging as a subject of interpretation; and it is this status of the ancient figure that ties it specifically to the experience of history today, according to Auerbach: "Thus while . . . the reality of the Old Testament presents itself as complete truth with a claim to sole authority, on the other hand that very claim forces it to a constant interpretative change in its own content; for millennia it undergoes an incessant and active development with the life of man in Europe" (*Mimesis*, pp. 11, 13).

Students of Auerbach have not missed the import of this passage, specifically its connection between *figura* and the historical reality of the individual. But the relation between them has been construed largely in terms of a mimetic model for representation: the original term in the structure "is like" its fulfillment in some way; both figure and fulfillment are thus "historical" because of the accord or similarity between them. And by following the succession of such figures through history, Auerbach offers us a "literary" model for understanding the "continuity of the individual."[20] Some readers have sought to fortify Auerbach's approach to figural realism by calling to mind that as a Jew in Nazi Germany he had every reason to preserve the integrity of the individual from disappearing into the tyranny of the moment. His interest in the historical reference of *figura* may well have something to do with this personal experience.[21]

I too have been suggesting a personal and political context for Auerbach's approach to representation, but not on the basis of the mimesis of *figura*. Though Auerbach himself sets up the continuity between the prior term and its fulfillment according to a formal principle of interpretation from Paul and the patristic exegetes, I have been suggesting that the so-called historicism of his claim for *figura* is based upon another consideration entirely. The resistance of Hebraic style to foregrounding assumptions about representation creates a sense of uncertainty and suspense in the story of Abraham or David which Auerbach aligns with his own experience of historical uncertainty in Germany and Turkey. The "historical" in this context is not being defined, in the long run, by a principle of accord or similarity among events, images, or persons, but by virtue of a stylistic resistance to representations that would compromise or occlude their "individuality." The suspension between a known past and an indeterminate future characterizes the difference from "legendary" experience in narrative; bondage to the suspense of the story is the point of connection between the individual of the ancient text and the philologian wondering about the fate of his colleagues and the outcome of his own history. Mimetic structure, in short, has little to do with the historicism of philology in this case, notwithstanding Auerbach's own concerted effort to establish it as the grounding principle of *figura*. Much more definitive was the strangeness and uncertainty he felt as a Jew and an exile. That experience inevitably found its way into his reading of history, not as an imitation of a distant Biblical analogue, but as a sensitivity to a literary style that persisted against compromising influences.

The extent to which strangeness or uncertainty plays a role in Auerbach's sense of *figura* becomes critical elsewhere in *Mimesis*, and one reader has pointed to it specifically in the closing remarks of chapter 2.[22] There Auerbach is concerned with the discontinuity between the sensory image, such as the birth of Eve from Adam's side, and its capacity to inspire an elaborate Christian interpretation, notably, the wound in Christ's side from which was born the mother of all people in the spirit, the Church. Compared with the power of this reading, says Auerbach, the "sensory occurrence pales." This disjunction in the structure of realism is the direct result of the tension between Hebraic and Hellenic tradition manifesting itself in "the antagonism between sensory appearance and meaning [*Erscheinung und Bedeutung*], an antagonism which permeates the early, indeed, the whole, Christian view of reality" (*Mimesis*, p. 43; German ed., p. 55).

But Auerbach does not find patristic and medieval commentators situating themselves in the "antagonism" of this split and playing out its possibilities, in the manner of a prescient experiment in deconstruction. It is critical to recognize, however, the degree of uncertainty that was potential in the "realism" of medieval figures, if we are to appreciate adequately the import of Auerbach's reading of them. For instance, considering the exegesis of Augustine in chapter 3 of *Mimesis*, Auerbach suggests a move away from uncertainty when he shows how classical learning and literary style are everywhere apparent in the reading of a fragmentary and discontinuous Hebraic style. That is, the Hellenic expectation for temporal and causal sequence, for symmetrical and rationalized balance among parts, runs up against an inherently irrational explanation of terms, one based upon an understanding of events from the perspective of Divine Providence, as "already consummated in the realm of fragmentary earthly event." Such a conception of history, he observes, "is completely alien to the mentality of classical antiquity, [and] it annihilated that mentality down to the very structure of its language . . . with all its ingenious and nicely shaded conjunctions, its wealth of devices for syntactic arrangement, its carefully elaborated system of tenses." The result, however, was that "whenever the two conceptions met, there was of necessity a conflict and an attempt to compromise—between, on the one hand, a presentation which carefully interrelated the elements of history, which respected temporal and causal sequence, remained within the domain of the earthly foreground, and, on the other hand, a fragmentary, discrete presentation, constantly seeking an interpretation from above" (*Mimesis*, p. 65).

In the exegesis of Augustine, the "compromise" of the two styles is unmistakable, as he mediates between them, constantly endeavoring "to fill in the lacunae of the Biblical account, to supplement it by other passages from the Bible . . . to establish a continuous connection of events, and in general to give the highest measure of rational plausibility to an intrinsically irrational interpretation." Attempting thus "to reconcile" fragmentary figures to rational sequence, according to Auerbach, is a powerful assertion of "classical antiquity" in the pages of *The City of God*, a struggle in which "two worlds were engaged in matters of language as well as in matters of fact" (*Mimesis*, p. 66). He concludes, as we know, by attributing the end of the struggle to the weakening of the "antique mentality" and the strengthening of Christian interpretation.

But this familiar dichotomy leaves out a critical element in Auerbach's own assessment of *figura*, namely its inherent persistence against what he calls "rationalization" and "syntactic organization." In view of the fact that he levels the same criticism against other harbingers of Hellenic style, Clement and Origen, is it not possible that their influential allegorizing forms became the vehicle of a "rationality" and "syntax" which compromised the fragmentariness of *figura*? It seems to me that the roots of figurality in the uncertainty, suspense, and disjunction of Hebraic style establish clear ground for resisting a literary mode that would import the compromising preoccupation with order, symmetry, sequence, and rationality—all those attitudes which qualify, or more accurately disqualify, the experience of strangeness in Auerbach's sense of historical experience, past or present.

We need only return, by way of conclusion, to some of the key statements in the 1938 essay to see how the strangeness of *figura* distinguishes it fundamentally from allegory. He says as much, after all, in the essay itself: "the strangeness [*die Fremdartigkeit*] of the medieval view of reality has prevented modern scholars from distinguishing between figuration and allegory."[23] But the "strangeness" of his own experience, as he wrote about it to Benjamin, is just as relevant here as his reading of patristic and medieval evidence. We may characterize such reading, he explains, by recognizing that "beside the opposition between *figura* and fulfillment or truth, there appears another, between *figura* and *historia*; *historia* or *littera* is the literal sense or the event related; *figura* is the same literal meaning or event in reference to the fulfillment cloaked in it, and this fulfillment itself is *veritas*, so that *figura* becomes a middle term between *littera-historia* and *veritas*" ("Figura," p. 47). Neither literal event or signified meaning, source or copy, the figure is a "middle term" perfectly coincidental with Auerbach's subsequent illustration of Abraham caught between his obedience to God and his love for his son, suspended "between what is past and what lies ahead." Being "inbetween," the condition of "inbetweenness" (if I may so use the term), is the experience not to be compromised in the reception of *figura*. In a certain sense, it is the condition of *figura* itself, which is not only an image of the past but the agent of disqualifying its claim on the present: as he says in one of the most poignant remarks in the essay, the figure "both fulfills *and annuls* the work of the precursor" ("Figura," p. 51; my emphasis). And yet the annulment does not erase history; rather, the past is recreated as a "concrete dramatic actuality" — actual by virtue of the "overwhelming suspense" which he says distinguishes the Abraham story as "tragedy" ("Figura," p. 51; *Mimesis*, p. 8).

Allegory, in contrast, threatens this drama of the past and present by rationalizing and resolving it into "an abstraction or a sign." But "figural interpretation establishes a connection between two events or persons, the first of which signifies not only itself but also the second, while the second encompasses or fulfills the first." In other words, *figura* sounds like allegory, but it acts differently. Existing "in time" as an event of history, it is also another subsequent event, and this middle position is what constitutes it "within the stream of historical life." The historicity of a figure, in the final analysis, does not consist in an identity with a previous or subsequent model, but in the uncertainty of the form, its role in the "stream" of time between origin and fulfillment. And Auerbach nearly tips his argument back into his own life experience when he generalizes a definition of "history" out of his formulation of *figura*: "History, with all its concrete force, remains forever a figure, cloaked and needful of interpretation. In this light the history of no epoch ever has the practical self-sufficiency which . . . resides in the accomplished fact; all history, rather, remains open and questionable, points to something still concealed. . . . Events are considered not in their unbroken relation to one another, but torn apart, individually, each in relation to something other that is promised and yet not present" ("Figura," pp. 53, 59).

One wonders, in passages like this, whether biography or history has priority in the project of philology. It seems to me a moot question in this case. And the argument against allegory in the essay so declares it. Though Auerbach says figural interpretation is "allegorical" in the broad sense, he appeals to the historical foundation of sign and signified for the purpose of separating the two modes. He objects, as noted, to the "abstraction" of the signified in allegory; but his definition offers another reflection, the simple equivalence of terms that appears to evacuate the prior term of any import in its own right: "most of the allegories we find in literature or art represent a virtue (e.g., wisdom), or a passion (jealousy), an institution (justice), or at most a very gen-

eral synthesis of historical phenomena (peace, the fatherland)—never
a definite event in its full historicity. Such are the allegories of late
antiquity and the Middle Ages" ("Figura," p. 54).

Another way to put the objection here is to say that such allegories
lack sufficient strangeness. "One could not write *Adam est allegoria
Christi*" ("Figura," p. 48). Or even more to the point, Dante's Beatrice,
says Auerbach, is no allegory since she is and is not Beatrice Portinari.
She illustrates a "deep chasm between reality and meaning," insofar as
explanations of what she signifies (Christ, Church, Virgin Mary) can
never dissolve what she is or was: "and thus she is not exhausted by
such explanations" ("Figura," p. 75). Allegory, on the other hand, denies the inbetweenness so crucial to Auerbach's reading, not to say his
response to his own experience in Germany and Turkey.

This appreciation of uncertainty was clearly still on his mind as
late as the reflections on his own methods in his last book, where he
connects his early work with his perception of the "crisis" in European
civilization of his own contemporary moment. By comparison with
the work of Spitzer or Curtius, Auerbach indicates that his own work
illustrates "a clearer awareness of European crisis. At an early date . . .
I ceased to look upon the European possibilities of Romance philology as mere possibilities and came to regard them as a task specific
to our time—a task which could not have been envisaged yesterday
and will no longer be conceivable tomorrow. European civilization is
approaching the term of its existence."[24] Between the opening of his
career and the present moment, the early Middle Ages and modern
culture, his own philological project occupies a middle position, not
unlike the structure of *figura* itself; and he even thinks of his own essays
as so many "fragments."[25]

Why Auerbach responded to the uncertainty of *figura* and his own
philology may be suggested, finally, by returning to Benjamin, but this
time for the remarks on allegory set forth in the *Ursprung des deutschen
Trauerspiels*, published ten years prior to Auerbach's essay on *figura*. It is
not possible to do justice here to the involved discussion of allegorical language in this treatise, or to the various points of comparison it
may share with Auerbach's discussions in the 1938 essay and his other
publications. But it is possible, I think, to see Auerbach's distinction
between *figura* and allegory as an indication of his own separation from
Benjamin on the problem of uncertainty and strangeness. My sense is

that Auerbach would not have embraced the vision of despair, ruin, and dejection Benjamin saw in the allegorical imagery of the German tragic drama, and that *figura* is his alternative to the exhaustion of allegory.

As a point of clarification, it must be noted that Benjamin's frame of reference does not reach back to the antique forms in Clement and Origen which Auerbach documents in his essay. Benjamin is concerned primarily with baroque allegory of the recent past, which he sees as a development out of medieval forms; and for this distinction, he relies extensively on the 1915 study of allegory by Karl Gielow.[26] But still, Benjamin draws continuously on medieval frames of reference for his discussion, and they are pertinent in several ways to the evidence Auerbach has in mind for allegory, as well as for *figura*. That is, much of what Benjamin argues about allegorical properties corresponds to the features of *figura* developed by Auerbach. Perhaps the most prominent point of comparison is Benjamin's spirited defense of allegory as a mode of temporality. His motive, however, is essentially apologetic, insofar as he would rescue allegory from the repudiations of the German romantics, principally Goethe and the Schlegel brothers, who disparaged allegorical language in favor of the transcendence of symbol. Auerbach, presumably, would not disagree, since he was aware of the medieval identification of allegory with the historical level of reading Scripture as illustrated, for instance, by Tertullian. But Auerbach, as I have already suggested, would maintain that under the allegorical rubric we really have the historical and figural method of reading. He is right, of course, but the fact that he insists on the category of *figura* for such reading marks his separation from Benjamin on the roots of allegory in time.

For Benjamin "man's subjection to nature is most obvious" in allegorical forms. More vividly than other kinds of representation, they render the "biographical historicity of the individual," which is "the heart of the allegorical way of seeing." The mode derives from a focus on fragmented, discontinuous, and time-bound images, an appreciation of what he calls the "script" of nature.[27] But this designation is manifestly not the medieval commonplace of the "book nature" understood as a metaphor of God's voice or the *liber praesentiae Dei*.[28] To the contrary, Benjamin has in mind the materiality of a writing dislocated from speech or voice, and distinct from the symbolic presence of a transcendent ideal of beauty.[29] As a writing awaiting voice, the allegory of the *Trauerspiel* is present in the form of the "ruin." "In the ruin history . . . does not assume the form of the process of an eternal life so much as that of irresistible decay. Allegory thereby declares itself to be beyond beauty. Allegories are, in the realm of thoughts, what ruins are in the realm of things."[30]

Auerbach would not disapprove of the references to "ruin" and "fragment" in Benjamin's remarks, since he too uses the word "fragment." But, he uses it for *figura* rather than for allegory, because he would preserve it as a "middle term" existing within the "stream" of historical life, proceeding from a source to a completion yet unrealized. The fragment is always capable of prefiguring, whereas for Benjamin the allegorical image is a writing not capable of emanating any meaning on its own. Meaning is up to the allegorist (the interpreter), who speaks through it. In itself, allegory is an exhausted form, an empty "schema," capable of reflecting only on itself. And that is why he says, "It means precisely the non-existence of what it presents."[31]

This statement has a distant echo in the concluding sentence of chapter 2 in *Mimesis*, about the split between sensory appearance and meaning. But, as already indicated, Auerbach does not approach that split as the occasion of exhaustion in Western realism. Allegory, as he uses the term in the Hellenic sense, betokens its own exhaustion when it voids the signifier in the name of identifying a signified idea—be it wisdom or the fatherland. He favored instead the tension and suspense occasioned by the Hebraic resistance to such compromises, and thus preferred the middle term of Abraham's situation as his *Ansatzpunkt*. In that kind of illustration of uncertainty, Auerbach differs markedly from Benjamin, who accepted no alternatives to the exhausted image. In this respect, Benjamin's reading of allegory has been appropriated as a prescient deconstruction of the romantic symbol and a precursor of postmodern allegories of reading.[32] Auerbach's sense of *figura* admits a similar reflexivity for the image that looks backward and forward between texts; but he stops short of saying that such action invalidates language as the representation of reality.

It is possible to see the exhaustion of allegory acknowledged by both Auerbach and Benjamin as a reading of the cultural exhaustion of their time.[33] But they obviously responded to it differently. Benjamin apparently found little reason for embracing it, except as a critique of romantic idealism and a demystification of its continuing presence in his own time — eventually manifested for him in the mad idealizations of history propagandized by the Third Reich. Auerbach, on the other hand, had a different reaction to the strangeness of uncertainty that he saw in the medieval world. It was apparently an occasion for appreciating the historicity of his own world in a new way, rather than turning from it in pessimism as a disgruntled academic out of place in America.[34] To the contrary, instead of seeing, with Benjamin, the images of ruin and decay as empty forms in which allegory reflects itself alone, Auerbach looked to the situation of images inbetween a certain past and an unknown future, and found in that middling position a strange alignment with his own life circumstance. Seeking to recognize the figure in the fulfillment, he postulated neither the truth of abstraction nor the disclosure of the accomplished fact. He conserved, rather, the resistance to compromising one term with another, past with present, and thus kept alive the history he read and the history he was living.

Hayden White

Auerbach's Literary History: Figural Causation and Modernist Historicism

In the Preface to *The Political Unconscious* (1981), Fredric Jameson re-marked: "of literary history today we may observe that its task is at one with that proposed by Louis Althusser for historiography in general: not to elaborate some achieved and lifelike simulacrum of its sup-posed object, but rather to 'produce' the latter's 'concept.'"[1] Jameson then went on to cite Erich Auerbach's *Mimesis* as an example of the kind of work he had in mind. "This is indeed," Jameson writes, "what the greatest modern or modernizing literary histories—such as Erich Auerbach's *Mimesis*—have sought to do, in their critical practice, if not in their theory."[2] In this essay, I intend to follow out the line of thought adumbrated by Jameson and to inquire into the "concept" of literary history elaborated in Auerbach's work and especially in *Mimesis*. I shall argue that Auerbach advances a distinctively "modernist" version of that "historicism" of which he was both historian and theoretician and that *Mimesis* itself consists in an application of this modernist histori-cism to the history of western literature.[3] Finally, I will suggest that the notion of "figural causation" might provide a key to an under-standing of what is distinctively historicist *and* modernist in Auerbach's "concept" of literary history, if not of history in general.

If *Mimesis* is—as Jameson averred—an example of an attempt to "produce" literary history's "concept," the concept in question is a peculiarly aesthetic one. In *Mimesis*, the specific "content" of the history of western literary realism is shown to consist in the figure of "figurality" itself and its "idea" to inhere within the notion of the progressive "fulfillment" (*Erfüllung*) of that figure. In a word, *Mimesis* presents western literary history as a story of the "fulfillment" of the "figure" of figurality.[4] This is only to say that western literature's "concept" consists in the recognition that every "representation" (*Vorstellung*) is also a "presentation" (*Darstellung*) and as such inspires western writers to the development of a practice of stylistic innovation ever better adapted to the depiction of a "reality" as various in its forms as it is multiple in its meanings. The history of western literature displays an ever fuller consciousness of western literature's unique project, which is nothing other than the "fulfillment" of its unique "promise" to "represent reality realistically." And because this reality is construed as consisting in a human nature that is historically inflected, the history of its representation can never come to a definitive closure or end, any more than its ultimate origin can be identified.[5] Thus, although the history of western literature displays the plot structure of a redemption, this redemption takes the form less of a fulfillment of a promise than of an ever renewed promise of fulfillment.

The notion of "fulfillment" (*Erfüllung*) is crucial for understanding the peculiar nature of Auerbach's conception of historical redemption. It provides him with a modern equivalent of classical "telos" and a secular equivalent of Christian "apocalypse." It allows him to endow history with the meaning of a *progressus* towards a goal that is never ultimately realizable nor even fully specifiable. It gives him a concept of a peculiarly "historical" mode of causation, different from ancient teleological notions, on the one side, and modern scientific, mechanistic notions, on the other. This distinctively historical mode of causation I propose to call "figural causation." It informs the process in which humanity makes itself through its unique capacity to "fulfill" the multiple "figures" in which and by which "reality" is at once "represented" as an object for contemplation and "presented" as a prize, a *pretium*, an object of desire worthy of the human effort to comprehend and control it.

Erfüllung must here be understood as a kind of anomalous, nondetermining causal force or ateleological end. A "fulfillment" is not the determined effect of a prior cause, the teleologically governed realization of an inherent potential, or the Hegelian actualization (*Ver-*

wicklichung) of an informing notion (*Begriff*). The kind of *Er-füllung* envisaged by Auerbach is the kind adumbrated by such synonymous prefixed-lexemes as English "per-formance," "con-summation," "compliance," "ac-complishment," and the like, all of which are suggestive of the kinds of *actions* of which morally responsible *persons* are thought to be capable, actions such as fulfilling a promise, cleaving to the terms of an oath, carrying out assumed duties, remaining faithful to a friend, and the like. In this respect, then, to say, for example, that a given historical event is a "fulfillment" of an earlier one is not to say that the prior event *caused* or *determined* the later event or that the later event is the "actualization" or "effect" of the prior one. It is to say that historical events can be related to one another in the way that a "figure" is related to its "fulfillment" in a narrative or a poem. The "fulfillment" of a figure over the course of a given period of time or narrative diachrony is not predictable on the basis of whatever might be known about the "figure" itself apart from its fulfilled form. No more could one predict that a promise will necessarily be fulfilled on the basis of whatever might be known about the person who made the promise. For while it is true that a promise could not be fulfilled unless it had first been made, the making of a promise itself is only a necessary, not a sufficient, condition for the fulfillment thereof. This is why the making of a promise can be deduced *retro*spectively from a fulfillment, but a fulfillment cannot be inferred *pro*spectively from the making of a promise.

And so it is with the relationships between the kinds of events we wish to call "historical," as against, say, "natural" events. A given historical event can be viewed as the fulfillment of an earlier and apparently utterly unconnected event when the agents responsible for the occurrence of the later event link it "genealogically" to the earlier one.[6] The linkage between historical events of this kind is neither causal nor genetic. For example, there is no necessity at all governing the relation between, say, Italian Renaissance culture and classical Greek-Latin civilization. The relationships between the earlier and the later phenomena are purely retrospective, consisting of the decisions on the parts of a number of historical agents, from the time of Dante or thereabouts on into the sixteenth century, to choose to regard themselves and their cultural endowment *as if* they had actually descended from the earlier prototype.[7] The linkage is established from the point

in time experienced as a "present" to a "past," not, as in genetic relationships, from the past to the present. To view an event such as the
Italian Renaissance as a "fulfillment" of the much earlier Greek-Latin
culture (and that whole series of other "renascences," which preceded
the Italian Renaissance, from the eighth through the twelfth centuries)
is to direct attention to what is new and original in Renaissance culture rather than to what is old and traditional about it. To be sure,
the fifteenth-century Italian "renaissance" was one in that series of
"renascences" the occurrence of which established the "possibility"
of the fifteenth-century version thereof. In this sense, the fifteenth-
century Renaissance "repeats" those earlier ones, but with important
differences: the choices of the specific aspects of Greek-Latin culture
that will serve as putative "ancestors" of the Italian Renaissance "re-
vivalists" are unique to this later period. These choices, taken in their
entirety, not only define the nature of the fifteenth-century Renaissance but retrospectively redefine the nature of the earlier Greek-Latin
cultural model, which is now constituted as a "figure" that achieves a
(new) "fulfillment" in a later "affiliation."

We can deduce the occurrence of the earlier event insofar as it is
linked by necessity to the later one: there could not have been any
"revival" of Greek-Latin culture had there not already been such a culture to revive. So, too, we can use the earlier event to illuminate the
later event insofar as the later one "fulfills" the earlier. But fulfillment
must be understood on the analogy of a specifically aesthetic, rather
than a theological, model of figuralism. Thus, for example, the exodus
of the Ancient Hebrews from Egypt as related in the Old Testament
was traditionally treated by medieval biblical exegetes as a "figure" that
was fulfilled in the liberation of humanity from the Old Law promised in the New Testament; but this is an example of a theological and
specifically Christian expropriation of Hebrew religion. There are no
objective grounds for linking the two events as elements of the same
historical sequence; and, indeed, modern Jewish exegetes quite explicitly reject this interpretation of the meaning of the earlier event. In
fact, the only "historical" ground for viewing the liberation from the
Law stressed by Saint Paul especially as having been prefigured in the
Flight from Egypt consists in the long process of expropriation of
the Hebrew Bible by its Christian interpreters since the time of Saint
Paul himself. Which is to say that "figuralism" has its own history—

as Auerbach pointed out in both *Mimesis* and the well-known essay "Figura" a number of times. The Christian interpreters view the relation between the earlier and the later events as "genetic" and "causal," as willed by God and therefore "providential." The *aesthetic* conception of the relation places the principal weight of meaning on the act of retrospective appropriation of an earlier event by the treatment of it as a "figure" of a later one. It is not a matter of "factuality"; the "facts" of the earlier event remain the same even after appropriation. What has changed is the *relationship* which agents of a later time retrospectively establish with the earlier event as an element in their own "past"—a past on the basis of which a specific present is defined.

It is in this sense that later events in the history of literature are to be viewed, in Auerbachian terms, as "fulfillments" of earlier ones. The later events are not "caused" by the earlier ones, certainly are not "determined" by them. Nor are the later events predictable on any grounds of teleology as realizations of earlier potentialities. They are related in the way that a rhetorical figure, such as a pun or metaphor, appearing in an early passage of a text, might be related to another figure, such as a catachresis or irony, appearing in a later passage— in the way that a premise of a joke is fulfilled in its punchline, or the "conflicts" in an opening scene of a play are fulfilled in its ending. The later figure "fulfills" the earlier by repeating the elements thereof but with a difference.

The model is most pertinently utilizable in the study of literary styles and genres. Thus, for example, the relationships obtaining among the Homeric, Virgilian, and Dantean kinds of epic (as well as the relationship between these three and the early modern novel) constitute a sequence of figure-fulfillment relationships. And so too for the relationships which Auerbach posits among the various incarnations or instantiations of the tradition of "realistic representation," from the Gospels and the *sermo humilis*, through Dantean "figural realism," down to "aesthetic historism," romantic figuralism, historistic realism, and modernism.[8]

What I have been suggesting is that Auerbach's *Mimesis* is not only a history of a specific kind of literary representation, that is, "figuralism," but also a history conceived as a sequence of figure-fulfillment relationships. In other words, the figure-fulfillment model is used by

Auerbach to provide the diachronic "plot" of the history of western literature. It provides the principle of mediation between successive periods of literary history or at least between successive periods within a common tradition of literary practice. Indeed, it would appear that, in his view, an actual figure-fulfillment-figure relationship, a gene-alogical relationship of successive expropriations, is what constitutes a tradition as such. The figure-fulfillment model is, therefore, a model for comprehending the syntagmatic dimensions of historical happening and for constructing the narrative line for the presentation of that history.

But what about the paradigmatic or synchronic dimension of literary history? If Auerbach uses the figure-fulfillment model as a way of delineating periods in the evolution of literary realism, how does he conceptualize relationships intrinsic to a given period—such questions as those of the integrity and coherence of an age, epoch, or era and those of the text-context relationship and, more specifically, the "representative" nature of the text? To put it in Jameson's terms once again, here the problem of "representation" takes precedence over that of "presentation." In what sense can a text be said to "represent" the "period" or the "context" in which it was composed?

The text-context relationship is a problem that formalisms typically moot and the various historicisms treat as having been resolved in the theory of "reflection." For example, an older Marxist criticism typically posited the social-historical context in terms of class membership, class structure, class conflict, and so on, and then proceeded to look for "reflected" images of this context in the literary text. The relative realism or ideological deformation of a given literary representation was then to be measured in terms of the extent to which the context thus posited was adequately—veraciously or undistortedly—reflected in the text. The text itself was considered to have no special illumina-tive function; its status as evidence of the historical period in which it was produced resided in the extent to which it confirmed evidence found in nonliterary, documentary sources.

For Auerbach, on the other hand, the literary text appears as a synecdoche of its context, which is to say it is a particular kind of "fulfillment" of the "figure" of the context. In his actual hermeneutic practice, Auerbach tends to "present" the text as a "representation," not so much of its social, political, and economic milieux as of its author's *experience* of those milieux; and as such, the text appears or is presented as a "fulfillment" of a figure of this "experience."

In this case, the relationship of the figure (the author's experience of the context) to its fulfillment (the text) is that of the implicit to the explicit. It is exactly the kind of relationship which, according to Auerbach, Balzac posits, in *Le Père Goriot*, between Mme. Vauquer and the pension over which she presides as *patronne*. Thus, Auerbach quotes Balzac, who says of Mme. Vauquer's relationship to her milieu: "enfin toute sa personne *explique* la pension, come la pension *implique* sa personne" (*Mimesis*, p. 469; my emphases). This relationship of the implicit to the explicit, is not—Auerbach stresses in his comment on the Balzac passage—logical; the one term of the relationship is not "deducible" from the other: "The entire description [of Mme. Vauquer and her *pension*] is directed at the mimetic imagination of the reader . . . ; the thesis of the stylistic unity of the milieu, which includes the people in it, is not established rationally but is represented [*vorgestellt*] as a striking and immediately apprehended state of things, purely suggestively, without any proof" (Eng. p. 471; Ger., p. 439). The representation is structured by what Auerbach calls "einem Hauptmotiv, . . . das Motiv der Harmonie zwischen ihrer Person einerseits und dem Raum, . . . der Pension, etc., . . . anderseits" (Eng., p. 470; Ger., 438). This "harmony-thesis," as Auerbach calls it, is simply "presupposed" (*vorausgesetzt*) (Eng., p. 471; Ger., p. 439) by Balzac; it appears in the form of "merely suggestive comparisons, not proofs nor even beginnings of proof" (ibid.). Thus, Auerbach concludes, "what confronts us [in the passage from Balzac] is the unity of a particular milieu, felt as a total concept of a demonic-organic nature and presented entirely by suggestive and sensory means" (Eng., p. 472). This does not mean that Balzac's "realism" is superior to other or earlier forms of representation. It is simply different, and different because it is itself a "product" (*ein Erzeugnis*) of its "period" (*Epoche*), which is to say, Auerbach adds, that Balzac's realism "is itself *a part and a result* of an *atmosphere*" (Eng., p. 473; Ger., p. 441; my emphases).

"A part and a result of an atmosphere": it might seem that Balzac has mystified the fundamental relationships between author and milieu, author and text, text and context, and the parts and the whole of any context by using the metaphor of "atmosphere" to describe a "period." What could be murkier? But just after he has remarked on the cogency of this notion of "atmosphere," he continues: "it is far more difficult to describe with any accuracy the intellectual attitude which dominates Balzac's own particular manner of presentation" (p. 474). This is because, Auerbach says, Balzac's "temperament" ("emotional, fiery, and uncritical") is itself a fulfillment of a milieu grasped by Balzac himself as an "umbra" and "imago": "[Balzac] bombastically takes every entanglement as tragic, every urge as a great passion; he is always ready to declare every person in misfortune a hero or a saint; if it is a woman he compares her to an angel or the Madonna; every energetic scoundrel, . . . he converts into a demon, etc." (Eng., p. 482; Ger. p. 449). This tendency "to sense hidden demonic forces everywhere and to exaggerate expression to the point of melodrama" is taken to be "in conformity with" (es entsprach) the temperament of the author, on the one side, and "the Romantic way of life," on the other (Eng., p. 482; Ger., p. 449). In other words, Balzac's style—which unites a specific generic form or mode (melodrama) with a distinct content ("demonic forces")—is itself a "figura" that unites his milieu with his work as an "imago" to a "veritas."

Thus, what is most characteristic of Auerbach's "concept" of literary history is the way he uses the figuralist model to explicate not only the relation between various literary texts but also the relation between "literature," on the one side, and its "historical contexts," on the other. For him, the representative literary text may be at once (1) a "fulfillment" of a previous text and (2) a potential "prefiguration" of some later text, but also (3) a "figuration" of its author's experience of a historical milieu, and therefore (4) a fulfillment of a prefiguration of a piece of "historical reality." In other words, it is not a matter of an author's having an "experience" of a historical milieu and then representing it, in a figurative way, in his text. On the contrary, the "experience" is already a "figure," and insofar as it will serve as a content or referent of a further representation, it is a "prefiguration" which is "fulfilled" only in a literary text.

Thus, if what Auerbach called "Figuralstruktur" serves as a model for transforming a series of literary periods into a sequence of figures and their fulfillments, thereby providing the paradigm for a mapping of the syntagmatic axis of historical happening, so too does it serve as a model for characterizing the relation between a specific text and a period style, on the one hand, and the style of a text and its context, on the other. The linkage between a prefigurative aspect of a given culture (a text, a style, a period) and its "fulfilled" form is suggested by mere "similarity" — of their forms, their contents, or the relations obtaining between forms and contents. But the perception and subsequent demonstration of a general similarity, such as between, say, Dante's "figural realism" and Balzac's "atmospheric realism," do not end the analysis. The two terms linked by similarity or resemblance must be subjected to a double articulation: the earlier terms must themselves be shown to be "fulfillments" of even earlier "figures" and the later terms be shown to be "prefigurations" of even later styles.

Moreover, the "figure" which is implicit in one and explicit in the other must be named and the modality of their relationship specified. The later terms in a series of "presentations" (*Darstellungen*) have an explanatory function vis-à-vis the earlier ones: the later terms "complete," "consummate," or otherwise "explicate" the earlier ones. In the way, for example, that Balzac's "atmospheric realism" can be said to complete, consummate, or explicate Dante's "figural realism." By the same token, however, the earlier term "explains" the later one insofar as it serves as a necessary precondition of the latter. But not a sufficient precondition, because this could be provided only by the particular temperament of a specific author in which a milieu is converted into a "figure" by the "poetic imagination."[9]

On the face of it, *Mimesis: Dargestellte Wirklichkeit in der abendländischen Literatur* is a historical treatment of the ways in which "reality" (*Wirklichkeit*) has been "presented" (*dargestellte*) in western "literary" discourse.[10] But the subject of this history, named in the title as *mimesis* (imitation), is not to be understood as the effort to produce a verbal mirror-image of some extraverbal reality. Rather, Auerbach writes the history of *mimesis* as a story of the development of a specific kind of *figuration*; and he seeks to document — by offering a series of specific examples — the transformations in the dominant modes of mimesis-as-figuration in western literary discourse from the time of the Evangelists to the middle of the twentieth century.[11]

There is nothing very mysterious about the idea of mimesis-as-figuration. Auerbach's idea of figuration is based upon Christian interpretations of ancient Judaism as an anticipation or prolepsis of Christianity. According to the Christian exegetes, those personages, events, and actions reported in the Old Testament are to be understood as having both a literal and a figurative dimension. On the one hand, they are to be apprehended as "real" and not merely as "fictions." On the other, they are to be apprehended as indicators of yet-to-come personages, events, and actions which will fulfill, that is, both complete and reveal, the relevance of the earlier ones to the promised revelation of God's will and purpose for His Creation. This notion of a real event that was complete in itself and full in its meaning at the moment of its happening, but was at the same time the bearer of a meaning that would be revealed only in a different and equally complete event at a later time, supplied Auerbach with a model for conceptualizing the relationships among specifically historical events. The relationships in question are of the kind which, since Nietzsche, have come to be called genealogical.

The Christian schema of the figure and its fulfillment (used by Christian thinkers to interpret the relation between the Old Testament and the New, between Judaism and Christianity, between This World and the Beyond, between the Present and the Future, and [in Dante] even between paganism and Christianity) is grasped by Auerbach as itself a "figure" that will be "fulfilled" in the modern idea of "history." Indeed, Auerbach holds that "history" is precisely that mode of existence in which events can be at once "fulfillments" of earlier events and "figures" of later ones. Such a schema provided him with a way of characterizing the peculiar combination of novelty and continuity which distinguished historical from natural existence. This combination was a mystery for both Aristotelian teleology and Newtonian physical science, both of which could conceive of causation as going in one direction only, from a cause to its effect and from an earlier to a later moment. The truth contained latently in the idea of God's purpose being revealed in the schema of figure and fulfillment was that the meaning of events happening in present history is contained precisely in what they reveal about certain earlier events to which they may bear no causal or genetic relationship whatsoever. Their relationship is "genealogical" precisely insofar as the agents responsible for the occurrence of the later event will have "chosen" the earlier event as an element of the later event's "genealogy."

Thus, for example, in *The Eighteenth Brumaire of Louis Buonaparte*, Marx does not suggest that the French Revolution of (February) 1848 was "caused" in any mechanistic way by the French Revolution of 1789. Nor does he represent the two revolutions as related genetically. The later revolution is affiliated genealogically with the earlier one inasmuch as the agents responsible for the later one identify their revolution (however justly or unjustly) as a completion of the earlier one. When Marx says that, in biological evolution, it is man that explains the monkey, rather than the other way around, he is advancing a distinctively historicist way of relating the later to an earlier phenomenon. So, too, in historical evolution, the Revolution of 1789 may have been an "effect" of, say, the Protestant Reformation or the Enlightenment and, as such, an ending of a process rather than a prefiguration of events yet to come.[12] But as a historical event, it remains open to retrospective appropriation by any later group which may choose it as the legitimating prototype of its own project of self-making and hence an element of its "genealogy."

In *Mimesis*, figuralism is presented as an enormously difficult, profound, but above all characteristic achievement of western culture, emerging in the Gospels' notion of the "seriousness," even tragic nature, of the lives of ordinary human beings, extending through Dante, the Renaissance, Rousseau, the "atmospheric realism" of Balzac, and the "descriptivism" of Flaubert, down to the modernism of Woolf, Proust, and Joyce in the twentieth century.[13] Obviously, Auerbach wished to write a historical account of that attitude or worldview known as "realism," which arose in the west and infused the dominant stream, not only of modern western literature but also of western (Baconian) science and (bourgeois) historiography.[14] He wished to account for the fact that western culture sought, in particular, to resist surrendering to the "blooming buzzing confusion" of mere sense data, on the one side, without falling prey to the transcendentalizing impulses of religion and Platonic philosophy, on the other.[15] For him, it was "figuralism" that accounted for western culture's unique achievement of identifying "reality" as "history."

In what sense can it be said, then, that Auerbach's work and *Mimesis* especially contributed to the production of a "concept" of literary history specifically modernist ("modern or modernizing") in kind?

Superficially, of course, Auerbach's own literary historiography, especially as represented by *Mimesis*, incarnates the *historicist* position of which he was both a theoretician and a historian. Indeed, in many respects, the doctrine of historicism is the key to the understanding of his history of literary realism. The growth of "realism" in western literature is chronicled by Auerbach in *Mimesis* as coextensive and even synonymous with the growth of that "historicist" point of view which crystallized in Germany at the beginning of the nineteenth century.[16] At one point, he even states that literary realism, as represented by Balzac, is nothing other than a product of the specifically historicist impulse to view "the present as history." Viewing social reality under the aspect of history was what western literature had been working toward since the representation in the Gospels of the "tragic seriousness" of the everyday life of ordinary human beings and the dissolution of a sense of qualitative differences among members of different social classes that this representation implied. Historicism was nothing other than the discovery that human life and society found whatever meaning they might possess in history, not in any metaphysical beyond or transcendental religious realm.[17] Literary realism in its classic, nineteenth-century incarnation was the application of this perspective to the representation of *present* social reality. Thus, Auerbach could write:

When people realize that epochs and societies are not to be judged in terms of a pattern concept of what is desirable absolutely speaking but rather in terms of their own premises; when people reckon among such premises not only natural factors like climate and soil but also the intellectual and historical factors; when, in other words, they come to develop a sense of historical dynamics, of the incomparability of historical phenomena and of their constant inner mobility; when they come to appreciate the vital unity of individual epochs, so that each epoch appears as a whole whose character is reflected in each of its manifestations; when, finally, they accept the conviction that the meaning of events cannot be grasped in abstract and general forms of cognition and that the material needed to understand it must not be sought exclusively in the upper strata of society and in major political events but also in art, economy, material and intellectual culture, in the depths of the workaday world and its men and women, because it is only there that one can grasp what is unique, what is animated by inner forces, and what, in both a more concrete and a more profound sense, is universally valid: then it is to be expected that those insights will also be transferred to the present and that, in consequence, the present too will be seen as incomparable and unique, as animated by inner forces and in a constant state of development; in other words, as a piece of history, whose everyday depths and total inner structure lay claim to our interest both in their origins and in the direction taken by their development. Now, we know that the insights which I have just enumerated and which, taken all together, represent the intellectual trend known as Historism, ...[18]

A realist literary criticism would apply this perspective in the study of literary texts. That is to say, it would find the meaning of a literary text in its relations to a *historical* context, not to some Platonic archetype of literature or art or beauty, nor to any changeless canon of classics which putatively incarnated the essence of literarity. And surely this is what Auerbach sought to do in that series of diachronic contextualizations of specific literary texts which comprises the manifest content of *Mimesis*.

It must be recalled, however, that Auerbach historicizes historicism itself in the same way that he historicizes realism. He does not treat historicism as a transcendental perspective on human reality. It is a specifically eighteenth- and nineteenth-century *Weltanschauung*, the meaning and authority of which were intimately linked to a social system (a society of classes), political apparatus (that of the emerging nation-states), and cultural endowment (that of a revised, classical humanism) that would sustain fatal blows in the first half of the twentieth century. If he regarded historicism as a progressive, even lastingly valuable moment in the history of western culture, he also recognized that historicism itself had a history. Like "realism" itself, historicism would undergo transmutations and metamorphoses, as its contexts—social, political, cultural—changed. And, indeed, in the famous last chapter of *Mimesis* ("Der braune Strumpf"), in which he tries to divine the relation between literary modernism (Joyce, Woolf, Proust) and realism (Stendhal, Balzac, Flaubert), Auerbach posits a form of modernist historicism so radically different from its nineteenth-century prototype as to appear to consist in a repudiation of "history" itself. But, as Auerbach makes quite clear in a passage in which he likens his own method of textual analysis to the style of Virginia Woolf,[19] it remains possible to be a modernist and a historicist at the same time. It only requires a different way of construing the field of historical occurrences or, at least, the field of literary-historical events. And it turns out that, when viewed from the perspective provided by Auerbach's analysis of literary modernism, his history of "the representation of reality in western literature" is an example of this very modernist historicism. In

Mimesis, Auerbach produces the concept of a distinctively "modernist historicist" literary history.

The manifest story told by Auerbach is of the twofold order of changes that have taken place in the relations between the classical hierarchy of "literary"[20] (poetic or discursive) styles (high, middle, and low or humble) and genres (tragedy, comedy, epic, romance, novel, history, essay, satire), on the one side, and a "social reality" in which people are divided into classes and treated as more or less human and consequently considered to be more or less worthy of being represented as the "subjects" of these styles and genres, on the other. On the manifest level, the story works out very well indeed: in the literary practice of the West, the styles are progressively defetishized, democratized, and mixed, and the human subject is progressively declassed and even—so the famous analysis of a passage from *To the Lighthouse* suggests—degendered. Thus, the various "periods" in the history of western literary realism can be defined in terms of their characteristic mixtures of styles, on the one hand, and the extent to which they succeed in grasping the content of "history" as a "social reality" delivered from class division, on the other.

However, running across this periodization and uniting its parts into a larger whole at the level of plot or *dianoia* is an account of the filling out, exfoliation, or elaboration of a specifically figural conception of the *relations* among those things that inhabit "history." Indeed, if, in many respects, *Mimesis* is ultimately the story of how western "literature" came to grasp "historicity" as humanity's distinctive mode of being in the world, this mode of being in the world is represented as one in which individuals, events, institutions, and (obviously) discourses are apprehended as bearing a distinctively "figural" relationship to one another. Unlike other natural things, which are related to one another only by material causality, historical things are related to one another as elements of structures of figuration (*Figuralstrukturn*). This means that things historical can be apprehended in their historicity only insofar as they can be grasped as elements of a whole which, in both their synchronic and diachronic dimensions, are related as linguistic "figures" are related to their "fulfillments." This particular insight and this particular concept of historicity inform the specifically *modernist* version of literary realism as represented by Joyce, Woolf, and Proust in *Mimesis*.

Auerbach is quite explicit in characterizing modernism as a kind of "fulfillment" of rather than as a reaction to earlier "realisms."[21] Auerbach does not present literary modernism as a flight from "history." To be sure, Auerbach's characterization of modernism's principal stylistic and semantic features amounts to a claim that it has transcended nineteenth-century "historicism." But it seems to me that Auerbach interprets modernism as a further development of nineteenth-century realism, hence as a "fulfillment" of nineteenth-century realism's identification of "reality" with "history" — and hence as a further elaboration of the notion of "history" itself. What appears to be a "rejection" of history is a further elaboration of its *nineteenth-century form*, which now appears as a figure beginning to be "fulfilled" in the mid-twentieth century.[22] It is not "history" that is being rejected, but the nineteenth-century form of it.

As thus envisaged, modernism effects the closure of the gap between "history" and the premodernist version of "literature" called "fiction." The rigid opposition between "history" and "fiction" which authorizes the nineteenth-century, "historicist" idea of history, in which the term "history" names both "reality" and the very criterion of "realism" as representational practices, is canceled in modernism's implicit critique of nineteenth-century notions of "reality" and its rejection of nineteenth-century realism's idea of what "realistic representation" consisted in. In modernism, "literature" takes shape as a manner of writing that effectively transcends the older oppositions between the literal and the figurative dimensions of language, on the one hand, and between the factual and fictional modes of discourse, on the other. Consequently, modernism is to be seen as setting aside as well the long-standing distinction between "history" and "fiction," not in order to collapse one into the other, but in order to image a historical reality purged of the myths of such "grand narratives" as Fate, Providence, Geist, Progress, the Dialectic, and even the myth of the final realization of Realism itself.

Recall Auerbach's well-known summary of the characteristic features of the modernist style in his exegesis of a passage from Virginia Woolf's *To the Lighthouse*. Among the "distinguishing stylistic characteristics" of that "modernism" which the passage has been chosen to exemplify, Auerbach lists:

1. The disappearance of the "writer *as narrator of objective facts*; almost everything stated appears by way of reflection in the consciousness of the *dramatis personae*";

2. the *dissolution of any "viewpoint . . . outside the novel* from which the people and events within it are observed";

3. the predominance of *a "tone of doubt and questioning" in the narrator's interpretation* of those events seemingly described in an "objective" manner;

4. the employment of such devices as "*erlebte Rede*, stream of consciousness, *monologue interieur*" for "aesthetic purposes" that "*obscure and obliterate the impression of an objective reality* completely known to the author";

5. the use of *new techniques for the representation of the experience of time and temporality*, for example, use of the "chance occasion" to release "processes of consciousness" which remain unconnected to a "specific subject of thought"; *obliteration of the distinction between "exterior" and "interior" time*; and *representation of "events," not as "successive episodes of [a] story" but as random occurrences* (my emphases).

This list of attributes does not, of course, describe the manifest level on which *Mimesis* unfolds. But Auerbach's suggestion that the technique of representation found in Woolf's work approximates to the method used in *Mimesis* for the analysis both of the structures of texts and of their relations to their contexts permits us to look for the similarities between *Mimesis* and the classic texts of literary modernism.

Part IV

Turning Points in Literary History

Brian Stock

Literary Realism in
the Later Ancient Period

The finest tribute that can be paid to a scholar by those who have the privilege of a historical perspective on his achievement is to renew and develop his thinking. My contribution to this volume is a modest attempt to broaden the context of reflection on some issues that arise out of *Mimesis*, chapters 2 to 4, and *Literary Language and Its Public*, chapters 1 and 2.[1] These essays on late Latin antiquity are among the least accessible of Auerbach's statements to contemporary readers. Yet their importance in the consolidation of his outlook is unquestionable. Taken together, they offer a foundation for his views on continuity and discontinuity in literary history, and, through his study of Vico, on his deeper perceptions of cultural change.

My remarks are limited to the early centuries that he touches upon, that is, to the period between Tacitus (A.D. 55–120) and Gregory the Great (ca. 540–604), and within that time span to a critical 150 years between the end of the third and the beginning of the fifth century.

One of the innovative features of his view of later ancient literature arose from his belief that the Latin version of the Bible played an important role in shaping stylistic conventions. As a Romance philologist, he was inclined to look on the Jerome translation as a text in its own right, not as a reflection of oral or written originals in Hebrew or Greek. He thereby contributed a new dimension to the literary criticism of the Bible. His biblical studies also helped to set up stylistic guidelines for writing the literary history of the patristic age. Using Eduard Norden's *Antike Kunstprosa*[2] as a point of departure, he mapped

a territory that lay between theology and style, especially in two remarkable essays, "Figura" (1939) and "Sermo humilis" parts I and II
(1952 and 1954).[3]

Given the direction of his interests, there was an inevitable failure to come to terms with the evolution of Greek ideas in the Latin
West. The obvious weakness lay in the field of allegory, as witness his
insufficient attention to writers like Prudentius, Johannes Scottus Eriu-
gena, or Alan of Lille, who were all important influences on medieval
vernacular literature. Also, early Latin authors whose style and methods were indebted to Greek exemplars were not singled out for special
attention in his critical writings (e.g., Horace, Cicero, or the young Augustine). It is legitimate to ask what happens to Auerbach's interpretive
scheme when issues in Greek thought are introduced.

In what follows, I briefly examine some themes in a Greek work
that deals with problems that reappear, somewhat transformed, in a
text that is well known through Auerbach's *Mimesis*. Then, I have a
second look at the Latin text on which he based his analysis. In conclusion, I hazard some observations concerning the role of the ancient
or modern outsider in setting up stylistic boundaries for "representations" and "reality."

I

My specific concern is the relationship of Augustine to one of his
acknowledged sources, Porphyry. Auerbach recognized Augustine's
central role in the creation of western literary realism both in theory
and stylistic practice. However, he did not seek the sources of Augustine's outlook in the authors whom the bishop of Hippo read, studied,
and used as a point of departure for his own speculations. Porphyry is
one of several such figures who make no appearance in either *Mimesis*
or *Literary Language and Its Public*.

Porphyry was the editor and biographer of Plotinus (A.D. 205–270).
He published his master's philosophical writings sometime between
301 and 305, organizing the corpus into the six *Enneads*, that is, "groups
of nine." It was a selection of these together with now vanished writings of Porphyry that Augustine read in Milan in the spring of 386
in the Latin translation of the rhetorician Marius Victorinus.[4] Plotinus
and Porphyry were largely responsible for turning him into a Christian

Platonist under the tutelage of Saint Ambrose just prior to his conversion to the religious life.[5] The Platonic (and neoplatonic) contrast between the data of the senses and the mind was the chief philosophical force shaping Augustine's notions about the literary perception and expression of "reality." Moreover, among the platonizing influences at work in his thought, a key role was played by some combination of the ideas of Plotinus and Porphyry. There is as well an important chronological relationship between the evolution of his philosophical outlook and its embodiment in a hermeneutical theory. It was only after his assimilation of Platonic views during 386–87 that he synthesized his thinking on prefigural symbolism and other methods of interpretation in the manner in which Auerbach presented them in his seminal essay on *figura*. He gave some indication of what was to come in *De Magistro*, which was completed in 389, and in *De Utilitate Credendi*, which was written in the year of his ordination, 391.

   Augustine's transformation of Porphyrian influences can be illustrated through a brief comparison of the styles of representing the self in the two writers. Porphyry's contribution is found in his *Vita Plotini* (which was not a "source" for Augustine, although he knew details of Plotinus's life). In the absence of letters, an autobiography,[6] or other relevant information, this text tells us practically all that we know about late antiquity's most remarkable pagan mind. And the lack of information appears to have been Plotinus's intention. According to Porphyry, he was ashamed of his body; he was also embarrassed to talk about his race, his upbringing, or his native land.[7]

   Porphyry illustrates the point through an interesting anecdote. Amelius, one of the members of his circle,[8] suggested that Plotinus should have his portrait painted. He refused, giving this reason: "Is it not enough to have to carry the image in which nature has encased us, without asking me to leave behind a longer-lasting image of the image, as if it were genuinely worth looking at?" (*Vita* 1.5–10). Amelius was not discouraged. He invited a well-known artist, Carterius, to attend Plotinus's lectures, which were open to the public. He then taught him how to produce a mental picture of his master based on observation. Carterius later created a likeness of Plotinus from memory.

   This is an unusual statement in ancient aesthetics, suggesting that an artistic representation of a person can come about indirectly, as a by-product of a recollected physical image. I will have something to say about it later; for the moment, I focus on Porphyry's reason for placing the anecdote at the beginning of the life. He knew that Plotinus's response to the suggestion of a portrait was typical of his position on sensory images in general. Plotinus denied that a picture apprehensible to the senses could convey the reality of his person, which was accessible only to the mind. If *Mimesis*, chapters 2 to 4, is taken into consideration, the philosopher's renunciation of the sensory would appear to be the opposite of what Auerbach sees taking shape in a number of later ancient authors—Tacitus, Apuleius, Ammianus Marcellinus, Augustine, and Gregory of Tours. All affirm some version of neoplatonic idealism as a philosophical doctrine; yet they are fascinated with the stylistic representation of the sensory, even to the point of endowing it with an autonomous if uncertain reality of its own.

What Plotinus's students conceal from their master is a puerile desire for an icon, a symbolic reminder of a nonmaterial presence. By contrast, the philosopher is portrayed as training his thoughts on the invisible—on the soul. This is Porphyry's (or Plotinus's) way of correcting a standard error of beginning students of neoplatonism, namely the inability to get beyond the superficialities of the senses. Plotinus's approach (if Porphyry can be trusted) is to deny the value of the memory of the body, while admitting its philosophically troubling existence. For the Latin writers whose stories fill the pages of *Mimesis* 2–4, corporeal memory is essential to a reconstruction of the real, since (in Augustinian terms) our memories are inseparable from our awareness of the passage of time in which sensory reality is perceived. Augustine thus differs from what Porphyry tells us was the position of Plotinus, inasmuch as his aim is not to transcend the body but to overcome it, using the images in his memory as an aid. (He spells this theory out in detail in *De Trinitate*, Book Fourteen.) Given what we are told in the *Vita*, we cannot imagine Plotinus representing reality through a story, while, if we look forward to Augustine's thinking on the subject, we cannot imagine reality being represented in any other way than in a narrative which is perceived by the senses through verbal signs. In both authors, philosophies and styles of presentation are deliberately being played with. The question is why.

Some light is shed on the issues if we note another feature of Porphyry's life. The philosopher who refused to have his portrait painted took care to designate a literary executor, whereas Augustine offered us his self-portrait and acted as his own editor and publisher. Plotinus thereby ensured that posterity would know him almost exclusively through his thought. This was to represent the reality of his self in terms of abstractions and their moral implications.

But that is not the whole story. By 253–54, when Porphyry had taken up residence in Rome, Plotinus, who was then 59, had himself written some 21 treatises (*Vita* 4.10–14). He wrote hesitantly, and his comments were circulated to a small band of followers as guides to his lectures. One reason for his diffidence was a typically ancient commitment to philosophical esotericism. He had made an agreement with two other followers of Ammonius (ca. 175–242), Erennius and Origen, not to disclose their master's teachings; he lectured on Ammonius for some ten years without writing a word (3.33–35) and only betrayed the pact when he learned that the other pair had done so. In second place, Plotinus was an exponent of the standard method of teaching philosophy in late antiquity, which was oral:[9] a text of an earlier philosopher, usually Plato or Aristotle, was usually read aloud with a commentary and then discussed by a master and students. Plotinus's classes consisted of such "questions and answers" (in which, Porphyry notes, there was a good deal of disorder, misplaced emotion, and needless verbiage).[10] Porphyry speaks at length of Plotinus's listening audience, which, despite the diverse origins of the members, appears to have formed a cohesive group (7.1–2). In fact, within the *Vita*, we learn more about the participants in his school than we do about Plotinus himself. Our attention is directed toward the audience rather than toward the source of his views: this is a necessary reorientation if we are fully to appreciate Porphyry's contribution to Plotinus's oeuvre. And this is what Porphyry wants.

Finally, it appears that Plotinus was not a successful writer for personal reasons. "When [he] had written anything he could never bear to go over it twice; even to read it through once was too much for him, as his eyesight did not serve him well for reading. In writing he did not form the letters with any regard to appearance or divide his syllables correctly, and he paid no attention to spelling. He was wholly concerned with what he thought" (*Vita* 8.1–8). Furthermore, "in the meetings of the school he showed an adequate command of language and the greatest power of discovering and considering what was relevant to the subject in hand, but he made mistakes in certain words . . .

which he also committed in his writing" (13.1–6). This may be an early
example of dyslexia;[11] even if it is not, Plotinus's psychological limitations admirably serve Porphyry's literary purposes. It was he, after all,
who rearranged Plotinus's writings in a fashion that made relations between his and his master's thought difficult to sort out. If we recall the
anecdote with which the life opens, it would appear that a set of literary
works is replacing a portrait based on memory as the symbolic icon of
the master. This is another indirect link with Augustine.

II

With these thoughts in mind, I turn to a text brilliantly analyzed
by Auerbach in *Mimesis*. This is an anecdote from the so-called "Life of
Alypius," which Augustine incorporated into Book Six of the *Confessions*.

There are, in fact, three anecdotes, of which Auerbach made use of
one: this is the story of Alypius's inability to resist the sensory appeal
of gladiatorial matches. The story provides a vivid illustration of Auerbach's thesis concerning the rise of irrationalism in everyday life in late
antiquity. In his memorable account of the passage, he sums up the
issues in this way:

Here, . . . the forces of the time are at work: sadism, frenetic bloodlust,
and the triumph of magic and sense over reason and ethics. But there is a
struggle going on. The enemy is known, and the soul's counterforces are
mobilized to meet him. In this case the enemy appears in the guise of a bloodlust produced by mass suggestion and affecting all of the senses at once. . . .
Against the increasing dominance of the mob, against irrational and immod-
erate lust, against the spell of magical powers, enlightened classical culture
possessed the weapon of individualistic, aristocratic, moderate, and rational
self-discipline. The various systems of ethics all agreed that a well-bred, self-
aware, and self-reliant individual could through his own resources keep from
intemperance. . . . So Alypius is not overly concerned when he is dragged
familiari violentia into the amphitheater. He trusts in his closed eyes and his
determined will. But his proud individualistic self-reliance is overwhelmed in
no time. (*Mimesis*, pp. 59–60)

Before turning to the three interlocked anecdotes, a few words are
necessary concerning their place in the *Confessions* and what they tell

us about narrative representation at the turn of the fourth century. By the time the *Confessions* was written, between 397 and 401, Alypius, who is their subject, had himself converted, entered the religious life, and become bishop in Thagaste, near Hippo. His reputation for asceticism had spread as far as Italy, from where Paulinus of Nola and his wife, Therasia, had written Augustine in 394, asking him for the story of his life. A scholarly debate has taken place on whether that uncompleted *vita* was the starting point for the *Confessions*[12]—however, the important issue here is the role that the stories play in changing the direction of the narrative books. They mark the beginning of a transitional phase, in which distant persons and remote models of virtue are gradually replaced by those nearer at hand, that is, by individuals whose lives are recorded within the living memory of Augustine's own time. The climax of this development is the introduction of the life of Saint Anthony in Book Eight.

In contrast to Plotinus, who envisages the problem of self-representation in terms of images, Augustine speaks of interlocking narratives. Within that context, he retains from neoplatonic idealism his ambivalence about the sensory. The point of Plotinus's retort to Amelius's suggestion of a portrait is that the soul is unknowable through outer representations. Augustine would agree, but his manner of getting at the issues differs. Alypius, whose stories are related in Book Six, is the appropriate witness to his conversion in Book Eight. However, he is a witness on the outside: he tells the story of the changes in his friend as a narrative understood through what he observes. He does not penetrate Augustine's mind. In the end, Augustine has to tell him that he has decided to follow the religious life. When Alypius makes a similar decision, he too has to relate what has transpired within to his friend. One would expect the anecdotes about Alypius in Book Six to prepare the way for this situation. This is what they do.

The problem of gladiatorial combat does not arise in anecdote two, to which Auerbach refers. It is recalled from the first story. In anecdote one, it is not attractions of the senses that are in question but the problem of other minds. The tale begins with Augustine reflecting nostalgically on the conversations that he had with Nebridius and Alypius in Milan prior to the conversion in August 386, when it was he, not his friend, who was chiefly tempted by money, honors, and the prospect of a good marriage. It was during this period that he read Plotinus and Porphyry—figures whose ideas hover in the background of the stories he tells.

Anecdote one takes place during the period in which Alypius was his student in Thagaste. They held each other in high personal esteem; yet, looking back on events from the vantage point of his bishopric, Augustine the author does not think that either of them was particularly meritorious. He was then engaged in teaching rhetoric, an activity that he subsequently repudiated. This was a type of instruction designed to show his students how to deal with words, whereas he should have offered them a hermeneutic method for revealing Christian truths in the Bible. Alypius was irresistibly attracted to the bloodshed of gladiatorial combat; he was neglecting his studies to the point that a promising legal career was threatened. To make matters worse, Augustine had recently quarreled with his father. As a result, Alypius was forbidden to attend class, and Augustine had no opportunity to offer him moral counsel. Alypius was too attached to his mentor to obey his father literally. He appeared in class from time to time, although as an auditor. The idea of reproving him gradually slipped from Augustine's mind: this is an apparently innocent detail, but it introduces the notion of forgetfulness into the story and thereby provides another underground link with neoplatonism through reminiscence.

The climax of the episode came about in this way. One day Alypius entered class after the lesson had begun. Augustine was lecturing, book in hand, and had come to the point where it was necessary to provide a moral example. By coincidence he hit on the gladiatorial games. He did not have Alypius's misconduct in mind, but his student was convinced of the opposite and afterwards took care to mend his ways. As we know from anecdote two, he subsequently relapsed. Augustine, who later became his mentor again, continued to play an ambivalent role in his moral development. Having misled his students into taking pagan rhetoric too seriously, he now embarked on a career of converting them to Manichaeism, a substitute for Catholic Christianity which he encountered in Carthage. Sensory delusion was thus introduced from another direction—through the dualist belief in the power of physical images—only to be answered in *Confessions* 7 through a combination of Plotinian doctrines and the Christianized Platonism of the Gospel of John.

The story is constructed around a well-known ancient *exemplum*,[13] which is related by Diogenes Laertius, among others, concerning Polemo, the son of Philostratus, who renounced his dissolute life and turned to philosophy after hearing a lecture by Xenocrates on the virtue of temperance. Augustine's direct source may be Ambrose, who refers to it in *De Helia et Ieiunio*. However, in the original, Polemo subsequently takes over the Academy and teaches the virtues of philosophy: Alypius merely passes from one type of illusion to another. Also, while the exemplar has two characters, Augustine's story has only one, since Alypius is a stand-in for the author himself. Augustine disobeyed his parents and went from Thagaste to Carthage for his education; he too was mesmerized by spectacles. As the anecdote is related, there is a change of emphasis from other persons' lives to Augustine's life. The hidden subject of Book Six is the bishop of Hippo's youthful attempt and failure to achieve a literary, that is, vicarious, remodeling of his self. The story ends without Alypius knowing what is in store for him. This is Augustine's way of reminding us that God's inscrutable ways determine the course of the narrative of his life throughout the *Confessions*.

Literary representation is thus caught up with problems of knowledge and ignorance; these themes in turn are loosely linked to metaphysically oriented notions of remembering and forgetting. There are two potential sources of human ignorance: minds cannot understand each other, and individuals cannot understand divine providence. In the second anecdote of Book Six, which Auerbach quotes, the same forces are at work. Nothing takes place by chance; and again the story's effect depends on Alypius's self-delusion. But a third element is added: this is the force of memory, not in Alypius or Augustine, but in us, as readers of the *Confessions*. Our vantage point in the account is that of Alypius's friends, who drag him off to the games to tempt him and wait to see whether he is able to resist. Auerbach overlooked the factor of memory, which is critical, I believe, to following the manner in which the three narratives are intertwined: they reinforce each other in Alypius's life just as the conversion stories of Book Eight have a cumulative effect on Augustine. It is in our reconstruction of the two sets of narratives in memory, moreover, that their moral force is realized. The audience, as a group of later readers and rememberers, thereby takes on some of the omniscience of the deity.

For this reason, the time frame of anecdote two is different, while the situation reiterates what has come before: Alypius is now in Rome, several years later, although still pursuing a worldly career and addicted to the sight of blood. The moral of the story is that Alypius should have relied on God, when he put all of his trust in himself. Augustine believed that self-confident rationalism was the weak link in pagan philosophies, as well as in Manichaeism. He disagreed with those who trusted in human reason to resolve the difficulties facing the individual in the moral and religious sphere. Alypius fails not because he lacks self-discipline, as Auerbach proposed, but because he places too much faith in it. He is weak, not because he is unaware of his inner life but because he refuses to seek support for it outside himself. Like Augustine, he lives in what Plato called "a region of dissemblance."

III

This Platonic phrase, *regio dissimilitudinis*, which echoes down through the centuries after it is Latinized by Augustine,[14] raises a third issue, the status of the outsider. If we compare the views of Plotinus and Augustine on this subject, we see a subtle transition taking place. Understanding its nature helps to place Auerbach's contribution in perspective.

Taking Plotinus first, what sort of an outsider was he? Essentially a person seeking an alternative lifestyle. After his training in western philosophy under Ammonius, he appears to have embraced the religious philosophies of Persia and India—we are not told which ones. He even tried to get to the East as a soldier. When the young emperor Gordian III was murdered at Zaitha in Mesopotamia in 244, he narrowly escaped to Antioch, returning to Rome at age 40 during the reign of Philippus I (A.D. 244–249) (*Vita* 3.13–24). There, despite his foreignness, he proceeded to acquire great intellectual prestige. Three senators were regular members of his entourage. One of them, Rogatianus, underwent a change of direction (echoed at a lower social level by Augustine's imperial converts in Trier): he renounced his property, dismissed his servants, and resigned from office; he gave up the house in which he normally lived and stayed as a guest with his friends, eating a meal only once every two days (incidentally, curing himself of gout) (7.32–44). Other men and women of high rank in the city entrusted their property to the disinterested Plotinus (9.6–9), who kept their accounts in order, thereby freeing them from worldly matters and enabling them to devote their attention to philosophy. He frequently judged disputes, and was said never to have made an official enemy (9.16–23)—no mean feat for an academic. He was "honoured and venerated" by the emperor Gallienus and his wife (12.1–3), who allegedly supported the scheme of founding a city of philosophers in the Campania to be called Platonopolis (12.3–10).

Augustine was something of an outsider himself in Rome—a fact that is no secret in the *Confessions*. When he came from Carthage to teach, hoping for better students, he was singled out as a provincial and cheated out of his fees (*Confessions* 5.8). Later, in Milan, he was sensitive to the social and intellectual distance that separated him from his would-be mentor, Saint Ambrose. The famous silent-reading scene at *Confessions* 6.3 is a study in isolation on Ambrose's part and of perceived alienation on Augustine's. When at length he found himself in the bishop's presence, he appears to have behaved like an undergraduate who is brought before a teacher he has longed to meet, only to find that the teacher has nothing to say to him. As Augustine sums matters up, he had achieved the status of an imperial chair of rhetoric, yet he could still envy a drunken beggar, who knew better than he the simple pleasures that he wanted out of life (6.6). Even in his maturity, Augustine was more at ease on the periphery than at the center of the empire: his conception of himself as an outsider gives his rhetoric much of its ironic force.

Porphyry takes pains to contrast the description of Plotinus's physical disabilities in old age with his otherworldly position on philosophical matters. Indirectly, the life also stresses the difference between his personal habits and his political influence. In chapter two, we hear of a variety of ailments that the philosopher endured: bowel disease, ulceration of the hands and feet, and, as death neared, the inability to lecture (*Vita* 2.1–20). Yet, through his ascetic withdrawal from society, Plotinus wielded considerable spiritual influence. He was imitated by many persons who did not understand the subtleties of his ideas. His alienation, in short, was one not of nationality (although he spoke Greek in a Latin world) but of beliefs. It was not imposed on him; he imposed it on himself.

In Plotinus, then, there is no reality to be illustrated by a story; as a result, there can be no narrative text of a life to be followed: the reality that hovers between self and otherness remains a philosophical and psychological problem for the individual. If we look forward to Augustine and beyond, the personal imitation of the holy person is supplemented by the living, reading, and writing of lives, all of which have become a single process: we are halfway to Freud and Lacan. The ideals that Augustine implants into Alypius's stories are not so different from those that Plotinus exemplifies to the senator Rogatianus. Yet, only in Augustine's scheme is it interlocking narratives that instruct Alypius and ultimately us as well. While Plotinus begins within the concept of the soul, Augustine begins with the senses, above all sight and hearing, through which narratives are understood as a sequence of meaningful words. As in poets and prose writers who follow him down to Dante, it is the earthly world, as Auerbach elsewhere argued, that is the starting point for understanding lived reality.

Augustine is not the first writer to hold such views about narrative, although he may be the first to offer a synthetic statement. Even here, however, other forces are at work in concert with his interpretation of the three levels of oratorical style. The chief of these is his rethinking of notions of memory, time, and the powers of the soul, which takes us back by a different route to Plotinus.

In my summary of the anecdote that begins Porphyry's life of the philosopher, I postponed a discussion of the important statement about memory. Amelius, as noted, taught Carterius how to paint from memory, instructing him through a type of visual mnemotechnics. This was an application of standard teaching on the art of memory.[15] Plotinus would have opposed the imagism, as Porphyry suggests, but not the theory of memory on which it is based. In fact, what Porphyry says sounds rather like what Plotinus says about remembering at *Enneads* 4.6.3.29–35, where he notes that "exercises to improve our mental grasp show that what is going on [in memory] is an empowering of the soul, just like the physical training of our arms and legs . . . by continuous exercise. For why, when one has heard something once or twice, does one not remember it, but [only] when one has heard it many times . . . ?" Augustine shared Plotinus's view that memory operates through an active element in the soul, not just recording sense-impressions but permitting mental images to pass from potentiality to actuality. He also saw memory as the locus for reconstructed narratives; this was his adaptation of Platonic reminiscence.

It was through his theory of memory that Augustine was able to transform a philosophical problem in neoplatonism into a literary problem for the West. The psychological awareness of alienation thus became the literary expression of alienation. A problem in the soul became a problem in narrative representation, and, with it, the inwardness of the mind became identified with the inner discourse of the text. There is no truly literary awareness of the issues in Plotinus, whereas in Augustine they are already so sophisticated in their presentation that the following ten centuries of literary criticism is largely a gloss on his ideas.

I would argue, therefore, that a turning point in the tradition of self-representation occurs in late antiquity, one that is disguised by the continuity of stylistic development between Tacitus and Gregory of Tours. The relativism that Plotinus associates with the sensory impressions in the soul reemerges as the relativism of the observer's point of view on a series of events. That is the rationale that lies behind Augustine's transformation of Plotinus's ideas in his well-known discussions of memory and time. Later writers in the West, while not reproducing the subtlety of his arguments, nonetheless perpetuate the literary tradition which they support. Auerbach saw in later ancient narrative a growing fascination with irrationalism and the cult of violence. Surely this was a reflection on his own age as much as on antiquity. The forces that he observed in the Roman period were there at the beginning as they were at the end. What the ancient narratives on this topic lack is not a description of evil in the world but an acceptable explanation of it. Augustine thought he had an answer. Some would disagree: yet, in supplementing the action of the soul with the remembered action of narratives, he took western literary theory in a new direction.

Kevin Brownlee

The Ideology of Periodization:
Mimesis 10 and
the Late Medieval Aesthetic

I would like to begin with a brief personal aside. My present reading of Erich Auerbach's *Mimesis* is a deeply critical one, and I have discovered in the process of writing that this critical stance is somewhat difficult for me for reasons of "filial piety" in an important intellectual sense. Well do I remember the reverence with which *Mimesis* was treated as a centerpiece in Columbia University's Humanities course which I took as a freshman in 1964, seven years after Auerbach's death in 1957. And well do I remember the galvanizing effect my first reading of Auerbach's study had not only on my engagement with literary texts but also on my notion of what being an intellectual meant. My current awareness of the epoch-making importance of *Mimesis* in imposing its literary-historical vision as canonical, especially in American university milieux almost from its first appearance in English-language translation, is now highly critical in many respects. And, indeed, I now see a critical consideration of this reception in terms of our contemporary perspectives on cultural ideology to be a fruitful (even a necessary) undertaking. Nonetheless, I feel the need to reaffirm my conviction that Auerbach's *Mimesis* is a great work of interpretative scholarship, both in terms of its overall conception of literary history and in its many specific microtextual readings. And part of the effect of a great work of scholarship is to call forth—that is, both to require and to empower—revisionist readings. In the case of Auerbach, these readings involve not only his book itself but also many of the central preoccupations of contemporary cultural and literary studies. This is, of course, an indication of the book's enduring intellectual vitality: investigating its limitations calls forth new insights. And it is in this spirit that I undertake my own revisionist reading.

I will be engaging in a kind of radical period-specificity: pressing very hard the single literary-historical period normally referred to as "the late Middle Ages"—and then "reading out" from this perspective into *Mimesis* as a whole, *against Mimesis* as a whole. As a corollary, I will be questioning the status of the Auerbachian textual starting point, the *Ansatz*, with regard precisely to its putative "particularity."

My overall approach is thus to interrogate Auerbach's notion in *Mimesis* of literary periodization by focusing upon this particular period construct—the late Middle Ages—and on the various broad assumptions (and categories), both ideological and methodological, that underlie it. At the same time, this interrogation will involve a critical probing of Auerbach's notion of mimesis itself within the historico-literary context of this particular period. This means a rereading of the textual excerpts he privileges as "representational" in chapter 10 largely by recontextualizing them—that is, by replacing them within the complex nexus of structural and discursive contexts through which they signify. Furthermore, I am interested in how Auerbach's vision of the late Middle Ages is, on the one hand, something of a special case in terms of his ideology of periodization; and how, on the other hand, his construct of the late Middle Ages is related to that of other "liminal" ("decadent") periods—especially to his double vision of late antiquity (i.e., pre- and post-imperial fall) in chapters 3 and 4; but also, I suggest, his vision of contemporary twentieth-century European letters in chapter 20.

Let me begin by considering three basic aspects of Auerbach's method which are particularly relevant to his concept of the late Middle Ages in chapter 10. First, there is the systematic privileging of the textual fragment, presented as a self-sufficient unit. The various contexts within which (and against which) the privileged fragments work to produce meaning are repeatedly downplayed, rendered virtually invisible, even suppressed as irrelevant. This includes the context provided by the work from which the fragment is extracted, the diachronic literary context in which both work and fragment are situated, and the synchronic socioliterary context to which both the work and the fragment respond, and which they often visibly inscribe. Chapters proceed from a decontextualized fragment or fragments which are presented as containing in embryo (or as a kind of essence) the basic mimetic attitude of a particular period of western literary history.

Second, there is Auerbach's construct of the literary-historical period as such, conceived as a unit, a coherent *mentalité*, a discrete segment in which a basic set of attitudes towards "reality" and its representation are incarnated. Now, this often involves opposing tendencies which are in implicit or even explicit conflict, but the presupposition is that this defining set of attitudes is so pervasive that any piece of mimetic discourse from the period will incorporate it, and that it can therefore be "derived" from any necessarily characteristic fragment. There is of course a kind of reciprocity (or circularity) at issue here. Auerbach's construct of the period can be read back into the textual fragments from which it has, in theory, been abstracted, and vice versa.

At the same time, each of Auerbach's literary-historical periods exists within a diachronic dimension: an overarching forward movement toward the goal of a fully actualized, universal realism, in which the limitations of style separation and "class boundaries" are overcome, and a profound and informed awareness of "creatural" sensoriness is maintained in tandem with a full consciousness of historical process. In addition, this "full" realism includes an ethical dimension in which humanistic values and a sense of the tragic coexist. In effect, the final goal of Auerbach's teleological literary history appears as a fully adequate blend of the two opposing mimetic modes adumbrated in chapter 1. We have a modified Hegelian model in which literary discourses play the role of historico-political forces. An ideology of progress is built into this model, with the nineteenth-century "realistic" French novel serving as a provisional end-point, and a hypothetically perfect mimesis situated in an elusive but attainable future period as the ideal end-point of literary history.

In chapter 10 of *Mimesis*, Auerbach turns to a negatively marked period within his teleological literary history: the late Middle Ages, which he characterizes as involving "Franco-Burgundian realism." This is a low point, a retrograde moment, in the Auerbachian schema: on the one hand, a falling away from the mimetic high point of trecento Italy (incarnated by Dante's *Commedia* and Boccaccio's *De-*

cameron); on the other hand, an inadvertent "preparation" for the impending high point of the Renaissance.[1] The primary literary-historical value of the late Middle Ages lies in its status as a literary-historical conduit which "transfers" from the High Middle Ages (including the trecento) to the Renaissance a sensibility that will be a key component in that new period's dominant collective mimetic mode, and one which, otherwise, might have been neglected, that is, the Christian preoccupation with the sensory and the creatural, otherwise at risk before the programmatic neoclassicism of the humanist aesthetic, especially with regard to the doctrine of the separation of styles.[2]

Auerbach's conception of the dominant period-aesthetic of the late French Middle Ages involves three interrelated features.

First, it is a question of an *exaggerated* "creatural realism," a morbid (almost pathological) focus on those corporeal details of earthly human life that most exemplify its weakness and its transitoriness— bodily vulnerability to pain, to disease, to aging, and to death. This focus is at once derived from what can be called Christian Incarnational poetics, and, in Auerbach's view, is radically detached from the essence of that poetics, in terms both of language and of ontology. That is, the late-medieval Franco-Burgundian obsession with "serious, creatural realism" is ultimately a consequence of the Christian figuralism that endows both "ignoble" human suffering (on the model of the Crucifixion) and domestic intimacy (on the model of the Annunciation and the Nativity) with an absolute spiritual, cosmic, universal seriousness. Yet this late-medieval outlook so deprivileges the spiritual dimension of Christian Incarnational history as to detach its realistic mimesis from any overarching worldview, from any redemptive, or even coherent, set of universal values.

This detachment is the second defining feature of late-medieval mimesis from Auerbach's point of view: "it has freed itself from serving the concept of a Christian universal order; indeed, it no longer serves any concept of order whatsoever. It is fully independent; it has become an end in itself" (p. 258). The late medieval aesthetic, in other words, involves no truly functional transcendent principle.

Third, Auerbach characterizes the period's realistic mimesis as fundamentally non–self-reflective. In literary-historical terms, this means a lack of awareness concerning the "progressive" period ideology that Auerbach assumes to be factually valid: "while the old order declines, there is nothing . . . to announce the rise of a new one" (p. 259). In socio-literary terms, this means a noncritical valorization of "class insignia" (p. 249), a "class-boundedness" from which no late-medieval mimetic discourse can escape. In Auerbach's usage, this seems to mean both highly ceremonial, "feudal-heraldic" mimetic art associated with the (putatively declining) nobility and a quotidian, domestic focus associated with the (inexorably rising) bourgeoisie. The extremely interesting set of conflicts built into this double (and, indeed, contradictory) kind of class consciousness in most official discourses of the late Middle Ages is not taken into account in Auerbach's conceptualization of the period. Nor does he consider the period's elaborate and highly self-conscious mimesis in literary works of patronage relations, whose necessary and ambiguous crossing of class lines—especially in first-person contexts—becomes increasingly part of the complex discourse of the late-medieval professional writer as such. It is in addition, I suggest parenthetically, difficult to understand exactly how "class-boundedness" differentiates fourteenth- and fifteenth-century Franco-Burgundian mimetic art from either that of trecento Italy or that of the High French Middle Ages, especially given that "class" is a notion which Auerbach does not scrutinize in any serious way but takes to be self-evident.

This construct of the literary-historical period of the late Middle Ages both presents itself as derived from Auerbach's readings of specific texts and informs these readings in all essential ways. This kind of circularity is of course built into the overall procedure of *Mimesis*, but is particularly visible in chapter 10, where the period construct seems to play a more important role than elsewhere. The dominant notions of decline, decadence, and dead end, resulting, in large part, from Auerbach's "progressivist" vision of the unfolding of literary history in the West—and overly dependent on Johan Huizinga—end up by oversimplifying and impoverishing, abstracting and flattening out his global presentation of fourteenth- and fifteenth-century French literary discourse. This period *mentalité* is presented as particularly homogeneous, somewhat paradoxically, by virtue of the putative status of the late Middle Ages as a time of cultural exhaustion.

The principal text at issue in chapter 10, serving both to establish and to illustrate the characteristic features of late-medieval mimesis according to Auerbach's conceptualization of the period, is Antoine de

La Sale's *Réconfort de Madame de Fresne* (1457), or, rather, a set of excerpts from the first of the two narrative exempla contained in that work.[3] As is standard practice for Auerbach, a bare summary of the overall structure of the work serves to situate the extracts on which he focuses his attention as philologist and literary historian. The first extract (*Mimesis*, pp. 233–38) presents the extended nocturnal discussion between M. and Mme du Chastel concerning the excruciating choice imposed upon them by the Black Prince, who is beseiging the fortress of Brest, commanded by M. du Chastel. The choice is between the preservation of the husband's honor and the imminent execution of their son. The second extract (pp. 238–40) is the narration by du Chastel's herald of the son's execution. The third and fourth excerpts (pp. 240–41) from the *Réconfort* involve the private and the public reactions of the father to the news of his son's death.

Auerbach's close reading of these passages involves a series of complementary perspectives, determined by a rigorous selectivity, and excluding and minimizing the multiple contexts within which the passages are embedded. First, he considers the language and the style of the *Réconfort* as a function of the work's author, who is constructed as synonymous with a simplified socio-biographical portrait. The stylistic considerations are consistently—and arbitrarily—evaluative. To take a particularly striking example, the interaction between legal and literary discourses so deeply characteristic of the late Middle Ages in France—and so deeply linked to the problematic of personal identity, coherence, and authority which was so obsessively engaged, and staged, by fourteenth- and fifteenth-century writers—is evaluated by Auerbach as a stylistic "flaw." He denigrates certain characteristic features of the *Réconfort*'s language as "reminiscent of the pompous style of legal and diplomatic documents" (p. 241), without considering how this "style" functions in that work.

This judgment is part of Auerbach's larger characterization of La Sale's language as "syntactically confused" (p. 242) and semantically repetitive (p. 241), which leads to generalizations concerning the inadequacy, the exhaustion, of late-medieval literary language as such. La Sale's use of the rhetorical traditions of antiquity is characterized as involving "its pedantic medieval transformation," and contrasted negatively with "the humanistic renewal of its original character" (ibid.). This period ideology informs virtually every aspect of Auerbach's putatively neutral use of "philology" to define and to interpret La Sale's language at both the syntactic and the semantic levels. His dismissive characterization of "the solemnly invocational accumulation of pleonastic or quasi-pleonastic expressions like *nourry, amé et tenu chier*" (ibid.) is typical. Not only is this formula semantically significant for the chronology of maternal love with regard to late-medieval physio-psychology (body-affect-intellect); not only is the tripartite sequence syntactically functional in terms of the late-medieval stylistic trait of hierarchical semantic overdetermination (i.e., the final term is privileged, as demonstrated in the recent work of Theo Venckeleer); but further, the fact that—within the plot line—a mother prepares to accept the untimely death of her child in visibly legalistic, formulaic language involves, among other things, an implicit guarantee of the apparently unbelievable content of her speech. The augmented authority conveyed by this legalistic articulation of what amounts to a renunciation of a gendered maternal identity is also deeply linked to the functioning of the entire *récit* as exemplum.[4]

Auerbach's consideration of what he calls the "content of the story" (p. 243), as opposed to its linguistic "form," is equally unaware of the generic status of the *Réconfort* as exemplum, as *confort*, and of the significance of genre (and, indeed, of the sociohistorical patronage situation) as discursive context. Thus, for example, he faults La Sale for not writing politico-military history, and finds the absence of detail in this connection to be "striking . . . to a modern reader" (p. 243). In point of fact, of course, the basic politico-historical presupposition of the story is purely fictional; that is, the city of Brest was in the hands of the English throughout the entire period during which the Black Prince campaigned in France.[5] The determining principle is the generic discourse of the *Réconfort*, itself a function of its dedicatee and privileged audience, Madame de Fresne. Again, Auerbach's period ideology imposes itself in his anachronistic and decontextualized evaluative reading.

An even more fundamental aspect of Auerbach's ideological readerly perspective is at issue in his opposition between La Sale's form and content, between his language and the "factuality" of his subject matter. The language is viewed as "class-determined" (p. 243), that is to say, as a naïvely closed linguistic system which supposedly reflects in its "solemn and circumstantial rhetoric, with its abundance of formulas, its superabundance of conventional gestures and invocations . . .

the stable class-determined order of life in which everything has and keeps its place" (p. 242). Thus Auerbach reads back into La Sale's language the authorial class-mentality traits that he derives from that same language. This circularity is all the more striking in that this putative naïveté of form and of approach is absolutely essential to Auerbach's notion of the late Middle Ages as profoundly "unconscious" of itself as a period of historical "transition," equally oblivious to the fact that the "old order" was crumbling and to the fact that a "new order" was already taking incipient shape. La Sale's representational status with regard to this period construct requires a similar kind of "microcosmic" naïveté and unself-consciousness. Thus, La Sale's style is "heavily pompous" (p. 243), his syntax is confused and repetitive (a failed and superficial hypotaxis), his compositional principles are simple chronology and mere enumeration (ibid.). Style, syntax, and structure all recall (in Auerbach's revelatory metaphor) an extended (though somewhat muddled) heraldic procession (pp. 241–42).

It is important to stress that Auerbach is rigorously consistent in his application of this reading, and nowhere more surprisingly than with regard to narrative structure: "as for the structure of the narrative as a whole, it is hardly possible to speak of any conscious organization" (p. 243). This, as I will attempt to demonstrate, is simply not true of either the *récit*'s internal narrative structure or of the structure provided for the *récit* by the *Réconfort* as a whole.

The final aspect of Auerbach's close reading of his excerpts from La Sale's text that concern me here involves what he terms the author's "approach" to his subject matter, and is directly linked to certain basic assumptions concerning the nature of mimetic verbal art which underlie Auerbach's book as a whole. The basic construct posits "reality" as an extratextual, extralinguistic referent, whose ontological status is unproblematic. Mimetic language is conceived of as a mirror, more or less fully adequate, more or less artificially distorting. In La Sale's du Chastel narrative, the inherent reality of the events of the story line involves a kind of life of its own. The spontaneous reality of the subject matter imposes itself upon the inadequate and artificial linguistic medium employed by La Sale. In spite of the author's profoundly limited class- and period-determined approach, there is an explosion of tragic conflict in terms of real events. And Auerbach treats these as if they have a life of their own.

This is the point at which Auerbach's evaluative criticism turns positive. The du Chastel couple's discussion of the impending death of their child is "a genuinely tragic and genuinely real scene" (p. 246). Here La Sale's otherwise mimetically inadequate discourse represents "a perfectly simple, directly human action" (ibid.). This achievement takes place almost in spite of La Sale's conscious authorial intentionality: "despite the solemn and ceremonious language, what takes place is very simple and very naive. . . . There is no question of any stylistic separation between the tragic and everyday realism . . . [everything is] so real and 'creatural' [*kreatürliches*]" (ibid.).

This exceptional moment of Auerbachian praise for the La Sale excerpts that he subjects to a philological and literary-historical close reading will serve as my point of transition to a contextualized rereading of the *Réconfort*. For virtually every detail of Auerbach's laudatory analysis involves a serious misreading in terms of context.

Let me start with the bedroom scene between husband and wife. The first key context established for the reading of this scene involves the frame provided by the prologue and the epilogue of the *Réconfort*. This context combines the two generic discourses of *consolatio* and *exemplum* in the specific setting of a young wife disconsolate at the loss of her first child. The work as a whole is addressed directly to this wife (identified by the vocative *vous*) and, through her, indirectly, to her husband (addressed either as part of the couple or in the third person). The discussion that takes place in the conjugal bed between M. and Mme du Chastel is thus meant to provide an example for Mme de Fresne to imitate and to be consoled by. Every word of La Sale's exemplary uxorial character functions in this double way. The narrative events that give rise to her exemplary reaction are not recounted for their own sake, or because that is how La Sale thinks that a series of "real" events transpired. Rather, these narrative events provide an example for Mme de Fresne to imitate, and are thus part of an overall, coherent, discursive strategy. While Auerbach sees that Mme du Chastel provides an intradiegetic[6] example for her husband (p. 245), his exclusion of overall context means that the full exemplarly charge of Mme du Chastel — with regard to the work's inscribed target audience — remains invisible.

Similarly, the primacy of the couple in the du Chastel story and the absolute subjugation by Mme du Chastel of her feelings toward her son in favor of her primary loyalty to her husband are both meant to

be read as part of the discourse of exemplum.[7] Far from being an un-
motivated "real" personality whose "natural simplicity and sensitivity"
erupt—accidently, as it were—into La Sale's naive story line, Mme du
Chastel is a powerful model, constructed rhetorically so as to compel
imitation and provide consolation.

A second key context which informs this same bedroom scene, and
which reinforces its status as exemplum, involves the functional presence of a subtext, the fact that the scene is immediately perceptable
to a fifteenth-century audience as a corrective rewriting of a standard
misogynist and anti-marriage topos: the wife in bed who makes the
husband reveal his secrets to his own detriment. This topos is here inverted, made good. Part of the effectiveness (indeed, of the very functioning) of La Sale's scene qua discourse involves its being read correc-
tively against this topos. Furthermore, there is a specific master model
text for this topos in the late French Middle Ages: the famous sequence
in the *Roman de la Rose* (ll. 16347–700, ed. Langlois) where Genius discourses to Nature on woman's inability to keep men's secrets, with
its central, illustrative, bedroom scene. Not only is this motif repeatedly deployed in the *Rose* itself—see the speeches of Le Jaloux and La
Vieille—but it also figures prominently in the early-fifteenth-century
Débat sur le "Roman de la Rose" as articulated by Christine de Pizan, and—
to take one particularly striking later example—in François Villon's
Grand Testament in the character of the Belle Heaulmière. Indeed, this
scene in the *Rose* clearly lies behind the sequence of the first of the
Quinze joyes de mariage cited by Auerbach himself in chapter 10 of
Mimesis, though without any awareness of this intertextual dimension.
Again, in the bedroom scene of the *Réconfort*, it is a question not of
"representing reality" (i.e., an unproblematic extratextual referent) but
of the *mediation* of La Sale's mimetic language by preexisting textual
models.

An equally important set of mediating contexts obtains in the second scene Auerbach excerpts from La Sale's du Chastel exemplum: the
child's execution.

First of all, there is the carefully structured drama of progressive
revelation and comprehension which culminates in the actual depiction
of the death scene. Several different, limited perspectives are deployed
in sequence (beginning in line 596), which present the events leading
up to the child's execution in increasingly greater detail and certainty,

stressing the excruciating distance and impotence of the parental (especially the paternal) point of view. Even the final narration of the death
scene itself involves a double narrative distance. The reader learns of
the event at the same diegetic moment as M. du Chastel, and at two
removes: the herald recounts to the father events recounted to him by
a direct witness, events that occurred after the herald had fainted from
horror. This highly self-conscious and intricate play of direct and indirect witnessing and narrating not only explodes Auerbach's bizarre
remark concerning the work's lack of "any conscious organization" or
narrative structure (p. 243) but also functions to heighten the pathos of
this death scene (and of *these* parents' sufferings), in contradistinction to
those of M. and Mme de Fresne, the work's addressees. Part of the way
in which the du Chastel narrative functions as exemplum lies precisely
in the fact that it is an extreme case. Its very extremity makes it more
effective as consolation for the privileged audience of La Sale's dedi-
catees, the death of whose son did not involve, by contrast, this sort of
absolute parental—and especially maternal—testing.

A second context for the death of the du Chastel son is provided
by the contrasting case of what La Sale calls his "deuxième example"
for Madame de Fresne, that is, the story of the heroic death of the son
of the anonymous "ancienne dame, baronnesse de Portugal," during
the Portuguese conquest of Ceuta in 1415. This heroic knight is none
other than the guardian (*gouverneur*) of Don Henry, son of John I, king
of Portugal. In La Sale's story, this knight sacrifices himself to save the
life of his royal charge, whose grief and gratitude know no bounds.
There follows a carefully structured sequence in which the king first
withholds, then progressively reveals the news of the son's death to his
mother at court—a sequence that recalls (not, of course, accidentally!)
the similar drama of concealment and revelation around the death of
the du Chastel son in the first of the *Réconfort*'s two exempla. King
John I functions as an exemplary source of *confort*, first for his own
disconsolate son and then for the mother for the death of her son. In
this second exemplum of La Sale, we have a careful and suggestively
symmetrical reversal of gender and parental roles: here a father (who
is also the absolute father figure, i.e., the king) comforts the mother.
This aspect of the exemplum is, in part, aimed at M. de Fresne in his
capacity as part of the couple. The fact that he is addressed indirectly
within the diegesis of the Ceuta story accords with the indirect address

(in the third person as "Monsieur vostre mari") of the prologue and epilogue of the *Réconfort* as a whole.

In addition, this second story of the death of a son involves a set of extreme contrasts with the first. With the du Chastel child's youth and innocence are contrasted the Portuguese knight's adulthood and maturity; the former's physical helplessness and passivity are contrasted with the latter's physical strength and control; the first is a passive object, the second, an acting subject; the former's contingent status (i.e., his death is the result of the choices of others) is contrasted with the latter's full autonomy (i.e., his fully exercised free will); finally, the former's pitiful—and ignobly borne—execution is contrasted with the latter's noble death in battle.

In terms of the global generic status of the *Réconfort* as exemplum, the deaths of the two sons in the two exemplary stories present two extreme cases, providing a kind of full context within which the death of the de Fresne son is situated. The overall focus is on La Sale's inscribed audience, M. and Mme de Fresne, and it is this that controls the details of the work's various narrative components.

A third context for the death of the du Chastel son in the first exemplum simultaneously involves both the death of the Portuguese knight in the second exemplary story and La Sale's authorial presentation of how Mme de Fresne should react to the death of her son in the *Réconfort*'s prologue and epilogue. This is the work's overall religious context, which functions consistently and powerfully to inform our reading. That is to say, La Sale presents both his work as a whole and each of its component parts as teaching a lesson. And a proper reading is intended to instill this lesson both in the "ideal" reader—that is, a parent who has recently lost a child—and in the "metaphoric" or "secondary" reader, namely, one who has suffered a similar devastating loss in earthly terms.

This didactic Christian reading program is first articulated in the *Réconfort*'s prologue. The general Christian reader's situation (specifically incarnated by Mme de Fresne) is set forth in terms of an imminent danger that a proper reading of La Sale's work is intended first to neutralize, then to transform into something positive. There is thus a dynamic readerly configuration inscribed into the text itself: the target audience needs to read in order to be cured, in order to be saved. Every aspect of the work that compels attention, identification, and self-consciousness operates to further this basic Christian readerly paradigm, which works as follows.

The grief experienced by Mme de Fresne over the death of her son is presented as a danger: if yielded to, "vostre dueil et voz tristesses vous porroient l'ame et le corps trop empirer" (ll. 28–29; "your mourning and your lamenting can greatly damage your soul and your body"). The presupposition, then, for the generic discourse of the *Réconfort* is that the reader is in a state of physical and spiritual danger as the result of overly-worldly grieving for a worldly loss. Virtually every detail of the *Réconfort* as a whole is determined by the requirements of this inscribed reader in terms of La Sale's Christian spiritual vision and his conception of himself as an authoritative spokesman for this vision.

The prologue repeatedly emphasizes the danger of excessive grief in terms of a single, capital sin: despair—the antonym of Hope: "telles doulleurs et tristresses de cueur souvent sont procurées par l'instirgacion de l'Ennemy" (ll. 38–39; "such pains and sadnesses of the heart are often caused by the intervention of the Devil"). The "désespoir" (despair) aimed at by Satan will "nous grever jusques à la mort espirituelle et corporelle" (ll. 43–44; "harm us so much as to cause spiritual and physical death"). In addition to citing classical and biblical *sententiae* (Seneca, Saint Bernard, Tobias, and the Gospel), La Sale recounts a "preliminary" narrative *"exemple"* (l. 66) in the prologue. This involves a mother whose excessive grief on the untimely death of her young son retards his spiritual progress in the afterworld. He comes to her in a vision and explains that "l'effusion des larmes que pour moy avez tant gettées" (l. 86; "the profusion of tears that you have shed for me") prevents his accession into Heaven. Her subsequently rightly directed prayers succeed in "saving" him (l. 95). The spiritual condition of both the (living) mother and the (deceased) son is thus at issue in this initial appeal to the bereaved Mme de Fresne.

The concomitant earthly part of this Christian didactic program for overcoming despair in the *Réconfort*'s prologue involves the imperative to have new children. This evokes of course a biblical model text (Genesis 1:22), which figures critically, be it noted in passing, in the Genius section of the *Roman de la Rose*. This literal earthly making good of the loss appears first in the conclusion to the prologue. Here, La Sale the author figure exhorts Mme and M. de Fresne to pray to Saint

Jehan Michiel (of Angers) to intervene on their behalf with God for a new son: "tant que je sçay et puis, tous deux vous requiers et prie que ad ce glorieux saint . . . vous recommandez et priez que . . . envers Dieu face prière telle que briefment vous doinst ung beau filz, ainssy qu'il a fait à maintz aultres" (ll. 170–75; "as much as I know how, I beg and entreat that you both commend yourselves to this glorious saint and pray that he pray God that you soon be given a beautiful son, as he has done to many others").

This key segment of the Christian didactic dimension is picked up by each of the work's two major exemplary characters: positively by Mme du Chastel (who declares both her capability and her intention to have another child even before the execution of her first child takes place), and negatively by the Portuguese baroness (who, while no longer physically able to have another child, declares her affective and spiritual satisfaction with her son's noble death).

In addition, each of these two narratives (though in different— indeed, complementary—ways) repeatedly inscribes this Christian didactic context at the level of plot. Both characters and readers are explicitly directed heavenward for an adequate understanding of and reaction to the events of the story line. At the same time, the earthly component is unrelentingly positive, even (for Mme du Chastel) optimistic: the confident anticipation of the birth of a new child.

The programmatic inscription of this Christian didactic dimension brings me to the fourth kind of context that the *Réconfort* provides for its narrative account of the death of the du Chastel son: that of a visibly articulated authorial subjectivity. From the *Réconfort*'s opening rubric, La Sale writes himself into his text as its linguistic and ontological point of origin. In the double heading "A MA TRES HONNOREE DAME ET MA TRESBONNE FILLE, MADAME KATERINE DE NEUFVILLE, DAME DE FRESNE" ("to my most honored lady and my very good daughter, Madame Catherine of Neufville, Lady of Fresne"), the component of La Sale's authorial identity that is a function of the sociopolitical reality of his patronage situation (a nonnoble *serviteur* of a noble *dame*) is overwritten by the authoritative *persona* of the conventional "wise old man," the Christian *senex*. The work's final rubric restates this hierarchized double identity in a pseudo-epistolary closing salutation and "signature": "VOSTRE SERVITEUR ET PERE ANTHOINE DE LA SALLE" (ll. 1225–26). As a writerly voice, therefore, La Sale from the first assumes the authoritative stance of the sage whose long years have provided him with both detachment and wisdom, whose philosophical perspective is combined with Christian spiritual insight. The entire religio-didactic dimension of the *Réconfort* is ultimately a mere function of this authorial stance. Its Christian "spiritual" context emanates from La Sale–*auctor*.

If the discursive stance that La Sale initially assumes by addressing his patroness/dedicatee as "fille" carries with it the authoritative identity of "father" (in the sense of priest and/or confessor), this paternal component of his authorial identity will be elaborated and nuanced as the work unfolds.

In the prologue, it is a question of the inscribed speech situation in which the typically late-medieval double narrator's voice (socially inferior but intellectually, spiritually, and chronologically superior) addresses a patron in the vocative in order to push that patron in the direction of his or her own best interests. The basic illocutionary situation involves a pseudo-dialogue, a *je/vous* configuration in which the *je* speaks and the silent *vous* is expected to react. In the prologue, therefore, the *je* of La Sale–author is repeatedly inscribed exhorting both Mme. and M. de Fresne to turn away from their potentially self-destructive grief (e.g., ll. 17–29, 135–49). In addition, this authorial *je* asserts both its existential and its verbal authority in the prologue's final lines. Existentially, we have the authoritative status of the authorial *je* as witness to the past miracles of Saint Jehan Michiel with regard to fertility and childbirth. The effective intervention of the saint in this context is guaranteed by the author as witness: "ainssy qu'il [i.e., le saint] a fait à maintz aultres, dont pluiseurs enffans en sont estez neez de femme tres anciennes et de gens qui n'en avoient eulz nulz, desquelx j'en ay veu pluiseurs" (ll. 175–78; "as the saint has done for many others, of whom several children have been born from very old women and from people who did not have any, of whom I have seen many").

Verbally, this authorial voice closes the prologue by an authoritative self-affirmation as enunciative source: "et pour vous confforter Madame, à votre consolacion, Madame vous reduis à memoire deux exemples de deux nobles et très prudentes dames" (ll. 179–81; "and in order to comfort you, my lady, in order to console you, I commend to your memory, my lady, two examples of two noble and very wise ladies"). At the same time, he expands his inscribed audience from the initial "vous" of Mme. (and M.) de Fresne to include "tous ceulx et celles qui les liront et orront lire" (ll. 182–83; "all those, men and women, who will read them [i.e., these stories] and hear them read"), thus making explicit his envisioned double readership: the "general" Christian reader of La Sale will both read these two exempla "meta-phorically" in terms of the Christian problematic of over-grieving and despair and read, as it were, Mme. de Fresne reading the exempla from her particular position of the moral-affective-spiritual crisis of a mother grieving over the recent death of her child.[8]

The prologue concludes with a final explicit appropriation of the language of the ensuing exempla as emanating from, and belonging to, La Sale the author figure. His deployment of the standard "false modesty topos," combined with the Christian topos of "rude (linguis-tic) exterior/pure (intentional) interior" finally serves both to mark the language of the *Réconfort* as his and, reciprocally, to present that language as a sign pointing back to him as *auctor*-origin: "[je vous prie] . . . que de mon simple, rude, [compendieux] reciter en veuilliez prendre ma bonne voullenté" (ll. 182–84; "I beg that you accept with good grace my simple, crude, overly long narrative").

Each of the two narrative exempla is filtered through, mediated by, La Sale's automimesis as speaking/writing subject in another impor-tant way as well. Each story is introduced as metonymically linked to La Sale's personal subjective past. Thus the du Chastel story opens as follows: "*au temps de ma jonesse, je oys* à aucuns preux et preudommes che-valliers loer les vertus de ce seigneur . . . [et] especialement de madame sa femme" (ll. 185–87, emphasis mine; "*in the time of my youth, I heard* several noble and worthy knights praise the virtues of this lord . . . and especially of my lady his wife"). The Portuguese story is even more elaborately linked to La Sale as authorial subject: he identifies himself as a direct witness-participant vis-à-vis the narrative events he is about to recount. Among the non-Portuguese soldiers who participated in the capture of Ceuta is "moy, Anthoine de la Salle, escuier de la conté de Provence" (ll. 942–43; "I, Antoine de la Salle, squire of the County of Provence").

We have, then, an authorial subject with existential roots in the dis-tant past, extending up to the privileged present moment of wise old age in which the *actor* has become an *author*. At the same time, this tem-poral dimension involves an important kind of self-authorization. The

existential witness stance of the youth guarantees the sage interpretation of the aged writer. And all of this, of course, is a construct. Thus,
the narrative mimesis of the two exempla is always mediated by the
figure of the remembering, writing self, which is represented as such.[9]

In Antoine de La Sale's *Réconfort de Madame de Fresne*, therefore,
mimesis is always mediated; it is never "direct." The various contexts I
have all too briefly sketched out above all inform—and give meaning
to—the narrative events of the story lines: each exemplum's narrative
and perspectival structure, the functional presence of inscribed literary
models, the "dialogic" relation between the two exempla, the Christian
didactic context of the work as a whole,[10] its generic discourse as *confort*
and as exemplum, the inscribed audience and the politics of patronage,
and, finally, the sustained mimesis of authorial subjectivity.

By way of conclusion I would like to suggest as a kind of final
context a tentative view of the late-medieval aesthetic as a whole. I
do not claim to derive it from La Sale's text, but rather suggest that
this text can better be understood as participating in a broad set of
(often conflicting) "period" preoccupations. Four of these strike me as
fundamentally important.

First, late-medieval French literature is characterized by an extremely heightened degree of literary self-consciousness.[11] This is particularly evident in the period's dominant lyrico-narrative form, the *dit*,
which involves as part of its very generic discourse a visible awareness
of the writing process as such.[12] At the same time the *dit*'s consistent staging of its relationship to preexistent models entails a constitutive part of its status as genre, beginning with Rutebeuf in the
late thirteenth century and continuing in the fourteenth and fifteenth
centuries from Nicole de Margivale and Jean de Condé to Guillaume
de Machaut, Jean Froissart, and Christine de Pizan. In the words of
Jacqueline Cerquiglini, "le dit est un genre qui se définit par son jeu
au second degré" ("the dit is a genre defined by its functioning at
a 'second level' of literary consciousness").[13] And in this regard, the
dit is symptomatic of the larger late medieval phenomenon of genre
hybridization.

Second, the period is deeply preoccupied with the status (and the
representation) of the writing subject.[14] There is virtually always a
simultaneous twofold mimesis in the dominant literary forms, from
lyric to historiography: the mimesis of the self writing, and that of the

story the writing self recounts, its *matière* (what Auerbach would call "reality"). On the one hand, this is found in the florescence of first-person forms: the extremely varied *dits amoureux*; the *Pelerinages* of Guillaume de Digulleville; the new poeticization of the lyric collection by Jean le Seneschel, Christine de Pizan, and Charles d'Orléans; the *Livre du cuer d'amours espris* of René d'Anjou; and the *Testament* of François Villon.[15] On the other hand, there is a new first-person dimension woven into forms which had hitherto been third-person: biography, historiography, and didacticism; from Jean de Joinville's *Vie de Saint Louis*, to Froissart's *Voyage en Béarn*, to Philippe de Mézières's *Songe du vieil pelerin*.[16]

Third, the late French Middle Ages is characterized by a series of self-conscious attempts to renew past forms. This enterprise of *renovatio* necessarily involves the kind of literary self-consciousness we have just mentioned as built into the period as a whole, and it transcends the humanist/nonhumanist opposition: extending as it does from the *Dit de la Panthère* and the *Roman de Perceforest* in the early fourteenth century to Froissart's *Roman de Méliador* in the late fourteenth and Georges Chastellain's *Temple de Bocace* in the mid–fifteenth century.[17] Linked to these discursive *renovationes* is the late-medieval preoccupation with (historical, or historicized) authority: the repeated thematization of authoritative literary lineages which becomes a powerful topos. If the primary model is provided by Jean de Meun's inscription of the Latin elegiac tradition at the approximate midpoint of the conjoined *Rose* text, French and Italian model authors (including Jean de Meun himself) are quickly incorporated into this figure in works such as Christine de Pizan's *Epistre au dieu d'amour*, Martin le Franc's *Champion des dames*, and René d'Anjou's *Livre du cuer d'amour espris*. This literary process also quite literally builds on itself: Eustache Deschamps names Machaut; Christine names Deschamps (as well as Jean de Meun, Boccaccio, and Dante); Martin names Christine; René combines (in 1457) Ovid, Machaut, Boccaccio, Jean de Meun, Petrarch, and Alain Chartier. What we have is the mimesis of the "French" literary self in literary history, using its awareness of that history for the purposes of self-authorization in a context that at once incorporates Italian literary innovations and does *not* point towards the retro-construction we now call the "Renaissance."[18]

The fourth and last period feature of the late French Middle Ages

I want to mention involves the staging of discursive conflict, of dialogism, within individual works, in a way which simultaneously interro-
gates the concept of the closed, self-contained work and experiments
with new ways of effecting closure, of defining the new discursive as
well as material status of the BOOK. The two exemples I cite in this connection are Christine de Pizan's *Cent ballades d'amant et de dame*, in which
courtly and anticourtly discourses and ideologies exist simultaneously
in violent opposition, and, most especially, Antoine de La Sale's *Petit
Jehan de Saintré*, bizarrely dismissed by Auerbach in chapter 10 of *Mimesis*
as an "eloquent though unintentional testimony to the ostentatious and
parasitic senselessness of knightly feats of arms at this epoch" (p. 244).
The fundamental organizing principle of the *Saintré* is the unresolved
(and unresolvable) conflict between the discursive world of courtly romance (in the first two-thirds of the text) and that of the sublimated
fabliau, a kind of celebratory, carnivalized mimesis of sensual appetite
(in the final third). It is as if—to speak anachronistically—Chrétien
de Troyes were pitted against Rabelais, or Guillaume de Lorris were
pitted against Jean de Meun's Genius, within a single work. But these
anachronistic comparisons necessarily oversimplify: the *Saintré* also in-
terrogates courtly-idealizing languages and values as well as sensual-
fabliau ones. At the same time, it exploits these conflicts in the interest
of a coherent but dynamic literary experiment. In all these senses, the
Saintré is an extraordinarily *representative* late-medieval text, antedating
by a single year (1456 vs. 1457) the *Réconfort de Madame de Fresne*. One can
well understand the desire of the young Julia Kristéva to consider the
Saintré—again anachronistically of course, but also with a certain deep-
structure sureness of touch—as "le premier roman moderne" (in her
thesis, published as *Le Texte du roman: Approche sémiologique d'une structure
discursive transformationelle*, 1970).[19]
    What emerges from my tentative sketch is a two-hundred-plus year
period of extraordinary literary vitality: a period of consistent and far-
reaching experimentation with literary forms and with the very notions
of literary discourse and of author. Self-conscious inscriptions both of
authorial subjectivity and of the tension-laden sociopolitical (patronage) dimension of literary production repeatedly characterize the dominant mimetic discourses of the late French Middle Ages in ways that
preclude any treatment of the period as a whole in Auerbachian terms
of "direct" versus "indirect" mimesis of an extralinguistic "reality."
At the same time, the impending "developments" of an approaching

and soon-to-be-dominant "Renaissance" are seen to be quite literally irrelevant to a reading of the late Middle Ages on its own terms.

In identifying these "period" characteristics—and even in speaking of a "late French Middle Ages"—I am, of course, assuming a certain self-evident coherence in terms of literary-historical corpus: for my present purposes, let's say the fourteenth and fifteenth centuries; or, better perhaps, from the *Roman de la Rose* of Jean de Meun to the *Grand Testament* of François Villon. On the other hand, a case could be made for a period extending from Machaut and Froissart in the late fourteenth century to Charles d'Orléans and Philippe Commynes in the late fifteenth. Yet another relevant factor would involve the degree to which Franco-Italian literary relations are seen to loom as primary: the so-called "proto-Humanist Parisian intellectual circle" of the first decade of the fifteenth century can be posited as a "period tendency" against which a "Franco-Burgundian realist current" would struggle until a literary-historical synthesis is reached with Jean le Maire de Belge, Rabelais, and Du Bellay.

Though perhaps most spectacularly in the case of the Franco-Italian scenario (which is also, in part, the scenario of Auerbach as an archetypal German *romanist*), each of these period constructs is accomplished after the fact. That is, not only the period characteristics but the very chronological limitations of a given period result from a backwards-looking perspective, one that would have been—by definition—invisible to those writing in the period itself. Historiographically speaking, it is a cliché to say that politico-military victors necessarily and automatically rewrite the past as if their victories were inevitable, thus giving historiography a teleological orientation. The present is presented as the *goal* towards which the past has been progressing. To avoid a similar kind of limiting perspective in literary history, we need to interrogate the very notion of "period" as a unit within a progressively evolving overall process. Auerbach's impoverished notion of the late Middle Ages is a function (and a result) of the evolutionary period-ideology which privileges the High Middle Ages and the Renaissance. An alternative approach would attempt to define a given literary historical period on its own (often lost) terms; to privilege its view(s) of its past over our views of its "future"; and to view every period as always containing seeds, currents, potentials that have nothing to do with the way things finally turned out.

Part V

Legacies

Carl Landauer

Auerbach's Performance and the American Academy, or How New Haven Stole the Idea of *Mimesis*

Auerbach opens the final chapter of his *Literary Language and Its Public in Late Latin Antiquity and in the Middle Ages* with a short anecdote. "One day," he begins, "at the games—so we are told by Pliny the Younger—Tacitus struck up a conversation on literature with a member of the equestrian order who was sitting next to him. After a time the knight asked: 'Are you from Italy or one of the provinces?' Tacitus answered: 'You know me by my writings.' Whereupon the knight: 'Are you Tacitus or Pliny?'"[1] The retelling of this tale is designed to introduce Auerbach's reader directly into the thematic of Auerbach's chapter, "The Western Public and Its Language," to give a concrete sense of what it must have been like to live in a literary public. In that final chapter of *Literary Language and Its Public*, Auerbach sets that literary public apart from "the great mass of the uneducated" as well as from "those who made literature and learning their profession."[2] And it is clear that with the opening anecdote Auerbach re-creates a moment that may be lost forever.

As I will suggest, this romance of a literary class has a complicated relationship with the core narrative of Auerbach's *Mimesis*, which plays so much on the Judaeo-Christian democratization of literary realism and speaks so often of the narrowness of the class-bound literature of the classical tradition. But the final words of *Mimesis*—Auerbach's wartime hope that his study "will reach its readers" and that the book "may contribute to bringing together again those whose love of our western history has serenely persevered" — suggest a fragmented literary public made invisible by the war but one defined by certain common values and commitments.[3] And it is clear that, with the revival of that literary society, Auerbach's membership is assured.[4]

Auerbach carefully situates the writing of *Mimesis*, telling his reader on the page facing the opening text of the original German edition that it was "written between May 1942 and April 1945." When Auerbach comes to tell the story from Pliny the Younger, he does so from a secure home in New Haven with his reputation assured. Although he registers a certain loss, the despair mixed with hope of the final sentence of *Mimesis* is gone. In his new mood, he writes after telling the Pliny story: "In relating this anecdote, with which he was understandably delighted, Pliny quite unintentionally gives us certain information about the literary public at the height of the empire."[5] But it is also clear to Auerbach's reader that he is telling it with obvious delight himself, and the fantasy of being asked "Are you Auerbach or Pliny?" is hard to miss. That fantasy leads us back to the persona Auerbach molded for himself in *Mimesis* as a virtuoso performer among the various monuments of western culture and, as I have suggested elsewhere, as the outsider turned ultimate insider in the culture of Europe.[6]

It turns out, however, that the virtuoso performer created by the author of *Mimesis* in Istanbul in the 1940's played perfectly to American audiences of the 1950's. For the mid-century attempt to apotheosize culture, in a sense to create an Americanized *Kultur*, *Mimesis* was an exemplary text.[7] But Auerbach was not alone, for a number of émigré scholars with their obvious erudition and their mastery of an enormous range of cultural artifacts became prized possessions of their adopted culture, so that reviews of books by Kantorowicz, Panofsky, Cassirer, Jaeger, Spitzer, Kristeller, and Auerbach seem to blend into one another. It was not just an encyclopedic range that marked these scholars but a sense that they brought a certain "depth" to the study of culture and history from which Americans could learn. It was, then, as a masterful scholar and a translator of European "depth" that the author of *Mimesis* made his name in an American academy looking for exactly such exemplars.

The Complex of Virtuosity

As Auerbach explains in his epilogue, the central narrative of *Mimesis* focuses on the career of the classical doctrine of the levels of style and its interruption first during the Christian Middle Ages and later under the force of nineteenth-century realism. Over against a classical commitment to the separation of a high literary style suited for high subjects from a low style intended for more commonplace subject matter, Auerbach's book privileges moments in the history of western realism in which the common and everyday came to be the subject of truly serious literature. And although there is a good deal of shifting and movement in Auerbach's book, he generally means literature that focuses on the life of the lower strata of European society.

Auerbach repeatedly criticizes literary works for their class narrowness. He tells us, for example, that as "different as Petronius and Tacitus may be in a great many respects, they have the same viewpoint—they look down from above" (*Mimesis*, p. 46). Shakespeare, he explains, never renders the middle and lower classes tragically, for Shakespeare's "conception of the sublime and tragic is altogether aristocratic" (p. 315). And Auerbach tells us that "with the first great realists of the [nineteenth] century, with Stendhal, Balzac, and even with Flaubert, the lower strata of the people, and indeed the people as such in general, hardly appear. And when it appears, it is seen not on its own premises, within its own life, but from above" (p. 497). Thus, these authors—each of whose realism is admired for some aspect by Auerbach—are susceptible to the criticism that their art suffers from a narrowness of class.

If a viewing "from above" earns Auerbach's censure, the aristocratic ideal in various forms over the centuries falls under similar attack. In his chapter on the twelfth-century courtly romance, Auerbach maintains that from "the very beginning, at the height of its cultural florescence, [the feudal] ruling class adopted an ethos and an ideal which concealed its real function. And it proceeded to describe its own life in extrahistorical terms, as an absolute aesthetic configuration without practical purpose" (p. 138). Auerbach makes quite clear that this aestheticizing courtly ideal was closely aligned to the separation of styles. Indeed, he explains, that ideal was one of the sources of "the idea of an elevated style, as it gradually developed during the Renaissance" (ibid.).

As part of the ideology of seventeenth-century French absolutism, the same ideal would reemerge as the "ideal of an all-around and uniformly perfected personality" as well as a cultivation of generalized knowledge (p. 307). For Auerbach, the knowledge envisioned by this ideal led away from concrete reality: "For the more general a man's culture and the less it recognizes a specialized knowledge and a specialized activity, at least as a point of departure for a more general survey of things, the further removed from the sphere of the concrete, the lifelike, and the practical will be the type of all-around perfection striven after" (p. 308).

Auerbach's reading of this cultural configuration is, of course, over-determined by the fact that it lies at the core of the German ideal of self-cultivation, an ideal at once closely associated with the name of Goethe and central to the self-image of the educated German. Against this highly textured background, then, Auerbach voices his complaint against Goethe's bourgeois appropriation of the aristocratic ideal. I have elsewhere interpreted this reproach as part of an effort by Auerbach to separate himself from German culture during his exile in Istanbul and to establish himself as a European.[8] But his brief against Goethe also gives particular force to his broader indictment against the aristocratic ideal.

At the same time, however, Auerbach's very indictment of Goethe —which stands out all the more because Auerbach devotes so little space to Goethe—provokes questions about the sincerity of his critique of the ideal of self-cultivation.[9] In this context, it is interesting to note that Auerbach seemed personally to have cut a rather aristocratic figure: Yakov Malkiel once described Auerbach as making "the impression of someone born into a family of some distinction."[10] Similarly, it is interesting to note the appearance of the word "aristocratic" in Arthur Evans's review of Auerbach's *Gesammelte Aufsätze zur romanischen Philologie* when he remarked on Auerbach's "aristocratic urbanity."[11] This characterization is not by chance: whether or not Auerbach cultivated his personal image, it is clear that he carefully crafted the author's persona in *Mimesis*. Indeed, when Auerbach comes to speak of Montaigne's embodiment of the uniformly perfected personality, it is hard not to think of the author of *Mimesis*: "There is, to be sure, a certain element of self-satisfaction in all this. Montaigne is pleased with himself; he knows that he is in all respects a free, a richly fitted, a full, a remarkably well-rounded human being, and despite all his self-irony he cannot completely conceal this delight in his own person" (p. 303).

Auerbach's encyclopedic range is, of course, one of the recurring motifs of reviews of *Mimesis*, so that, for example, the poet Delmore Schwartz wrote in his review for the *New York Times* that "the compass and richness of the book can hardly be exaggerated."[12] Apparently, the author of *Mimesis* knows absolutely everything about absolutely everything, and that is exactly the way Auerbach wanted it. The authority Auerbach commands in *Mimesis* is immense as he ranges over what seems to be the whole of western literature with obvious comfort and familiarity. Often, his rhetoric implies that his reader shares his experience and his insights. The very first sentence of the book assumes that "[r]eaders of the Odyssey will remember" exactly what Auerbach remembers, so that *Mimesis* begins with an implicit challenge, with an "of course" that may not be so certain for Auerbach's reader. Repeatedly, Auerbach voices his assumption of collective experience with his reader. During his discussion of Shakespeare, he asserts that "[n]o reader or spectator can fail to sense this" (p. 324). Similarly, before quoting a long passage of Racine's *Esther*, he states that "what Racine made of the scene where Esther appears unsummoned before the King is remembered by every reader."[13]

At one point, Auerbach begins a sentence: "Should this analysis find any readers but little versed in medieval vernacular literature . . ." (p. 182). But that clause makes essentially the same point that Auerbach's "remembered by every reader" does: he expects that his reader's literary experience matches his. With somewhat less expectation of his reader's literary equipment, Auerbach writes: "I suppose anyone who has read enough of Montaigne to feel at home in the essays must have had the same experience as I. I had been reading him for some time, and when I had finally acquired a certain familiarity with his manner, I thought I could hear him speak and see his gestures" (p. 290). Obviously, the author of *Mimesis* has thoroughly internalized his subject.

In his chapter devoted to Virginia Woolf, James Joyce, and Marcel Proust, Auerbach describes the modernist conviction that "in any random fragment plucked from the course of a life at any time the totality of its fate is contained and can be portrayed" (p. 547). When Auerbach uses the word "random" (*beliebig*) in this context it is a word that has already appeared in many places in his book.[14] It is, thus, not surprising that Auerbach moves from his discussion of the modernists' use of the random moment to an explanation that "certain modern philologists" proceed with the conviction that the random literary fragment is a particularly fruitful starting point for literary study, and Auerbach quickly includes himself in their number (p. 548). He explains, "I am convinced that these basic motifs in the history of the representation of reality—provided I have seen them correctly—must be demonstrable in any random realistic text" (p. 548).

As he describes the technique of *Mimesis*, Auerbach makes clear that a "systematic and chronological" treatment would have been impossible: "I could never have written anything in the nature of a history of European realism; the material would have swamped me" (ibid.). In part, Auerbach makes a virtue out of necessity, his refuge in Istanbul, "where the libraries are not well equipped for European studies" (p. 557). Auerbach, in fact, ventures that "it is quite possible that the book owes its existence to just this lack of a rich and specialized library" (ibid.). So situating the writing of *Mimesis* as he does at the end of the book serves to underline the fact that the immense work that the reader has just completed did not require a specialized library, just as it did not require the advantages of the "international communications" impeded by the war. Rather, the book derives from modest resources—basically, Auerbach himself.

Auerbach is known for launching each of his chapters from a specific passage cited at length at the start of his discussion and then moving from the passage to his chosen themes. In the epilogue to *Mimesis*, he explains that "the great majority of the texts were chosen at random, on the basis of accidental acquaintance and personal preference" (p. 556). With this definition of "random" in mind, it is clear that the textual passages were not truly random, for they are passages of particular interest to Auerbach. And yet, the range of those passages is so great and Auerbach's familiarity so powerful that what constitutes Auerbach's "accidental acquaintance" (*zufällige Begegnung*) must be truly staggering. And those places where he admits limitation to his knowledge or his capacity seem only to emphasize his range. Thus, Auerbach's comment that an analysis of Russian literature would be "impossible when one cannot read the works in their original language" serves as a reminder of just how many different linguistic skills Auerbach summoned to write *Mimesis*.

Occasionally, Auerbach will note that a particular author's prose is especially difficult, as when he comments that were Ammianus's Latin "not so hard to understand and so untranslatable, he might well be one

of the most influential authors of antique literature" (p. 56)—a comment which, of course, does not limit Auerbach's "accidental acquaintance" with and "personal preference" for Ammianus's text. When
Auerbach begins a sentence in his discussion of Gregory of Tours with
the clause "even if one is not put off by the irregular orthography and
inflections" (p. 81), it is inconceivable that Auerbach himself could be
so easily "put off."

Far from presenting any difficulty, western literature is a realm of
play for Auerbach. Indeed, *Mimesis* is full of little parlor games in
which Auerbach opens books at random and, of course, chances upon
passages that work perfectly to prove his points. For example, directly
after citing two quotations from books by Eduard Norden and Michael
Rostovtzeff, he writes: "As I open Rostovtzeff's work to check the quotation above, my eyes fall on this sentence . . ." (p. 39). Similarly, it
just so happens that Auerbach can write: "In the introduction to an
edition of Shakespeare which I have before me . . . I find it expressed
in the following terms . . ." (p. 318). And we see Auerbach "turn a few
pages" in *Macbeth* to happen upon lines that conveniently continue his
analysis. We may think something amiss when he chances upon the
"full of sound and fury" soliloquy, but that seems to be how the pages
of books turn for Auerbach. Perhaps, coming upon so famous a passage other than by its chance placement a few pages after his last-cited
quotation would have proved an embarrassment.

The parlor games of *Mimesis* are, in part, an exaggeration of Auerbach's conviction that his critical method should work on any random
realistic text. And they show the author of *Mimesis* to be a virtuoso
performer, capable of dealing with any text or fragment that comes his
way.[15] The games are also just that, games, which tie into the general
playfulness of *Mimesis*, the fact that Auerbach describes his method as
constantly in play—"im Spiel"—with the texts of western literature.[16]
The play of *Mimesis*, along with all of the facility and ease of its author's activity, suggests less the traditional image of scholarly activity
than the exemplar of the aestheticizing aristocratic ideal. In *Literary
Language and Its Public*, Auerbach mourned those periods of European
history that lacked a broad-based literary public. In those fallow times,
scholars were isolated and their work was arid. Thus, for example, the
writing one finds from England under Alfred the Great "is clerical,
erudite, and didactic, and there is no sign of the liberal-mindedness

characteristic of a true literary movement."[17] It quickly becomes clear that the Auerbach of *Literary Language and Its Public* shares Montaigne's preference for general knowledge over that of the specialist. And despite all of the criticism in *Mimesis* leveled at the aristocratic ideal with its impractical aestheticism and its remove from the concrete, the persona Auerbach develops for himself in *Mimesis* is fully within the orbit of that same aestheticizing aristocratic ideal.

In his review of *Mimesis*, René Wellek wrote that the book "must be judged as something of a work of art."[18] Indeed, Auerbach conveyed a sense of his work as art. Such, for example, is the implication of his comparison of his method to that of Virginia Woolf and the other modernists. And Auerbach consciously moved away from scholarly conventions—a move that was not occasioned merely by his taking up residence in Istanbul. Thus, for example, his prose was marked by exclamation points, and his pages were unmarred by footnotes.

In Germany, the unfootnoted volume of literary criticism as well as the notion of literary criticism as art would have been identified with the stream of literary biographies written by the followers of the poet Stefan George. Auerbach would hardly have welcomed such a comparison. His *Mimesis* was far from the "Dichter und Helden" myth-making of the Georgekreis critics as one finds, for example, in Ernst Bertram's fashioning of a modern myth in his *Nietzsche*. Yet, despite the fact that the core argument of *Mimesis*—with its emphasis on the everyday reality of the lower social strata of European society—would have been alien to the likes of Friedrich Gundolf, Ernst Bertram, and Max Kommerell, in his aestheticizing nobility the author of *Mimesis* bears some resemblance to the literary critics of the Georgekreis.

In the preface to his book on the medieval Hohenstaufen emperor Frederick II, Georgekreis member Ernst Kantorowicz cited a wreath placed on the sarcophagus of Frederick II during the celebration of the 700th anniversary of the University of Naples reading: "To Its Emperors and Heroes/The Secret Germany."[19] Kantorowicz espoused an overwhelmingly cosmopolitan nationalism, creating an exotic, intellectual Frederick the Second who was half Arab in spirit as an emblem of his Germany. His "Secret Germany" was consequently cosmopolitan and intellectual if still waiting for its emperors and heroes. There is something of the same bittersweet longing in the final sentences of *Mimesis*: "Nothing now remains but to find him—to find the reader, that is. I hope that my study will reach its readers — both my friends of former years, if they are still alive, as well as all the others for whom it was intended. And it may contribute to bringing together again those whose love for our western history has serenely persevered" (p. 557). One might say that *Mimesis* is addressed to Auerbach's "Secret Readership," a scattered literary public in a European cultural landscape ravaged by the Second World War. The displays of mastery in *Mimesis*, then, are meant for this particular audience. Ironically, this literary gentility provides the backdrop for Auerbach's democratic thematics, creating a strange complex of democracy and elitism.

The Virtue of Complexity

On a visit to the United States, the German romance philologist Ernst Robert Curtius — a scholar whose name is often mentioned in the same breath with Auerbach's — was heard to complain that "one hardly hears anything but *Mimesis*."[20] The obvious exaggerations of rivalry aside, it is clear that *Mimesis* quickly assumed the position of an American classic. One must, then, ask why a book on western literary realism that totally overlooks the contribution of American authors, a book that ignores Whitman and Melville, James and Wharton, and mentions only Pearl Buck in the context of the cultural leveling process, a book that is so obviously addressed to Auerbach's secret European readership should attain such stature in the United States.

The answer must be found in the resonance Auerbach's book produced for those working in the humanities in mid-century America. Even Auerbach's method of playing with the texts of the western literary tradition seemed to be in sync with the trends of the American academy. In describing how a "Great Texts of Literature" course should be taught, the "Redbook," the influential Harvard faculty report on general education produced over the same period that Auerbach was writing *Mimesis*, asserted: "Freedom for the instructor is essential. He only teaches, in this field, by letting his students watch the play of a mind with a mind that their minds may play in turn."[21] What better text to use to show that sort of play at work than *Mimesis*?

Indeed, the development of the personality that was a concomitant part of the aristocratic ideal embodied by Auerbach, as well as the critique of specialization, were touchstones of the various general

education and great-books courses established in American colleges
and universities. As Daniel Bell explained, the reaction of the liberal-
arts college to specialization was to strike out against it: "The rallying
cry, in this respect, was *humanitas*."[22] That was also the rallying cry of
Goethe and the other Weimar classicists in their harmonious development of the individual. Ironically, the specialization of the American
university had been based on the German model of the university, and
now in its reaction to that specialization, the American university was
approaching another German tradition. The Germans were, of course,
not the only source for that ideal. It was recognized as one of the
prized legacies of the Renaissance.[23] And Lionel Trilling pointed out
in his book on Matthew Arnold that for Arnold and John Stuart Mill,
"the idea of development of the full personality was precious."[24] But at
that very place in his text, Trilling jumped to a footnote to explain that
both Arnold and Mill had been influenced by Wilhelm von Humboldt.
Whether or not American humanists were conscious of the German
precursors to their newfound ideology, Auerbach's *Mimesis* seemed to
share the spirit of their enterprise completely.

More broadly, Auerbach's *Mimesis* seemed responsive to a general
attempt in the American humanities to apotheosize culture. This effort
weaves together very different and often quite antagonistic parties in
the American humanities from the great-books crowd at the University of Chicago, with its Aristotelian bent, and the followers of the
New Humanists and T. S. Eliot, through the New Critics, to Clement
Greenberg and the high modernists who wrote for the *Partisan Review*.
There were many significant divides, whether political or cultural-
political, among the various groups engaged in this effort. In our
historical discussions of the humanities, for example, there has been
a fair amount of attention given to the seemingly never-ending conflict between formalists and contextualists, such as described by Gerald
Graff in his *Professing Literature*.[25] Usually, the formalists are depicted as
having an uncompromising art-for-art's-sake enthusiasm, which would
make them the obvious apotheosizers of culture, since, as in the case
of the New Critics, they would be seen as being preoccupied with the
poem, the work of art itself abstracted from reality. René Wellek—no
matter how self-serving his discussion may seem—is correct when he
argues in the sixth volume of his history of modern criticism that such
a view is a caricature of New Criticism.[26] Similarly, those at the contex-

tualist end of the spectrum were hardly tone-deaf to the artistic aspect of art.

The work of German scholars like Erich Auerbach tended to carry the stamp of *Geistesgeschichte*, and perhaps the *geistesgeschichtlich* character of their work seemed to offer a historical embedding of texts to contextualists and a formal intensity to formalists. Certainly, Auerbach focused much of his energy on historical structure while providing those gemlike *explications de texte*, focusing as he did on rhetorical detail. More important, however, than the twin appeal of Auerbach's method was the sheer magnitude of his mastery seemingly over the whole range of western literature. In the context of a mid-century effort to apotheosize culture, to produce an Americanized version of *Kultur*, what better symbol of culture could there be than such a consummate *Kulturträger* as Erich Auerbach? Auerbach was, of course, not alone: a number of German émigré scholars gained eminence in the American humanities. The very erudition and methodological sophistication of Leo Spitzer, Ernst Kantorowicz, Erwin Panofsky, Walter Friedlaender, Ernst Cassirer, and Leo Strauss made them exemplary figures for the American academy.

This did not mean that the WASP departments of Ivy League schools automatically opened their doors to the influx of German Jewish refugees—indeed, the resistance of the Ivy League to the refugee scholar is a significant story in its own right.[27] Nevertheless, by the 1960's, the German refugee scholar became the subject of a mythology that climaxed with the publication of Donald Fleming and Bernard Bailyn's *The Intellectual Migration* in 1969.[28] In part, the mythology resulted from the fact that the refugee scholars were the teachers of so many American academics trained in the 1940's and 1950's. But the mythology was ultimately driven by the place the German refugee scholar assumed in the American mythology of culture.

In a sense, the German scholar was the perfect tutor to the American academic. The mythology of the American innocent being tutored by the European has a long history, much of it chronicled by R. W. B. Lewis in *The American Adam*.[29] In the career of the American cultural inferiority complex, however, the middle of the century witnessed an emergence of American culture and literature as a serious subject of study in its own right. In that development, F. O. Matthiessen's *American Renaissance* was the great text, urging the complexity and profundity of Emerson, Thoreau, Hawthorne, Melville, and Whitman.[30] But even the American Renaissance was in Matthiessen's reading a *renaissance*, drawing much of its insight from the seventeenth-century metaphysical poets, especially Donne and Browne, as well as from Shakespeare. Consequently, in addition to the significant overlays represented by the importance of the German model for the American research university and the prominence of German academics in international associations, the mythology that surrounded the German professor on the American campus fed into one of the central myths of American culture.

A number of the German refugee scholars quickly identified their position in the mythology of the American academy and made the most of it. In this mode, Panofsky advised American humanists—in an essay published alongside contributions by Franz Neumann, Henri Peyre, Wolfgang Koehler, and Paul Tillich in *The Cultural Migration*— that "humanists cannot be 'trained'; they must be allowed to mature or, if I may use so homely a simile, to marinate. It is not the reading matter assigned for Course 301 but a line of Erasmus of Rotterdam, or Spenser, or Dante, or some obscure mythographer of the fourteenth century, which will 'light our candle'; and it is mostly where we have no business to seek that we shall find." [31] The explicit message of this passage was a critique of the structure of learning in the United States, but implicitly, Panofsky's American readers were set to wonder how they could replicate the marinating of the young Erwin Panofsky. In fact, only two pages later Panofsky relates: "The man who taught me Latin was a friend of Theodor Mommsen and one of the most respected Cicero specialists. The man who taught me Greek was the editor of the *Berliner Philologische Wochenschrift*, and I shall never forget the impression which this lovable pedant made on us boys of fifteen when he apologized for having overlooked the misplacement of a comma in a Plato passage." [32]

With this sort of cultivation always visible in the background, a number of German émigré scholars showed a particular playfulness with popular culture. Panofsky wrote an essay on the Rolls Royce grill, and Spitzer devoted an article to an analysis of Sunkist orange advertisements.[33] But if those essays appeared as self-indulgent romps, they simply emphasized the Mandarinism and the special authority of their authors. The playfulness of such subjects served to underline the general comfort that was assumed to be part of the cultural gentility of the German professor.

If Erich Auerbach's *Mimesis* entered so well into the mythology of cultural gentility and the apotheosis of culture in the United States, what happened to his message about the "fourth estate" and the "lower strata of the people"? Auerbach himself undermined what at times seems the guiding passion of the book. Whether or not because of the era-specific *geistesgeschichtlich* relativism of *Mimesis*, Auerbach was not very consistent about keeping social and political realism in the forefront: what, for example, does the experiential realism of Mrs. Ramsay's sewing the brown stocking in *To the Lighthouse* have to do with the class concerns Auerbach expresses elsewhere in *Mimesis*? More important perhaps is the fact that, ultimately, Auerbach's book is about how certain subjects, including the everyday life of the lower classes, were treated by serious literature. As much as the book catalogues the failures of so many forms of western realism to come to grips with certain aspects of social life, *Mimesis* nevertheless reads as a celebration of literature. Indeed, much of the passion of *Mimesis* concerns the fate of the western heritage. If Arthur Evans discovered that "beneath the surface of scholarly detachment and aristocratic urbanity there is a pathos," it was "an urgency of involvement born of a passionate commitment to the variety of attitudes and the shared values and assumptions of Western civilization." [34]

Still, the mixture of a social and political thematic within the context of an immense, aesthetically reverent, scholarly work suggests comparison with F. O. Matthiessen's *American Renaissance*, which appeared in 1941. As Wellek describes it, *American Renaissance*, "undoubtedly a great achievement in its scope and penetration, bursts at its seams; the combination of social pathos, close reading, and critical theories about tragedy, allegory, and symbolism set in the tradition of Coleridgean aesthetics or organic form holds together with difficulty." [35] One might expect "social pathos" from Matthiessen the fellow traveler. But the politics of *American Renaissance* is quite muted. Jonathan Arac has commented on the "absence of class analysis" in the book. [36] Although that is not entirely true — Matthiessen observes, for example, that "Thoreau came about as close to the status of proletarian writer as was possible in his simple environment" [37] — the overall politics of *American Renaissance* is a broad affirmation of democratic culture: "The one common denominator of my five writers, uniting even Hawthorne and Melville, was their devotion to the possibilities of democracy" (*American Renaissance*, p. ix). In essence, the social sensibility of *American Renaissance* was not very far from that of *Mimesis*. At the same time, Matthiessen also made clear his aesthetic impulse, using Vernon Parrington—who did not want "to evaluate reputations or weigh literary methods"—as a foil (quoted ibid.).

More significantly, Matthiessen applauded the realistic representation of concrete reality. His Emerson even turns to Dante on the point: "I think, if I were professor of Rhetoric—teacher of the art of writing well to young men—I should use Dante for my textbook. . . . Dante knew how to throw the weight of his body into each act, and is, like Byron, Burke, and Carlyle, the Rhetorician" (quoted p. 33). For Matthiessen's Emerson, Dante demonstrated that your daily surroundings "are the very best basis of poetry, and the material which you must work up" (quoted ibid.). Thus, a Dante not so far from Auerbach's made his way into *American Renaissance*.

A similar discussion of Thoreau leads Matthiessen back to the seventeenth-century metaphysical poets and their wedding of concrete reality and idea. "This power," he writes, "to unite thought with sense impression, the immediate feeling with the reflection upon it, is what Eliot has discerned to be the distinguishing attribute of the English metaphysical poets" (p. 98). Largely the legacy of T. S. Eliot, the metaphysical poets loom large over the literary criticism of mid-century America. They are of immense importance to the New Critics. The metaphysical poets as precursors of the modernists are the heroes of Cleanth Brooks's *Modern Poetry and the Tradition*: for him, the modernist draws directly from the metaphysical poets' use of metaphor, their practice of bringing together unlikely combinations.[38] In a chapter entitled "Wit and High Seriousness," Brooks explained that the metaphysical poets indulged in witty comparisons that would not fit what Matthew Arnold would later call the "high seriousness." The interesting point is that Arnold "believed in a poetic subject matter," and the metaphysical poets along with the modernists did not. Moreover, wit and sincerity were not polar opposites.[39] In his book on Matthew Arnold, Lionel Trilling similarly criticized Arnold's poetic prejudices: he found it troubling that Arnold would confuse seriousness with solemnity and consequently exclude important poets from his personal pantheon.[40]

The idea that only certain subjects were appropriate for serious poetic effort was, of course, the exact line Auerbach was attacking in *Mimesis*, even if the particular targets of the American critics—Arnold and Wordsworth—did not appear in his book. And if the metaphysical poets appear in *Mimesis* only in the epigraph taken from Andrew Marvell—"Had we but world enough and time . . ."—Auerbach shared with Brooks, Trilling, and Matthiessen the reference to modernism.

As mentioned above, Auerbach identified his critical method with that of the high modernists, seeing in his work a mirroring of their focus on the random particular. Auerbach understood that the focus on the random was connected to a privileging of multiplicity. "These are," he wrote, "the forms of order and interpretation which the modern writers here under discussion attempt to grasp in the random moment—not one order and one interpretation, but many, which may either be those of different persons or of the same person at different times; so that overlapping, complementing, and contradiction yield something that we might call a synthesized cosmic view or at least a challenge to the reader's will to interpretive synthesis" (*Mimesis*, p. 549). Basically, Auerbach saw reality as complexity, which is why he was so interested in a treatment of everyday reality that was tragic, or perhaps more accurately, "problematic." One can understand his attraction for an American academy that had begun to fetishize complexity.

Auerbach's commitment to multiplicity was closely tied to his perspectivism. Much has been made of Auerbach's perspectivism or relativism. Auerbach, in fact, fully understood his own work as historically contingent. Thus, for example, he concluded his "Epilegomena zu *Mimesis*," appearing in 1953, with an assertion that *Mimesis* was without doubt "a book that a particular man in a particular place wrote in the early 1940's."[41] A radical perspectivism would probably have been too much for Auerbach's American audience—for all of the American academics I have cited would have wanted finally to be led back to a moral core. Ultimately, Auerbach's *Mimesis* suggests just such a moral center of gravity. And if Wolfgang Fleischmann depicts Auerbach as "seeming effortlessly to make the chaos whole,"[42] Auerbach makes the impression that he does finally have a claim on truth. In this context, then, one may return to Auerbach's description of the Elohist's relation to truth: "What he produced, then, was not primarily oriented toward 'realism' (if he succeeded in being realistic, it was merely a means, not an end); it was oriented toward truth" (*Mimesis*, p. 14). Indeed, *Mimesis* was similarly oriented toward truth, and Wellek caught this in the final words of his obituary for Auerbach in *Comparative Literature*, asserting that Auerbach "*has* achieved insights which are 'true' unhistorically and that, in *Mimesis* he has written a book which is not only a great work of scholarship and a symptomatic pronouncement of our age, but a work of truth, insight, and art which cannot be superseded or made obsolete by mere historical change."[43] Perhaps others would not have so contradicted Auerbach's explicit words, but some of the success of Auerbach's *Mimesis* resides in its suggesting chaos and multiplicity and promising the reader, through the person of the author, a realm of calm.

Herbert Lindenberger

On the Reception of *Mimesis*

I

Some thirty years ago, before the study of reception had come into vogue, my students in a seminar on modern criticism expressed curiosity about how the books they were reading were first received. Had these books been recognized by their reviewers as the major works we now knew them to be? Did they seem significant for the same reasons that we were now assigning significance to them? Were they, as we suspected, neglected or misunderstood? We tracked the reviews of two books: Auerbach's *Mimesis* and Northrop Frye's *Anatomy of Criticism*. For Auerbach I sought out the reviews of the original German-language edition of 1946 as well as of the English translation, which appeared seven years later—less than a decade before the time of our class exercise.[1]

Somehow we expected that a book we so much admired would have to fight its way to fame after first being ignored or treated in a demeaning way. Imagine our surprise to find that this work which we were admiring in class was by no means a neglected masterpiece—that, with very few exceptions, its uniqueness and its distinction were acknowledged from the start. The theologian Nathan Scott, for example, spoke of its "truly monumental greatness."[2] Or, to cite the Romance scholar Theophil Spoerri, "In the area of literature one has never encountered so perfect a combination of synchronic and diachronic observation."[3] Here, most reviewers agreed, was a large-minded vision of the past that encompassed the whole of western culture with a boldness that few scholars had ever dared to display. Methodologically, as a number of reviewers pointed out, Auerbach had officiated over a most happy match between *explication de texte* and *Geistesgeschichte*. Perhaps the only serious jarring note appeared in an article—not a review—by Ernst Robert Curtius, one of the very few among Auerbach's contemporaries who could be called his peer (in fact, some of the early reviews had made connections between Auerbach's book and Curtius's *Europäische Literatur und lateinisches Mittelalter*, a work written during virtually the same years as *Mimesis*). Curtius, whose article did not appear until six years after the publication of *Mimesis*, took issue with a number of Auerbach's central assertions, most notably his interpretation of the separation of styles,[4] and Auerbach, in a vigorously argued defense of his book in 1953, not only clarified his intention on this issue but used the opportunity to declare his fealty to historical perspectivism, and particularly to that long-standing tradition within German historical thought that stemmed from Hegel and his romantic predecessors.[5]

Yet Auerbach's stress on his perspectivism was also a response to a form of criticism present within many of the reviews. Even the most laudatory reviews, especially those by German scholars, more often than not quibbled about the texts and authors that Auerbach chose to highlight in his study. Since it was Auerbach's aim to portray those privileged moments in western literature when everyday reality was treated in a serious or a tragic manner, his reviewers took a special pride in pointing out other moments which, they claimed, could have fit his model at least as well as, if not better than, those that made it into his book. Why, as an eminent classical scholar, Ludwig Edelstein, asked, did Auerbach give short shrift to Greek realism and leave out such figures as the watchman in the *Agamemnon*, the nurse in *The Libation Bearers*, or the various characters of Menander?[6] Another classical scholar, Otto Regenbogen, attempted to absorb some of the ancient historians, above all Herodotus and Thucydides,[7] within Auerbach's definition of realism. A Latinist, Harry E. Wedeck, suggested the appropriateness that Tertullian's "diatribes against sumptuary excesses and women" might have had to Auerbach's thesis.[8] Several Romance scholars, Helmut Hatzfeld, Gerhard Hess, and Ulrich Leo, argued for the special relevance of Spanish texts—for example the *Celestina*, the picaresque novels, and *Don Quijote*—none of which served as examples in the original edition of *Mimesis*.[9] (Auerbach may well have been responding to this complaint when, a few years after the publication of

Mimesis, he added a chapter on the *Quijote* for a Spanish translation of his book.)[10] The American critic Robert Gorham Davis complained that Auerbach "does almost nothing with English fiction before 1900," nor does he so much as "mention American literature."[11] The German-ist Norbert Fuerst complained of Auerbach's disapproving remarks on Goethe, Schiller, and German literature in general.[12] The Chaucerian Charles Muscatine, though mentioning no specific texts that the au-thor might have included, reminds Auerbach that "there are half a dozen medieval realisms," of which figural realism, the principal one discussed in the book, is only one.[13]

As one looks over the complaints about what Auerbach left out, one notes a specific institutional bias that motivates most of them: since the works that Auerbach finds at once "serious" and "realistic" form a special and privileged canon in this book, the reviewers obvi-ously wish to see texts from their own specialized fields represented in this new canon. As one reviewer, Donald Heiney, put it baldly, "The perfectionist will do well to skip those chapters concerned with his field of specialization; he will enjoy the rest."[14] This chorus of pro-tests, for those of us caught up in the canon debates during recent years in our own universities, seems an eerie prediction: the complaints that earlier emanated from interest groups defending their entrenched fields have now come from groups with specific ethnic, gender, and sexual-orientation programs that seek their places in the academic sun. As I shall show later in this paper, Auerbach's book throughout its near half-century of life has served definable institutional needs and, by the same token, has been ignored when it was not perceived to meet such needs.

To return to the early complaints made about *Mimesis*, the many au-thors whom various reviewers nominated for inclusion in Auerbach's canon run the gamut of western literature—from Hesiod and Xeno-phon at one end to Grimmelshausen, Thackeray, and Pirandello at the other. As one hears these names, one can formulate the replies that Auerbach would have made, indeed sometimes did make.[15] Thackeray, he would have protested, presented everyday reality within a comic per-spective distinctly different from the more earnest mode of his French realist contemporaries. The occasional appearance of simple folk in Greek tragedy was scarcely enough to give them any prominence—in fact, these figures are subsumed within a larger structure that stresses the fate of the heroic figures. But behind the reviewers' suggestions about what the author should have included there lurks a suspicion not simply that he left something out, but, even more important, that a certain arbitrariness guided Auerbach's method. Can one, after all, acknowledge the legitimacy of a historical narrative whose primary examples have been chosen arbitrarily? What if some other examples, especially from a different period or culture, could have served Auerbach's argument just as well, perhaps even better? Might these counterexamples not render his whole argument unconvincing? One answer, of course, is that this book was being judged by the notions that prevailed at the time as to what constituted literary scholarship. Thus, a number of reviewers note, if only in passing, that *Mimesis* is shaped much like a literary work.

Certainly Auerbach was the first to admit an arbitrariness in the examples he chose—not only in the authors and in the texts, but even in the brief passages picked for close analysis. It is significant that he discussed his method within the last chapter of *Mimesis*, directly after the analysis of passages on the brown stocking and the madeleine in Virginia Woolf and Proust. In fact, Auerbach openly identifies his own habit of choosing what he calls random realistic texts with the modernist novelist's exploitation of random everyday events. Moreover, Auerbach uses the same word, "random" (*beliebig*), to characterize the way that the modern novelists chose seemingly inconsequential events to organize their books as well as the way that he himself chose the texts around which his own book was organized.[16] Auerbach thus points to a key characteristic of literary modernism, a category to which, incidentally, he is conscious that *Mimesis* itself belongs. I refer to that tendency of modernist writing to give particular prominence to data and events that first strike one as odd, or insignificant, or randomly chosen—while managing, by means of the verbal structures that the writer improvises, to convince the reader that these strange materials are fraught with significance, indeed that they constitute the most appropriate possible embodiment for what the author has been trying to articulate. In the hands of a master craftsman—whether he calls his vocation that of novelist or of literary critic—what may seem arbitrary comes to assume the guise of inevitability.

Just as early readers of modernist literature often complained that they were expected to attach undue significance to inconsequential

and randomly selected objects and events, so it seems perfectly under-
standable that Auerbach's early reviewers tempered their admiration
for his achievement with complaints about the randomness of his examples. Like his novelist contemporaries, Auerbach recognized that
the nineteenth-century conception of history, whether in the form of
public history or private novelistic history, assumed that the author
retained a firm confidence in the naturalness of his narrative choices
and narrative connections. Yet this confidence was no longer possible
to a twentieth-century mind. Just as Virginia Woolf could not have
concocted a narrative in the mode of *Vanity Fair* or *Middlemarch*, so
Auerbach could not, as he himself makes clear, have written a history
of realism in the manner of nineteenth-century literary historians.

Yet with our present hindsight on *Mimesis*, we have come to accept
the particular choices and placement of its materials as appropriate and
natural—just as we have come to see a naturalness in the temporal dis-
placements and stylistic eccentricities of *To the Lighthouse* and *Ulysses*.
Partly this is due to the aura that automatically surrounds those works
we now accept as classics. But in Auerbach's case one can point to
another factor—namely, his perspectivism. In his defense of 1953 that I
referred to earlier, Auerbach not only asserted his tie to the perspectiv-
istic view of history within German historical thought but also stressed
the unique perspective from which he viewed the whole of western culture—that of a German Romance scholar who happened to be writing
in Istanbul during World War II: "*Mimesis* is quite consciously a book
written by a particular person in a particular place during the early
1940's."[17] By means of this perspective, at once personal and intellectual, with which he saw the past, he was able to create a narrative that
allowed the diverse texts he had chosen to fall temporally into place
with what seems uncommon precision. We are all now familiar with
Auerbach's guiding narrative—the struggle between historicity and a
static, moralistically colored, eternal view of things; the changing for-
tunes between Judeo-Christian egalitarianism and classical class stratification; the ultimate victory of tragically perceived everyday reality in
the great French realists of the nineteenth century. In this tightly controlled historical drama that structures Auerbach's *Mimesis*, the arbitrary
triumphantly achieves the status of inevitability.

Indeed, from the point of view of our own so-called postmodern
time, is it possible that Auerbach's narrative is *too* highly determined?

Might we perhaps prefer a random method that does not seek the illusion of the inevitable? At a time when many of us have challenged the boundaries that separate scholarly discourse from what used to be called imaginative writing, it scarcely seems strange to read a scholarly work that, like *Mimesis*, shares some of the methods present in the art about which it is concerned. In fact, as we look back at it half a century after it was begun, Auerbach's book now strikes us as being just as distant from us, and also every bit as classic, as those early-twentieth-century novels that bring his own narrative to a conclusion.

II

Symptomatic of the distance we have come to feel between Auerbach's classic and our own time is the fact that among four recent anthologies of criticism designed for the academic market in the United States and Britain, three omit Auerbach entirely. One of the latter group, entitled *Contemporary Critical Theory*, is mostly devoted to critics of a later generation, but it does include such contemporaries of Auerbach as Ernst Bloch, Walter Benjamin, Mikhail Bakhtin, Martin Heidegger, Roman Jakobson, and Georges Bataille.[18] Another anthology, *The Critical Tradition: Classic Texts and Contemporary Contexts*, does not even include an Auerbach selection among its so-called "classic texts," though it finds spots in this section for such slightly younger critics as Kenneth Burke and Lionel Trilling as well as the considerably younger (though apparently now "classic") Susan Sontag![19] Moreover, the so-called "contemporary contexts" section of this anthology includes other figures of Auerbach's generation, such as I. A. Richards and Jan Mukarovsky. David Lodge, though he had included the first chapter of *Mimesis* in his 1972 anthology, *20th Century Literary Criticism*, found no room for Auerbach in the collection entitled *Modern Criticism and Theory*, which he edited sixteen years later;[20] through his other career as chronicler of academic foibles, Lodge doubtless knew what would sell in the classroom by the late 1980's. It is significant that the temporally wide-ranging *Literary Criticism and Theory: The Greeks to the Present*, the only one of these four recent anthologies that includes any part of *Mimesis*, prefaces its selection with the seemingly up-to-date (if also somewhat confused) statement "Narrative is the performance of a culture of a moment in history, history being a rhetorical construct."[21]

The most obvious explanation for Auerbach's near-omission from what counts as the critical canon among publishing houses is that his "method" does not lend itself to easy classification. Thus, whereas Bloch, Benjamin, and Bakhtin are placed in the first of these anthologies in the section called "Marxism" (however uncomfortably the last two of these figures may fit this rubric), and Heidegger and Bataille under "Deconstruction," Auerbach would not seem to lend himself to easy categorizations—unless an anthologist should choose to install such categories as "stylistics" or "Geistesgeschichte," neither of which has ever really acclimated itself to the British or American critical scene. On the basis of these omissions, one suspects that Auerbach does not serve the perceived institutional needs of literary study at the present time. And one also suspects that for any critic of Auerbach's generation to maintain academic currency he or she would need to stand at the head of some particular genealogy, as Lukács does for Marxist and Freud for psychoanalytical criticism in two of these anthologies. It is significant that Trilling, who *did* include the first chapter of *Mimesis* in his 1970 anthology, *Literary Criticism: An Introductory Reader*, said in his introductory remarks: "*Mimesis* remains unique, unclassifiable, without imitation even. It is as though Auerbach had exhausted the subject in the very process of bringing it into existence."[22]

If one looks back at the uses to which *Mimesis* was put during the first generation after its publication, one notes that throughout this time it served quite discernible institutional purposes. Before the English-language translation of the book had even appeared, the Dante chapter was printed in the *Kenyon Review*, one of the key journals associated with the New Criticism, at that time the reigning critical paradigm in North American universities.[23] The chapter formed part of a special Dante issue together with essays by such New Critics as Allen Tate and Francis Fergusson, as well as a statement by T. S. Eliot about the effect of Dante on his own poetry. Although Auerbach's historical approach to Dante is far removed from the distinctly nonhistorical approach of these critics, readers at the time would have felt an affinity between Auerbach's commitment to stylistic analysis and what in those days was called "close reading." Certainly the praise that the American reviewers heaped on *Mimesis* for its attention to individual texts suggests a certain congruence between the interpretive aims of Romance stylistics and the New Criticism. I might add that another Auerbach essay, his close analysis of Pascal's *Pensée* fragment 298 (not included in *Mimesis*), had earlier appeared, in shortened form, in another major New Critical journal, the *Hudson Review*;[24] as with the Dante chapter, whatever close reading one can find in this essay is always subsumed within Auerbach's larger historical perspective.

If Auerbach, to the extent that he practiced stylistic analysis, suited the New Critical program, he also served as a model within another institutional configuration, namely the field of comparative literature, which gradually emerged as a presence within North American universities during the 1950's and 1960's and later in the United Kingdom. Closely associated at Yale with René Wellek, who was the chairman of Comparative Literature at that university as well as one of the early reviewers of the English-language edition of *Mimesis*, Auerbach could exemplify the linguistic and cultural breadth that this new field sought to encourage among its practitioners. If one looks at the various handbooks written during the past generation to introduce students and teachers to the field, one generally finds *Mimesis* listed as a prime model for comparative scholarship.[25] To the extent that comparative literature was long defined primarily as a discipline that broke down the boundaries separating national literary traditions, Auerbach's book, whatever its own rhetorical aims, lent itself readily to pedagogical use among those who called themselves "comparatists."

Yet *Mimesis* served as still another type of pedagogical model during this period. Since it was organized around a series of texts extending chronologically from Homer to Virginia Woolf, it covered much the same material included in the so-called "Western Culture" courses required at the time of freshman students in many American universities. One could argue, in fact, that the anxieties that Auerbach voiced from his Turkish exile about the fate of the western tradition coincided with the anxieties that motivated these courses in the first place.[26] It scarcely seems coincidental that a chapter from *Mimesis* (in this instance the chapter on Homer and the Old Testament) should find itself anthologized in a volume of 1962 entitled *The Proper Study: Essays on Western Classics* designed by two scholars, Questin Anderson and Joseph A. Mazzeo, both actively associated with the required freshman humanities course at Columbia University, which had fathered this type of course soon after World War I and had also inspired various textbooks used throughout the United States during subsequent decades.[27] More-

over, Auerbach's place in the anthology of criticism by Trilling mentioned earlier can also be related to the concerns of Western Culture
courses. Trilling, who was also closely associated with the Columbia
course, introduces his selection of *Mimesis* by praising, among other
things, the book's "precision [in tracing] the evolution of the realities
that have been distilled into words by Western writers from Homer to
the modernists of this century."[28]

Another aspect of Auerbach, one that is only tangentially related
to *Mimesis*, gained attention during the later 1960's and the 1970's with
the emerging interest in the social roots of literature. In certain individual essays, above all "La Cour et la ville," as well as in his ambitious
final volume on the Latin literary public in late antiquity, Auerbach
had provided models for the investigation of readerships, an area that
did not become prominent within literary study until well after his
death. A British anthology of 1973, Elizabeth and Tom Burns's *Sociology
of Literature and Drama*, includes a selection from Auerbach's last book
together with models by such other socially oriented critics as Lukács,
Raymond Williams, and Ian Watt, while a German volume of 1968,
Wege der Literatursoziologie, edited by Hans Norbert Fügen, includes "La
Cour et la ville."[29]

Whatever new relevance Auerbach's investigations of the literary
public may have come to possess, it remains clear that the currency enjoyed by *Mimesis*—above all in North America—at the time (the early
1960's) that my class examined the reviews cannot be recaptured in our
present intellectual milieu.[30] The traditionally special place that *Mimesis*
awards to major literary texts has come to seem questionable at a time
when the boundary separating literary discourse from other discursive forms has lost its authority. Moreover, the many younger scholars
who profess some form of historicism borrow their frameworks for
historical change from Foucault or the Frankfurt school and not from
Auerbach's historicist tradition, itself a quite individual blend of Vico
with German thinkers from Herder to Meinecke.[31] Even Auerbach's
perspectivism, which would seem to assure his contemporaneity for
readers skeptical of critics with pretensions to some timeless objec-
tivity, has been challenged as still another absolute: conspicuously in-
voking the authority of Derrida in the pages of *Diacritics* in 1975, David
Carroll questions Auerbach's claim that the uniqueness of his point
of view "convey[s] to us his presence, exactly who he is."[32] Carroll's

essay reveals Auerbach to be a relatively easy target for a deconstructive exercise, with Auerbach's various oppositions—"between philosophical systems and the real, between class perspective and the real, and between purely literary and the real"—all being exposed for their "philosophical and ideological implications."[33] Paul Bové, writing in the mid-1980's and trying to account for Auerbach's high prestige in the United States during the preceding generation, describes Auerbach's "function" in American intellectual life at mid-century "not as a philological model but as a sign that in an antihistorical, antihumanistic age of relativism, mass-cultural leveling, and the increasing irrelevance of writers and critics, it is not only possible for critics . . . to construct monumental synthetic texts in the face of massive specialization . . . but also, in so doing, to relegitimate culturally a certain image of the responsible and responsive authoritative critical voice."[34] If Auerbach earlier counted as a model for cultural criticism, the authority he could once exercise in that role has now been questioned by still another, less distinctly humanistic form of cultural criticism.

In our present critical climate, in which multiculturalism has emerged within American universities as a rallying point for progressive thought, *Mimesis* must look particularly vulnerable for its exclusive focus upon the European literary tradition. What earlier seemed one of its academic virtues, namely its use as a legitimizing text for the Western Culture courses once deemed central to civilizing the young in America, now becomes a burden that his advocates must explain or excuse. Looking at the final page of *Mimesis*, with its boast that the poor library facilities in Istanbul actually freed the author to rethink the European tradition from which he felt himself cut off, a reader in our own time might well complain with terms such as "elitism" and "ethnocentrism." Indeed, if one notes the linguistic origins of the various texts with which he begins each chapter, it is clear that fully thirteen of the book's twenty chapters start with texts belonging to the field of *Romanistik*, Auerbach's professional homeland. Since ten of these thirteen chapters—half the book!—start with French texts, those on the lookout for cultural biases could surely charge Auerbach not simply with Eurocentrism but with Gallocentrism as well.[35] Auerbach's famous *Ansatzpunkte* are perhaps not as arbitrarily chosen as he led us to believe.

Certainly Auerbach can be credited with foresight in giving pride of place in his chapter on modernism to a text by Virginia Woolf: when he wrote about her soon after her death, she was relatively little read or written about and still far from being the cultural icon that she became during the 1970's with the emergence of feminist criticism. Yet nothing in his lengthy analysis of the stocking passage in *To the Lighthouse* displays what today would be labeled a sensitivity to the gender of the writer or of the character through whose point of view the novel's world is presented. Since the chapter culminates in a comparison of Woolf's modernist techniques with those of Joyce and Proust, a present-day reader might well chide Auerbach for ignoring how an apparently similar group of techniques is employed in significantly different ways according to the author's gender and sexual orientation. Those who feel the need to invoke narrow criteria such as these to judge the contemporary relevance of older critical texts are bound to find fault with, perhaps even to reject, *Mimesis*.

III

The rapidity with which *Mimesis* was granted a kind of classic status—at least to judge by its reviews and by the inclusion of chapters in anthologies during the first two decades after its appearance—may well have helped make the book seem old-fashioned once a new set of priorities and expectations had settled into the critical marketplace. Whatever the intrinsic interest of the book, it could easily be condemned for those very virtues—its traditional humanism, its older form of historicism, its reliance on the close verbal analysis of canonized texts—for which its earlier advocates chose to praise it. And doubtless, as time went by, a reader's attitude toward the book became colored by whatever attitude one held toward these advocates themselves.

How, one might ask, can one best define its usefulness to us today? Since Auerbach, as I mentioned earlier, recognized the affinities of his method to that of the modernist novelists whom he treated in his final chapter, one might simply relegate his book to the category of "high-modernist text"—to be treated with something of the respect we accord the novels that he discussed in this chapter, but also to be kept at a discrete distance from the concerns with which we are at present engaged. As it turns out, the blurring taking place these days of the boundaries between what has traditionally been called literature and what we call criticism has allowed *Mimesis* to be subjected to the sort of treatment formerly accorded works classified as "literature." Thus, W. Wolfgang Holdheim, declaring that Auerbach's "way of writing history (in *Mimesis*, for example) is strikingly aesthetic," has read the first eight chapters of the book as a narrative with closely interweaving themes that come to a climax in the Dante chapter.[36] Timothy Bahti uses Auerbach's figural method of interpretation to read *Mimesis* itself as an "allegory of history" (to cite the title of Bahti's own book), with Auerbach's Dante chapter as the *figura* and the climactic chapter on French realism as its fulfillment.[37] In another quite recent study, Suzanne Gearhart performs a close reading of the section on *Manon Lescaut*, to whose tragic content she finds Auerbach unresponsive because an acknowledgment of this content would "interrupt the dialectic" (to cite the title of her own book) that, for Auerbach, culminates in the triumph of French tragic realism during the succeeding century.[38] Or *Mimesis* can be approached less as literature than as a classic of German historical writing, even philosophy of history, as Klaus Gronau, in a dissertation of 1979, chose to treat it.[39]

But the continuing life of an interpretative or historical work—and *Mimesis* belongs to both these categories—can perhaps be measured less by its readiness to allow the application of new critical methods than by its ability to generate later modes of thought, even of an antithetical sort. Unlike many respected critical works, the book has not easily lent itself to imitation, if only because its scope and its mixture of methods do not easily transfer to other contexts. Over the years since it was published, one can find occasional imitations of sorts: for example, Walter Höllerer's *Zwischen Klassik und Moderne*, written a decade after Auerbach's German edition and which, like its unacknowledged model, begins each section with a quotation that is then subjected to close interpretation, after which the author expands his inquiry to other works by the same writer and to the historical milieu surrounding them.[40] Yet any attempt to set these books next to one another exposes the narrowness of Höllerer's project, which consists of readings of German writers of the mid–nineteenth century, with even the historical "context" already, as it were, predetermined by the formalistic concerns prevalent in both German and Anglo-American criticism of that period.

Indeed, one might say that the synoptic quality of *Mimesis*, that quality which frustrated the attempts of anthologists to fit it into genealogies, has also militated against the book's ability to inspire and generate later scholarship. As David Lodge put it in his introductory note to the selection he anthologized in 1972, "[Auerbach's] ability to respond knowledgeably and sympathetically to so many different cultures and authors is amazing, and it is unlikely that research in the humanities will ever again produce a monument of scholarship so catholic in scope and so unpedantically learned."[41] Doubtless few could come up with titles of later books that might dispute Lodge's judgment.

If Auerbach's writing has experienced a significant afterlife in our own time, it has not done so by means of imitation or emulation but rather in the inspiration it has given to a critic whose work would not seem to share many affinities with *Mimesis*. I refer to Edward Said, whose *Orientalism*, published in 1978, played a decisive role in making American critics conscious of the Eurocentrism that marked their work and that, once they recognized their biases, could also be used to display the limitations of Auerbach's book.[42] Yet Said's own writings, above all his major recent work, *Culture and Imperialism*, reveal themselves to be strongly affected by Auerbach's example, a fact that Said has never failed to acknowledge.[43] For instance, Auerbach's *Ansatzpunkt* is central to Said's concept of what constitutes a text's or a writer's "beginning," the subject of his book entitled *Beginnings*.[44] For his understanding of Auerbach's own concept, Said refers repeatedly to Auerbach's "Philologie der Weltliteratur," an essay that Said cotranslated in 1969 and that itself could be said to create an *Ansatzpunkt* helping to shape his own subsequent work.[45]

Perhaps even more important than the *Ansatzpunkt* as a link between *Mimesis* and Said's writings is the fact that in this essay, published six years after *Mimesis*, Auerbach recognizes the need for literary study to expand its focus beyond the confines of the European tradition. To quote from Said's translation, "We possess literatures ranging over six thousand years, from all parts of the world, in perhaps fifty literary languages. Many cultures known to us today were unknown a hundred years ago; many of the ones already known to us in the past were known only partially."[46] Throughout this essay, essentially a meditation on Goethe's concept of *Weltliteratur* (the term used in the title of the festschrift in which the essay appeared), Auerbach seeks ways in which literary and historical scholars can make sense of and synthesize the new and larger bodies of knowledge that the modern world imposes upon them.

Those who would criticize *Mimesis* for its Eurocentrism (or wonder why the author of *Orientalism* should be drawn to this book) will find a wider view of the world in this later essay, but for Said, despite the European focus of the earlier book, *Mimesis* has proved exemplary for his own work. On the surface, *Culture and Imperialism* surely does not look like a continuation of Auerbach's project. Though it provides readings of a number of novels and what we have come to classify as "cultural texts"—for example, *The Wretched of the Earth* and *The Black Jacobins*—it does not attempt the detailed analysis of brief passages that marked the earlier book as the heir to the tradition of Romance stylistics. Nor, given its focus on the effect of imperialism upon modern culture, can it claim anything near the time span that marked *Mimesis*; it is as though Said, like any contemporary scholar, acknowledges from the start that the learning possessed by Auerbach and his generation of *Romanisten* cannot be duplicated in our time. Although Said does not aim for temporal breadth, *Culture and Imperialism* extends itself spatially to a degree that one rarely encounters in a serious work of criticism. It is most obviously like *Mimesis* in the way it balances insights into specific texts with larger theoretical principles—more precisely, in the way that theory comes directly out of each author's critical practice, indeed the way that theory and practice correct and reshape one another in the course of the argument. Just as *Mimesis* proposes a theory of fiction by means of the changing concepts of the "real" in a series of texts, so Said, looking at the imperialist subtext within certain classic works, self-consciously proposes a theory of the novel that, like those deriving from Lukács and Proust, is based not on the primacy of temporality, but rather on "the function of space, geography, and location" (*Culture and Imperialism*, p. 84).

Said has complained on several occasions of the "trivial uses" to which *Mimesis* has been put, by which he meant that it was often praised as a work of "rich analysis" without a "sense of its mission."[47] Even more than the affinities I suggested above, what ties *Mimesis* and *Culture and Imperialism* most closely together is this larger "sense of mission." Both books, as Said likes to remind his readers, are written from the perspective of an exile. To conclude his "Epilegomena zu *Mimesis*" Auerbach had written the sentence I quoted earlier in this essay: "*Mimesis* is quite consciously a book written by a particular person in a particular place during the early 1940's." For Said, Auerbach's perspectivism is not simply a matter of the point of view from which the analyst looks at his materials. The western tradition, seen from the perspective of an exile in Istanbul during the early 1940's, has itself been transformed in the very process of an author's contemplating it. Said, as a Palestinian who has spent most of his life in the United States, gives exemplary readings of classic western texts such as *Mansfield Park*, *Kim*, and *L'Etranger* by means of what he calls a "contrapuntal" method—reading them at once on their "own," seemingly literal terms and at the same time noting the larger, unspoken history of colonialism embedded under their surface.[48]

Yet though Auerbach and Said both write out of what one might call their "situatedness," the latter reminds us to what a high degree exile has become central to much of the significant writing since the time Auerbach's book was written: "Exile, far from being the fate of nearly forgotten unfortunates who are dispossessed and expatriated, becomes something closer to a norm, an experience of crossing boundaries and charting new territories in defiance of the classic canonic enclosures, however much its loss and sadness should be acknowledged and registered" (*Culture and Imperialism*, p. 317). Learning to deal with, indeed to transcend the experience of exile becomes a crucial challenge, one that Said finds expressed in a medieval text by Hugo of Saint Victor that Auerbach uses to bring "Philologie der *Weltliteratur*" to conclusion and that Said later quotes in several places: "The person who finds his homeland sweet is still a tender beginner; he to whom every soil is as his native one is already strong; but he is perfect to whom the entire world is as a foreign place. The tender soul has fixed his love on one spot in the world; the strong person has extended his love to all places; the perfect man has extinguished his."[49]

In his most recent citation of these lines Said reminds us that for Hugo "the 'strong' or 'perfect' person achieves independence and detachment by *working through* attachments, not by rejecting them" (*Culture and Imperialism*, p. 336). Of both *Mimesis* and *Culture and Imperialism* one can say that, however different their focus or their methods may look, each book can be characterized by its fine balance of engagedness and

detachment; to put it specifically in Said's terms, each author has succeeded in "working through" his attachments to achieve a stance that is
neither sectarian nor neutral and that discourages the reader from ex-
pecting easy or formulaic responses to the questions posed in the book.
At one point he describes his method as a "homemade resolution of
the antitheses between involvement and theory" (p. 194). It is significant that Said, in a book devoted to uncovering the imperialist subtexts
in the literature and culture of the last two centuries, self-consciously
avoids what he calls "the rhetoric of blame, so often now employed
by subaltern, minority, or disadvantaged voices" (p. 96), nor does he
wish to "indict [texts] wholesale or suggest that they are less interesting
as art for being in complex ways part of the imperialist undertaking"
(p. 186). And he seeks to avoid as well the type of reading "rigorously
based in one or another of the advanced theoretical schools" (p. 95).
The intellectual generosity displayed in these statements, indeed in the
book as a whole, seems to me the chief legacy with which Auerbach's
writing has endowed the work of Said. In avoiding the sharp polemics
that had marked *Orientalism*, Said also seeks to assume the cultural authority that Bové described Auerbach as exercising within the English-
speaking world in the preceding generation; and since this type of
authority had long been associated in this world with the examples of
Matthew Arnold and Lionel Trilling (whose actual office at Columbia
Said also happened to inhabit for a while), *Culture and Imperialism* seeks
to communicate with an audience wider than those "advanced theoretical schools" he had addressed in his earlier books—a more general
audience that presumably has not yet questioned the Eurocentric views
associated with Said's distinguished predecessors.[50]

The appearance of *Culture and Imperialism* has demonstrated that
Mimesis has had more of an afterlife than one might have thought in
view of the misapprehensions to which it has been subjected or in view
of the fact that it has come to be ignored in recent years. Although
nobody expects a literary scholar of our time to produce a work as
synoptic and self-assured as Auerbach's unique book, the particular
stimulation that *Mimesis* offered to Said suggests at least one of several directions in which it might lead future thinkers. Can one, for
instance, imagine a "new stylistics" different from the one practiced
by Auerbach's generation of Romance scholars, a stylistics based not
only on canonical or even written texts but also on a wider variety of

evidence—gestures, habits, visual artifacts—that can provide insights into both the differences separating and the continuities binding diverse historical moments or cultures? Or might one imagine a new historicism different from Auerbach's historicism as well as from the recent movement that bears this name and that has fast become routinized? Can one imagine, for instance, a historicism that would create significant and convincing connections among cultures that have developed independently of one another? And might one also imagine a new synthesis of formal and historical methods which, though necessarily different from the synthesis achieved by Auerbach, can claim something of the latter's rigor and audacity? It is the function of major works such as *Mimesis* to help us formulate the questions and the methods by means of which we seek to move beyond them.

Appendix:
Early Reviews and Discussions of *Mimesis*

Adolf, Helen. *Modern Language Quarterly* 10 (1949): 249–50.

Anon. *New Yorker*, June 26, 1954, p. 92.

Auerbach, Erich. "Epilegomena zu *Mimesis.*" *Romanische Forschungen* 65 (1953): 1–18.

Baldensperger, Fernand. *Revue de littérature comparée* 21 (1947): 619–21.

Barrett, William. "Words and Masks." *Saturday Review of Literature* 37 (Mar. 13, 1954): 21.

Barron, Louis. *Library Journal* 79 (Jan. 15, 1954): 143.

Baum, P. F. *South Atlantic Quarterly* 53 (1954): 428–30.

Bergholz, Harry. *Modern Language Journal* 39 (1955): 109.

Bezzola, Reto R. *Anzeiger für deutsches Altertum und deutsche Literatur* 65 (1951): 77–85.

Curtius, Ernst Robert. "Die Lehre von den drei Stilen in Altertum und Mittelalter (zu Auerbachs *Mimesis*)." *Romanische Forschungen* 64 (1952): 57–70.

D., W. H. *The Personalist* 36 (1955): 90–91.

Davis, Robert Gorham. "The Imitation of Life." *Partisan Review* 21 (1954): 321–26.

Dieckmann, Herbert. *Romanic Review* 39 (1948): 331–35.

Edelstein, Ludwig. *Modern Language Notes* 65 (1950): 426–31.

Ethier-Blais, Jean. "*Mimesis*: Réalisme et transcendance." *Études françaises* 6 (1970): 7–24.

Fergusson, Francis. "Two Perspectives on European Literature." *Hudson Review* 7 (1954): 119–27. (Reviews *Mimesis* together with Curtius's *European Literature and the Latin Middle Ages*.)

Fuerst, Norbert. *JEGP* 47 (1948): 289–90.

George, Albert J. *Symposium* 9 (1955): 152–54.

Gogarten, Friedrich. "Das abendländische Geschichtsdenken: Bemerkungen zu dem Buch von Erich Auerbach *Mimesis.*" *Zeitschrift für Theologie und Kirche* 51 (1954): 270–360.

Gruenter, Rainer. "Begriff der mittelalterlichen Stilrevolution." *Anzeiger für deutsches Altertum und deutsche Literatur* 65 (1951): 85–88.

Hatzfeld, Helmut. *Romance Philology* 2 (1949): 333–38.

Heiney, Donald. *Western Humanities Review* 8 (1954): 69–71.

Hess, Gerhard. "MIMESIS: Zu Erich Auerbachs Geschichte des abendländischen Realismus." *Romanische Forschungen* 61 (1948): 173–211.

Horst, Karl August. *Merkur* 6 (May 1952): 482–84.

Hughes, Serge. "The Creation of Literary Style." *The Commonweal* 59 (Feb. 5, 1954): 454.

Isenberg, Arnold. *Journal of Aesthetics and Art Criticism* 12 (1954): 526–27.

Kuhn, Helmut. "Literaturgeschichte als Geschichtsphilosophie." *Philosophische Rundschau* 11 (1963): 222–48.

Leo, Ulrich. *Comparative Literature* 1 (1949): 92–95.

Mortier, Roland. *Revue belge de philologie et d'histoire* 28 (1950): 189–92.

Muscatine, Charles. *Romance Philology* 9 (1956): 448–57.

Naumann, Walter. *Modern Philology* 45 (1947): 211–12.

Nykl, A. R. *Speculum* 22 (1947): 461.

Oras, Ants. *JEGP* 53 (1954): 444–48.

Regenbogen, Otto. Reprinted in *Kleine Schriften*, ed. Franz Dirlmeier. Munich: Beck, 1961. Pp. 600–17.

Roncaglia, Aurelio. "Introduzione" to Auerbach, *Mimesis: Il realismo nella letteratura occidentale*. Turin: Giulio Einaudi, 1956. Pp. ix–xxxv.

Schalk, Fritz. *Deutsche Vierteljahrsschrift* 24 (1950): 281–85.

Schwartz, Delmore. "The King Asked, 'What Time Is It?'" *The New York Times Book Review*, Nov. 29, 1953, p. 40.

Scott, Nathan A., Jr. *Christian Scholar* 37 (1954): 538–47.

Seaton, Ethel. *Year's Work in English Studies* 27 (1946): 10–11.

Sharrock, Roger. *Modern Language Review* 50 (1955): 61–62.

Spoerri, Theophil. *Trivium* 6 (1948): 297–308.

Svendsen, Kester. *Books Abroad* 29 (1955): 95.

Tuve, Rosemond. *Yale Review* 43 (1954): 619–22.

Wedeck, Harry E. *Latomus* 13 (1954): 610–13.

Wellek, René. "Auerbach's Special Realism." *Kenyon Review* 16 (1954): 299–307. See also Wellek's memorial note, "Erich Auerbach (1892–1957)," *Comparative Literature* 10 (1958): 93–94, and the detailed treatment of *Mimesis* in Wellek's *A History of Modern Criticism: 1750–1950*, vol. 7 (New Haven, Conn.: Yale University Press, 1991), pp. 113–23.

Geoffrey Green

Erich Auerbach and the "Inner Dream" of Transcendence

I

The decades that have passed since Erich Auerbach's death in 1957 serve to remind us of his greatness—as a philologist, as a literary historian, as a unique critical voice in the ongoing narration of modernity. Often the process of time provides a changed or altered context with which readers may assess and appreciate anew certain aspects of a writer's contribution. New critical associations or nuances may prompt us to focus on details that were previously seen as unimportant; a passage thought to be relatively obscure may then fairly leap out for significant attention. So it is with Auerbach's relation to modernity. In the course of reading him, one might duly note (especially but not exclusively in *Mimesis*) a measured ambiguity toward the modern, the present, the literature of the future. In his later writings, it was not unusual for Auerbach to stake out for himself a careful critical position and then, in a few ironic phrases, separate himself from the implications of that position. This personal trait is evident as well in the deeply poignant ending of *Mimesis*. How contemporary readers react to these passages depends on the associations we bring to Auerbach's writing: if we evaluate him as a philologist in relation to the standards of the early twentieth century, then Auerbach's late themes of contradiction and self-estrangement—an apparent doubling of himself—are inconsequential and insignificant. If, however, we opt to consider certain refrains in Auerbach as exemplifying familiar choruses now understood as representing more contemporary expressions and modes of thought, then we become aware of Auerbach as an avatar of postmodernity. Born in 1892, Auerbach was nine years junior to Kafka, seven years senior to Borges and Nabokov; he wrote and lived while Freud completed his densely textured and richly ambiguous late writings; he was the exact contemporary of Walter Benjamin.

There is a shared quality in Benjamin and Auerbach: a sense that each writer is not only writing about a text, but also highlighting his particular circumstances as an element to be included in the text and its analysis. This passage from Walter Benjamin's "Unpacking My Library" is an example: "Instead, I must ask you to join me in the disorder of crates that have been wrenched open, the air saturated with the dust of wood, the floor covered with torn paper, to join me among piles of volumes that are seeing daylight again after two years of darkness, so that you may be ready to share with me a bit of the mood—it is certainly not an elegiac mood but, rather, one of anticipation—which these books arouse in a genuine collector. For such a man is speaking to you, and on closer scrutiny he proves to be speaking only about himself."[1] Auerbach's insistence in *Mimesis* that the circumstances of his book's composition—involuntary exile from Germany coupled with an environment unsuitable for scholarly research—be considered as part of his narrative may be understood in terms of Benjamin's similar assertion. Rather than continue the fiction of constructing a hypothetical book collector, Benjamin's narrator confesses that he *is* that hypothetical collector: Walter Benjamin is the writer who presented to us this confession about himself. Auerbach makes an analogous statement (at the end of *Mimesis*) when he presents *Mimesis* as an instance of the modernist theme of using the fragment to exemplify the whole. Auerbach, however, is the writer who uses this personal statement to present the contradiction he wishes us to perceive: *Mimesis* exemplifies certain aspects of modernism—its author, however, does not care for modernist works.

Who has written *Mimesis*, one may consequently wonder: the Auerbach who presents himself and his book as exemplifying the historical trend of modernism, or the Auerbach who disapproves of modernism for its rejection of his historicism? Several years after Auerbach wrote *Mimesis*, Jorge Luis Borges wrote the following lines: "I live, let myself go on living, so that Borges may contrive his literature, and this literature justifies me. It is no effort for me to confess that he has achieved some valid pages, but those pages cannot save me, perhaps because what is good belongs to no one, not even to him, but rather to language and to tradition. . . . Thus, my life is a flight and I lose everything and everything belongs to oblivion, or to him. I do not know which of us has written this page."[2] I wish to draw into emphasis this strand of self-irony, of self-contradiction. We are quite familiar with self-negation as an inherent element of postmodern or postcontemporary art. It is perhaps not so customary to suggest that Auerbach expressed affiliative notions at precisely the same period.

Borges's insistence (in "Kafka and His Precursors") that, once perceived, the Kafkaesque may be detected in writers who lived *before* Kafka suggests that the reader possesses an ability to sift and order historical materials from a *radical relativist* position: we read, in other words, from and through our own vantage point. This is conveyed in these lines from Borges's meditation: "The fact is that every writer *creates* his own precursors. His work modifies our conception of the past as it will modify the future."[3] Do we hear a sympathetic voice in Auerbach's "Purpose and Method" from *Literary Language and Its Public in Late Latin Antiquity and in the Middle Ages*?

Has such an approach scientific validity? It matters little. My own experience, and by that I mean not merely my scientific experience, is responsible for the choice of problems, the starting points, the reasoning and the intention expressed in my writings. No other approval is sought but the consent (which is bound to be variable and never complete) of those who have arrived at similar experience by other paths, so that my experience may serve to clarify, to complement, and perhaps to stimulate theirs.[4]

Auerbach's refrain that who he is, when he lives, and under what circumstances serve to determine his critical vantage point underscores the postmodern flavor that we can detect in his writings.

Auerbach recognized that standards of judgment in literature and history are relative to one's personal circumstances. Courageously, he acknowledged this limitation but did not forswear the endeavor to discriminate and form critical estimations. In the "Purpose and Method" section of *Literary Language*, he proclaimed,

Historical relativism is relative in two respects—of the material and of those who are striving to understand it. It is a radical relativism, but that is no reason to fear it. The area in which we move in this effort at understanding is the world of men, to which we ourselves belong. . . . In such activity we do not lose the faculty of judgment; on the contrary, we acquire it. We cease, it is true, to judge on the basis of extrahistorical and absolute categories, and we cease to look for such categories. (*Literary Language*, pp. 12–13)

In this willingness to admit that one's system of analysis was relative and yet functional, Auerbach was a kinsman of Freud in his late writings. Consider, for example, this passage from "Analysis Terminable and Interminable," the essay in which Freud grants that the appropriate ending of a psychoanalysis is not inherent but rather constructed or devised when there are no clear indications that an end has arrived: "We know that the first step towards attaining intellectual mastery of our environment is to discover generalizations, rules and laws which bring order into chaos. In doing this we simplify the world of phenomena; but we cannot avoid falsifying it, specially if we are dealing with processes of development and change." In that same essay, Freud posited that "a normal ego . . . is, like normality in general, an ideal fiction." [5] "Normality" is an "ideal fiction," and yet we use such contrivances to recognize ourselves and our desires. Freud's confession was his seasoned recognition that contradiction was crucial to all modernity and its devices. Interpretation and categorization do not cease merely by our recognition that we are proceeding out of our own subjectivity.

For Auerbach, *Weltliteratur* was the double, the foil, for our individually relative perspective of isolation. The words of Maire and Edward Said are eloquent in their introduction to their translation of Auerbach's "Philology and *Weltliteratur*": "It is, of course, Goethe's own word (which he used increasingly after 1827 for universal literature, or literature which expresses *Humanität*, humanity), and this expression is literature's ultimate purpose. *Weltliteratur* is therefore a visionary concept for it transcends national literatures without, at the same time, destroying their individualities." [6] In that essay, Auerbach refers to "a scientifically ordered and conducted research of reality" as our "Myth": it "stirs us most deeply and compels us most forcibly to a consciousness of ourselves." [7] Here we detect a meaningful echo of Freud in the assertion that our myths achieve a "relative" or constructed reality for us because they express the deep hermeneutic truth of our inner states of desire.

Auerbach, in "Philology and *Weltliteratur*," establishes that "history therefore includes the present. The inner history of the last thousand years is the history of mankind achieving self-expression." This is history without an objective vantage point—a process of narrating events from within their unfolding sequence. It is thus an "inner" history rather than an objective one, and it results in "self-expression" rather than absolute knowledge. Auerbach refers to our "adventurous advance to a consciousness of [our] human condition" as the "unfold[ing]" of "an inner dream." Despite these qualifications, he nevertheless asserts that "collecting material and forming it into a whole that will continue to have effect" is a "duty" that is "urgent." Our "historic perspectivism" enables us to transcend this innate contradiction: "The reason we still possess this sense [of historic perspectivism] is that we live the experience of historical multiplicity, and without this experience, I fear, the sense would quickly lose its living concreteness" ("Philology and *Weltliteratur*," p. 5). Compare Auerbach's emphasis to the concluding epiphany of his fellow emigré, Vladimir Nabokov, in his novel, *The Real Life of Sebastian Knight*: "The soul is but a manner of being—not a constant state—. . . [and] any soul may be yours, if you find and follow its undulations. The hereafter may be the full ability of consciously living in any chosen soul, in any number of souls, all of them unconscious of their interchangeable burden. . . . I am Sebastian, or Sebastian is I, or perhaps we both are someone whom neither of us knows."[8]

Living the "experience of historical multiplicity" is the quintessence of postmodernism. It is the recognition that we may enter the hermeneutic circle at any appropriate point as long as that entry point is inherently true, narratively true—expressive, in some deep sense, of the state of human desire. Auerbach understood, as did Benjamin, that each historian is telling his own story, narrating a set of circumstances that corresponds to the unfolding of an "inner dream." In psychoanalysis, the dream is interpreted dialogically between the analyst and the analysand; we come to "self-expression" by following the "undulations" of our opposing self. The writers we most value as achieving a resonance of our self-contradictory postmodernity have a knowing awareness that we are in flux, that we are multiple, that there is an "I" overlooking "Borges," that we are always in a state of becoming. As Auerbach expressed it, "the subject at hand . . . needs constant rediscovery." Representing himself as a philologist, Auerbach, the contemporary man, embraced the contradictions of our era: "Our philological home is the earth: it can no longer be the nation." But only when a philologist is "separated" from that "most priceless and indispensable" heritage, "his own nation's culture and language . . . , and then transcends it does it become truly effective. . . . *Geist* is not national" ("Philology and *Weltliteratur*," pp. 15, 17).

II

"The Brown Stocking," the final chapter of Erich Auerbach's landmark critical study, *Mimesis*, describes a dilemma that has significant applicability for an understanding of contemporary literary history and theory. I would like to consider briefly a few elements of that chapter in order to focus on one aspect that I consider to be highly significant among Auerbach's many legacies. In his analysis of Virginia Woolf's *To the Lighthouse*, Auerbach reveals a perceptive and subtle insight as to what constitutes modernism: "Writers present minor happenings . . . as points of departure for the development of motifs, for a penetration which opens up a new perspective into a milieu or a consciousness or the given historical setting." Modernists have "discarded presenting the story of their characters with any claim to exterior completeness, in chronological order, and with the emphasis on important exterior turning points of destiny." In the modernist novel, a conspicuous worldview is never enunciated directly; rather, the modernist places "greater confidence in syntheses gained through full exploitation of an everyday occurrence."[9]

In the discussion that follows, Auerbach emphasizes the similarity between modernism and his own approach to philology. "The interpretation of a few passages from *Hamlet*, *Phèdre*, or *Faust* can be made to yield more, and more decisive, information about Shakespeare, Racine, or Goethe and their times than would a systematic and chronological treatment of their lives and works." *Mimesis* itself could never have been completed had not Auerbach utilized a decidedly modernist technique—the isolated fragment being perceived as symbolically significant of a larger whole. Modernist novelists and philologists are "guided by the consideration that it is a hopeless venture to try to be really complete within the total exterior continuum and yet to make

what is essential stand out." Identifying his project and his methodology with modernism, Auerbach continues: "Our lives appear in our
own conception as total entities—which to be sure are always changing, more or less radically, more or less rapidly, depending on the
extent to which we are obliged, inclined, and able to assimilate the
onrush of new experience." Modernists embrace "not one order and
one interpretation, but many, which may either be those of different
persons or of the same person at different times" (*Mimesis*, pp. 548, 549).

What I find most intriguing, poignant, and insightful is Auerbach's
admission of his disaffection from modernist texts even though he is
himself a modernist. "In a Europe unsure of itself, overflowing with
unsettled ideologies and ways of life, and pregnant with disaster—
[modernist] writers distinguished by instinct and insight find a method
which dissolves reality into multiple and multivalent reflections of consciousness. That this method should have been developed at this time is
not hard to understand." Although there is "a good deal to be said for
such a view," Auerbach finds modernism wanting: modernism contains
an "atmosphere of universal doom," an "impression of hopelessness";
there is, in modernist texts, "something hostile to the reality which
they represent," a "turning away from the practical will to live"—there
is, in short, "an air of vague and hopeless sadness." To the extent to
which modernism represents "an economic and cultural leveling process" of undifferentiation, it gives voice to a "very simple solution."
At this point, Auerbach evokes himself: "Perhaps it will be too simple
to please those who, despite all its dangers and catastrophes, admire
and love our epoch for the sake of its abundance of life and the incomparable historical vantage point which it affords. But they are few
in number, and probably they will not live to see much more than the
first forewarnings of the approaching unification and simplification"
(*Mimesis*, pp. 551, 552, 553).

This estrangement from self in *Mimesis* emerges as a moving and
affecting culmination of Auerbach's study of realism from antiquity
to modernity. Having disassociated himself from the modernism with
which he had earlier proclaimed allegiance, Auerbach ends his own
study with an "air of vague and hopeless sadness" analogous to that
which he had condemned in modernist novels. But estrangement from
self also stands as an appropriate description of an inherent *postmod-
ernist* strategy: the simultaneous engagement and detachment of self
within the text.

This affinity for doubling, self-contradiction, and self-cancellation is present in later significant Auerbach texts. The introductory "Purpose and Method" section of *Literary Language* addresses the goal of achieving "an insight into the diverse implications of a process from which we stem, and in which we participate, a definition of our present situation. . . . Such a method compels us to look within ourselves and to set forth our consciousness of ourselves here and now, in all its wealth and limitations." Auerbach here stresses that he is implicated in his writing—as a result of his perspective, his method, his individual self. His writing about the past is dictated by his "own experience" in modernity—professional as well as personal (*Literary Language*, pp. 21, 22). Having described his method and proclaimed that "it matters little" whether there is "validity" to his approach, he confesses that he "should have liked to make more evident [in the text that follows] the connecting thread that unites the whole. In this light the book is still in search of its theme." Auerbach calls on his readers to "sense the unity behind" his project (pp. 22, 24). Now it may be argued that such a dissociation is a function of Auerbach's hermeneutics in which the part is taken to suggest the whole but with an intrinsic awareness of the whole throughout existent in the fragments: "It is patently impossible to establish a synthesis by assembling all the particulars," but "fertile areas" or "key problems" may "open up a knowledge of a broader context and cast a light" (p. 18).

But I would also suggest that one enduring and increasingly relevant aspect of Auerbach's legacy is his willingness to describe his human desires as influencing and contextualizing his hermeneutic, philological, and historical endeavors. Indeed, what Auerbach presents in his later work as the culmination of his interpretive career is the interplay of the subjective with the maintenance of human critical standards of evaluation. Auerbach's essay in *Scenes from the Drama of European Literature*, "The Aesthetic Dignity of the *Fleurs du Mal*," displays his willingness to share with his readers his sense of paradox, dynamic contradiction, and self-estrangement. It is a brave and audacious act to ask at the end of a stylistic explication of a writer, "But what then of the hope? How can nothingness be a new sun that will bring flowers to unfolding? I know no answer." Here Auerbach is willing to stake his own interpretive gifts, his own aesthetic preferences and desires, as part of an assessment of Baudelaire. Auerbach praises Baudelaire's "unswerving honesty" as his "greatness" and declares that he gave the modern age a "new poetic style." He expressed the "naked, concrete existence of an epoch."[10] But the historical perspective is not the end of Auerbach's process; his desire (as he noted in *Literary Language*) "is always to write history," a history that "shows a much clearer awareness of the European crisis" than that of other philologists (*Literary Language*, pp. 20, 6).

Thus, he brings the discussion of Baudelaire directly into his own historical and critical context:

Now that the crisis of our civilizations (which at Baudelaire's time was still latent, presaged by only a few)—now that the crisis is approaching a decision, we may perhaps expect a decline in Baudelaire's influence; in a totally changed world that is perhaps moving toward a new order, the coming generations may lose contact with his problems and his attitude. But the historic importance of *Les Fleurs du mal* can never be shaken. . . . Baudelaire's style, the mixture we have attempted to describe, is as much alive as ever. (*Scenes*, p. 225)

Having described Baudelaire's stylistic originality, historical decisiveness, and literary influence, Auerbach nonetheless feels that something else is missing, something addressing the "European crisis" and the contemporary moment of history. Baudelaire, he concludes, has written a "book of gruesome hopelessness, of futile and absurd attempts to escape by inebriation and narcosis." Those critics who rejected Baudelaire may have had a "better understanding" of him than his admirers: "A statement of horror is better understood by those who feel the horror in their bones, even if they react against it, than by those who express nothing but their rapture over the artistic achievement." Auerbach here identifies with those critics of Baudelaire even as he stylistically presents Baudelaire's poetic greatness. In so doing, Auerbach exposes the subjectivity lurking within the methodology of the interpretive act: "It seems to us that aesthetic criticism alone is unequal to the task" (*Scenes*, p. 226).

Should it be supposed that I am reading too much into Auerbach's written texts, too much of a degree of personal interaction and profound deliberate inner contradiction, I would like to consider briefly the account provided by Robert Fitzgerald of Auerbach's presentation and improvisational delivery of the Baudelaire paper at the Princeton Seminars in 1949: "All who know modern poetry, said Auerbach, find Baudelaire the initiator; he is the point where everything converges, then radiates again. 'But I have a personal confession,' he said. 'I don't like him very much.'"[11] It is clear that Auerbach wishes to bring himself into the explication; he wants to confront the element of himself that is inclined to observe Baudelaire as a creature of history with the element of himself that finds such poetry repugnant despite his stylistic, historical, and aesthetic appreciation.

Fitzgerald's account of Auerbach's second presentation on Baudelaire makes this perspective even clearer: "In the new style that [Baudelaire] gave to poetry were to be found for the first time in literature certain surprising and incoherent combinations of ideas whose visionary power was a revelation to later poets; perhaps a revelation of present anarchy and dawning order. . . . Auerbach's final point was that he, nevertheless, did not like the poetry of Baudelaire. This poetry is horrible, he said emphatically, and smiling."[12] Thus, Auerbach's conception may be recognized and observed: at the conclusion of a learned and focused hermeneutic, Auerbach's design is to acknowledge the inner contradictions of his own methodology: his own human desires contaminate the outcome of his purely philological judgment; "aesthetic criticism alone is unequal to the task." If we define the task as the "European crisis," then I believe we derive a sense of Auerbach's importance, his originality, and his legacy.

With what should an interpreter be concerned? If trained in philology and stylistics, if rooted in hermeneutics, ought one to remain, narrowly, in the realm of aesthetic criticism? Or does one recognize and, as a consequence, bring into one's work the influence of one's world, one's time, one's life, one's personal experience? Auerbach doubles himself because he understands that he is not able to say what he has to say singly, to or from one discrete perspective. In so doing, Auerbach's legacy resonates with profound collective tendencies in contemporary writing. The double of the self and its estranged other is an important theme in Freud's work as expressed in the simultaneous subjectivity and detachment of psychoanalytic discourse. It may be viewed as well as a crucial criterion for postmodernism: in Borges and Nabokov, for instance, in Benjamin, Roland Barthes, Mikhail Bakhtin, and Jacques Lacan, we find writing that parodies cultural and historical values and, simultaneously, conveys and is a product of these modes of thought. *Mimesis* concludes, "Nothing now remains but to find . . .

the reader" (*Mimesis*, p. 557). One hundred years after his birth, it is an honor to read—and be read by—Erich Auerbach.

III

"For such a man is speaking to you, and on closer scrutiny he proves to be speaking only about himself": Benjamin's words underline the haunting implications of expression (or self-expression) in a postmodern age.[13] One is speaking, always, unavoidably, for oneself—but the self is fragmented, a multitude. Benjamin's narrator speaks to "you" about "himself," in the hope that his "I" will be you. Reader and writer are doubles, shadows, traces each of the other. Auerbach ends *Mimesis* with the mimetic echo of the act of writing: "Nothing now remains but to find [the reader]. I hope that my study will reach its readers—both my friends of former years, if they are still alive, as well as all the others for whom it was intended" (*Mimesis*, p. 557). For whom did Auerbach intend his writings? His "Purpose and Method" section of *Literary Language* brings this to light: "No other approval is sought but the consent (which is bound to be variable and never complete) of those who have arrived at similar experience by other paths, so that my experience may serve to clarify, to complement, and perhaps to stimulate theirs" (*Literary Language*, p. 22). Through the faces of the crowd, the writer seeks out that face that is, if not his or her own, linked by a mimetic attitude of shared perspective. The writer, affirming the uniqueness of identity, is simultaneously formulating that identity in the plural. I exist in you, through you, among you—if I exist at all.

Reaching one's readers, obtaining their empathy and identification, has the consequence of "bringing together again" those who were fragmented, estranged, isolated (*Mimesis*, p. 557). One part of Auerbach's writerly self understands this estrangement and allows it to attain rich and poetic expression. On the other hand, *Weltliteratur* provides for a bridge, a transcendence, a "bringing together again" that may compensate, in part, for the postmodern situation of fragmentation and centerlessness. The ability of literature to speak to multitudes while yet remaining singular is, for Auerbach, a powerful expression of our "inner dream . . . whose scope and depth entirely animate the spectator, enabling him at the same time to find peace in his given potential by the enrichment he gains from having witnessed the drama" ("Philology and *Weltliteratur*," p. 5). Here we may recall the words from Nabokov's *The Real Life of Sebastian Knight*: "Any soul may be yours, if you find and follow its undulations. The hereafter may be the full ability of consciously living in any chosen soul, in any number of souls, all of them unconscious of their interchangeable burden."[14] If *Geist* is not national, then "any soul may be yours." The basis of writing — regardless of the genre and form of its expression — is to provide a representation of the writer's soul in order to live among any number of souls. This commitment, for Auerbach, for Nabokov, for Benjamin, for Freud, is one that remains deeply expressive of our contemporary desires. For, if anything, we have become more fragmented, more standardized, more estranged from each other and ourselves than during the years in which Auerbach wrote.

The reader of a novel, Walter Benjamin emphasized, "is isolated, more so than any other reader. . . . He is ready to make [the novel] completely his own, to devour it, as it were."[15] In these words by Benjamin, we may detect that spirit that conveys a good measure of Auerbach's "inner dream" of human transcendence:

Seen in this way, the storyteller joins the ranks of the teachers and the sages. . . . For it is granted to him to reach back to a whole lifetime (a life, incidentally, that comprises not only his own experience but no little of the experience of others . . .). His gift is the ability to relate his life; his distinction, to be able to tell his entire life. The storyteller: he is the man who could let the wick of his life be consumed completely by the gentle flame of his story.[16]

These may appear to be curious words to apply to a great philologist and literary historian. But I would suggest that Auerbach's gift was his commitment to narrative: he dramatized the story of our literary evolution — with himself as the storyteller; he sought, in his own words, to write "an inner history of mankind . . . a conception of man unified in his multiplicity" ("Philology and *Weltliteratur*," p. 4). And, like Benjamin, he recognized himself in the estrangement and fragmentation of his day and sought, with his writing, to achieve a "bringing together again."

Auerbach wrote that Zola was "one of the very few authors of the century who created their work out of the great problems of the age" (*Mimesis*, p. 512). Certainly, this applies equally to Auerbach. As we approach him now, we appreciate how crucially his themes and concerns remain our own: representation as a figure of reality, marginalization, the aesthetic depiction of human dignity, the mixing of styles as a correlative for multiple voices, human multiplicity, the volatile flow of living change. "Whatever we are, we became in history, and only in history can we remain the way we are and develop therefrom": so Auerbach insisted that we constitute ourselves in relation to the past in order to create and fulfill the promise of the future. Auerbach called for a "history-from-within," a hermeneutic voyage into the text of our own historical lives ("Philology and *Weltliteratur*," pp. 6, 12). As he embodied his ironic self-contradictions, so do we see ourselves vividly in the questions he asked and the problems he addressed.

Twelve years have passed since the publication of my book, *Literary Criticism and the Structures of History: Erich Auerbach and Leo Spitzer*.[17] In that time, interest in Auerbach has increased: this is as it should be—there is no literary historian more worthy of our renewed attention. It is my fervent hope that readers will continue in their efforts to negotiate the Auerbachian space: between history and language; between writing and experience; between life and art. In this way, Erich Auerbach's "inner dream" of human "self-expression" will achieve fulfillment in each of us.

Thomas R. Hart

Literature as Language:
Auerbach, Spitzer, Jakobson

Erich Auerbach's *Introduction aux études de philologie romane* is generally, and rightly, considered the least personal of his books; Alberto Vàrvaro calls it "distressingly superficial."[1] It was first published in a Turkish translation in 1944; Auerbach presumably undertook it only because his contract with the Turkish State University required him to do so. It is perhaps surprising that a letter to his former Marburg colleague Werner Krauss written on June 22, 1946, when Auerbach was planning to give up his position in Istanbul and anxious to make his work better known abroad, expresses his interest in publishing the original French version and notes that he had sent it to the firm of A. Francke in Bern, which was to bring out *Mimesis* in the fall.[2] In another letter to Krauss, of July 9, 1947, he again notes that he had submitted the book to Francke the year before and adds that he had refused the publishers permission to publish the chapters on literary history alone, and to replace the linguistic section with one by Walther von Wartburg. Auerbach feared that von Wartburg would not complete his portion of the work, but he also insists that "my book . . . is a whole."[3]

In it, Auerbach defines philology as "the ensemble of activities that deal methodically with human language and with the works of art composed in it."[4] He notes that "literary history often makes use of linguistic concepts" and observes that his own preferred method, the *explication des textes*, occupies the middle ground between literary history and linguistics (*Philologie romane*, p. 33). Auerbach did not, however, teach Romance linguistics at Yale, where he joined the faculty in 1950 and became Sterling Professor of Romance Philology in 1956, nor, so far as I know, at Marburg. His linguistic publications are limited to studies in historical semantics. The treatment of Romance historical linguistics in *Philologie romane* is sketchy and even inaccurate in a few details.

Auerbach's conviction that the study of literature cannot be separated from that of language links his work to that of two other European scholars of the same generation who ended their teaching careers in the United States: Leo Spitzer (1887–1960) and Roman Jakobson (1896–1982). The three treat language, and hence literature, in quite different ways. Auerbach sees language as a key to the character of a particular society. For him, close readings of a text "almost always have a general significance, which goes beyond the text itself and reveals something about the writer, the period in which he wrote, the development of a mode of thought, an artistic form, or a way of life" (*Philologie romane*, p. 36). Spitzer is interested primarily in the use of language by individual writers, seeking the clue to a writer's personality in his deviations from the norm. Jakobson is concerned with the timeless and universal laws that govern language in all its manifestations, spoken and written, and that link it with other, nonverbal systems of signs; linguistics includes poetics and is itself included in semiotics.[5]

Spitzer did not share Auerbach's preoccupation with history, though his interpretations invariably rest on a vast fund of historical knowledge, by no means confined to the history of literature. Jakobson is closer to Auerbach in his interest in the epistemological problems posed by the writing of literary history. He was keenly aware of the interplay between synchronic and diachronic factors in both language and literature. His lectures on Ferdinand de Saussure's *Cours de linguistique générale*, given at the Ecole Libre des Hautes Etudes in New York in 1942 and published only after his death, offer both an excellent introduction to Saussure's thought and a searching critique of the Swiss linguist's distinction between *langue* and *parole*.[6] In an important programmatic statement, written in collaboration with Jurij Tynjanov, Jakobson insists that pure synchrony is an illusion, both in language and in literature; every stage in the development of a language, like every period in the history of literature, contains reminiscences of earlier periods and hints of future developments.[7]

In the manual he wrote for his Turkish students, Auerbach notes that the practice of *explication des textes* "has been considerably developed and enriched by certain modern philologists (among Romanists, one must mention especially L. Spitzer). . . . It is no longer solely a method of confirming what was already known but a research tool that leads to new discoveries" (*Philologie romane*, p. 35). Spitzer similarly asserts that "the direct observation of concrete works helps us to discover characteristics of a poet that must remain hidden when whole works are treated in a general and summary fashion."[8] Jakobson insists that "any unbiased, attentive, exhaustive, total description of [the linguistic features of a text] surprises the examiner himself by unexpected, striking symmetries and asymmetries" (*Language in Literature*, p. 127).

Auerbach cautions his Turkish students that "one must consider only the text itself . . . ; one must read freshly, spontaneously and carefully and guard scrupulously against premature classifications" (*Philologie romane*, p. 36). One must also know what one is looking for. At the end of the introduction to his last, posthumously published book Auerbach quotes Augustine's "nonnulla enim pars inventionis est nosse quid quaeras." Earlier in the same introduction, which constitutes the fullest statement of his method, he declares that "I never approach a text as an isolated phenomenon; I address a question to it, and my question, not the text, is my primary point of departure." Auerbach explicitly distinguishes his textual analyses from those of Spitzer: "My purpose is always to write history."[9]

Auerbach's ten years in Istanbul as professor of Romance philology at the Turkish State University may have made him more sensitive to both the continuity and the ruptures in the European cultural tradition, although Hans Ulrich Gumbrecht is surely right in stressing that Auerbach's "passionate and distanced view of European culture" was formed before he left Germany.[10] The impact of Turkey on Auerbach was probably greater than its impact on Spitzer (who left Istanbul in 1936 to teach at Johns Hopkins), partly because Auerbach remained in Turkey for a much longer time, but primarily, I think, because his interest in literary works centered on discovering what they reveal about relationships between the individual and society in a particular time and place. Auerbach's experience in Turkey may have made him more sensitive to the interplay of continuity and change in cultural history, a feature that distinguishes his thought from that of Spitzer, and still more from that of Ernst Robert Curtius.

Auerbach was, of course, familiar with Rome before he emigrated to Turkey. I do not know whether or not he had visited Greece. Even if he had, Ephesus and Pergamon must have been a revelation; both give a more intense sense of the life of a whole Greek city than any site in Greece itself. Turkey is even richer in reminders that the Roman Empire extended far into Asia Minor. One is the great aqueduct of Valens in Istanbul, which stands only a few blocks away from the University where Auerbach taught. And there are also great monuments of Byzantine civilization like Haghia Sophia. Auerbach must have seen the marvelous mosaics in the church of Saint Savior in Chora, just outside the walls of Istanbul; he may have visited the cave churches of Cappadocia, where the frescoes recall those of Romanesque churches in western Europe. Both Haghia Sophia and the church at Chora were transformed into mosques; both are now state museums. Turkey offers many other striking examples both of the continuity of classical and postclassical civilization and of how one phase of civilization sometimes assimilates, sometimes transforms, and sometimes obliterates its predecessor.

Auerbach's experience in Turkey must have heightened his awareness of the speed with which a language, and with it a way of life, can change. His contract with the University required him to "make every effort" to learn Turkish and to prepare himself to lecture in the language after his first three years in Istanbul. He could not have failed to notice that virtually all aspects of modern life are designated in Turkish by words borrowed from a western language, usually French. One cannot walk down a street in a Turkish town without seeing signs offering goods and services named by French words respelled according to the conventions of the modern Turkish orthography imposed by Atatürk to replace the traditional Arabic script, which was a major obstacle to his efforts to increase literacy.

Atatürk's banning of the Arabic script marked a deliberate break with a rich cultural tradition, as did his attempts to outlaw the indiscriminate use of words and idioms borrowed from Arabic and Persian that had made the Ottoman literary language almost unintelligible to the vast majority of Turks who knew neither language. The break may have reminded Auerbach of the loss entailed by the decline of classical studies in the West. In a letter to Walter Benjamin of December 12, 1936, a few months after his arrival in Istanbul, he notes,

Here all traditions have been thrown overboard in an attempt to build a thoroughly rationalized state that will be both European and extremely Turconationalistic. The whole process is being carried out with a fantastic and unearthly speed [*es geht phantastisch und gespenstisch schnell*]; already it is hard to find anyone who can read Arabic or Persian or even Turkish texts written in the last century, since the language has been modernized and reoriented along purely Turkish lines and is now written in roman letters.[11]

Another letter to Benjamin, written a few weeks later, on January 3, 1937, gives further details. Auerbach finds Istanbul "wonderfully situated but unlovable and unwelcoming." "Atatürk and his Anatolian Turks" are "a naïve, mistrustful, honorable, somewhat awkward and boorish race," and Atatürk himself is "a likable autocrat, clever, generous, and witty, completely different from his European counterparts." But Auerbach notes also that Atatürk's program of Europeanization has brought about "a fanatically antitraditional nationalism: rejection of all existing Islamic cultural traditions [and] adherence to an imaginary purely Turkish origin [*Anknüpfung an ein phantastisches Urtürkentum*]":

The result is both an exaggerated nationalism and the destruction of the national character shaped by history. . . . The linguistic reform is both fantastically nationalistic [*phantastisch urtürkisch*], freeing the language from the impact of Arabic and Persian, and dedicated to the creation of new technical terms; no one under the age of twenty-five can read a literary, philosophical or religious text more than ten years old and the individual character of the language is rapidly being destroyed by the introduction of the Latin alphabet, which was made compulsory a few years ago. . . . It is becoming increasingly clear to me that the present political situation is nothing more than a stratagem of providence to lead us down a gory and tormenting road toward an *Internationale* of triviality and to Esperanto culture. I had already suspected this in Germany and Italy . . . but here I have become almost certain of it.[12]

Auerbach's firsthand experience of Atatürk's attempt to transform his country into a modern secular state may have contributed to his pessimism about the rapidly increasing uniformity of twentieth-century civilization reflected more than a dozen years later in his essay "Philologie der Weltliteratur."[13]

For Roman Jakobson, "the main subject of poetics is the *differentia specifica* of verbal art in relation to other arts and in relation to other kinds of verbal behavior" (*Language in Literature*, p. 63). This specific difference is the dominance of what Jakobson calls "the aesthetic function," though he recognizes that "just as a poetic work is not exhausted by its aesthetic function, similarly the aesthetic function is not limited to poetic works" (p. 43). Both Spitzer and Jakobson sometimes study the literary devices used in nonliterary texts. Spitzer analyzes a poster for *Sunkist* orange juice in "American Advertising Explained as Popular Art"; Jakobson examines the relationship between form and meaning in the campaign slogan "I like Ike."[14] Their practice is quite different from that of Auerbach, for whom the language of both literary and nonliterary texts is a key to the conception of everyday reality in a particular time and place.

In his *History of Modern Criticism*, René Wellek observes that Auerbach "mingles passages from poetry, drama, and novels with passages from histories, memoirs, chronicles, essays, personal letters, and critical manifestos. The limits of literature as fiction are constantly overstepped." Wellek acknowledges that Auerbach's refusal to limit his account to works of imaginative literature is deliberate and that *Mimesis* is not "literary history—does not even pretend to be—but a history of man's attitude toward reality and existence."[15]

Auerbach's preoccupation with man's place in a particular society extends throughout his career. In the preface to his doctoral dissertation in Romance philology, he notes that, while tragedy and epic deal directly with God and destiny,

in the novella the subject is always society [*die Gesellschaft*], and its object is therefore the form of earthly life [*Diesseitigkeit*] we call culture. The novella does not seek a ground or essence but the concrete; it therefore presupposes a closed circle of individuals who have achieved a well-defined place in society and take an interest in recognizing and judging themselves. Thus the novella always takes place in time and space; it is a piece of history, though it is [in Friedrich Schlegel's words] "a history that, strictly speaking, is not a part of history, and brings with it a predisposition to irony."[16]

Auerbach's concentration on an individual's relationship to society rather than on more abstract or metaphysical issues distinguishes his work from that of Georges Poulet. Wellek observes that a reader of Poulet's *L'Espace proustien*, which he considers "a particularly successful example" of his work, "would hardly have any idea of the Balzacian social picture" developed at such length in Proust's novel, which is "reduced to a series of memories and abstractions."[17]

Auerbach also differs from Poulet in that he does not seek to identify with the writers he studies. His position is closer to that of the nineteenth-century classical scholar August Boeckh, for whom the goal of philology "is the task of reproducing all that alien thought so that it becomes mine. . . . At the same time, however, the task of philology is to *dominate* what it has thus reproduced . . . for only then can I assign it a place in my own thought, which is an act of judgment."[18] Auerbach insists that "it is a grave mistake to suppose that historical relativism results in an eclectic incapacity for judgment" (*Literary Language*, p. 20).

Both in *Mimesis* and in the introduction to *Literary Language* Auerbach sets forth the principles that govern his practice of literary history. He does so, however, almost wholly without reference to his own life, although he acknowledges that "my own experience, and by that I mean not merely my scholarly experience, is responsible for the choice of problems, the starting points, the reasoning and the intention expressed in my writings" (*Literary Language*, p. 22; I substitute "scholarly" for Manheim's "scientific" [*wissenschaftlich*]. Auerbach published no autobiographical essays like Leo Spitzer's "Linguistics and Literary History" and "The Development of a Method," both reprinted in *Representative Essays*, or Jakobson's account of his own career in interviews with his wife Krystyna Pomorska.[19] Many readers have nevertheless noted the strongly personal tone of Auerbach's scholarly writing, though it suggests a personality very different from the exuberance of Spitzer or Jakobson. In the classroom, too, Auerbach was far less charismatic than either of his great contemporaries. His reticence in writing about himself, however, never suggests that he is unsure of his purpose or that he doubts the validity of his method. If his work seems more personal than that of Spitzer or Jakobson, the reason is perhaps that he addresses his reader not as an academic specialist but as an individual human being. Like Montaigne, Auerbach knows that "every kind of specialization falsifies the moral picture; it presents us in but one of our roles."[20] In this he differs from Spitzer, who often invites his reader, a specialist like himself, to judge a quarrel with a rival specialist, and also from Jakobson, whose interest in a problem often lies in the possibilities it offers for further research, whether by Jakobson himself or by others.

Louis O. Mink remarks that whereas "scientists can note each other's results, historians must read each other's books." The reason is that "the significant conclusions of historical arguments are embedded or incorporated in the narrative structure of historical writing itself" and cannot be detached from it or even stated as propositions.[21] Auerbach seems to have shared this conviction. At the end of the introduction to *Literary Language*, he observes that "I should like [my book] to be read as a whole, and with that in mind I have tried to make its form as inviting as possible." He insists that his book "is a fragment or rather a series of fragments. It lacks even the loose but always perceptible unity of *Mimesis*" (*Literary Language*, pp. 23–24). Auerbach must have wanted readers of *Mimesis*, too, to read it as a whole, though I suspect that few readers actually do so. It is a very oddly organized book. Auerbach uses the terms "realism" and "reality" repeatedly throughout, but the special sense he gives to the representation of reality (*dargestellte Wirklichkeit*) is made explicit only toward the end of the book. His "Epilogue" to *Mimesis* contains material most other scholars would have placed in an introduction or preface.

Most of the texts Auerbach discusses do not exemplify his conception of the representation of everyday reality, which he gradually defines by making clear what it is not. Thus, he notes that "the riches of [Rabelais's] style are not without their limits; the grotesque frame in itself excludes deep feeling and high tragedy. . . . Hence it might be doubted whether he has rightfully been given a place in our study, since *what we are tracing is the combination of the everyday with tragic seriousness*" (*Mimesis*, p. 282; my emphasis). Again, he concedes that "there is no denying the presence, in many of [Voltaire's] works, of colorful, vivid, *everyday reality*. But it is incomplete, consciously simplified, and hence — despite the serious didactic purpose — nonchalant and superficial" (p. 411; my emphasis). *Mimesis* resists summary because each text is shown to be interesting in its own right, even though most of them fail to meet Auerbach's criteria for the serious representation of everyday reality. His book is not a history of repeated failures, but of the most varied kinds of literary success. Robert Alter argues that most serious fiction presents "an intent, verisimilar representation of moral situations in their social contexts."[22] *Mimesis* shows what a late development this is and helps us to understand earlier works—*Gargantua et Pantagruel, Don Quixote, Candide*—that have quite different claims to our attention.

Auerbach insists in *Mimesis* that he "could never have written anything in the nature of a history of European realism. . . . As opposed to this I see the possibility of success and profit in a method which consists in letting myself be guided by a few motifs which I have worked out gradually and without a specific purpose." He is confident that the essential characteristics he discerns in the history of representations of everyday reality "must be demonstrable in any random realistic text [*jedem beliebigen realistischen Text*]" (*Mimesis*, p. 548). Elsewhere in the book Auerbach cites Stendhal's "je prends au hasard ce qui se trouve sur ma route" and observes that "this method, as Montaigne knew, is the best for eliminating the arbitrariness of one's own constructions, and for surrendering oneself to reality as given" (pp. 462–63).

Auerbach notes that for Montaigne "Know Thyself is not only a pragmatic and moral precept but an epistemological precept too. . . . In his study of his own random life [*des beliebigen eigenen Lebens*] Montaigne's sole aim is an investigation of the *humaine condition* in general; and with that he reveals the heuristic principle which we constantly employ . . . when we endeavor to understand and judge the acts of others" (*Mimesis*, p. 301). The *random* events of Montaigne's life, like the *random* realistic texts examined in *Mimesis*, yield insights into the human condition only if we interpret them in the light of our own experience: "*Mirer sa vie dans celle d'autrui*: in these words [of Montaigne] lies the complete method of an activity which sets itself the goal of understanding the actions or thoughts of others" (pp. 302–3).

One reason *Mimesis* appeals to many readers who are not otherwise attracted to literary criticism is that Auerbach's true subject is not texts but the lives of individuals, both the authors of the texts he examines and the men and women who figure in the texts. Sometimes he shifts almost imperceptibly from author to character or character to author, or treats both at once, as in his presentation of the merchant Dindenault,

a choleric and pompous person [who] is endowed with the crafty, idiomatic, and subtle wit which is natural to almost all of Rabelais' personages. . . . Rabelais has, as usual, stuffed [Dindenault's speech] with the most various and grotesque erudition . . . and adorned [it], as usual, with mythology, medicine, and strange alchemical lore. Yet this time the center of interest does not lie in the multifarious outpouring of ideas which come to Dindenault in his praise of sheep, it lies in the copious portrait which he gives of his own character. . . . He perishes because . . . in his blind folly and vaingloriousness, he runs straight forward, like Picrochole or the *écolier limousin*, his one-track mind incapable of registering his surroundings. . . . Thick-headedness, inability to adjust, one-track arrogance which blinds a man to the complexity of the real situation, are vices to Rabelais. (pp. 274–75)

Auerbach's reluctance to define his conception of realism, often remarked by students of his work, reflects his wish that he had been able to write a book "without any general expressions."[23] It helps to explain his insistence that "to describe [Rabelais's intellectual attitude] more in detail is not a wise undertaking — for one would immediately find oneself forced into competition with Rabelais. He himself is constantly describing it, and he can do it better than we can" (*Mimesis*, p. 281).

The same refusal to summarize complex issues in a word or phrase is evident in Auerbach's treatment of "the difficult question . . . : what is the 'something' which orders the whole [of *Don Quixote*] and makes it appear in a definite, 'Cervantean' light?" Auerbach begins his answer with a series of negations: "It is not a philosophy; it is no didactic purpose; it is not even a being stirred by the uncertainty of human existence, as in the case of Montaigne and Shakespeare. It is an attitude . . . in which bravery and equanimity play a major part" (*Mimesis*, p. 355). One is tempted to say that Auerbach never really defines this attitude and that the remaining pages of the essay veer off in a different direction, or in several different ones; a more careful reading may suggest that these pages, which could not be summed up in a brief formula, are themselves the promised definition.

The same insistence on examining phenomena in all their complexity may explain why Auerbach, unlike Spitzer or Jakobson, never defines a writer by his use of a single linguistic feature. Spitzer constantly seeks "a common denominator for all or most of [a writer's] deviations" from the usage of his contemporaries. He finds this "common spiritual etymon" or "psychological root" in such features as Charles-Louis Philippe's frequent use of the phrase *à cause de*, which Spitzer calls "pseudo-objective motivation" and considers "the clue to Philippe's *Weltanschauung*; he sees the world functioning wrongly with an appearance of rightness, of objective logic" (*Representative Essays*, pp. 13–16). Spitzer interprets Cervantes's fondness for "polyonomasia (and polyetymologia)" in *Don Quixote* as evidence that "perspectivism informs the structure of the novel as a whole: we find it in Cervantes's treatment of the plot, of ideological themes, as well in his attitude of distantiation toward the reader" (*Representative Essays*, p. 225).[24] Jakobson, too, believed that a single dominant linguistic trait can hold the key to a writer's work. In Pasternak's *Safe Conduct*, "we learn what he lives on, this lyric hero outlined by metonymies, split up by synecdoches into individual attributes, reactions, and situations. . . . But the truly heroic element, the hero's activity, eludes our perception; action is replaced by topography" (*Language in Literature*, p. 313). Nevertheless, one must not exaggerate the difference between their work, particularly Spitzer's, and Auerbach's. A sentence like this one from Auerbach's chapter on Rabelais would be perfectly at home in one of Spitzer's essays: "Our analysis has permitted us . . . to recognize an essential principle of [Rabelais's] manner of seeing and comprehending the world: the principle of the promiscuous intermingling of the categories of event, experience, and knowledge, as well as of dimensions and styles" (*Mimesis*, p. 272).

Auerbach might have justified his practice by appealing to the authority of Montaigne, who remarks that "even good authors are wrong to insist on fashioning a consistent and solid fabric out of us. They choose one general characteristic, and go and arrange and interpret all a man's actions to fit their picture. . . . He who would judge them in detail and distinctly, bit by bit, would more often hit upon the truth."[25] But if Auerbach is wary of definitions and summary formulations, he is generous with descriptions that typically embrace both form and content. His treatment of tempo, a term he does not define, in Voltaire and Rabelais offers a splendid example. He says of Voltaire: "Especially his own is his tempo. His rapid, keen summary of the development, his quick shifting of scenes, his surprisingly sudden confronting of things which are not usually seen together — in all this he comes close to being unique and incomparable. . . . Voltaire's tempo is part of his philosophy" (*Mimesis*, pp. 405–6). Rabelais's tempo is equally rapid, but quite different: he "purposely jumble[s] together all the categories of style and knowledge," while Voltaire always retains "the pleasing clarity, *l'agréable et le fin*" of seventeenth-century French classicism (*Mimesis*, pp. 273, 406).

Not surprisingly, Auerbach is especially attracted to such writers as Montaigne, whose subject is always "his own *random* life" and Saint-Simon, who "knows how to use the *random* and idiosyncratic [*dem beliebig Einzelnen*], the unselected, . . . as points of departure for sudden descents into the depths of human existence" (*Mimesis*, pp. 301, 432; my emphasis). Auerbach's own gift for assessing character is comparable to that of the two French masters; one may say of him, as René Wellek says of Paul Valéry, that "every artist recommends the art he himself practices." [26] Saint-Simon's pell-mell accumulation of physical and psychological details, which Auerbach analyzes with exemplary precision, is nonetheless wholly unlike his own calm and orderly exposition. Auerbach makes us want to read or reread Saint-Simon. He is enthusiastic about the authors he studies, not, as we sometimes feel when reading Spitzer or Jakobson, about the way he himself studies them.

Most of all, of course, Auerbach's interpretations of individual texts differ from those of Spitzer or Jakobson in that they do not stand alone but form part of a narrative history of one aspect of western literature from Homer to Virginia Woolf. *Mimesis* is an odd sort of historical account, but it is not merely a series of individual explications arranged in the chronological order of the texts studied. There are many reminders, only some of which are explicit, that we have met a particular phenomenon before or that we shall come across it again. Auerbach does not attempt to account for every feature of his texts although he often tells us much more than the minimum necessary to show how they fit into his scheme. Other texts might have been chosen; Auerbach's fine essay on *Les Fleurs du mal* would require only a little adjustment to make it fit smoothly into his account of nineteenth-century realism.[27] One may argue that Auerbach misinterprets a particular text without damaging *Mimesis* as a whole; to do that one would need to show that no other text of the same period fits the description of the one he has chosen to represent it. Conversely, one may question his historical account of the representation of everyday reality in literature while recognizing the excellence of many or even most of his interpretations of individual texts.

Kevin Brownlee, in his contribution to this volume, observes that Auerbach's literary history is teleological and built on a modified Hegelian model: "An ideology of progress is built into this model, with the nineteenth-century 'realistic' French novel serving as a provisional endpoint, and a hypothetical perfect mimesis situated in an elusive but attainable future period as the ideal endpoint of literary history."[28] I think it may be argued, however, that nineteenth-century French realism is not the first but the second peak in Auerbach's chart of the rise of representations of everyday reality. It is much less complete than Dante's realism, which offers a view of earthly life in all its political and social complexity and completes it with an ethics, cosmology, and metaphysics. No such view is attainable today, even for those who share Dante's Catholic faith, and Auerbach gives no reason to suppose that one will arise in the future.

Auerbach's conception of western history cannot easily be classified as either tragic or comic, though it is surely much closer to the first. A more complete representation in literature of some aspects of everyday reality is now possible, but it falls far short of Dante's achievement, which rests on bases neither Auerbach nor most of our contemporaries can accept. The tragic aspect of Auerbach's view of history is that Dante's unity has been replaced by another kind that erases the individually inadequate but infinitely varied representations of reality examined in *Mimesis*. In doing so it destroys something Auerbach considers of supreme value, the conception of history he learned from Vico, which offers "a possibility of 'modifications' within ourselves" (*eine Möglichkeit von uns selbst*) (*Literary Language*, p. 12). Auerbach develops this point, touched on in the reference to *Esperantokultur* in his letter to Benjamin, in "Philologie der Weltliteratur": "The history of the last millennia, which treat philology as a historical discipline, is the history of man's achievement of self expression. . . . It offers a spectacle whose depth and fullness stimulate all the beholder's powers and enable him, through the enrichment it offers, to accept his own situation. The loss of this spectacle, which becomes accessible only when presented and interpreted, would be an impoverishment for which nothing could compensate us."[29]

Reference Matter

Notes

Lerer, "Introduction"

1. Erich Auerbach, *Mimesis: The Representation of Reality in Western Literature*, trans. Willard R. Trask (Princeton, N.J.: Princeton University Press, 1953), pp. 19–20. In the original German, the passage reads: "Nun ist der Unterschied zwischen Sage und Geschichte für einen etwas erfahrenen Leser in den meisten Fällen leicht zu entdecken. So schwer es ist, und so sorgfältiger historisch-philologischer Ausbildung es bedarf, um innerhalb eines geschichtlichen Berichts das Wahre vom Gefälschten oder einseitig Beleuchteten zu unterscheiden, so leicht ist es im allgemeinen, Sage und Geschichte überhaupt auseinanderzuhalten. . . . Geschichte zu schreiben ist so schwierig, daß die meisten Geschichtsschreiber genötigt sind, Konzessionen an die Sagentechnik zu machen" (*Mimesis: dargestellte Wirklichkeit in der abendländischen Literatur* [Bern: A Francke, 1946], pp. 24–25).

2. "Wer etwa das Verhalten der einzelnen Menschen und Menschengruppen beim Aufkommen des Nationalsozialismus in Deutschland, oder das Verhalten der einzelnen Völker und Staaten vor und während des gegenwärtigen (1942) Krieges erwägt, der wird fühlen, wie schwer darstellbar geschichtliche Gegenstände überhaupt, und wie unbrauchbar sie für die Sage sind" (*Mimesis*, p. 25).

3. In addition to the reviews of scholarship and criticism contained in the essays in this volume, see Jan Ziolkowski's survey of the large bibliography on Auerbach in his foreword to the paperback reprinting of *Literary Language and Its Public in Late Latin Antiquity and in the Middle Ages*, trans. Ralph Manheim (Princeton, N.J.: Princeton University Press, 1993), pp. ix–xxxii, with a comprehensive listing of works cited on pp. xxxiii–xxxix.

4. On Spitzer, see Alban Forcione, Herbert Lindenberger, and Madeline Sutherland, eds., *Leo Spitzer: Representative Essays* (Stanford, Calif.: Stanford University Press, 1988), especially John Freccero's sensitive foreword on Spit-

zer as teacher (pp. xi–xx). Spitzer and Auerbach are often paired in the
impressions of midcentury German émigré medievalists. See, for example,
the reflections of Paul Zumthor: "The work of the gentle Auerbach, with
his large eyes and his expression of timid goodness, marked a generation,
otherwise but no less than the work of the brilliant Spitzer, that great con-
versationalist, self-confident and beloved by women" (*Speaking of the Middle
Ages*, trans. Sarah White, [Lincoln: University of Nebraska Press, 1985], p. 21).
See, too, Harry Levin, "Two *Romanisten* in America," in Donald Fleming and
Bernard Bailyn, eds., *The Intellectual Migration: Europe and America, 1930–1960*
(Cambridge, Mass.: Harvard University Press, 1969), pp. 467–83. On Spitzer
and Auerbach, see Geoffrey Green, *Literary Criticism and the Structures of His-
tory: Erich Auerbach and Leo Spitzer* (Lincoln: University of Nebraska Press,
1982). For a discussion of Auerbach's response to Curtius's *European Litera-
ture and the Latin Middle Ages* in his "Philologie der Weltliteratur" of 1952, see
Paul Bové, *Intellectuals in Power: A Genealogy of Critical Humanism* (New York:
Columbia University Press, 1986), pp. 205–6. For an amusing anecdote about
Auerbach's encounter with Curtius in Princeton in 1949, related as an icon of
their respective scholarly and emotional personalities, see Robert Fitzgerald,
Enlarging the Change: The Princeton Seminars in Literary Criticism 1949–1951 (Boston:
Northeastern University Press, 1985), pp. 21–22.

    5. While there is, to my knowledge, no full-length biography of Auerbach,
a brief sketch of his life and a bibliography of his works may be found in Ziolkowski's foreword to *Literary Language and Its Public*, and in the chronology
appended to the book, pp. 393–407. An impressionistic account of Auerbach's
institutional wanderings begins Luiz Costa-Lima's "Erich Auerbach: History
and Metahistory," *New Literary History* 19 (1988): 467–68. Hans-Ulrich Gumbrecht's contribution to this volume, "'Pathos of the Earthly Progress': Erich
Auerbach's Everydays," marks an important and revisionary approach to the
relationship between Auerbach's life and work.

    6. "La philologie est l'ensemble des activités qui s'occupent méthodique-
ment du langage de l'homme, et des oeuvres d'art composées dans ce langage. . . . Le besoin de constituer des textes authentiques se fait sentir quand
un peuple d'une haute civilisation prend conscience de cette civilisation, et
qu'il veut préserver des ravages du temps les oeuvres qui constituent son patrimoine spirituel" (Auerbach, *Introduction aux études de philologie romane* [Frankfurt
am Main: Vittorio Klostermann, 1949], p. 9, translated by Suzanne Fleischman).

    7. Among the many recent reassessments of the history of Romance phi-
lology in Europe, see in particular Hans-Ulrich Gumbrecht, "'Un Souffle
d'Allemagne ayant passé': Friedrich Diez, Gaston Paris, and the Genesis of
National Philologies," *Romance Philology* 40 (1986): 1–37 (with a full bibliogra-

phy of primary and secondary sources). The January 1990 issue of *Speculum* (volume 65) is devoted to "The New Philology" and contains several essays relevant to the analysis sketched here: Stephen G. Nichols, "Introduction: Philology in a Manuscript Culture," pp. 1–10; R. Howard Bloch, "New Philology and Old French," pp. 38–58; Lee Patterson, "On the Margin: Postmodernism, Ironic History, and Medieval Studies," pp. 87–108.

8. From Diez's remarks on his candidacy for a lectureship at the University of Bonn, quoted in Gumbrecht, " 'Un Souffle,' " p. 18.

9. From the opening of Aubertin's *Histoire de la langue et de la littérature française au moyen age d'après les travaux le plus récents*, quoted in Gumbrecht, " 'Un Souffle,' " pp. 26–27.

10. For a chronicle of these attempts, see Gumbrecht, " 'Un Souffle,' " and Bloch, "New Philology and Old French."

11. On the agendas of Franco-German philology in the nineteenth and twentieth centuries, see the studies cited above. For the responses of postwar American New Criticism, see Bové, *Intellectuals in Power*, especially pp. 106–7. For a history of the *Grundriß der romanischen Literaturen des Mittelalters* and the larger context of postwar German philology, see Hans-Ulrich Gumbrecht, "Tenacious Semen: The Sad and Weary History of the *Grundriss der romanischen Literaturen des Mittelalters*," in R. Howard Bloch and Stephen G. Nichols, eds., *Medievalism and the Modernist Temper: On the Discipline of Medieval Studies* (Stanford, Calif.: Stanford University Press, 1994). On the changing canons of professional training in medieval studies, see Lee Patterson, *Negotiating the Past: The Historical Study of Medieval Literature* (Madison: University of Wisconsin Press, 1987), pp. 3–74, and Allen J. Frantzen, *Desire for Origins: New Language, Old English, and Teaching the Tradition* (New Brunswick, N.J.: Rutgers University Press, 1990).

12. See, for example, the discussions in Luiz Costa-Lima, "Erich Auerbach: History and Metahistory"; Thomas M. DePietro, "Literary Criticism as History: The Example of Auerbach's *Mimesis*," *Clio* 8 (1979): 377–87; W. Wolfgang Holdheim, "Auerbach's *Mimesis*: Aesthetics as Historical Understanding," *Clio* 10 (1981): 143–54; and the treatment of Bové, *Intellectuals in Power*, pp. 131–208. See, too, Edward Said, *Beginnings: Intention and Method* (Baltimore: Johns Hopkins University Press, 1975), pp. 68–70. "Philologie der Weltliteratur" appeared originally in *Weltliteratur, Festgabe für Fritz Strich* (Bern: A Francke, 1952), and has been translated as "Philology and *Weltliteratur*," by Marie and Edward Said in *The Centennial Review* 13 (1969): 1–17. "Epilegomena zu *Mimesis*" appeared in *Romanische Forschungen* 65 (1953): 1–18. *Dante als Dichter des irdischen Welt* (Berlin: Walter de Gruyter, 1929), has been translated by Ralph Manheim as *Dante, Poet of the Secular World* (Chicago: University of Chicago Press, 1961).

13. "Philology and *Weltliteratur*," p. 5.

14. *Literary Language and Its Public*, pp. 114–19.

15. *Mimesis*, trans. Trask, pp. 183–84.

16. Ibid., pp. 525–53, especially the remarks on p. 536.

17. The idea of "sermo humilis" is developed in the discussion of Augustine in *Mimesis*, pp. 66–74, in the essay "Sermo humilis," *Romanische Forschungen* 64 (1952): 304–64, and in the first essay of *Literary Language and Its Public*, pp. 25–66. The concept of figura and the idea of figural interpretation form the spine of many of the readings of the Late Antique and medieval texts in *Mimesis* (see the account in chap. 7, "Adam and Eve," esp. pp. 156–62, and in chap. 8, "Farinata and Cavalcante," esp. pp. 194–202) and has also been widely disseminated in the translation of the essay "Figura," originally published in *Archivum Romanicum* 22 (1938), by Ralph Manheim in *Scenes from the Drama of European Literature* (New York: Meridian Books, 1959). For some reconsiderations of the utility of both of these sets of classifications, see the essays by Brownlee, White, and Lerer in this volume.

18. *Literary Language and Its Public*, p. 255. For a review of early medieval literary culture and cultural literacy that develops these observations, see Franz Bäuml, "Varieties and Consequences of Medieval Literacy and Illiteracy," *Speculum* 55 (1980): 237–65.

19. See, for example, Timothy Bahti, "Vico, Auerbach, and Literary History," in Giogrio Tagliacozzo, ed., *Vico Past and Present* (Atlantic Highlands, N.J.: Humanities Press, 1981), pp. 249–66, and his discussion of Auerbach in *Allegories of History* (Baltimore: Johns Hopkins University Press, 1992); Said, *Beginnings*, p. 363 (who calls Auerbach "Vico's principal and most profound literary student"); and Costa-Lima, "Erich Auerbach," pp. 469–85.

20. For such a chronicle, see Bové, *Intellectuals in Power*, pp. 79–208.

21. *Intellectuals in Power*, pp. 96–113.

22. One exception to this dehistoricized *Mimesis* among the early reviews is René Wellek, "Auerbach's Special Realism," *Kenyon Review* 16 (1954): 299–306. For a detailed reconsideration of the early reviews of *Mimesis*, see Lindenberger's essay in this volume.

23. *Romance Philology* 2 (1949): 338.

24. Robert Fitzgerald, *Enlarging the Change*, p. 15. Fitzgerald's account, while published in 1985, is based on reports he prepared at the time of the original seminars, and its tone reproduces the clubroom atmosphere of Princeton in the 1940's.

25. For a personal account of the German émigré intelligentsia in Istanbul during the war, see Liselotte Dieckmann, "Akademische Emigranten in der Türkei," in Egon Schwarz and Matthias Wegner, eds., *Verbannung: Aufzeichnungen deutscher Schriftsteller im Exil* (Hamburg: Christian Wegner, 1964), pp. 122–26.

26. From Gerhard Hess, *"Mimesis:* Zu Erich Auerbachs Geschichte des abendländischen Realismus," *Romanische Forschungen* 60 (1948): 173–211, who assessed the overall effect of reading *Mimesis:* "Der Leser lebt in einer wohltuend humanen Atmosphäre" (p. 174).

27. Bové, *Intellectuals in Power,* and Bahti, *Allegories of History: Literary Historiography after Hegel* (Baltimore: Johns Hopkins University Press, 1982).

28. Ziolkowski, foreword to *Literary Language and Its Public,* pp. xxvi–xxvii.

29. Michael Holquist, "The Last European: Erich Auerbach as Precursor in the History of Cultural Criticism," *Modern Language Quarterly* 54 (1993): 373.

30. Ibid., p. 390.

Gumbrecht, " 'Pathos of the Earthly Progress' "

In its original version, this essay was a contribution to the colloquium on "The Legacy of Erich Auerbach," held at Stanford University in October 1992. I want to thank Seth Lerer, the organizer of the Stanford conference, for his encouragement and advice, and R. Howard Bloch, Luiz Costa-Lima, Thomas Hart, Steven Nichols, and Hayden White for criticism and important suggestions. The description of the German intellectual environment during the 1920's greatly profited from remarks by Judith Butler and David Wellbery, who heard my Auerbach paper at The Johns Hopkins University in December 1992. It will not relativize my gratitude to these colleagues, however, if I emphasize that by far the most important contribution to my research was a number of long conversations with Erich Auerbach's son Clemens. For the documentary basis of my work, I received invaluable help from Inge Auerbach (who is not related to Erich Auerbach's family!) at the Hessisches Staatsarchiv Marburg, from U. Bredehorn (Handschriftenabteilung der Universitätsbibliothek Marburg), Andreas Mahal (Landesarchiv Berlin), Mr. Klauss (Geheimes Staatsarchiv / Preussischer Kulturbesitz Berlin), Eva Ziesche (Staatsbibliothek zu Berlin / Preussischer Kulturbesitz), Carola Schmidt (Bibliothek der Humboldt-Universität zu Berlin), Christian Velder (Französisches Gymnasium Berlin), Gerhild Atze (Universitätsbibliothek Greifswald), Mr. Herling (Universitätsarchiv Greifswald), Christian Renger (Archivleiter der Universitätsbibliothek Heidelberg), and William R. Massa, Jr. (Public Services Archivist at the Yale University Library). Karlheinz Barck (Berlin), and Wolf-Dieter Stempel (Munich) shared important Auerbach letters with me. My friend Paul Rottmann and my father Hanni Gumbrecht provided me with a copy of Auerbach's (difficult to obtain) legal dissertation. Last but not least, I want to thank Melissa Goldman for editing my original text.

1. The role of "philologist" seems to have been Auerbach's favorite—and ultimately successful—form of self-presentation. During the Stanford colloquium in October 1992 and through my own research, I have become increas-

ingly convinced that it rather fits his deliberately modest personal style than his true intellectual profile.

2. The Latin meaning of "Clemens," the name of Erich Auerbach's only son, appears to be emblematic for the dominant tonality in his private life and in the presentation of his work.

3. For the history of the concept "everyday life," see my essay " 'Alltagswelt' und 'Lebenswelt' als philosophische Begriffe: Eine genealogische Untersuchung," in Thomas Kniesche, ed., *Deutsche Intellektuelle in Kalifornien* (forthcoming).

4. *Literatursprache und Publikum in der lateinischen Spätantike und im Mittelalter* (Bern: Francke, 1958), p. 14.

5. See Erich Auerbach, "Epilegomena zu Mimesis": "I call that realism which was unknown to the classical antiquity serious, problematizing, or tragical—and I explicitly set it into contrast with 'moralist' realism. Perhaps I should have called it 'existential realism,' but I was reluctant to use this all-too-contemporary expression for phenomena of a remote past" (*Romanische Forschungen* 65 [1953]: 4).

6. Clemens Auerbach supposes that their contact was established through his aunt, who was more familiar with Jewish intellectual circles in Berlin than Erich Auerbach.

7. See Walter Benjamin, *Gesammelte Schriften*. VII/1 (Frankfurt, 1989), p. 515.

8. Karlheinz Barck, ed., "Fünf Briefe Erich Auerbachs an Walter Benjamin in Paris," *Zeitschrift für Germanistik* 6 (1988): 689–90.

9. In general, Auerbach's seminars and *Vorlesungen* as they were announced in the course programs of the University of Marburg between the years 1929–30 and 1935–36 appear rather conventional. The fact that some of them were directly related to his contemporary research interests is typical for the German academic principle of maintaining a "unity of research and teaching."

10. The position of the *Universitätskurator* was equivalent to that of the provost at American universities. Although von Hülsen, after being removed from his office in 1933, joined the National Socialist Party (which certainly contributed to his restoration as *Universitätskurator*), Auerbach and other Jewish professors appreciated the conservative—and therefore comparatively liberal—style of his administration. See Klaus Ewald, "Ernst von Hülsen (1875–1950)/Kurator der Philipps-Universität," in Ingeborg Schnack, ed., *Marburger Gelehrte in der ersten Hälfte des 20, Jahrhunderts* (Marburg, 1977), pp. 210–18.

11. Hessisches Staatsarchiv Best. 310, acc. 1978/15, no. 2261. Personalakte Professor Dr. Erich Auerbach. Bd. 2. 1936–66.

12. Friedrich Schürr, who was born in Vienna in 1888, had not reached the rank of full professor at Graz. After his appointment at Marburg, where he

became *Prorektor* of the university between 1937 and 1939, he enjoyed a very successful career which brought him to Cologne in 1940, to Strasburg (as codirector of the *Petrarca-Haus*) in 1941, and to Tübingen during the winter 1944–45. Schürr was not reappointed to a regular professorship after the end of World War II. See Inge Auerbach, *Catalogus professorum academiae Marburgensis* (Marburg, 1979), 2:607–8.

13. Barck, ed., "Fünf Briefe Erich Auerbachs an Walter Benjamin in Paris," p. 690.

14. See my article "Karl Vosslers noble Einsamkeit: Über die Ambivalenzen der 'inneren Emigration'" in R. Geissler and W. Popp, eds., *Wissenschaft und Nationalsozialismus* (Essen, 1988), pp. 275–98.

15. *Privatdozenten* have the right of independent teaching, which, in the German academic tradition, is a prerequisite for the appointment to a professorship. Without necessarily implying a remunerated employment, this status is acquired through the procedure of the *Habilitation* whose core element is the judgment of a senior faculty committee on a second book manuscript and on a public lecture. Rumor has it that Krauss was about to leave Marburg on the morning before his *Habilitationsvorlesung* on April 30, 1932, and could only be convinced to deliver this lecture by Auerbach's last-minute intervention (see the documents concerning Krauss's *Habilitation* and further academic career in Marburg, Hessisches Staatsarchiv 307 d, acc. 1966/10, no. 141 a/b). In a letter to his mentor Vossler from June 22, 1931 (Bayerische Staatsbibliothek, Ana 350, 12A), Krauss describes the beginning of his "Marburg adventure" in very self-critical terms and emphasizes that "Auerbach's friendliness and great human support are absolutely on the positive side of my account."

16. See the documents on Krauss in the Hessisches Staatsarchiv and at the Bundesarchiv Koblenz (M 996 A 7).

17. See Regina Griebel, Marlies Coburger, and Heinrich Scheel, eds., *Erfasst? Das Gestapo-Album zur Roten Kapelle, Eine Foto-Dokumentation* (Berlin, 1992), pp. 260–61. Krauss's student Karlheinz Barck has analyzed the documents of this trial: Werner Krauss im Widerstand und vor dem Reichskriegsgerichtshof. Ms. Berlin 1992. The file of the Krauss/Vossler correspondence at the Bayerische Staatsbibliothek contains three letters that Krauss sent to his former academic teacher from the prison for death candidates in Plötzensee. The first of these letters was written on January 20, 1943, two days after the end of Krauss's trial: "For a long time I have felt an urgent necessity to write you, but in the meantime—I don't know whether the rumor has reached you—a dark current has taken possession of myself, and it now carries me away so far that I have to say farewell. The memory of your teaching and your awakening, of your example and your friendship, is penetrating into the reign of ghosts, and while I am taking this last step, I thus remain one of those who

can only thank you by continuing to accept your gifts. . . . For the realization of all your great projects I wish you the confidence of those who give joy and light in the darkness of misery; the time of future generations will be yours at any rate. In thankful friendship and admiration, I remain he who was yours, Werner Krauss."

18. One of them was the Anglicist Max Deutschbein who, in 1930, had officially complained about a lack of "German spirit" in Auerbach's *Habilitationsschrift*. Barck supposes that Ernst Robert Curtius and Karl Vossler participated in the initiative.

19. According to Thea Gumbrecht, who was Kretschmer's (enthusiastic) student during the 1940's.

20. Kretschmer's letter is part of the Krauss file at the Hessisches Staatsarchiv.

21. An impressive document for the bankruptcy of the traditional "humanistic" discourse is a letter of congratulation on the occasion of Krauss's marriage written on June 6, 1945, by Dean Ebbinghaus, who had continued in his office after the end of the war: "Only very late it dawned on me that the dramatic events around your person were but a chapter of a novel. And if I see this novel from the perspective of its future readers, I understand once more how much all bureaucratic matters have to remain on the bare surface of human existence. Now that the knot is untied, you seem to be at a stage of your life which, at a mature age, can only be reached by those whose entire existence has been at stake; you are entering a chapter of your life where everything is new, free from the past, and full of hope. For the voyage on this sea of your future which no ship has yet undertaken, please receive, together with your wife, my very best wishes."

22. In Hessisches Staatsarchiv Best. 310, acc. 1978/15, no. 2261. A handwritten remark on Auerbach's letter seems to indicate that it was directly taken to his file without being submitted to the *Rektor*.

23. See Horst Widmann, *Exil und Bildungshilfe: Die deutschsprachige akademische Emigration in die Türkei nach 1933* (Bern: Herbert Lang, 1973).

24. Auerbach's lawyer indeed visited the dean's office at Marburg (on December 28, 1936), as a remark on his calling card in the Auerbach file at the Hessisches Staatsarchiv shows. The calling card reads "Dr jur. Carl Haensel. Rechtsanwalt und Notar. Berlin W 15. Kurfürstendamm 26a."

25. Kurt Düring was born in 1898 and passed the *Habilitation* in geography on July 28, 1934. His career with the NSDAP was characterized by a series of high-ranking appointments and subsequent removals as an academic representative of the party. He died on August 11, 1945, in Yugoslavia. See Inge Auerbach, ed., *Catalogus*, vol. 2, p. 793.

26. It states that there are no negative observations, but highlights, at the

same time, that Auerbach was the superior of at least one "full Arian" assistant and had recently received unfavorable comments from a female Turkish colleague.

27. During the summer of 1937, Auerbach came back to Germany for a two-month vacation (at Berlin, the Lake of Konstanz, and Garmisch-Partenkirchen); Marie Auerbach returned again in 1938. Before taking notice, in 1992, of the documents quoted above, Clemens Auerbach, who was fourteen years old in 1937, was not aware of the fact that state and party authorities in Germany had been concerned with the legal status of his family's residence in Turkey after their emigration.

28. See the long series of Auerbach's Vico publications: his translation *Die neue Wissenschaft über die gemeinschaftliche Natur de Völker: Nach der Ausgabe von 1744 übersetzt und eingeleitet* (Munich: Allgemeine Verlaganstalt, 1925); *Benedetto Croce: Die Philosophie Giambattista Vicos.* Nach der 2. Auflage übersetzt (Tübingen: J. C. B. Mohr, 1927); "Giambattista Vico," *Der Neue Merkur* 6 (1922); "Vico," *Vossische Zeitung* (June 5, 1929); "Vico und Herder," *Deutsche Vierteljahrsschrift für Literaturwissenschaft und Geistesgeschichte* 10 (1932): 671–86; "Vico and Aesthetic Historism," *Journal of Aesthetics and Art Criticism* 8 (1948): 110–18; "Giambattista Vico e l'idea della filologia," *Convivium* 24 (1956): 394–403. The list of publications at the end of *Gesammelte Aufsätze zur romanischen Philologie* (Bern: Franke, 1967) mentions two further review articles concerning Vico. Auerbach summarized his Vico readings in the introduction to *Literatursprache und Publikum*, pp. 10ff. I will not address the question whether we can consider Auerbach's Vico interpretation as philosophically and historically adequate, which my colleague Robert Harrison quite convincingly raised during the Stanford colloquium.

29. "Über Absicht und Methode," p. 17: "[According to Vico,] philology investigates what the nations, at their different cultural stages, hold to be true (although they only hold it to be true within their limited perspective) and therefore take for the ground of their actions. . . . Philosophy, in contrast, deals with the unchangeable and absolute Truth."

30. This thought found its strongest expression in Auerbach's essay "Philologie der Weltliteratur," in *Gesammelte Aufsätze*, pp. 301–10.

31. In "Über Absicht und Methode," p. 10, Auerbach mentions that he had first found this meaning of the word "drama" in Vico. Most of the scholarly articles on Auerbach highlight the concepts of "drama" and "tragedy" as points of convergence between his life and his work. See Harry Levin, "Two *Romanisten* in America: Spitzer and Auerbach," in Donald Fleming and Bernard Bailyn, eds., *The Intellectual Migration: Europe and America, 1930–1960* (Cambridge, Mass.: Harvard University Press, 1969), p. 469; Lowry Nelson, Jr., "Erich Auerbach: Memoir of a Scholar," *The Yale Review* 69,

2 (1980): 312–320; Henri Peyre, "Erich Auerbach (1892/1957) / Romanist," in Ingeborg Schnack, ed., *Marburger Gelehrte*, p. 18; Geoffrey Green, *Literary Criticism and the Structures of History: Erich Auerbach and Leo Spitzer* (Lincoln: University of Nebraska Press, 1982), p. 55; Paul A. Bové: *Intellectuals in Power: A Genealogy of Critical Humanism* (New York: Columbia University Press, 1986), p. 116.

32. It is highly unusual that a book is accepted as *Habilitationsschrift after* its publication. By normally excluding this option the academic authorities reserve the possibility to impose changes on the final version of a book manuscript before going to print. Exceptions from this rule are granted either to applicants who have not gone through (and do often not pursue) a regular university career or in cases of exceptional quality.

33. Quoted after the English version, *Dante, Poet of the Secular World*, trans. Ralph Manheim (Chicago: University of Chicago Press, 1961), p. viii.

34. See the chapter on "artificiality" in my forthcoming book *In 1926: An Essay in Historical Simultaneity*.

35. *Dante, Poet of the Secular World*, p. 1.

36. Ibid., p. 177.

37. Ibid., p. 3.

38. See the two following paragraphs of this essay.

39. According to Clemens Auerbach, his father never actually worked as a librarian at Marburg.

40. See for these documents Hessisches Staatsarchiv Best. 307d, acc. 1966/ 10, no. 74.

41. Wolf-Dieter Stempel gave me copies of two Auerbach letters to Binswanger (from March 3, 1930, and October 28, 1932). After 1933, Ludwig Binswanger, who, to Auerbach's regret, was an admirer of Mussolini, emigrated to Italy where he ran a small hotel in Florence. A few years later, he went on to New Zealand and finally became a university professor. Auerbach had published a review of Binswanger's book *Die aesthetische Problematik Flauberts* (1934) in *Literaturblatt für germanische und romanische Philologie* 58 (1937): 111–13.

42. See, among the numerous Spitzer portraits, Fritz Schalk, "Leo Spitzer (1887–1960) / Romanist," in Schnack, ed., *Marburger Gelehrte*, pp. 523–35.

43. Auerbach uses the word *Geheimrat* ("secret counselor"), a title which some German states awarded to especially deserving civil servants (e.g., Karl Vossler). Auerbach's father, who owned a sugar factory, had received the equivalent title of *Kommerzienrat*.

44. There are no documents attesting to such a search in the Auerbach file or in the files of the dean's office at the Hessisches Staatsarchiv Marburg.

45. Auerbach's review appeared in the *Deutsche Literaturzeitung* 53 (1932): 360–63. I quote after *Gesammelte Aufsätze zur romanischen Philologie*, p. 344.

46. Quoted in Nelson, "Erich Auerbach: Memoir of a Scholar," p. 320. The second part of Auerbach's inscription is from *Purgatorio* XXXII, 102: "Quella Roma onde Cristo e romano."

47. Nelson, "Erich Auerbach: Memoir of a Scholar," p. 320.

48. Ernst Robert Curtius, *Deutscher Geist in Gefahr* (Stuttgart: Deutsche Verlagsanstalt, 1932), p. 9.

49. Beside its function as a political intervention, Curtius's book contains an argument about the necessary return to medieval culture within such a new humanism. This thought seems to have inspired Curtius's research toward *Europäische Literatur und lateinisches Mittelalter* (finally published in 1948). See *Deutscher Geist in Gefahr*, p. 31.

50. Letter to Ludwig Binswanger of October 28, 1932.

51. See my essay "Alltagswelt' und 'Lebenswelt' als philosophische Begriffe."

52. See Ferdinand Fellmann, *Phänomenologie und Expressionismus* (Freiburg, 1982), p. 52–53.

53. See Martin Heidegger, *Being and Time*, trans. John Macquarrie and Edward Robinson (San Francisco: HarperCollins, 1967, p. 69), and the historical analysis of *Sein und Zeit* in the final chapter of my book, *1926*.

54. See Ferdinand Fellmann, *Gelebte Philosophie in Deutschland: Denkformen der Lebensweltphilosophie und der kritischen Theorie* (Freiburg: Alber, 1983), pp. 80–98.

55. Oswald Spengler, *The Decline of the West*, trans. Charles Francis Atkinson (New York: Alfred Knopf, 1976), p. 506.

56. See Fellmann, *Gelebte Philosophie*, pp. 98–109.

57. I owe this hypothesis to conversations with Jeffrey Schnapp.

58. See my essay, "Karl Vosslers noble Einsamkeit."

59. This doubtless had to do with the fact that before World War II, the *Abitur*—and with it the access to a university education—was reached by only a very small group of the total population.

60. Translated from a quotation in Christian Velder, ed., *300 Jahre Französisches Gymnasium Berlin* (Berlin: Nicolai, 1989), pp. 455–59.

61. According to Clemens Auerbach, this step was taken without any pressure from his father's family. For those who could afford it, frequent changes of university were among the "joyful" aspects of a student's life.

62. The impression, however, that Auerbach was by no means a brilliant examinee is confirmed by the fact that he obtained the lowest possible degree (*rite*) which, on the other hand, was normal for doctors in law and medicine who did not try to qualify for an academic career. In this context, I have to mention that I am not completely sure whether I understand correctly the relevant passage in Auerbach's doctoral diploma:

GRADUM DOCTORIS
SUMMOS IN UTROOQUE IURE HONORES
RITE CONTULIMUS ET HOC DIPLOMATE SIGILLO ORDINIS
NOSTRI MUNDO TESTATI SUMUS

The double ambiguity of this text lies in the possibility to read the words *summos honores* either as a part of the phrase "in both laws" or as a grade (which would mean that Auerbach obtained the highest grade), and to understand the adverb *rite* either in the sense of "orderly" or as the lowest grade.

63. Auerbach, *Die Teilnahme in der Vorarbeiten zu einem neuen Strafgesetzbuch* (Berlin: Frensdorf, 1913), pp. 15–16.

64. On this occasion Auerbach was awarded the *Eiserne Kreuz zweiter Klasse.*

65. This Lommatzsch was not identical with Auerbach's examiner for Latin at Greifswald and later Marburg colleague. A historical linguist, Eberhard Lommatzsch would later on gain a reputation as editor of an *Altfranzösisches Wöterbuch.* Even more than Spitzer's commentary on Auerbach's *Habilitation,* Lommatzsch's very superficial evaluation of his dissertation makes it clear that Auerbach had developed his main line of argumentation independently. The degree *valde laudabile* referred exclusively to the dissertation manuscript, whereas in the oral part of the examination (*Rigorosum*) Auerbach obtained not only a *rite* in Latin but also a *kaum ausreichend* in philosophy.

66. Auerbach, *Zur Technik der Frührenaissancenovelle in Italien und Frankreich* (Heidelberg, 1921), p. 1.

67. Auerbach's father-in-law, too, had been awarded an honorary title, in his case the title of *Justizrat.*

68. Auerbach, "Racine und die Leidenschaften," *Germanisch-Romanische Monatsschrift* 14 (1926): 380. (The essay is republished in *Gesammelte Aufsätze,* pp. 196–203.) This article appears to have been the origin for Auerbach's groundbreaking study on the sociology of the French seventeenth-century public, *Das französische Publikum des 17. Jahrhunderts* (Munich: Hueber, 1933). From the perspective of the contemporary intellectual climate, it is interesting that the same issue of *Germanisch-Romanische Monatsschrift* contained a further article on "the tragic": Max J. Wolff, "Die Freude am Tragischen," pp. 390–97.

69. Auerbach, "Paul-Louis Courier," *Deutsche Vierteljahrsschrift für Literaturwissenschaft und Geistesgeschichte* 4 (1926): 520, 543.

70. Auerbach, "Über das Persönliche in der Wirkung des hl. Franz von Assisi, *Deutsche Vierteljahrsschrift für Literaturwissenschaft und Geistesgeschichte* 5 (1927): 70, 77. (The essay is republished in *Gesammelte Aufsätze,* pp. 33–42.)

71. See, for example, the chapter on Proust in Ernst Robert Curtius, *Französischer Geist im neuen Europa* (Stuttgart: Deutsche Verlagsanstalt, 1925).

72. "Marcel Proust: Der Roman von der verlorenen Zeit," *Die Neueren*

Sprachen 35 (1927): 16–22. (The essay is republished in *Gesammelte Aufsätze*, pp. 296–301).

73. From a letter to Krauss, written at Istanbul on August 27, 1946. See *Beiträge zur Romanischen Philologie* 26 (1987): 371.

74. A similar configuration seems to inform our relation to the work and the biography of Michel Foucault. See James Miller, *The Passion of Michel Foucault* (New York: Simon and Schuster, 1993), pp. 319ff., and my essay "Beyond Foucault / Foucault's Style," *Symptome* 10 (1992), pp. 40–45.

75. Stephen Spender, "German Impressions and Conversations," *Partisan Review* 18, 1 (Winter 1946): 8, 11.

76. *Beiträge zur Romanischen Philologie* 17 (1987): 316.

77. *Gesammelte Aufsätze*, p. 310.

78. See Peyre, "Erich Auerbach (1892–1857) / Romanist," in Schnack, ed., *Marburger Gelehrte*, pp. 10–21, 11.

Uhlig, "Auerbach's 'Hidden' Theory"

1. See Alexander Demandt, *Metaphern für Geschichte: Sprachbilder und Gleichnisse im historisch-politischen Denken* (Munich: Beck, 1978), p. 453.

2. See Frank E. Manuel, *Shapes of Philosophical History* (Stanford, Calif.: Stanford University Press, 1965), p. 5.

3. Ernst Robert Curtius, *Kritische Essays zur europäischen Literatur* (3d ed.; Bern: Francke, 1963), p. 317.

4. This is clearly evidenced by the table of contents already in Erich Auerbach, *Gesammelte Aufsätze zur romanischen Philologie* (Bern: Francke, 1967); see also Arthur R. Evans, Jr., "Erich Auerbach as European Critic," *Romance Philology* 25 (1971): 193–215, reviewing the volume; as well as Aurelio Roncaglia, "Erich Auerbach," *Giornale storico* 135 (1958): 679–82. *Gesammelte Aufsätze* also contains a classified bibliography of Auerbach's writings (pp. 365–69).

5. See Eduard Spranger, *Lebensformen: Geisteswissenschaftliche Psychologie und Ethik der Persönlichkeit* [1921], Siebenstern-Taschenbuch, 35–36 (Munich: Siebenstern, 1965), p. 145.

6. See Dante Della Terza, "Auerbach e Vico," in V. E. Alfieri et al., eds., *Critica e storia letteraria: Studi offerti a Mario Fubini* (Padova: Liviana, 1970); and René Wellek, "Auerbach and Vico," *Lettere Italiane* 30 (1978): 457–69.

7. Auerbach, *Literatursprache und Publikum in der lateinischen Spätantike und im Mittelalter* (Bern: Francke, 1958), pp. 9–24; translated by Ralph Manheim as *Literary Language and Its Public in Late Latin Antiquity and in the Middle Ages* (London: Routledge and Kegan Paul, 1965), pp. 3–24. This posthumous volume includes a chronological list of Auerbach's publications (pp. 391–405).

8. Auerbach, "Vico and Aesthetic Historism" (1948), *Gesammelte Aufsätze*, pp. 266–74, esp. p. 269; see also *Literary Language*, pp. 7–9.

9. See Giambattista Vico, *Die Neue Wissenschaft über die gemeinschaftliche Natur der Völker*. Trans. from the ed. of 1744 and introd. by Erich Auerbach (Munich: Allgemeine Verlagsanstalt, 1924; Berlin: de Guyter, [1929]), pp. 9–39, esp. p. 28.

10. See R. G. Collingwood, *The Idea of History*, ed. T. M. Knox (1946), Oxford Paperbacks 27 (Oxford: Oxford University Press, 1961; repr. 1973), pp. 282–302.

11. See Auerbach, *Gesammelte Aufsätze*, p. 269.

12. Vico, *Neue Wissenschaft*; Auerbach, *Literary Language*, pp. 9–11.

13. Auerbach, *Mimesis: Dargestellte Wirklichkeit in der abendländischen Literatur* (Bern: Francke, 1946), p. 390; translated by Willard R. Trask as *Mimesis: The Representation of Reality in Western Literature* (Princeton, N.J.: Princeton University Press, 1953), p. 443. The citation here is to the English translation, although as a rule I base my discussion on the German original as first published in 1946. In the present context, see also Charles Breslin, "Philosophy or Philology: Auerbach and Aesthetic Historicism," *Journal of the History of Ideas* 22 (1961): 369–81.

14. See Auerbach, *Literary Language*, pp. 20–21.

15. Karl R. Popper, *The Poverty of Historicism* (London: Routledge and Kegan Paul, 1960; repr. 1974), although, regrettably, Popper's title is a misnomer, since one can never entirely equate historicism with determinism in the way he does.

16. Auerbach, *Mimesis*, p. 390; trans. Trask, p. 444.

17. See Siegfried Kracauer, *History: The Last Things Before the Last* (New York: Oxford University Press, 1969), esp. pp. 144–50.

18. See Auerbach, "Giambattista Vico und die Idee der Philologie" (1936), in *Gesammelte Aufsätze*, pp. 233–41, esp. p. 238. See also Yvon Belaval, "Vico and Anti-Cartesianism," in Giorgio Tagliacozzo and Hayden V. White, eds., *Giambattista Vico: An International Symposium* (Baltimore: Johns Hopkins University Press, 1969), esp. p. 83.

19. Auerbach, *Literary Language*, pp. 16–17; see also Paul Zumthor, "Erich Auerbach ou l'éloge de la philologie," *Littérature* 2 (1972): 107–16.

20. See Auerbach, *Mimesis*, pp. 488–89.

21. Auerbach, "Philologie der Weltliteratur" (1952), in *Gesammelte Aufsätze*, esp. p. 309; see also *Literary Language*, pp. 16–20; and W. Wolfgang Holdheim, "The Hermeneutic Significance of Auerbach's *Ansatz*," *New Literary History* 16 (1985): 627–31.

22. Auerbach, *Literary Language*, pp. 19–20, comparing himself to Spitzer in that manner. See also Harry Levin, *Grounds for Comparison* (Cambridge, Mass.: Harvard University Press, 1972), pp. 110–30; and above all Geoffrey Green, *Literary Criticism and the Structures of History: Erich Auerbach and Leo Spitzer* (Lincoln: University of Nebraska Press, 1982), pp. 1–7, 161–66.

23. See, instead of many, David Couzens Hoy, *The Critical Circle: Literature, History, and Philosophical Hermeneutics* (Berkeley: University of California Press, 1978), pp. vii–viii, 166–68.

24. Auerbach, "Epilegomena zu Mimesis," *Romanische Forschungen* 65 (1953): 1–18, esp. p. 16. See also W. Wolfgang Holdheim, *The Hermeneutic Mode: Essays on Time in Literature and Literary Theory* (Ithaca, N.Y.: Cornell University Press, 1984), pp. 211–25, esp. p. 217.

25. Much like Spitzer in this respect again, according to Lowry Nelson, Jr., "Erich Auerbach: Memoir of a Scholar," *The Yale Review* 69 (1979): 312–20, esp. p. 314.

26. For an instance of objections to Auerbach's method along those lines, see Klaus Gronau, *Literarische Form und gesellschaftliche Entwicklung: Erich Auerbachs Beitrag zur Theorie und Methodologie der Literaturgeschichte*, Hochschulschriften Literaturwissenschaft 39 (Königstein/Taunus: Forum Academicum, 1979), pp. 79–89.

27. René Wellek, "Erich Auerbach (1892–1957)," *Comparative Literature* 10 (1958): 94.

28. See Henri Peyre, "Erich Auerbach," in Ingeborg Schnack, ed., *Marburger Gelehrte in der ersten Hälfte des 20. Jahrhunderts*, Veröffentlichungen der Historischen Kommission für Hessen 35, 1 (Marburg: Elwert, 1977), pp. 17, 20.

29. Auerbach, *Dante als Dichter der irdischen Welt* (Berlin: de Gruyter, 1929), pp. 5–33.

30. See, for instance, the review of the first edition of *Mimesis* by Otto Regenbogen in 1949, reprinted in his *Kleine Schriften*, ed. Franz Dirlmeier (Munich: Beck, 1961); or the account, for that matter, of Ludwig Edelstein in *Modern Language Notes* 65 (1950): 426–31.

31. See Auerbach, "Figura" (1939), in *Gesammelte Aufsätze*, pp. 74–82. This essay reached its full impact only somewhat later, when translated by Ralph Manheim in *Scenes from the Drama of European Literature*, Meridian Books 63 (New York: Meridian Books, 1959), where it occupies pride of place.

32. See Auerbach, "Franz von Assisi in der *Komödie*" (1945), "Figurative Texts Illustrating Certain Passages of Dante's *Commedia*" (1946), and "Typological Symbolism in Medieval Literature" (1952), all reprinted in *Gesammelte Aufsätze*, as well as *Typologische Motive in der mittelalterlichen Literatur*, Schriften und Vorträge des Petrarca-Instituts Köln 2 (Krefeld: Scherpe, 1953; 1964), esp. pp. 8–15.

33. See Auerbach, *Mimesis*, pp. 188–92. "Omnitemporality," by the way, is Holdheim's happy rendering for *"Jederzeitlichkeit"* in *The Hermeneutic Mode*, p. 215.

34. See Paul J. Korshin, *Typologies in England 1650–1820* (Princeton, N.J.: Princeton University Press, 1982), pp. 75–100.

35. See ibid., p. xiii. Rudolf Bultmann, one of Auerbach's colleagues at Marburg, must be named in this connection, although the latter's teaching in Romance philology was still far from "prefiguring" the concerns of *Mimesis* written in exile in Istanbul. Incidentally, sifting through the bulletins of Marburg University for the years from 1930 to 1936, the period of Auerbach's tenure, one notices that his academic teaching was fairly conventional, comprising as it did lectures and seminars on both historical linguistics and, with regard to French as well as Italian literature, the great names of the canon.

36. See also Demandt, *Metaphern für Geschichte*, pp. 409–11; and Northrop Frye, *The Great Code: The Bible and Literature* (London: Routledge and Kegan Paul, 1982), pp. 78–101, esp. pp. 80–83.

37. See Rudolf Bultmann, "Weissagung und Erfüllung" (1949), in his *Glauben und Verstehen*, 5th ed. (Tübingen: Mohr-Siebeck, 1968), 2:163; and Hoy, *The Critical Circle*, p. 88.

38. Auerbach, *Gesammelte Aufsätze*, pp. 111–13. On the principle of *contrapasso*, i.e., direct retributive justice, see Dante, *Die Göttliche Komödie*, italienisch und deutsch. Übers. und Komm. von Hermann Gmelin, 6 vols. (Stuttgart: Klett, 1949–57), *Inf.* 28.142; *Komm.* 1.424.

39. Green, *Literary Criticism and the Structures of History*, pp. 25–33.

40. On the generic opposition between profane history and sacred history, related as they are to Providence and the notion of judgment, see Krzysztof Pomian, *L'ordre du temps* (Paris: Gallimard, 1984), p. 26.

41. See also my *Theorie der Literarhistorie: Prinzipien und Paradigmen* (Heidelberg: Winter, 1982), p. 31.

42. See Wellek, "Auerbach's Special Realism," *Kenyon Review* 16 (1954): 299–307; see also his *History of Modern Criticism, 1750–1950*, vol. 7, *German, Russian, and Eastern European Criticism, 1900–1950* (New Haven, Conn.: Yale University Press, 1991), pp. 113–34, esp. pp. 117–21.

43. As to this methodic procedure, see Auerbach's own clarification in *Literary Language*, p. 20.

44. See Auerbach, *Mimesis*, pp. 7–30, esp. pp. 28–29 on the stylistic difference between Homer and the Bible.

45. *Mimesis*, pp. 169–96, esp. pp. 179–80, 188–94.

46. Reprinted in Auerbach, *Gesammelte Aufsätze*, pp. 21–26.

47. Auerbach, "Sermo Humilis" (1952), in *Literary Language*, pp. 65–66.

48. Auerbach, *Mimesis*, p. 291. As to repercussions of this chapter of *Mimesis* in later Montaigne studies, see Patrick Henry, "Auerbach et la critique actuelle de Montaigne," *Studi Francesi* 29 (1985): 324–33.

49. See also Jean Ethier-Blais, "*Mimesis*: réalisme et transcendance," *Études françaises* 6 (1970): 7–24.

50. Auerbach, *Mimesis*, p. 437; trans. Trask, p. 491.

51. See Wesley Morris, *Toward a New Historicism* (Princeton, N.J.: Princeton University Press, 1972), p. 150.

52. For a critique along those lines, see, for instance, Richard Brinkmann, *Wirklichkeit und Illusion: Studien über Gehalt und Grenzen des Begriffs Realismus für die erzählende Dichtung des neunzehnten Jahrhunderts* (Tübingen: Niemeyer, 1958), pp. 68–77.

53. For the sociological viewpoint in Auerbach criticism, and that not only with regard to *Mimesis*, see Franz Niedermayer, "Deutsche Romanistik zwischen Metaphysik und Soziologie?" *Die Neueren Sprachen*, n.s. 18 (1969): 394–99; Ulrich Knoke, "Erich Auerbach — eine erkenntnis- und methodenkritische Betrachtung," *Zeitschrift für Literaturwissenschaft und Linguistik* 17 (1975): 74–93; and Gronau, *Literarische Form und gesellschaftliche Entwicklung* (as above, n. 25), rev. Ulrich Knoke in *Lendemains* 24 (1981), 99–170. As to Marxist persuasions, see Franco Fortini, *Die Vollmacht: Literatur von heute und ihr sozialer Auftrag* (Vienna: Europa Verlag, 1968), pp. 143–50; or Joseph Venturini, "La *Mimesis* d'Auerbach appliquée à Dante," *Littérature* 2 (1972): 117–25.

54. See Käthe Hamburger, "Zwei Formen literatursoziologischer Betrachtung: Zu Erich Auerbachs *Mimesis* und Georg Lukács' *Goethe und seine Zeit*," *Orbis Litterarum* 7 (1949): 142–60; and Albert Junker, "Zum Problem des Realismus in der Literatur," *Die Neueren Sprachen*, n.s. 2 (1954): 446–52.

55. For objections to Auerbach in a similar vein, see Gerhard Hess, "*Mimesis*: Zu Erich Auerbachs Geschichte des abendländischen Realismus" (1948), in his *Gesellschaft-Literatur-Wissenschaft: Gesammelte Schriften 1938–1966*, eds. H. R. Jauss and C. Müller-Daehn (Munich: Fink, 1967), p. 203; and, above all, Helmut Kuhn, reviewing the second and enlarged German edition of *Mimesis* of 1959, in "Literaturgeschichte als Geschichtsphilosophie," *Philosophische Rundschau* 11 (1963): 222–48, esp. pp. 235–36.

56. Auerbach, "Vico and Aesthetic Historism," in *Gesammelte Aufsätze*, p. 267.

57. See, for instance, Robert Alter, *The Art of Biblical Narrative* (New York: Basic Books, 1981), pp. 17, 114; and Albert Cook, *History/Writing* (Cambridge: Cambridge University Press, 1988), pp. 11, 140, 149.

58. For the former, see Elizabeth Salter, "Medieval Poetry and the Figural View of Reality" (1968), in J. A. Burrow, ed., *Middle English Literature: British Academy Gollancz Lectures* (Oxford: Oxford University Press, 1989); and, for the latter, Lee Patterson, *Negotiating the Past: The Historical Understanding of Medieval Literature* (Madison: University of Wisconsin Press, 1987), pp. 24, 104–5, 170, 206.

59. See Wolfgang Bernard Fleischmann, "Erich Auerbach's Critical Theory and Practice: An Assessment," *Modern Language Notes* 81 (1966): 540. Strangely uncritical, in view of its date, and full of piety instead, is Hans-Jörg Neu-

schäfer's own assessment in his article "Sermo humilis. Oder: was wir mit
Erich Auerbach vertrieben haben," in *Deutsche und österreichische Romanisten als
Verfolgte des Nationalsozialismus*, ed. Hans H. Christmann, Frank-Rutger Haus-
mann, and Manfred Briegel (Tübingen: Stauffenburg, 1989).

60. David Carroll, "Mimesis Reconsidered: Literature-History-Ideology,"
Diacritics (summer 1975): 9.

61. For such a misguided departure, as it seems to me, see Nina Perlina,
"Auerbach e Bachtin sulla rappresentazione artistica della realtà," *L'immagine
riflessa* 7 (1984): 223–55.

62. Auerbach, *Literary Language*, p. 17.

63. See Auerbach, *Gesammelte Aufsätze*, pp. 301–10, esp. p. 310.

64. See Harold Bloom, writing on "the cultural prospects of American
Jewry," in *Agon: Towards a Theory of Revisionism* (Oxford: Oxford University
Press, 1982), pp. 318–29, esp. p. 319.

65. On this point, see Peyre, "Erich Auerbach," p. 10: "Israélite de naissance, agnostique de formation et de tour d'esprit, pénétré de culture gréco-
latine et lecteur assidu des Pères de l'Eglise et de Dante, il semblait incarner
pour nous les plus précieuses qualités de l'humaniste européen de l'époque de
Lessing, de Herder, et de Goethe."

Costa-Lima, *"Auerbach and Literary History"*

1. Quoted in Bernd Witte, "La Naissance de l'histoire littéraire dans l'esprit
de la révolution," in Michel Espagne and Michael Wener, eds., *Contributions
à l'histoire des disciplines littéraires en France et en Allemagne au XIXe siècle* (Paris:
Éditions de la Maison des Sciences de l'Homme, 1990), p. 77.

2. However, in a beautiful work, *Éloge de la variante: Histoire Critique de la
philologie* (Paris: Seuil, 1989), Bernard Cerquiglini shows that the distance between the analyst and his object was also wide in the generation of the fathers
of Romance philology, who saw the medieval texts they studied as examples
of a literary expression that was "au fond . . . un peu infantile et insouciante"
(p. 62). For a *petite histoire* of this generation, which indirectly points to the gap
opened between the philologist's scientific ideal and the literary object, see
also H. Bloch, " 'Mieux vaut jamais que tard': Romance, Philology, and Old
French Letters," *Representations* 36 (1991): 64–86.

3. See Hayden White, *The Content of Form: Narrative Discourse and Historical
Representation* (Baltimore: Johns Hopkins University Press, 1987).

4. We may understand in the same sense a marginal observation of Koselleck's: since *Geschichte* implied the unicity of the process of time, "increasingly, historical narrative was expected to provide the unity found in the epic
derived from the existence of Beginning and End" (R. Koselleck, *Vergan-
gene Zukunft: Zur Semantik geschichtlicher Zeiten* [1979]; translated by K. Tribe as

Futures Past: On the Semantics of Historical Time (Cambridge, Mass.: MIT Press, 1985), p. 29.

5. See David Lloyd, "Arnold, Ferguson, Schiller: Aesthetic Culture, the Politics of Aesthetics," *Culture Critique* 2 (1984–85): 137–69.

6. See Erich Auerbach, "Epilegomena zu Mimesis," *Romanische Forschungen* 65½ (1953): 15–16. Further page references to this essay are included in the text.

7. Auerbach, *Mimesis: The Representation of Reality in Western Literature*, trans. Willard R. Trask (Princeton, N.J.: Princeton University Press, 1968), p. 486. Further page references to *Mimesis* are included in the text.

8. In a letter to Max Brod, Kafka makes a similar comparison between the Greek and Hebrew legacies, and writes that the whole world of the gods was "a great national educational institution, which captured and held men's gaze. It was less profound than the Law of the Jews, but perhaps more democratic" (letter to Max Brod, 7 August 1920, in *Letters to Friends, Family, and Editors*, trans. R. and C. Winston [New York: Schocken, 1977]).

9. Auerbach, "Figura" (1944), reprinted in *Scenes*, p. 29.

10. See ibid., p. 34.

11. Timothy Bahti, "Auerbach's Mimesis: Figural Structure and Historical Narrative," in Gregory S. Jay and David L. Miller, eds., *After Strange Texts: The Role of Theory in the Study of Literature* (Tuscaloosa: University of Alabama Press, 1985), p. 138.

12. Robert Fitzgerald, who attended Auerbach's 1949 seminar at Princeton, recorded a surprising observation of his: though Auerbach agreed that Baudelaire was the initiator of modern poetry, he did not like him. See Robert Fitzgerald, *Enlarging the Change: The Princeton Seminars in Literary Criticism 1949–1951* (Boston: Northeastern University Press, 1985), p. 23.

13. Bahti, "Auerbach's Mimesis," p. 145.

14. Ibid., p. 143.

15. Gustave Flaubert to Louise Collet, 4 December 1852, in *Correspondance*, ed. J. Bruneau (Paris: Gallimard, 1973; 3 vols.), 2:151.

16. David Carroll, "Mimesis Reconsidered: Literature-History-Ideology," *Diacritics* (Summer 1975): 9, 11.

17. Dominick LaCapra, *"Madame Bovary" on Trial* (Ithaca, N.Y.: Cornell University Press, 1982), p. 140.

Nichols, "Philology in Auerbach's Drama of (Literary) History"

I would like to express my thanks to Professor Seth Lerer for conceiving the conference "Literary History and the Challenge of Philology" to honor the centennial of Erich Auerbach's birth, and for inviting me to participate. Although I have written this paper in my mind many times since 1959, it would not have seen the light of day, I fear, without Seth Lerer's initiative.

1. Giambattista Vico, *Die neue Wissenschaft über die gemeinschaftliche Natur der Völker* (Munich: Allgemeine Verlagsanstalt, 1924).

2. Erich Auerbach, *Literary Language and Its Public in Late Latin Antiquity and in the Middle Ages*, trans. Ralph Manheim, Bollingen series 74 (New York: Pantheon Books, 1965). German title: *Literatursprache und Publikum in der lateinischen Spätantike und im Mittelalter* (Bern: Francke, 1958). See his introduction, "Über Absicht und Methode."

3. "Each historian (we may also call him, with Vico's terminology, 'philologist') . . ." Erich Auerbach, "Vico's Contribution to Literary Criticism," in A. G. Hatcher and K. L. Selig, eds., *Studia philologica et letteraria in honorem L. Spitzer* (Bern: Francke, 1958); p. 36.

4. "Ein anderer Aspekt der vichianischen Erkenntnistheorie ist dieser, daß er das Geschichtliche mit dem Menschlichen gleichsetzt. Die Welt der Völker . . . umfaßt bei ihm nicht nur die politische Geschichte, sondern auch Geschichte des Denkens, des Ausdrucks (Sprache, Schrift und bildende Kunst), der Religion, des Rechts, der Wirtschaft: weil alle diese Dinge aus den gleichen Bedingungen, nämlich dem jeweiligen Kulturstande der menschlichen Gesellschaft, hervorgehen und somit entweder im Zusammenhang miteinander oder gar nicht verstanden werden können; *die Einsicht in einen dieser Teile menschlichen Gestaltens in einem bestimmten Stadium der Entwicklung muß zugleich den Schlüssel zu allen anderen Gestaltungen des gleichen Stadiums liefern.*" Auerbach, *Literatursparache und Publikum*, p. 11 (italics mine).

5. René Wellek, "Auerbach's Special Realism," *Kenyon Review* 16 (1954): 305. Auerbach later spiritedly denied the charge of eclecticism Wellek had leveled at him, while vigorously defending the "radical relativism" (*radikaler Relativismus*) of the approach. "Vor allem aber ist es nicht richtig, daß der historische Relativismus zur eklektischen Urteilsunfähigkeit führt und daß man, um zu urteilen, außerhistorischer Maßstäbe bedürfe. Wer den Historismus eklektisch versteht, der hat ihn nicht verstanden. Die Eigentümlichkeit einer jeden Epoche und eines jeden werkes sowie die Art ihrer Beziehungen untereinander sind durch Hingabe und Vertiefung zu erobern, eine unendliche Aufgabe, die jeder für sich, von seinem Standorte, zu lösen versuchen muß. Denn der historische Relativismus ist ein doppelter, er bezieht sich auf den Verstehenden ebenso wie auf das zu Verstehende. *Es ist en radikaler Relativismus: man sollte ihn deshalb aber nicht fürchten.* Der Raum, in dem man sich bei dieser Tätigkeit bewegt, ist die Welt der Menschen, zu der Verstehende selbst gehört." *Literatursprache und Publikum*, pp. 14–15.

6. Wellek, "Auerbach's Special Realism," pp. 305–6.

7. Ibid., p. 306. See also René Wellek, "The Concept of Realism in Literary Scholarship," in S. G. Nichols, ed., *Concepts of Criticism* (New Haven, Conn.:

Yale University Press, 1963), p. 236: "Historicism contradicts existentialism. Existentialism sees man exposed in his nakedness and solitude, it is unhistorical, even anti-historical. These two sides of Auerbach's conception of realism differ also in their historical provenience. 'Existence' descends from Kierkegaard, whose whole philosophy was a protest against Hegel, the ancestor of historicism and *Geistesgeschichte*."

8. "'Philology' is open to many misunderstandings. Historically it has been used to include not only all literary and linguistic studies but studies of all the products of the human mind. Though its greatest vogue was in nineteenth-century Germany, it still survived in the titles of such reviews as *Modern Philology*, *Philological Quarterly*, and *Studies in Philology*. . . . Today, because of its etymology and much of the actual work of specialists, philology is frequently understood to mean linguistics, especially historical grammar and the study of past forms of languages. Since the term has so many and such divergent meanings, it is best to abandon it." René Wellek and Austin Warren, *Theory of Literature*, Revised (Third) Edition (New York: Harcourt, Brace and World, 1968), p. 38.

9. "Man also . . . ebensowohl eine Philologie wie eine Philosophie nennen kann. Es handelt sich in dieser philologischen Philosophie oder philosophischen Philologie nur um uns, die Menschen auf dem Planeten Erde." Auerbach, *Literatursprache und Publikum*, pp. 17–18.

10. Engels formulated his ideas in the published version of a talk he had given to a congress of romance philology: "Philologie Romane—Linguistique—Études Littéraires," *Neophilologus* 37 (1953): 14–24.

11. The expression comes from Carlo Tagliavini's *Le Origini delle lingue neolatine*, 2nd ed. rielaborata (Bologna: R. Patron, 1952), p. 36. "La filologia, in senso più stretto, prende la lingua come oggetto di studio solo là dove essa comincia ad essere attestata letterariamente o comunque ad essere l'espressione di un pensiero artistico."

12. The entire paragraph excluding artistic language from the proper sphere of philology reads: "Pourtant, 'la langue qui commence à être l'expression d'une pensée artistique,' c'est là, à notre avis, précisément la définition de l'objet des *études littéraires*: la langue en tant que véhicule du beau littéraire. Employer ici le terme 'philologie' ne servirait qu'à créer des malentendus et des confusions. Je dis *études littéraires*, au pluriel, pour rendre possibles toutes les classifications et divisions ultérieures." Engels, "Philologie Romane," p. 20.

13. "La [philologie]-linguistique sera donc l'étude de la langue *comme moyen de communication*." Ibid., p. 21. Romance linguistics should not study style or rhetoric, but rather investigate the phonetico-morphological question of the endings -*ais*, -*ais*, -*ait* of the imperfect tense or the linguistic functions of the

subjunctive, or take part in discussions on the origin of the pronoun *on* (ibid., p. 22). Romance linguistics will not treat texts as such in any form, whether literary or non-literary (ibid.).

14. Brian Stock, "The Middle Ages as Subject and Object: Romantic Attitudes and Academic Medievalism," *New Literary History* 5 (1974): 527–47. Further page references to this essay are included in the text.

15. Erich Auerbach, *Mimesis: The Representation of Reality in Western Literature*, trans. Willard R. Trask (Princeton, N.J.: Princeton University Press, 1953), p. 6.

16. Erich Auerbach, "Vico and Aesthetic Historicism," in his *Scenes from the Drama of European Literature*, Theory and History of Literature, vol. 9 (Manchester: Manchester University Press, 1984), p. 197. This is a copublication with the University of Minnesota Press. The work was originally published in New York by Meridian Books in 1959. Mrs. Auerbach told me that permission had not been sought for the publication; a post-publication settlement was eventually reached. The title of the collection was thus emphatically not Auerbach's (as Paolo Valesio says in his introduction, p. ix, though without saying why the publisher rather than the author would have made so important a decision). Mrs. Auerbach indignantly denounced it as silly and pandering.

17. The manuscript does not put a discourse indicator for Adam at line 285; possibly it has been trimmed away as S. Etienne suggested in his "Note sur les vers 279–287 du *Jeu d'Adam*," *Romania* 48 (1922): 592–94. There has consequently been some hesitancy about accepting the MS discourse attributions. Paul Studer gives the prevailing opinion for the late nineteenth and early twentieth century: "281–87 in the MS this passage is very corrupt. . . . Moreover the scribe went hopelessly wrong in his division of the dialogue" (*Le Mystère d'Adam*, ed. Paul Studer [1918; reprint, Manchester: Manchester University Press, 1949], p. 50). But by the early 1920's a more moderate view prevailed; Etienne's article, against which Auerbach reacts so strongly, suggests giving more credance to the MS readings, while still proposing some editorial intervention.

18. One cannot fall back on the argument that he did not have access to a first-class library in Istanbul by way of explanation. Hans Ulrich Gumbrecht informs me that Auerbach taught a proseminar on the *Jeu d'Adam* in Marburg in 1934. He almost certainly used his notes from that seminar for his chapter, and so the question of the preferred edition becomes even more cogent. He would have had access to all of the relevant texts in Marburg, if, in fact, textual specificity were the issue for him, instead of a particular, medieval "voice." Of course, as one compassionate (unfortunately anonymous) reader of this essay pointed out, it may not be entirely fair to have expected Auerbach "to have written in his seminar notes the punctuation of a later edition. In

1934, he may not have foreseen that a decade later he would be without access to the later edition."

19. Auerbach, *Mimesis*, p. 149.

20. Luiz Costa-Lima, "The Fates of Subjectivity: History and Nature in Romanticism," chapter 2 of his *Control of the Imaginary: Reason and the Imagination in Modern Times*, trans. Ronald W. Sousa, Theory and History of Literature, vol. 50 (Minneapolis: University of Minnesota Press, 1988), p. 91.

21. Erich Auerbach, "Vico and Aesthetic Historicism," in *Gesammelte Aufsätze zur romanischen Philologie* (Bern: Francke, 1967), p. 272. See the trenchant discussion of Auerbach's use of Vico against eighteenth-century rationalism by Costa-Lima, *Control of the Imaginary*, p. 91. The theatricalization of Eve in the *Ordo*, in Auerbach's reading, would be an example of the "superiority of imagination over reason" that Auerbach formulated, in Costa-Lima's words, as Vico's "blatant contradiction" to Enlightenment historical politics.

22. Studer, *Le Mystère d'Adam*, p. 60.

23. *Le Mystère d'Adam, Drame religieux du XIIe siècle*, ed. Henri Chamard (Paris: 1925).

24. Michel de Certeau, *The Writing of History*, trans. Tom Conley (New York: Columbia University Press, 1988), p. 21.

Lerer, "Philology and Collaboration"

1. Erich Auerbach, *Mimesis: The Representation of Reality in Western Literature*, trans. Willard R. Trask (Princeton, N.J.: Princeton University Press, 1953), pp. 145–46. The epigraph to my essay is from p. 557. The German reads: "So daß ich auf fast alle Zeitschriften, auf die meisten neueren Untersuchungen, ja zuweilen selbst auf eine zuverlässige kritische Ausgabe meiner Texte verzichten mußte." *Mimesis: Dargestellte Wirklichkeit in der abendländischen Literatur* (Bern: A. Francke, 1946), p. 497. Throughout this essay, I will quote primarily from the English translation of *Mimesis*, save on those occasions when close attention to Auerbach's German necessitates a full quotation in the text. Page numbers after quotations in each language refer to the respective editions just cited. Throughout, unattributed translations are my own.

2. The canonicity of the *Jeu d'Adam* in Anglo-American studies of medieval drama is affirmed by its inclusion in David Bevington, *Medieval Drama* (Boston: Houghton Mifflin, 1975), with its introductory assessment heavily dependent on Auerbach's judgments (see my discussion at the close of this essay). For a supple counterargument to the Auerbachian tradition of interpretation, reading the play as primarily a liturgical Latin occasion rather than a popular vernacular one, see Steven Justice, "The Authority of Ritual in the *Jeu d'Adam*," *Speculum* 42 (1987): 851–64.

3. "Quant aux lacunes et aux passages irrémédiablement corrompus, il

peut essayer d'en reconstituer le texte par des conjectures, c'est-à-dire par sa propre hypothèse sur la forme originale du passage en question; bien entendu, il faut indiquer, dans ce cas, qu'il s'agit de sa propre reconstitution du texte, et il faut y ajouter encore les conjectures que d'autres ont faites pour le même passage, s'il y en a. On voit que l'édition critique est, en général, plus facile à faire s'il y a peu de manuscrits ou seulement un manuscrit unique; dans ce dernier cas, on n'a qu'à le faire imprimer, avec une exactitude scrupuleuse, et à y ajouter, le cas échéant, des conjectures." Erich Auerbach, *Introduction aux études de la philologie romane* (Frankfurt a.M.: Vittorio Klostermann, 1949), p. 12. For a full discussion of the genesis, importance, and reception of this work, see Fleischman's essay in this volume.

4. S. Etienne, "Note sur les verse 279–287 du *Jeu D'Adam*," *Romania* 48 (1922): 592–94.

5. Etienne, "Note," quotations are from pp. 592, 593 respectively.

6. ". . . les sauver non seulement de l'oubli, mais aussi des changements, mutilations et additions que l'usage populaire ou l'insouciance des copistes y apportent nécessairement," Auerbach, *Introduction*, p. 9.

7. See the discussion of the early reception of *Mimesis* in the essays by Green, Hart, Landauer, and Lindenberger in this collection.

8. Hans-Ulrich Gumbrecht, " 'Un Souffle d'Allemagne ayant passé': Friedrich Diez, Gaston Paris, and the Genesis of National Philologies," *Romance Philology* 40 (1986): 2.

9. Léon Gautier, "Chronique," *Revue des questions historiques* 9 (1870): 496, translated and quoted in R. Howard Bloch, "New Philology and Old French," *Speculum* 65 (1990): 40.

10. Henri Massis, *Les Jeunes gens d'aujourd'hui* (Paris, 1913), p. 107, translated and quoted in Bloch, "New Philology and Old French," p. 40.

11. On the rise of chairs of literature in France and Germany in the nineteenth century, see Gumbrecht, "Un souffle d'Allemagne," pp. 31–32. For the rise "of a new paradigm in the history of French scholarship, which will create its own publication outlets in *Romania* (from 1872 on) and the *Société des Anciens Textes Français* (from 1875)," see ibid., p. 27. For the phrasings of Gaston Paris, see his *Les Contes orientaux dans la littérature française du moyen âge* (Paris, 1875), p. 3, quoted in Bloch, "New Philology and Old French," pp. 41–42.

12. Bloch, "New Philology and Old French," p. 40. Auerbach had left Marburg in 1936.

13. Jean-Paul Sartre, "Qu'est-ce qu'un collaborateur?" in *Situations III* (Paris: Gallimard, 1949), pp. 43–61. Further page references are included in my text. For a treatment of this essay in the context of another episode of academic politics and collaboration, see Werner Hammacher, "Journals, Politics: Notes on Paul de Man's Wartime Journalism," in Werner Hammacher, Neil Hertz,

and Tom Keenan, eds., *Responses* (Lincoln: University of Nebraska Press, 1990), pp. 438–67, especially pp. 447–48.

14. Erich Auerbach, "Epilegomena zu *Mimesis*," *Romanische Forschungen* 65 (1953): 1–18. Further page references will be included in my text.

15. "*Mimesis* ist ganz bewußt ein Buch, das ein bestimmter Mensch, in einer bestimmten Lage, zu Anfang der 1940er Jahre geschrieben hat," ibid., p. 18.

16. Paul Aebischer, ed., *Le Mystère d'Adam*, Textes Littéraires Français (Geneva: Droz, 1963), pp. 51–52.

17. Leif Sletsjöe, ed., *Le Mystère D'Adam*, Bibliothèque Française et Romane (Paris: Klincksieck, 1968), pp. 21, 85.

18. Bevington, *Medieval Drama*, text on p. 94, discussion on p. 79, quoting Auerbach's discussion of the everyday element of the play's realism (from *Mimesis*, p. 151) in support of an argument that the play was "intended for an audience of ordinary men and women."

19. Erich Auerbach, *Literary Language and Its Public in Late Latin Antiquity and in the Middle Ages*, trans. Ralph Manheim, with a new Foreword by Jan Ziolkowski (Princeton, N.J.: Princeton University Press, 1993), p. 20. This passage, and the historicist sentiment imagined behind it, generates the discussion of Auerbach's method in Thomas M. De Pietro, "Literary Criticism as History: The Example of Auerbach's *Mimesis*," *Clio* 8 (1979): 377–87, and forms the point of argument for the critique of Auerbach's "understanding of humanism's contradictory development" in Paul Bové, *Intellectuals in Power: A Genealogy of Critical Humanism* (New York: Columbia University Press, 1986), pp. 206–7; see, too, pp. 183–84, from which the above phrase in quotation marks is taken.

Fleischman, "Medieval Vernaculars and the Myth of Monoglossia"

My thanks to Jonathan Beck for judiciously critiquing an earlier draft of this essay; if I have chosen not to follow certain of his suggestions, the onus is entirely on me.

1. Erich Auerbach, *Introduction aux études de la philologie romane* (Frankfurt a.m.: Vittorio Klostermann, 1949; reprint, 1965). Citations from this work are my translations, with page references to the 1949 French edition. Where appropriate, the original text is provided in notes. The English translation of this manual by Guy Daniels, entitled *Introduction to Romance Languages and Literatures* (New York: Capricorn, 1961), omits the introductory section on philology and literary history, from which all material quoted here is drawn. The editor for Capricorn Books deemed this section "unnecessary for Western students, although of considerable interest in itself" (p. 11).

2. "La philologie est l'ensemble des activités qui s'occupent méthodiquement du langage de l'homme, et des oeuvres d'art composés dans ce langage.

Comme c'est une science très ancienne, et qu'on peut s'occuper du langage de beaucoup de façons différentes, le mot philologie a un sens très large, et comprend des activités fort différentes. Une de ses plus anciennes formes, la forme pour ainsi dire classique, et qui jusqu'à ce jour est regardée par beaucoup d'érudits comme la plus noble et la plus authentique, c'est l'édition critique des textes." Auerbach, *Introduction*, p. 9.

3. "Le besoin de constituer des textes authentiques se fait sentir quand un peuple d'une haute civilisation prend conscience de cette civilisation, et qu'il veut préserver des ravages du temps les oeuvres qui constituent son patrimoine spirituel; les sauver non seulement de l'oubli, mais aussi des changements, mutilations et additions que l'usage populaire ou l'insouciance des copistes y apportent nécessairement." Ibid.

4. New data can be added to the corpus, but only when previously unknown *texts* are brought to light. Admittedly, the boundaries separating "old," "middle," and "modern" X (where X is any language documented to a certain time-depth) are somewhat arbitrary, having been established post hoc by language historians, who, moreover, do not always agree on where to locate them; but as long as we acknowledge this, and acknowledge furthermore that the term "text language" is but a convenient shorthand for referring to the earlier stages of a language as documented in surviving texts, then it seems reasonable to operate with this concept as a useful heuristic device. I discuss elsewhere, in more detail, the particular constraints text languages impose on linguistic methodology; see my "Philology, Linguistics and the Discourse of the Medieval Text," *Speculum* 65 (1990): 19–37, and "Methodologies and Ideologies in Historical Grammar: A Case Study from Old French," in S. G. Nichols and R. H. Bloch, eds., *Medievalism and the Modernist Temper: On the Discipline of Medieval Studies* (Baltimore: Johns Hopkins University Press, forthcoming). See also Christiane Marchello-Nizia, "Question de méthode," *Romania* 106 (1985): 481–92.

5. Original text given in n. 6 below.

6. "Il est évident que l'édition des textes n'est pas une tâche tout-à-fait indépendante; elle a besoin du concours d'autres branches de la philologie, et même souvent des sciences auxiliaires qui ne sont pas à proprement parler philologiques. . . . [I]l faut se rendre compte que les textes qu'on veut reconstituer sont presque toujours des textes anciens, écrits dans une langue morte ou dans une forme très ancienne d'une langue vivante. Il faut comprendre la langue du texte; donc, l'éditeur a besoin d'études linguistiques et grammaticales; d'autre part, le texte fournit souvent à ces études un matériel fort précieux; c'est sur la base des anciens textes que la grammaire historique, l'histoire du développement des différentes langues, a pu se développer; elle y a trouvé des formes anciennes qui ont permis aux érudits du 19ᵉ siècle de

se faire une idée nette, non pas seulement du développement de telle ou telle langue, mais aussi du développement linguistique en tant que phénomène général." Auerbach, *Introduction*, p. 14.

7. Roy Harris, *The Language Myth* (London: Duckworth, 1971), p. 31.

8. Jean-Claude Milner, *Introduction à une science du langage* (Paris: Seuil, 1989), p. 64.

9. Tony Crowley, "That Obscure Object of Desire: A Science of Language," in B. Joseph and T. Taylor, eds., *Ideologies of Language* (London: Routledge, 1990), p. 50.

10. Autonomous linguists approach a language "as a natural scientist would study a physical phenomenon, that is, by focusing on those of its properties that exist *apart from the beliefs and values of the individual speakers of a language or the nature of the society in which the language is spoken*" —whence the label "autonomous" (Frederick J. Newmeyer, *The Politics of Linguistics* [Chicago: University of Chicago Press, 1986], p. 5, my emphasis). Newmeyer adds (p. 12) that autonomous linguists have traditionally viewed theirs as the only *scientific* approach to language. Work in autonomous linguistics ranges from simple accounts of changes in pronunciation, to descriptive statements ("grammars") of the structural regularities in particular languages, to ambitious attempts to characterize universal limits within which languages may differ structurally.

11. Bernard Cerquiglini, *Eloge de la variante. Histoire critique de la philologie* (Paris: Seuil, 1989). Cerquiglini's periodization of French textual criticism is taken from Alfred Foulet and Mary Blakely Speer, *On Editing Old French Texts* (Lawrence: Regents Press of Kansas, 1979).

12. Cerquiglini offers a convincing demonstration (*Eloge*, pp. 105–8) of how the established practice of listing variants atomistically (i.e., by individual words or, at most, minimal word groups) often obscures or misrepresents syntactic phenomena operative at higher levels of linguistic structure such as the utterance or discourse.

13. Robert-Léon Wagner, *L'Ancien français* (Paris: Larousse, 1974), pp. 22, 11.

14. See Peter Rickard, *A History of the French Language*, 2d ed. (London: Unwin Hyman, 1989), p. 43.

15. Louis Remacle, *Le Problème de l'ancien wallon* (Liège: Bibliothèque de la Faculté de Philosophie et Lettres, 1948). See also Carl Theodor Gossen, *Französische Skriptastudien* (Vienna: Osterreichische Akademie der Wissenschaften, 1967).

16. In the field of medieval philology, unlike the sciences, there tends to be a significant time lag between the introduction of a new hypothesis (i.e., in specialized publications) and the point at which it finds its way into grammars and language histories, *a fortiori* if the hypothesis is controversial or challenges

received thinking. Granted, the necessity to spread the word about new discoveries may be less urgent in our field than in most sciences; but might we not also construe the time lag as a telling indication of medieval philology's reluctance to embrace new methodology or new interpretations of its data (which, unless new manuscripts are discovered, remain fairly stable)? This macro-question provides a major subtext of the recent issue of *Speculum* (1990) devoted to "The New Philology" (vol. 65, no. 1).

17. See the following works by Anthonij Dees: *Atlas des formes et constructions des chartes françaises du 13ᵉ siècle*, ZRPh, suppl. 178 (Tübingen: Niemeyer, 1980); "Dialectes et scriptae à l'époque de l'ancien français," *Revue de linguistique romane* 49 (1985): 87–117; and *Atlas des formes linguistiques des textes littéraires de l'ancien français*, ZRPh, suppl. 212 (Tübingen: Niemeyer, 1987).

18. The questionable status of Francian will be discussed below.

19. William W. Kibler, *An Introduction to Old French* (New York: Modern Language Association, 1984; 4th printing with revisions, 1989), p. xxv, my emphasis.

20. Pieter van Reenen, "La Linguistique des langues anciennes et la systématisation de ses données," in Anthonij Dees, ed., *Actes du IVᵉ Colloque sur le Moyen Français* (Amsterdam: Rodopi, 1985), pp. 433–70. In fairness, let me acknowledge that, notwithstanding the premise on which it is founded, I find this paper a useful piece of scholarship, providing rigorous and seemingly sound methodological guidelines for linguists seeking to extract descriptive generalizations from a data corpus shot through with irregularity.

21. Cerquiglini, *Eloge*, p. 111.

22. Noam Chomsky, *Aspects of the Theory of Syntax* (Cambridge, Mass.: MIT Press, 1965), p. 3.

23. "La thèse de la copie comme dégénerescence, qui fonde la philologie, présuppose un original sans faute: l'auteur n'a pas droit au lapsus. De même, l'idée de la dégradation langagière implique un original impeccable: l'auteur n'as pas droit non plus à l'incorrection, à l'à-peu-près, voire à la diversité de sa parlure. Tout manuscrit médiéval étant une copie, il est par définition la reproduction fautive (de par l'inadvertance des scribes) et disparate (de par la diversité de leurs interventions) d'un original par définition sans tache et qu'homogénise l'unicité d'un scripteur de talent. *Myope, la grammaire historique est de plus fort soupçonneuse, et recherche, sous les graphies dégradées, le système [linguistique] homogène que l'original avait entrepris de transcrire.*" Bernard Cerquiglini, *La Naissance du français*, "Que sais-je?" no. 2576 (Paris: Presses Universitaires de France, 1991), p. 105, my emphasis; see also Cerquiglini, *Eloge*, pp. 76–78.

24. It was this powerful ideology of language that united the goals of philology and historico-comparative linguistics during the later decades of the nineteenth century: while linguists busied themselves with classifying the

Indo-European languages and trying to reconstruct the primordial, perfect *Ursprache*, philologists busied *themselves* classifying manuscripts and trying to reconstruct the archetypal *Urtext*.

25. See Foulet and Speer, *On Editing Old French Texts*, p. 82.

26. Eugène Vinaver, "Principles of Textual Emendation" (1939), reprinted in Christopher Kleinhenz, ed., *Medieval Manuscripts and Textual Criticism*, UNCSRLL (Chapel Hill: University of North Carolina, Dept. of Romance Languages, 1976), pp. 139–66.

27. Cf. Pieter van Reenen and Lene Schøsler, "Le Problème de la prolifération des explications," *Vrije Universiteit Working Papers in Linguistics* 27 (1987): 12–13, and Cerquiglini, *Eloge*, pp. 93–94.

28. On the various "jobs" verb tense is called on to perform when it is not functioning to locate events in time, see Suzanne Fleischman, "Temporal Distance: A Basic Linguistic Metaphor," *Studies in Language* 13 (1989): 1–51; *Tense and Narrativity. From Medieval Performance to Modern Fiction* (Austin: University of Texas Press, and London: Routledge, Chapman and Hall, 1990); and "Verb Tense and Point of View in Narrative," in S. Fleischman and L. R. Waugh, eds., *Discourse Pragmatics and the Verb: The Evidence from Romance* (London: Routledge, 1991), pp. 26–54. See also Roger Lass, "How to Do Things with Junk: Exaptation in Language Evolution," *Journal of Linguistics* 26 (1990): 79–102.

29. For particulars, see Bernard Cerquiglini, Jacqueline Cerquiglini, Christiane Marchello-Nizia, and Michèle Perret-Minard, "L'Objet 'ancien français' et les conditions propres à sa description linguistique," in J.-C. Chevalier and M. Gross, eds., *Méthodes en grammaire française* (Paris: Klincksieck, 1976), pp. 185–200. It might be more accurate to say that case was no longer operative in actual *usage*, which is always at some distance from the *grammar* of written language. Reflecting on the broader implications of this observation, we might consider the idea that norms of correctness for written language exist for no other purpose than to preserve linguistic practices that are "no longer operative" in the spoken language.

30. This consecrated term of the metalanguage of historical linguistics— *loss*—is hardly innocent, participating as it does in a deeply rooted ideology of language change as a process of decline or decay.

31. The myth of monoglossia is the linguistic component of a broader impetus toward standardization which Blommaert and Verscheuren refer to as the "dogma of homogeneism"—a view of society in which differences are seen as dangerous and centrifugal, and in which the "best" society is one without intergroup differences. Jan Blommaert and Jef Verscheuren, "The Role of Language in European Nationalist Ideologies," *Pragmatics* 2 (1992): 362.

32. Cf. R. Anthony Lodge, *French: From Dialect to Standard* (London: Routledge), pp. 23–26.

33. Foulet and Speer, *On Editing Old French Texts*, p. 81, my emphasis.

34. Vinaver, "Principles of Textual Emendation," pp. 158–59; Kleinhenz, *Medieval Manuscripts*, p. 23. My emphasis in both instances.

35. Philologists of earlier periods would have had no qualms about acknowledging this explicitly. Comforted, no doubt, by the stability, regularity, and coherence of the text produced by his rigorous editorial toilette of the Hildesheim MS of *St. Alexis*, Gaston Paris writes: "Je pense qu'on voudra bien reconnaître que le texte de ce poème, tel que je le livre au public, offre un spécimen admissible de la bonne langue française telle qu'elle devait se parler et s'écrire au milieu du XIe siècle." ("Readers will surely acknowledge that the text of this poem, in the form in which I present it here, offers a reasonable specimen of good French as it was presumably spoken and written in the mid-eleventh century.") Cited by Cerquiglini, *Eloge*, p. 94.

36. Thus Wagner observes, "Est-il injuste d'avancer que quelques grammairiens médiévistes n'ont pas toujours résisté à la tentation d'enseigner comment un clerc médiéval *devait* s'exprimer, qu'il écrivît ou qu'il parlât? Ainsi en allait-il des premiers éditeurs de textes. En face de manuscrits reputés corrompus ils n'hésitaient pas à recomposer une oeuvre telle qu'elle *aurait dû* sortir de la plume de son auteur." *L'Ancien français*, p. 67.

37. See Lodge, *French*, especially pp. 175–82.

38. I.e., the doctrine according to which naming creates reality; what has no name has no conceptual existence. At the theoretical level, this view of the relationship between language and the extralinguistic world, i.e., that language has the capacity to shape our reality and the way we perceive, or conceptualize, the extralinguistic world, has been a subject of intense controversy among philosophers and linguists since ancient times. At the practical level, it undergirds the discourses (in the Foucauldian sense of the term) of every institution/ideology that has ever existed, from the rhetoric of advertising, to the feminist campaign for nonsexist usage, to the underlying nationalist agenda of nineteenth-century French philology (see below).

39. Gabriel Bergounioux, "Le Francien (1815–1914): La Linguistique au service de la patrie," *Mots/Les langages du politique* 19 (1989): 23–40.

40. This familiar formula of French linguistic historiography—"a patois that 'made it'"—provides to my mind a singularly brilliant catachresis for conceptualizing the history of the French language: while appearing to validate the devalorized patois (through the egalitarian myth of "poor boy makes good"), it simultaneously reaffirms the "ideology of the standard" so deeply rooted in French culture (the latter phrase is from J. Milroy and L. Milroy, *Authority in Language* [London: Routledge, 1985]).

41. A clear articulation of this ideology, with respect to French, is con-

tained in Gaston Paris's 1888 essay, now a classic, "Les Parlers de France" (*Revue des Patois gallo-romans* 2 [1888]: 161–75). The ideology of the standard has conceivably been the single most important ideological determinant operative in the history of French. As Anthony Lodge observes, "the way in which the history of the French language has traditionally been written (principally in France, but elsewhere too) has . . . been heavily conditioned by reverential attitudes to the standard language and by linguistic prescriptivism. . . . [M]any . . . studies are in essence histories of the standard variety only (principally in its literary manifestations), implying that the other varieties of French (e.g., colloquial, popular, and regional forms) are of little interest. . . . This concentration on the evolution of a single variety of French often cloaks a teleological yearning on the part of the historian for linguistic homogeneity. . . . [By contrast, a] multidimensional history would . . . assume that no speech community is ever linguistically homogeneous, and so would trace, within the severe limits imposed by the evidence available, the development of the whole amalgam of varieties which make up 'the language'" *French*, pp. 7–9.

42. This attitude toward the French language is summed up in the phrase "l'expression parfaite du génie de la race et de la nation" ("the consummate expression of the spirit of the race and of the [French] nation"), which I came across in the Preface to Alexis François's *Histoire de la langue française cultivée des origines à nos jours* (Geneva: Alexandre Julien, 1959), a monograph appropriately dedicated to the memory of Gaston Paris.

43. There is evidence suggesting that by the thirteenth century the speech of Paris had achieved "most favored dialect" status (Lodge, *French*, p. 102; Dees et al. say this occurred even later, as noted by van Reenen, "La Linguistique," pp. 449–50). Nonetheless, consensus is lacking as to when it *began* to be viewed in this special light. The preeminence of Paris as a social and economic center should not be dated before the twelfth century (Lodge, *French*, p. 103).

44. Bergounioux, "Le Francien," pp. 38–39. Quite independently, in an essay published the same year as Bergounioux's, Howard Bloch invokes this same historical circumstance—French-German rivalry and the intense nationalism of the period between the Franco-Prussian and First World wars—to account for "the birth of medieval studies" in France, with particular reference to two of its founding texts, the *Strasbourg Oaths* (see also Cerquiglini, *La Naissance du français*) and the *Song of Roland*. "The founding discourse of medieval studies," Bloch asserts, "makes no distinction between the genesis of France's earliest linguistic and literary monuments and the identity of the nation" ("842. The Birth of Medieval Studies," in D. Hollier, ed., *A*

New History of French Literature [Cambridge, Mass.: Harvard University Press, 1989], p. 13). To the first term of his equation I would add one more element: the genesis of the French language itself.

45. A "linguistic variable" is defined as "a linguistic unit [phoneme, morpheme, construction] with two or more variants involved in covariation with other social and/or linguistic variables" (J. K. Chambers and Peter Trudgill, *Dialectology* [Cambridge, Eng.: Cambridge University Press, 1980], p. 60). For a classic text of variationist sociolinguistics, see William Labov's *Sociolinguistic Patterns* (Philadelphia: University of Pennsylvania Press; Oxford: Blackwell, 1972).

Gellrich, "Figura, Allegory, and the Question of History"

1. "Figura," in *Archivum Romanicum* 22 (1938): 436–89, translated by Ralph Manheim as "Figura," in Auerbach's *Scenes from the Drama of European Literature* (Minneapolis: University of Minnesota Press, 1984), pp. 11–76. Auerbach, "Typological Symbolism in Medieval Literature," *Yale French Studies* 9 (1952): 3–10.

2. "Philologie der Weltliteratur," in W. Muschg and E. Staiger, eds., *Weltliteratur, Festgabe für Fritz Stich* (Bern: A. Francke, 1952), translated by Marie Said and Edward Said as "Philology and Weltliteratur," in *Centennial Review* 13 (1969): 1–17; see also Edward Said's comments on the originality of Auerbach's use of *Ansatzpunkt* in *Beginnings: Intention and Method* (New York: Basic Books, 1975), pp. 68–76, and Paul Bové's evaluation of Said's response in *Intellectuals in Power: A Genealogy of Critical Humanism* (New York: Columbia University Press, 1986), pp. 187–93.

3. "Typological Symbolism in Medieval Literature," p. 6.

4. See "Figura," pp. 49–52.

5. *Biblia Sacra iuxta Vulgatam Clementinam* (Madrid: Biblioteca de Autores Christianos, 1965). Translations throughout are from the Douay version.

6. See, e.g., Henri de Lubac, "Concorde des deux testaments," *Exégèse médiévale: les quartre sens de L'Écriture* (Paris: Aubier, 1959), part 1.1.328–41. It is relevant to note that de Lubac begins his assessment of the Scriptural foundations of medieval exegesis with a discussion of two principles in Pauline interpretation, which he names "allégorie" and "mystère," on the authority of the reference in Galatians 2.24 ("L'allégorie paulinienne," 1.2.373–83). *Figura* does not appear as an important term anywhere in his lengthy analysis, though he mentions Auerbach's essay once (p. 399), in a discussion of the mystical sense. In de Lubac's opinion, allegory is the operative term from as early as the first century, and by the time of Jerome, it is axiomatic, e.g., "iuxta allegoriam, id est, intelligentiam spiritalem" (Jerome, *In Amos*, in J.-P. Migne, ed., *Patrologia Latina*, 25.1025).

7. See "Figura," pp. 28–44, 54–55.

8. *Patrologia Latina*, 83.99.

9. Thomas Aquinas, *Summa Theologiae*, Article 10 (Cambridge: Blackfriars, 1964), I.38.

10. Pierre Bersuire, *Repertorium morale* in *Opera omnia* (Cologne, 1730–31), II.201A. But Bersuire also goes on to cite "parable," "aenigma," and the "ornaments" of conversation as characteristic *figurae*, and such uses reach back to the oratorical tradition of the term that Auerbach associates with its pagan origins.

11. *Literatursprache und Publikum in der lateinischen Spätantike und im Mittelalter* (Bern: Francke, 1958); "Introduction: Purpose and Method," *Literary Language and Its Public in Late Antiquity and in the Middle Ages*, trans. Ralph Manheim (New York: Pantheon, 1965), p. 20.

12. Years ago Charles Donahue tried to allay negative reaction to "allegory" in the study of medieval literature by appealing to Auerbach's distinction between Hebraic and Hellenic styles set forth in *Mimesis*, chapter 1: see "Summation," in Dorothy Bethurum, ed., *Critical Approaches to Medieval Literature, Selected Papers from the English Institute, 1958–1959*, pp. 61–82, 160–62 (New York: Columbia University Press, 1960). But the distinction between Hellenic and Hebraic that Donahue traces in medieval allegory is ultimately more useful in understanding Auerbach, as I am trying to do here, than in defining the "historicity" of medieval forms. In fact Donahue never refers to the 1938 essay where Auerbach discusses the Alexandrian texts. Moreover, tracing their influence on subsequent literature needs to be considered in light of recent qualifications that the Alexandrians themselves were developing already existing forms; see, e.g., David Dawson, *Allegorical Readers and Cultural Revision in Ancient Alexandria* (Berkeley: University of California Press, 1992). For this reference, and several other crucial points, I am grateful to Thomas G. Rosenmeyer.

13. Prior to the presentations in this volume, publications typically make only incidental reference to Auerbach's personal circumstances for understanding his philological arguments; but more extended considerations have been ventured, e.g., by Geoffrey Green, *Literary Criticism and the Structures of History: Erich Auerbach and Leo Spitzer* (Lincoln: University of Nebraska Press, 1982), pp. 11–82, and Bové, *Intellectuals in Power*, pp. 79–208.

14. This conclusion is derived, e.g., from the "Figura" essay, n. 34, in which Auerbach recalls a remark made by Rudolf Bultmann (on the Redemption as a second Exodus) and then observes: "the specialized literature is not available to me at the moment" (p. 234). But even more to the point is his response to Curtius' criticism of the *figura* essay in "Epilegomena zu Mimesis," in *Romanische Forschungen* 65 (1953): 10, n. 12. Here Auerbach says he was

only able to write about *figura* because he had access to the complete copy of Migne's *Patrology* owned by the Dominican monastery of San Pietro di Galata. Although the library containing the collection was closed to the public, Auerbach was given permission to use it by the good offices of the papal delegate to Istanbul, Msgr. Roncalli, who apparently tried to assist refugees from the Holocaust. It is most suggestive that some of the work on *figura* was done in the very context of refuge in an "attic room" offered to a Jewish scholar.

15. Auerbach's "Epilegomena zu Mimesis," pp. 1–18, discusses the problem of limited sources for the book. Chapter 7 is the only chapter with documentation, which is probably the result of his scholarship on the play in Marburg.

16. As Bové, e.g., illustrates in *Intellectuals in Power*, p. 208.

17. The presentation of this "reading" of "Auerbach's Everydays" by Hans Ulrich Gumbrecht at the symposium became the occasion for my reconsideration of the relation between allegory and *figura* in this essay. I am grateful for his many provocative suggestions and for the documentation he provided generously at the symposium, including the documents on Auerbach's dismissal from the University referred to above, from the Staatsarchiv Marburg, Best. 307d/74, acc. 1966/10.

18. "Von der Seltsamkeit meiner Lage eine Vorstellung zu geben ist unmöglich"; from the recently published letter (23 September 1935) in Karlheinz Barck, ed., "Neue Materialien," *Zeitschrift fuer Germanistik* 6 (1988): 689–90, also discussed by Hans Gumbrecht.

19. *Mimesis: Dargestellte Wirklichkeit in der abendländischen Literatur* (Bern: A. Francke, 1946), translated by Willard Trask as *Mimesis: The Representation of Reality in Western Literature* (New York: Anchor, 1957), p. 492.

20. This is the formulation of Luiz Costa-Lima, "Erich Auerbach: History and Metahistory," *New Literary History* 19 (1988): 485–94. See also Timothy Bahti, "Vico, Auerbach and Literary History," in *Vico: Past and Present*, ed. Giorgio Tagliacozzo (Atlantic Highlands, N.J.: Humanities Press, 1981), pp. 93–114.

21. See, e.g., Green, *Literary Criticism and the Structures of History*, pp. 29–53. See also Bové, *Intellectuals in Power*, pp. 87, 93–96; Karl F. Morrison, *The Mimetic Tradition of Reform in the West* (Princeton, N.J.: Princeton University Press, 1982), pp. 408–14.

22. Paul de Man, "Form and Intent in the American New Criticism," in *Blindness and Insight: Essays in the Rhetoric of Contemporary Criticism* (New York: Oxford University Press, 1971), p. 23, cited as a qualification of the "continuity" between style and theme presumed in American formalism. What de Man may have made of this potential "deconstruction" of Auerbach's con-

cept of mimesis is not carried out in the essay. It would seem to me that the split between allegory and *figura*, as I will continue to argue it, qualifies the view sometimes taken of mimesis as an organic structure of similarities and continuities.

23. "Bei den modernen Forschern hat die Fremdartigkeit der mittelalter-lichen Wirklichkeitsanschauung dahin geführt, das sie Figuration und Alle-gorie nicht von einander scheiden" ("Figura," in *Archivum Romanicum*, p. 487; Manheim trans., "Figura," p. 74). The use of *Seltsamkeit* in the letter to Benjamin (23 September 1935) signifies "strangeness" or "oddness" in the sense of "unusual" or "infrequent"; *Fremdartigkeit* in the 1938 essay signifies "strange-ness" or "oddness" in the sense of "unfamiliar," "alien," or even "un-German."

24. "Introduction," *Literary Language and Its Public*, p. 6.

25. Ibid.

26. *Die Hieroglyphenkunde des Humanismus in der Allegorie der Renaissance*, dis-cussed by Benjamin, *The Origin of German Tragic Drama*, trans. John Osborne (London: New Left Books, 1977), pp. 167–70. Judging from the familiar tone of Auerbach's correspondence with Benjamin in Paris in the mid-1930's, I am certain that Auerbach read this treatise prior to the publication of his essay on *figura*. But I am not aware of any comparative analysis of allegory in the two writers. For a recent discussion of Benjamin alone, see John McCole, *Walter Benjamin and the Antinomies of Tradition* (Ithaca, N.Y.: Cornell University Press, 1993), pp. 139–55. I have discussed the uncertainty of deconstruction and Benjamin's notion of allegory in "Deconstructing Allegory," *Genre* 18 (1985): 197–213.

27. Benjamin, *Origin of German Tragic Drama*, pp. 166, 175–77.

28. McCole does not make this distinction for the medieval reference and thus compromises the extent of Benjamin's departure from it: see *Walter Benjamin and the Antinomies of Tradition*, pp. 144–45. Cf. my discussion, "Decon-structing Allegory," p. 202 and n. 24.

29. See Benjamin, *Origin of German Tragic Drama*, pp. 195–202.

30. Ibid., pp. 178–79.

31. Ibid., pp. 194, 233.

32. Specifically by de Man, who quotes Benjamin's definition, "allegory means precisely the non-existence of what it represents" (without naming the publication), as a closing argument against organic form in "Form and Intent in the American New Criticism," p. 35. That he closes with this reference, rather than returning to his own point from Auerbach cited at the outset, is perhaps telling of the incompatibility of figural realism to Benjaminian allegory.

33. As already noted for Auerbach in the "Introduction" to *Literary Lan-*

guage and Its Public, p. 6; and for Benjamin throughout the essay on allegory in the *Origin of German Tragic Drama*, as remarked by McCole in *Walter Benjamin and the Antinomies of Tradition*, esp. chap. 4.

34. As Bové, for one, would make him out to be in *Intellectuals in Power*, p. 208. Consider, by contrast, Harry Levin's interview with Auerbach shortly after his arrival in the United States in "Two *Romanisten* in America: Spitzer and Auerbach," in *The Intellectual Migration: Europe and America, 1930–1960*, eds. Donald Fleming and Bernard Bailyn (Cambridge, Mass.: Harvard University Press, 1969), pp. 463–84. Let me also note that Cleanth Brooks, Auerbach's colleague at Yale in the 1950's, recently told me that Auerbach never spoke of Turkey or Germany to him, and gave no indication whatsoever of pessimism or dejection in his personal attitudes.

White, "Auerbach's Literary History"

1. Fredric Jameson, *The Political Unconscious: Narrative as a Socially Symbolic Act* (Ithaca, N.Y.: Cornell University Press, 1981), p. 12.

2. Ibid.

3. I use the by now more conventional translation, "historicism," for what Auerbach called "Historismus," translated "historism" in the English version of *Mimesis*. By "Historismus" Auerbach, following Meinecke, intended that worldview which identified "reality" with "history," rather than with a theological or metaphysical, noumenal "reality." Prior to the end of the eighteenth century, Meinecke argued, the meaning of history had always been referred to some extratemporal or transcendental ground. After Herder and Goethe and in Ranke especially, "history" itself becomes foundational and the meaning of human events established by purely "intrahistorical" reference. Auerbach locates the earliest statements of this worldview in the work of G. B. Vico, which, as Auerbach puts it, proceeds on the basis of the "identity" of "human nature" and "human history." See Erich Auerbach, "Vico and Aesthetic Historism," in his *Scenes from the Drama of European Literature: Six Essays* (New York: Meridian Books, 1959), p. 198. In discussion of *Mimesis* I use the following editions: *Mimesis: The Representation of Reality in Western Literature*, trans. Willard R. Trask (Princeton, N.J.: Princeton Univ. Press), and *Mimesis: Dargestellte Wirklichkeit in der abendländischen Literatur* (Bern: A. Francke, 1946). Page references are included in my text.

4. Here we might note Auerbach's insistence, in "Figura," on the distinction between figural and allegorical interpretation (*Scenes*, p. 54). He notes that, in Christian hermeneutics, the Greek myths are interpreted allegorically in Christian terms (as in the Christian expropriation of Virgil's *Eclogue* IV). But Auerbach notes how, in the *Commedia*, for example, Dante relates pagan to Christian things not allegorically but figurally (p. 63). Thus, Virgil is pre-

sented less as an "allegory for reason" than as a "figura" of the "poet-prophet-guide, now fulfilled in another world" (p. 69). "The historical Virgil is 'fulfilled' by the dweller in limbo" (ibid.). Then, in his commentary on Vico, in "Vico and Aesthetic Historicism," Auerbach suggests that Vico's philosophy of history is itself figural. The "poetic imagination" of Vico's "first men" (the Age of the Gods) is a "figura," Auerbach argues, of the "poetic imagination" of the "third age" (that of Men) which "fulfills" it. "Vico and Aesthetic Historism," p. 194.

5. The problem of the origin of western literary realism is of course dealt with in the positing of the originality of the representation of everyday life in the mode of tragic realism found in the Gospels. Whence the often remarked "gap," the leap from the descriptions of Homeric and Old Testament representations of "reality" in *Mimesis*, chapter 1, "Die Narbe des Odysseus," over the whole of Greek and Hellenistic literature, to the treatments of Petronius, Tacitus, and the Gospel according to Mark, in which the whole of classical proto-realism is transcended and western "figural" realism is set under way.

6. The term "genealogical" is intended to summon up the usage by Nietzsche and Foucault.

7. See Bernard Williams's discussion of how we are "related" to Greek culture in his recent book, *Shame and Necessity* (Berkeley: University of California Press, 1993).

8. This sequence, too, represents a series of figures and their fulfillments, with each fulfillment itself becoming another figure to be further fulfilled in its turn. This would all be quite justifiably called an example of a kind of Hegelian "expressivist" conception of historical causation providing the basis for a "dialectical" analysis of the relations between successive phases of the series, were it not for the fact that it is so specifically Vichian in its conceptualization. The relationships are dialectical in the Hegelian sense insofar as Hegel is the theoretician of a notion of historical change more tropical than logical in kind, but it is more Vichian insofar as Vico was not only a more overt theoretician of a "poetic logic" centered — as de Man would have said — upon rhetoric as trope rather than as persuasion, but also, by Auerbach's lights at least, the inventor of modern "aesthetic historism."

9. Recall that Balzac's creative powers are specifically referred, not to his "intellectual attitude," which is presented as a confused and contradictory set of "apothegms" hastily thrown off, but to his "temperament"—"emotional, fiery, and uncritical." *Mimesis*, p. 482.

10. Notice that the subtitle of *Mimesis* is *Dargestellte Wirklichkeit der abendländischen Literatur*. Although this subtitle is translated into English as "The Representation of Reality in Western Literature," in the German, the focal term is *Wirklichkeit* ("reality"), not "representation" (*Vorstellung*). Indeed, the

notion of "representation" appears only in the form of a gerundive adjective, "dargestellte," which suggests not so much a thing (a "representation") as, rather, an *activity*, specifically the activity of "presentation." Thus, the original subtitle of *Mimesis* comes to mean something like "*presented* reality in western literature"—with the connotation that specific "representations" of "reality" have been "worked up" or, more accurately, "styled" for presentation to someone or something for some purpose, aim, or end. In German, *darstellen* encompasses the meanings "to present," "show," "produce," and "exhibit," as well as "to sketch," "delineate," and "mimic," and, in theatrical usage, "to perform." So we might say that the phrase *Dargestellte Wirklichkeit*, which is translated into English as "the Representation of Reality" might be more accurately, though to be sure less elegantly, rendered as "the *presentation* of reality." Translating thus we could capture both the sense of the "constructed" nature of any "representation of reality" and Auerbach's point that there is no such thing as "the" (in the sense of a single or unitary) "representation" of "reality" (in the sense of a changeless substance or noumenon) whose "nature" is gradually being fully described by successive efforts to "represent" it "realistically." What he himself "presents" is a succession of efforts by writers working in a generally delineated tradition of "presented representations" to devise ways of capturing in written utterance the multiplicity and change characteristic of "social" and more generally "human" reality—and always failing in that process in the end. The inevitability of this failure is suggested by the epigraph of the book, a line from Andrew Marvell: "Had we but *world enough and time*" (my emphasis).

11. Note here that the famous first chapter of *Mimesis*, "Die Narbe des Odysseus," constitutes a veritable pre-history, prologue, or proema to the actual subject of *mimesis* as figuration. Here it is suggested that figuralist representation was unknown to both the Homeric and the most ancient biblical epics. The programmatic nature of Auerbach's interpretations of these texts is reflected in his stress on the elements of each which permit one to *oppose* it to the others. For example, Homer is all surface and detail, the Bible all depth and typological; the one is spatial, the other temporal; the one features metonymic, the other metaphorical relations, and so on. Figural realism, the history of which takes up the remaining nineteen chapters, supposedly mediates, dialectically as it were, between what Jakobson called the "two axes" of discourse, the paradigmatic and syntagmatic. As thus envisaged, Auerbach's "figuralism" is the tropical movement between the two axes of speech.

12. The idea that the Revolution of 1789 is not itself a revolution but only an eruption of forces long latent, a delayed effect of causes originating in the Reformation, has been a topos of historical interpretation at least since Tocqueville.

13. Considered as a figure fulfilled, however, any given text, such as, for example, Dante's *Commedia*, is itself a "prefiguration" of a later text, such as, for example, Balzac's *Comédie humaine*, which can be viewed in turn as the "fulfillment" of Dante's text. So, too, for texts within a single author's corpus: for example, the "Vita Nuova" is interpreted as a prefiguration of the *Commedia*, which in its turn is also a "fulfillment" of the *Aeneid* of Virgil. But this "prefiguration(figure)fulfillment" model can be used for the construction of whole traditions of writing, in which a later text is viewed not so much as an "effect," offspring, or descendent of an earlier text, but rather a product of an author's "choice" of an earlier text as a model. Finally, the "prefiguration(figure)fulfillment" paradigm can be used to characterize the relation between whole epochs, such as that between the Italian Renaissance, on the one hand, and classical antiquity, on the other.

14. The famous first chapter of *Mimesis*, "Odysseus's Scar," depicts two stylistic conventions, that of the Homeric and that of the ancient Hebrew epics, which do *not* prefigure the representational practices of western realism. They are different antitypes to western literary realism, which emerges, according to Auerbach, only with the Gospels. Whence the famous "gap" in the account of western literary realism, the omission of Greek and Hellenistic literature.

15. In this respect his project, originally published in 1946, resembled that of E. H. Gombrich in *Art and Illusion: A Study in the Psychology of Pictorial Representation* (New York: Pantheon, 1960).

16. Auerbach takes Meinecke's interpretation of the birth of historicism (*Historismus*) at face value. *Mimesis*, p. 444 (English edition).

17. This is not to suggest that either Auerbach or Meinecke identified *Historismus* with secularism *tout court*. See Friedrich Meinecke, *Historism: The Rise of a New Historical Outlook*, trans. by J. E. Anderson. (New York: Herder and Herder, 1972), p. 496ff.

18. *Mimesis*, 443–44.

19. See the passage on his own style of analysis compared with that of Woolf, in *Mimesis*, p. 548 (English edition).

20. It is worth recalling, it seems to me, that the notion of "literature" itself and the idea of a manner of writing that is specifically "literary" in nature are strictly modern concepts. Indeed, it is arguable that what "modernism" amounts to is the attempt to contrive a mode of language use which, in its transcendence of the dichotomy between "factual" and "fictional" discourse, produces a writing that is both "imaginary" and "cognitional." Auerbach appears to have grasped this in his discussions of the strain of realism which emerges in Flaubert and culminates (is fulfilled in) the style of Virginia Woolf.

21. This continuity is to be seen in Auerbach's description of the relation between the historical context of the twentieth and that of the nineteenth cen-

tury (*Mimesis*, p. 549, English edition). See also the last paragraph of *Mimesis*, in which Auerbach dilates on the "realism" of Virginia Woolf's style (ibid., p. 556).

22. The more "the random moment" is exploited, Auerbach writes, "the more the elementary things which our lives have in common come to light. The more numerous, varied, and simple the people are who appear as subjects of such random moments, the more effectively must what they have in common shine forth. In this unprejudiced and exploratory type of representation we cannot but see to what an extent—below the surface conflicts— the differences between men's way of life and forms of thought have already lessened. The strata of societies and their different ways of life have become inextricably mingled. . . . So the complicated process of dissolution which led to fragmentation of the exterior action, to reflection of consciousness, and to stratification of time seems to be tending toward a very simple solution. Perhaps it will be too simple to please those who, despite all its dangers and catastrophes, admire and love our epoch for the sake of its abundance of life and the incomparable historical vantage point which it affords. But they are few in number, and probably will not live to see much more than the first forewarnings of the approaching unification and simplification." Ibid., pp. 552–53.

Stock, "Literary Realism in the Later Ancient Period"

1. Throughout this essay, quotations from these works will be from the following editions: *Mimesis: The Representation of Reality in Western Literature*, trans. Willard R. Trask (Princeton, N.J.: Princeton University Press, 1953), and *Literary Language and Its Public in Late Latin Antiquity and in the Middle Ages*, trans. Ralph Manheim (Princeton, N.J.: Princeton University Press, 1965). Page references are included in my text.

2. Eduard Norden, *Die antike Kunstprosa vom VI. Jahrhundert vor Christ bis in die Zeit der Renaissance*, 2 vols. (Leipzig: Teubner, 1915). This is Norden's most frequently cited secondary work.

3. Erich Auerbach, "Figura," *Archivum Romanicum* 22 (1939): 436–89; "Sacrae scripturae sermo humilis," *Neuphilologische Mitteilungen* 42 (1941): 57–67 and *Garp Filolojileri Dergisi* 1 (1947): 15–22; "Sermo humilis I," *Romanische Forschungen* 64 (1952): 304–64; and "Lateinische Prosa des 9. und 10. Jahrhunderts (Sermo humilis II)," *Romanische Forschungen* 66 (1954): 1–64.

4. See the fundamental studies of Pierre Hadot, *Marius Victorinus. Recherches sur sa vie et ses oeuvres* (Paris: Etudes Augustiniennes, 1971), pp. 201–10; and *Porphyre et Victorinus*, 2 vols. (Paris: Etudes Augustiniennes, 1968).

5. For a succinct review of the considerable literature on this subject, see

Goulven Madec, *Saint Augustin et la philosophie. Notes critiques* (Paris: Institut catholique, 1992), pp. 27–33.

6. See Pierre Hadot, *Plotin ou la simplicité du regard*, 2nd ed. (Paris: Etudes Augustiniennes, 1973), pp. 21–39, especially p. 26.

7. Porphyry, *Vita Plotini*, 1. I use the edition and translation of A. H. Armstrong in the Loeb Classical Library, *Plotinus*, vol. 1, 2nd ed. (Cambridge, Mass.: Harvard University Press, 1989), which incorporates the changes in Henry-Schwyzer, *Plotini Opera*, vol. 3 (Oxford: Clarendon Press, 1982). Further passage references are included in my text.

8. On Amelius's views, see A. H. Armstrong, "Plotinus, Amelius, and Porphyry," in A. H. Armstrong, ed., *The Cambridge History of Later Greek and Early Medieval Philosophy* (Cambridge, Eng.: Cambridge University Press, 1967), pp. 264–68.

9. See Pierre Hadot, *La Citadelle intérieure. Introduction aux pensées de Marc Aurèle* (Paris: Fayard, 1992), pp. 8–9, and, on the notion of oral "spiritual exercises," see his recent statement, "La Philosophie antique. Une éthique ou une pratique?" in P. Demont, ed., *Problèmes de la morale antique* (Amiens: Université d'Amiens, 1993), pp. 7–37.

10. Porphyry's observation may in part be rhetorical, since it draws attention to the need for someone—namely Porphyry—to bring order to the discussion. *Vita* 3.36–38.

11. I make the claim with caution; for a description of the parameters of dyslexia, see Insup Taylor and M. Martin Taylor, *The Psychology of Reading* (New York: Academic Press, 1983), pp. 421–28, which is however limited to empirical research on dyslexic children.

12. For a summary of the evidence, see Pierre Courcelle, *Recherches sur les "Confessions" de saint Augustin*, 2nd ed. (Paris: Boccard, 1968), pp. 30–32. For a decisive refutation of Courcelle's view, see James J. O'Donnell, *Augustine. "Confessions"* (Oxford: Clarendon Press, 1992), vol. 2, pp. 360–62.

13. For a more thorough discussion of this point, see my forthcoming study, *Augustine the Reader*.

14. See the dossier compiled by Pierre Courcelle, "Tradition néo-platonicienne et traditions chrétiennes de la 'région de dissemblance,' (Platon, *Politique* 273d)," *Archives d'histoire doctrinale et littéraire du moyen âge*, année 1957 (1958): 5–33.

15. Two recent studies of this tradition are Mary Carruthers, *The Book of Memory: A Study in Medieval Culture* (Cambridge, Eng.: Cambridge University Press, 1990), and Janet Coleman, *Ancient and Medieval Memories: Studies in the Reconstruction of the Past* (Cambridge, Eng.: Cambridge University Press, 1992). A classic in the field remains Frances A. Yates, *The Art of Memory* (Chicago:

University of Chicago Press, 1966). On Augustine's notion of memory and his transformation (and criticism) of Neoplatonic views, see A. Solignac, "La Mémoire selon saint Augustin," in Augustine, *Les Confessions VIII–XIII* (Paris: Bibliothèque Augustinienne, 1962), pp. 557–67.

Brownlee, "The Ideology of Periodization"

1. As a low point, the late Middle Ages is also, and quite interestingly, comparable to the other key low point in the overall literary-historical sweep sketched by *Mimesis*: post-imperial late antiquity, treated in chapter 4, and focusing on Gregory of Tours.

2. Erich Auerbach, *Mimesis: The Representation of Reality in Western Literature*, trans. Willard R. Trask (Princeton, N.J.: Princeton University Press, 1953), pp. 260–61. All citations are from this edition; further page references will be included in my text. The German text I use is *Mimesis: Dargestellte Wirklickeit in der abendländischen Literatur* (Bern: A. Francke, 1946).

3. All citations are from Antoine de La Sale, *Le Réconfort de Madame de Fresne, édité d'après les mss. 10748 et II 7827 de la Bibliothèque Royale de Bruxelles*, ed. Ian Hill (Exeter: University of Exeter, 1979). Translations are mine.

4. Cf. the term *confort* (also present in Auerbach's excerpt) as semantically overdetermined in La Sale's text as a whole.

5. Brest was taken by the English in 1342 and remained in their possession until 1396; the Black Prince died in 1376; see Hill's comments in La Sale, *Réconfort*, p. ix. Pseudo-historicity and *effet de réel* are both key elements in La Sale's narrative. Cf. the forgetting of the heroine's name in his story number two.

6. For this useful narratological terminology, see Gérard Genette's now classic *Figures III* (Paris: Seuil, 1972), esp. pp. 67–267, "Discours du récit."

7. See John D. Lyons, *Exemplum: The Rhetoric of Example in Early Modern France and Italy* (Princeton, N.J.: Princeton University Press, 1989).

8. A similar kind of double audience and double exemplarity is at issue in Philippe de Mézières's treatment of the Griseldis story in his *Livre sur la vertu du sacrement de mariage* (ca. 1385–89). Cf. Auerbach's reference to the "story of Griselda" as "romantically moving" (*Mimesis*, p. 245). Given the MS diffusion, it is not impossible that Griseldis serves as an "inverted model" for the de Fresne couple. For the "polyvalence" of Griseldis as exemplum, see Kevin Brownlee, "Commentary and the Rhetoric of Exemplarity: Griseldis in Petrarch, Philippe de Mézières, and the *Estoire*," *South Atlantic Quarterly* 91 (1992): 865–90.

9. In this context it is worth recalling the other celebrated late-medieval story of the death of a noble child, cited by Auerbach in chapter 10 as an even more stark example of the "complete directness" characteristic of late-medieval mimesis at its "best." This is the narrative of how Gaston Fébus

kills his son and only legitimate heir, the younger Gaston, as recounted by Jean Froissart in his *Chroniques* 3.21 (*Chroniques. Livre III*, ed. Léon Mirot, in vol. 12 [Paris, 1931] of *Chroniques de J. Froissart*, ed. S. Luce et al., Société de l'Histoire de France, 15 vols. [Paris, 1869-), as part of the sequence at the beginning of Book 3 of the *Chroniques* known as the *Voyage en Béarn*. Again, Auerbach takes this episode out of context and misreads it as simple "detailed realism." Following Huizinga yet again, Auerbach cites the episode's "almost tragic power" (*Mimesis*, p. 258). Then he juxtaposes Froissart's narrative of a son's violent and premature death with that recounted by La Sale to illustrate extreme cases of a kind of one-dimensional late-medieval mimesis: with the deaths of the young du Chastel and the young Gaston, the reader has "nothing beyond the direct, concrete experience of the events narrated." The reader is left with "nothing but a sensory . . . horror from the experience of life's transitoriness" (p. 259).

When we consider Froissart's treatment of the death scene of the young Gaston, however, we see that, narratologically speaking, there is special emphasis on the multiple contexts which produce meaning through their interaction. At the same time, this kind of self-conscious reading activity is inscribed as part of the global discourse of *Chroniques* 3 in at least five different ways: (1) The story is progressively revealed and suspense is built up by careful narrative structuring, including the shifting of diegetic narrators. (2) The key intratextual model scene, Gaston's murder of his cousin, Pierre de Béarn (*Chron.* 3.14), informs the young-Gaston sequence in terms of juxtapositions and cross-readings, including a set of progressions, one of the most striking of which is the ludicrous reduction of the (in both cases uncourtly) murder weapon: "une dague" ("a dagger," p. 62) to kill Pierre de Béarn; to kill the young Gaston, "un petit long coustelet dont il appareilloit ses ongles et nettoioit" ("an elongated little knife with which he used to clean his fingernails," p. 88). (3) Froissart inscribes his (socioeconomic) relation to his patron(s) so that it functions as part of a built-in speech situation, which is thus fraught with patronage considerations. (4) The "autobiographical" component of *Chroniques* 3's opening presentation of "reality" is mediated by Froissart qua writer; this mediated mimetic construct then becomes an element of the plot of *Chroniques* 3. (5) Froissart repeatedly meditates on the limits of historiographic mimesis, i.e., the impossibility of knowing and/or telling the truth. Cf. the important study by Peter F. Ainsworth, *Jean Froissart and the Fabric of History: Truth, Myth, and Fiction in the "Chroniques"* (Oxford: Clarendon, 1990), esp. pp. 143–45, 153–71.

10. This context is bivalent, involving both heavenly and earthly dimensions and imperatives. It is also directly linked to the issues of procreation and lineage.

11. See Jacqueline Cerquiglini, *La Couleur de la mélancolie. La fréquentation des livres au XIVe siècle. 1300–1415* (Paris: Hatier, 1993); and Daniel Poirion, *Le Poète et le prince. L'évolution du lyrisme courtois de Guillaume de Machaut à Charles d'Orléans* (Paris: PUF, 1965).

12. See Jacqueline Cerquiglini, "Le Clerc et l'écriture: Le *Voir dit* de Guillaume de Machaut et la définition du *dit*," in Hans Ulrich Gumbrecht, ed., *Literatur in der Gesellschaft des Spätmittelalters* (Heidelberg: Winter, 1980), pp. 151–68.

13. Ibid., p. 158.

14. See Kevin Brownlee, "Ovide et le moi poétique 'moderne' à la fin du moyen âge: Jean Froissart et Christine de Pizan," in Brigitte Cazelles and Charles Méla, eds., *Modernité au moyen âge. Le défi du passé* (Geneva: Droz, 1990), pp. 153–73.

15. See Sylvia Huot, *The "Romance of the Rose" and Its Medieval Readers: Interpretation, Reception, Manuscript Transmission* (Cambridge, Eng.: Cambridge University Press, 1993, pp. 207–238; Poirion, *Poète*, pp. 271–310; Jean-Claude Mühlethaler, *Poétiques du quinzième siècle. Situation de François Villon et Michault Taillevent* (Paris: Nizet, 1983).

16. See Michel Zink, *La Subjectivité littéraire. Autour du siècle de saint Louis* (Paris: PUF, 1985); and Ainsworth, *Jean Froissart and the Fabric of History*, esp. pp. 140–71.

17. For the late-medieval poetics of *renovatio*, see Peter F. Dembowski, *Jean Froissart and His "Méliador": Context, Craft, and Sense* (Lexington: French Forum, 1983), esp. pp. 7–59. See also Jane Taylor, "The Fourteenth Century: Context, Text and Intertext," pp. 267–332 in Norris J. Lacy, Douglas Kelly, and Keith Busby, eds., *The Legacy of Chrétien de Troyes*, vol. 1 (Amsterdam: Rodopi, 1987).

18. See Kevin Brownlee, "Christine de Pizan et Dante: Généalogies littéraires et le problème du père," in Wolf-Dieter Stempel, ed., *Französische Lyrik des Spätmittelalters* (Munich: Fink, forthcoming).

19. See also the important study of Madeleine Jeay, "Une Théorie du roman: Le Manuscrit autographe de *Jehan de Saintré*," *Romance Philology* 47 (1994): 287–307. For another example of this kind of late-medieval dialogism (or, perhaps better, textual polyphony), see Kevin Brownlee, "Machaut's Motet 15 and the *Roman de la Rose*," *Early Music History* 10 (1991): 1–14.

Landauer, "Auerbach's Performance and the American Academy"

For their contributions to his thoughts in this essay, the author would like to thank David Hollinger and Herbert Lindenberger.

1. Erich Auerbach, *Literary Language and Its Public in Late Latin Antiquity and in the Middle Ages*, trans. Ralph Manheim (New York: Pantheon, 1965), p. 237.

2. Ibid., p. 239.

3. Erich Auerbach, *Mimesis: The Representation of Reality in Western Literature*, trans. Willard R. Trask (Princeton, N.J.: Princeton University Press, 1953), p. 557. Further page references to this edition and to the original German edition (identified by "Ger."), *Mimesis: Dargestellte Wirklichkeit in der abendländischen Literatur* (Bern: A. Franke, 1946), will be included in my text.

4. For Paul Bové, it is clear that the literary society of Auerbach's Europe had disappeared. Bové, *Intellectuals in Power: A Genealogy of Critical Humanism* (New York: Columbia University Press, 1986), p. 103. And yet, for Auerbach there are always those hopes of readers reached and throughout an image retained of a literary society in which he belonged.

5. Auerbach, *Literary Language*, p. 237.

6. Carl Landauer, "*Mimesis* and Erich Auerbach's Self-Mythologizing," *German Studies Review* 11, no. 1 (Feb. 1988): 83–96.

7. Bové, in his *Intellectuals in Power*, provides a fascinating study of the appropriation of Erich Auerbach by the American academy, the styling of Auerbach as a representative figure. However, Bové emphasizes that this audience misread Auerbach, "distort[ing] his achievement while establishing his authority" (p. 101). I will suggest not so much the distortions of cultural translation as the traits in Auerbach's *Mimesis* that were perfectly suited for American consumption.

8. Landauer, "*Mimesis* and Erich Auerbach's Self-Mythologizing," p. 89.

9. This is especially so in light of the fact that Goethe held particular significance to German Jews. On this point, see David Sorkin, *The Transformation of German Jewry, 1780–1840* (Oxford: Oxford University Press, 1987) and George Mosse, *German Jews Beyond Judaism* (Bloomington: Indiana University Press, 1985).

10. Yakov Malkiel, interview with the author, Dec. 16, 1987 (Berkeley, California).

11. Arthur Evans, "Erich Auerbach as European Critic," *Romance Philology* 25, no. 2 (1971): 200.

12. Delmore Schwartz, "The King Asked, 'What Time Is It?'" *New York Times*, Nov. 29, 1953, p. 40.

13. Auerbach, *Mimesis*, p. 373. In his review of *Mimesis* in the *Kenyon Review*, René Wellek called Auerbach's bluff: "Who has read the gruesome story of the arrest of Peter Valvomeres in Ammianus Marcellinus? Or the moving dialogue, in bed, between husband and wife, deciding the fate of their only boy, threatened with execution, from Antoine de la Sale? Or who remembers, even if he has dipped into the *Mémoires* of Saint-Simon, the scene of the Duke of Orleans sitting on his close-stool among his valets and officials?" Wellek, "Auerbach's Special Realism," *Kenyon Review* 16 (1954): 299.

14. Willard Trask translates "beliebig" as "random." Probably "arbitrary" or some other word suggesting choice rather than mere chance would provide

Notes to Pages 185–87

a better translation. Nevertheless, in many places in *Mimesis*, Trask's choice of "random" is not misleading.

15. In *Modern Language Notes*, Wolfgang Fleischmann described "an almost uncanny quality of the choice of texts for inclusion in *Mimesis*: Why do seemingly random passages from texts often of doubtfully representative quality for the period of literary history envisaged work so well in bringing not only the work from which they are taken but also the whole period of their origin to life?" And Fleischmann continues: "There is no doubt that *Mimesis* is infused with a kind of providential spirit, seemingly effortlessly to make the chaos whole." Wolfgang Bernard Fleischmann, "Erich Auerbach's Critical Theory and Practice: An Assessment," *Modern Language Notes* 81 (1966): 537.

16. Auerbach, *Mimesis* (Ger.), p. 517. In a provocative essay on Auerbach, Seth Lerer suggests that the early emphasis by some of Auerbach's critics on his sensitivity and belletrism "is not simply a misunderstanding on the part of Auerbach's contemporaries. It represents a conscious strategy to efface the disturbing political and personal themes of *Mimesis*: to make it safe for the reader in the study, the student in the library, the connoisseur in that literary gallery where we may all breathe that 'humane atmosphere' of intellectual comfort." Lerer, "Making *Mimesis*: Erich Auerbach and the Institutions of Medieval Studies," in R. Howard Bloch and Stephen G. Nichols, eds., *Medievalism and the Modernist Temper: On the Discipline of Medieval Studies* (Baltimore: Johns Hopkins University Press, 1996). Despite the tragic tones of *Mimesis*, however, there is also plenty of the parlor game and an unabashed playfulness.

17. Auerbach, *Literary Language*, p. 269.

18. Wellek, "Auerbach's Special Realism," p. 300. It must be mentioned that Wellek was suspicious of scholarship as art: "a work of scholarship and criticism can never be a work of art in the strict sense of the word." Ibid., p. 305.

19. Ernst Kantorowicz, *Kaiser Friedrich der Zweite* (Berlin: Georg Bondi, 1927), Preface.

20. Curtius, quoted by Konrad Bieber, letter to author, Feb. 2, 1986. In this context it is interesting to note that Auerbach in 1949 was the first speaker in the Princeton Seminars in Literary Criticism, the seminars organized by R. P. Blackmur that would develop into the Gauss Seminars; and that the small audience included Erwin Panofsky, Delmore Schwartz, John Berryman, Jacques Maritain, and Ernst Robert Curtius, as well as Blackmur. See Robert Fitzgerald, *Enlarging the Change: The Princeton Seminars in Literary Criticism, 1949–1951* (Boston: Northeastern University Press, 1985).

21. Auerbach, cited in Daniel Bell, *The Reforming of General Education: The Columbia College Experience in Its National Setting* (New York: Columbia University Press, 1966), p. 45. In his *Anatomy of Criticism*, Northrop Frye—the University of Toronto critic whom Frank Lentricchia depicts as the major

post–New Criticism critic—explains his approach as "based on Matthew Arnold's precept of letting the mind play freely around a subject in which there has been much endeavor and little attempt at perspective." Northrop Frye, *Anatomy of Criticism* (New York: Atheneum, 1958), p. 3.

22. Bell, *Reforming of General Education*, p. 51.

23. Ibid., p. 18.

24. Lionel Trilling, *Matthew Arnold* (New York: Harcourt Brace, 1939) p. 260.

25. Gerald Graff, *Professing Literature: An Institutional History* (Chicago: University of Chicago Press, 1987).

26. René Wellek, *A History of Modern Criticism: 1750–1950*, vol. 6 (New Haven, Conn.: Yale University Press, 1986), pp. 144–58.

27. See Karen Greenberg, "'Uphill Work': The German Refugee Historians and American Institutions of Higher Learning," in Harmut Lehman and James J. Sheehan, eds., *An Interrupted Past: German-Speaking Refugee Historians in the United States after 1933* (Washington, D.C. and Cambridge: German Historical Institute and Cambridge Univ. Press, 1991), pp. 94–101.

28. Donald Fleming and Bernard Bailyn, eds., *The Intellectual Migration: Europe and America, 1930–1960* (Cambridge, Mass.: Harvard University Press, 1969).

29. R. W. B. Lewis, *The American Adam* (Chicago: University of Chicago Press, 1955).

30. F. O. Matthiessen, *American Renaissance: Art and Expression in the Age of Emerson and Thoreau* (Oxford: Oxford University Press, 1941). Page references will be included in my text. In a recent article, Jonathan Arac explained: "Matthiessen played a decisive role in making possible the American academic study of American literature (for short, 'American studies')." Jonathan Arac, "F. O. Matthiessen: Authorizing an American Renaissance," in Walter Benn Michaels and Donald E. Pease, eds., *The American Renaissance Reconsidered* (Baltimore: Johns Hopkins University Press, 1985), p. 90.

31. Erwin Panofsky, "The History of Art," in W. Rex Crawford, ed., *The Cultural Migration: The European Scholar in America* (Philadelphia: University of Pennsylvania Press, 1953), p. 106.

32. Panofsky, "History of Art," p. 109.

33. Erwin Panofsky, "The Ideological Antecedents of the Rolls-Royce Radiator," *Proceedings of the American Philosophical Society* 107 (1963): 273–88; Leo Spitzer, "American Advertising Explained as Popular Art" (1949), reprinted in Leo Spitzer, *Representative Essays* (Stanford, Calif.: Stanford University Press, 1988), pp. 327–56.

34. Arthur Evans, "Erich Auerbach as European Critic," *Romance Philology* 25, no. 2 (Nov. 1971): 200–201.

35. Wellek, *History of Modern Criticism*, 6: 80.

36. Arac, "F. O. Matthiessen," p. 97.

37. Matthiessen, *American Renaissance*, p. 78. At that point in the text Matthiessen's footnote cites Marx and Engels.

38. Cleanth Brooks, *Modern Poetry and the Tradition* (Chapel Hill: University of North Carolina Press, 1939).

39. Ibid., pp. 18, 25.

40. Trilling, *Matthew Arnold*, p. 375.

41. Erich Auerbach, "Epilegomena zu *Mimesis*," *Romanische Forschungen* 65, nos. 1/2 (1953): 18, my translation.

42. Fleischmann, "Auerbach's Critical Theory and Practice," p. 537.

43. René Wellek, "Erich Auerbach (1892–1957)," *Comparative Literature* 10 (1958): 94.

Lindenberger, "On the Reception of Mimesis"

1. For a list of the reviews that I used, plus several others I located during the intervening years, see the appendix, "Early Reviews and Discussion of *Mimesis*," at the end of this chapter. Full information is given there for the reviews cited below.

2. Scott, review in *Christian Scholar*, p. 547.

3. "Auf dem Boden der Literatur [hat man] noch nie eine solch vollkommene Verbindung von synchronischer und diachronischer Betrachtung . . . gesehen." Spoerri, review in *Trivium*, p. 297.

4. Curtius, "Die Lehre von den drei Stilen in Altertum und Mittelalter (zu Auerbachs *Mimesis*)," review in *Romanische Forschungen*.

5. Auerbach, "Epilegomena zu *Mimesis*," *Romanische Forschungen*. For a brief discussion of Auerbach's perspectivism, see Geoffrey Green, *Literary Criticism and the Structures of History: Erich Auerbach and Leo Spitzer* (Lincoln: University of Nebraska Press, 1982), pp. 14–20.

6. Edelstein, review in *Modern Language Notes*, pp. 427–28.

7. Regenbogen, review reprinted in Regenbogen, *Kleine Schriften*, pp. 604, 610–13.

8. Wedeck, review in *Latomus*, p. 611.

9. Hatzfeld, review in *Romance Philology*, p. 337; Hess, "MIMESIS," pp. 177, 193, 199–200; Leo, review in *Comparative Literature*, p. 94.

10. Erich Auerbach, *La Representación de la realidad en la literatura occidental*, trans. I. Villanueva and E. Imaz (Mexico City and Buenos Aires: Fondo de Cultura Económica, 1950). The new chapter, entitled "La Dulcinea encantada," appears on pp. 314–39. The presence of this chapter may also have been motivated by the publisher's desire to provide Spanish-speaking readers with an analysis of one of their own classics; the dust jacket even calls attention to the fact that the chapter was written for this edition.

11. Davis, "Imitation of Life," review in *Partisan Review*, p. 325.

12. Fuerst, review in *JEGP*, p. 290.

13. Muscatine, review in *Romance Philology*, p. 454.

14. Heiney, review in *Western Humanities Review*, p. 71.

15. René Wellek claims that Auerbach could have avoided "the interminable series of misunderstandings" that mark the early reviews if he had consented "to define his terms and to make his suppositions clear from the outset." See Wellek, *A History of Modern Criticism: 1750–1950*, vol. 7 (New Haven, Conn.: Yale University Press, 1991), p. 118. I am doubtful that any such clarifications would have prevented reviewers from voicing their own institutional biases.

16. On Woolf: "Sie hält sich an kleine, unscheinbare, *beliebig* herausgegriffene Vorgänge." On his own method: "Denn ich bin überzeugt, dass jene Grundmotive der Geschichte der Wirklichkeitsdarstellung, wenn ich sie richtig gesehen habe, sich an jedem *beliebigen* realistischen Text aufweisen lassen müssen" (italics mine in both quotations). In *Mimesis: Dargestellte Wirklichkeit in der abendländischen Literatur*, 2nd ed. (Bern: A. Francke, 1959), pp. 508, 510 respectively. For the English translation of these passages, see *Mimesis: The Representation of Reality in Western Literature*, trans. Willard R. Trask (Princeton, N.J.: Princeton University Press, 1953), pp. 546, 548 respectively. See also Carl Landauer's discussion of Auerbach's conception of randomness in his essay within this volume.

17. "*Mimesis* ist ganz bewusst ein Buch, das ein bestimmter Mensch, in einer bestimmten Lage, zu Anfang der 1940er Jahre geschrieben hat." Auerbach, "Epilegomena zu *Mimesis*," p. 18.

18. Dan Latimer, ed., *Contemporary Critical Theory* (San Diego: Harcourt, Brace, 1989).

19. David H. Richter, ed., *The Critical Tradition: Classic Texts and Contemporary Trends* (New York: St. Martin's Press, 1989).

20. See David Lodge, ed., *20th Century Literary Criticism: A Reader* (London: Longman, 1972), pp. 315–32, and David Lodge, ed., *Modern Criticism and Theory: A Reader* (London: Longman, 1988). Note Lodge's change in title: whereas the term *criticism* could still encompass the whole field in 1972, by the late 1980's it was impossible to market a book of this sort without the term *theory*.

21. Robert Con Davis and Laurie Finke, eds., *Literary Criticism and Theory: The Greeks to the Present* (New York: Longman, 1989), p. 632. The selection from *Mimesis* (and, as with most anthologies, it is Auerbach's first chapter) occupies pp. 633–47.

22. Lionel Trilling, ed., *Literary Criticism: An Introductory Reader* (New York: Holt, Rinehart and Winston, 1970), p. 521. Despite Trilling's insistence on the book's uniqueness, those anthologists who included selections cited particu-

lar principles of criticism that they sought to exemplify. James L. Calderwood
and Harold E. Tolliver use the analyses of Homer and the Old Testament
to illustrate the New Critical principle that "what a work of fiction reveals
to us is inseparable from the manner in which it does so"; see their *Perspectives on Fiction* (New York: Oxford University Press, 1968), p. 4 (the Auerbach
selection occupies pp. 6–26). Lawrence Lipking and A. Walton Litz excerpt
Auerbach's passage on *Madame Bovary*, together with selections by Poulet,
Lukács, and Sartre, to exemplify another principle that teachers stressed at
the time, namely that there are multiple ways of looking at a single canonical
author, in this instance Flaubert; see Lipking and Litz, eds., *Modern Literary
Criticism: 1900–1970* (New York: Atheneum, 1972), pp. 458–64.

23. Erich Auerbach, "Farinata and Cavalcanti," *Kenyon Review* 14 (1952):
209–42.

24. Erich Auerbach, "The Triumph of Evil in Pascal," *Hudson Review* 4
(1951): 58–79.

25. I cite examples of Auerbach's appearance in handbooks in four different countries. Robert J. Clement's *Comparative Literature as Academic Discipline:
A Statement of Principles, Praxis, Standards* (New York: Modern Language Association, 1978) presents a model graduate seminar in which Auerbach is
listed with Wellek, Northrop Frye, and Leo Spitzer to provide "illustrations
of method" (p. 70). Henry Gifford's *Comparative Literature* (London: Routledge and Kegan Paul, 1969), designed for British academics, also presents a
model "postgraduate course" that recommends the final chapter of *Mimesis*
together with essays by Baudelaire, Pound, and Eliot as "writings that bear
on the topic of comparative literature" (p. 98). Zoran Konstantinovic's *Vergleichende Literaturwissenschaft: Bestandaufnahme und Ausblicke* (Bern: Peter Lang,
1988) recommends *Mimesis* as "ein immens wichtiges Buch" in a section on
"vergleichende Stilistik" (p. 146). The volume *Qu'est-ce que la Littérature comparée?*, by P. Brunel, Cl. Pichois, and A.-M. Rousseau (Paris: Armand Colin,
1983), lists *Mimesis* among a small group of "ouvrages de réflexion" together
with books by critics such as Étiemble, Cleanth Brooks, and Emil Staiger (pp.
160–61). All these handbooks, published between 1969 and 1988, present views
of literary study that would have counted as extremely conservative at their
various moments of publication.

26. For more detailed descriptions of the rationale behind these courses,
see W. B. Carnochan, *The Battleground of the Curriculum: Liberal Education and
American Experience* (Stanford, Calif.: Stanford University Press, 1993), pp. 68–
87, and my discussion in *The History in Literature: On Value, Genre, Institutions*
(New York: Columbia University Press, 1990), pp. 148–62.

27. Questin Anderson and Joseph A. Mazzeo, eds., *The Proper Study: Essays
on Western Classics*, together with its accompanying *Student Manual* (New York:

St. Martin's Press, 1962), includes a selection by various authorities—for example, Américo Castro on Cervantes and Stuart Hampshire on Spinoza—about each of its major texts from Homer to Freud. Since Auerbach wrote about the *Odyssey*, the editors chose another authority, Simone Weil, to represent the *Iliad*. Weil's famous essay, like *Mimesis*, was written by a Jew during World War II and self-consciously looks at a classic text from the perspective of events that the author is herself experiencing. Despite the editors' attempts to find critical texts with a high degree of contemporary relevance, they remain conscious of American college students' need for training in writing: thus, the *Student Manual* advertises that "Auerbach on Homer, for example, gives a lesson in organizing an extended comparison" (p. iii).

28. Trilling, *Literary Criticism*, p. 521.

29. Elizabeth Burns and Tom Burns, *Sociology of Literature and Drama* (Harmondsworth, Eng.: Penguin, 1973), pp. 418–32, and Hans Norbert Fügen, *Wege der Literatursoziologie* (Neuwied: Luchterhand, 1968), pp. 344–88.

30. I confess that by the mid-1980's I had stopped including *Mimesis* in my graduate theory seminars after student evaluations showed it to be the least popular of the assigned texts. Despite my own commitment to the book, I recognized that it did not pack the same wallop among students as the writings of, say, Bakhtin, Barthes, and Benjamin. I have continued assigning *Mimesis* in undergraduate honors courses, where the book seems to have lost none of its power.

31. For detailed studies of Auerbach's relation to these earlier forms of historicism, see Charles Breslin, "Philosophy or Philology: Auerbach and Aesthetic Historicism," *Journal of the History of Ideas* 22 (1961): 369–81; Helmut Kuhn, "Literaturgeschichte als Geschichtsphilosophie," *Philosophische Rundschau* 11 (1963): 222–48; Klaus Gronau, *Literarische Form und gesellschaftliche Entwicklung: Erich Auerbachs Beitrag zur Theorie und Methodologie der Literaturgeschichte*, Hochschulschriften Literaturwissenschaft 39 (Königstein: Hain, 1979); and Paul Bové, *Intellectuals in Power: A Genealogy of Critical Humanism* (New York: Columbia University Press, 1986), pp. 79–208.

32. David Carroll, "*Mimesis* Reconsidered: Literature, History, Ideology," *Diacritics* 5 (Summer 1975): 10. Similarly, Timothy Bahti, in a much more recent essay, deconstructs Auerbach's opposition between prefiguration and fulfillment as "reduplicated in, or more accurately, . . . already implied in, the *figurative* structure of figural interpretation." See Bahti, *Allegories of History: Literary Historiography after Hegel* (Baltimore: Johns Hopkins University Press, 1992), p. 144. Unlike Carroll, Bahti treats Auerbach as a proto-poststructuralist for whom "historical reality is canceled or annihilated in its fulfillment in literature" (p. 155).

33. Carroll, "*Mimesis* Reconsidered," pp. 8–9.

34. Bové, *Intellectuals in Power*, pp. 80–81.

35. Despite this Gallocentrism, one might note that whereas *Mimesis* had appeared in Spanish, English, and Italian translation within a decade after the original edition, a French translation was not issued until 1968.

36. W. Wolfgang Holdheim, *The Hermeneutic Mode: Essays on Time in Literature and Literary Theory* (Ithaca, N.Y.: Cornell University Press, 1984), pp. 211–25. My quotation is from p. 212.

37. Bahti, *Allegories of History*, pp. 145–55.

38. Suzanne Gearhart, *The Interrupted Dialectic: Philosophy, Psychoanalysis, and Their Tragic Other* (Baltimore: Johns Hopkins University Press, 1992), pp. 133–56.

39. Gronau, *Literarische Form und gesellschaftliche Entwicklung*.

40. Walter Höllerer, *Zwischen Klassik und Moderne: Lachen und Weinen in der Dichtung einer Übergangszeit* (Stuttgart: Klett, 1958).

41. Lodge, *20th Century Literary Criticism*, p. 315.

42. Edward Said, *Orientalism* (New York: Pantheon, 1978).

43. Edward Said, *Culture and Imperialism* (New York: Knopf, 1993); page references will be included in my text. Indeed, the influence of Auerbach has been used by one of Said's harshest critics, Aijaz Ahmad, to attack *Orientalism*, which Ahmad sees as "deriving from the ambition to write a counter-history that could be posed against *Mimesis*." See Ahmad, *In Theory: Classes, Nations, Literatures* (London: Verso, 1992), p. 163. Ahmad, writing from a Marxist point of view, locates a "High Humanist" strain in Said's work that he attributes to the influence of Auerbach and to what he labels "Comparative Literature and Philology" (p. 167).

44. Edward Said, *Beginnings: Intention and Method* (New York: Basic Books, 1975). For Said's discussions of Auerbach on this issue, see pp. 68–69, 72–73, 76, 324. For an analysis of Said's relation to Auerbach's notion of the *Ansatzpunkt*, see Bové, *Intellectuals in Power*, pp. 187–91. For a discussion of Auerbach's *Ansatzpunkt* in relation to the German hermeneutic tradition, see W. Wolfgang Holdheim, "The Hermeneutic Significance of Auerbach's *Ansatz*," *New Literary History* 16 (1985): 627–31.

45. Auerbach's essay, first published in 1952 in a festschrift for Fritz Strich, can be found in *Gesammelte Aufsätze zur romanischen Philologie* (Bern: A. Francke, 1967), pp. 301–12. Said's translation, under the title "Philology and *Weltliteratur*," appeared in *Centennial Review* 13 (1969): 1–17. Said's specific references to the ideas in this essay can be found in *Beginnings*, pp. 36, 68–69, 72–73, 76, 324; *Orientalism*, pp. 259–60; *The World, the Text and the Critic* (Cambridge, Mass.: Harvard University Press, 1983), pp. 7–8, 16; *Culture and Imperialism*, pp. 45, 317–18, 335–36.

46. Auerbach, "Philology and *Weltliteratur*," p. 8.

47. Said, *Culture and Imperialism*, p. 47. See also *The World, the Text and the*

Critic, where he complains of readers approaching Auerbach and Spitzer as though they "were rather old-fashioned versions of Brooks or Warren" (pp. 148–49).

48. On his concept of "contrapuntal" reading, see *Culture and Imperialism*, pp. 32, 51, 66–67, 111, 114, 146, 178–79, 194, 259, 279, 318, 336.

49. Quoted by Auerbach in "Philology and *Weltliteratur*," p. 17. Said reproduces this quotation in two of his books, *The World, the Text and the Critic*, p. 7, and *Culture and Imperialism*, p. 335, where Hugo's statement and Said's commentary upon it bring the book to conclusion.

50. One might note that *Culture and Imperialism* is unique among recent scholarly books for being issued not by an academic press but by one of the major New York commercial houses.

Green, "The 'Inner Dream' of Transcendence"

1. Walter Benjamin, "Unpacking My Library," trans. Harry Zohn, in *Illuminations* (New York: Schocken, 1969), p. 59.

2. Jorge Luis Borges, "Borges and I," trans. James E. Irby, in *Labyrinths*, eds. Donald A. Yeates and James E. Irby (New York: New Directions, 1964), pp. 246–47.

3. Borges, "Kafka and His Precursors," trans. James E. Irby, *Labyrinths*, p. 201.

4. Erich Auerbach, *Literary Language and Its Public in Late Latin Antiquity and in the Middle Ages*, trans. Ralph Manheim (Princeton, N.J.: Princeton University Press, 1965), p. 22.

5. Sigmund Freud, "Analysis Terminable and Interminable," in *The Standard Edition of the Complete Psychological Works of Sigmund Freud*, 24 vols., ed. and trans. James Strachey (London: Hogarth, 1953–74), 23:228, 235.

6. Maire Said and Edward Said, introduction to "Philology and *Weltliteratur*," by Erich Auerbach, *Centennial Review* 13, no. 1 (1969): 1.

7. Auerbach, "Philology and *Weltliteratur*," trans. Maire Said and Edward Said, *Centennial Review* 13, no. 1 (1969): 4–5.

8. Vladimir Nabokov, *The Real Life of Sebastian Knight* (New York: New Directions, 1959), pp. 204–5.

9. Auerbach, *Mimesis: The Representation of Reality in Western Literature*, trans. Willard R. Trask (Princeton, N.J.: Princeton University Press, 1953), pp. 547–48.

10. Auerbach, "The Aesthetic Dignity of the *Fleurs du Mal*," trans. Ralph Manheim, in *Scenes from the Drama of European Literature*, (Gloucester, Massachusetts: Peter Smith, 1973), pp. 223, 224, 225.

11. Robert Fitzgerald, *Enlarging the Change: The Princeton Seminars in Literary Criticism, 1949–1951* (Boston: Northeastern University Press, 1985), p. 23.

12. Ibid., p. 26.

13. Benjamin, "Unpacking My Library," p. 59.

14. Nabokov, *The Real Life of Sebastian Knight*, pp. 204–5.

15. Benjamin, "The Storyteller," trans. Harry Zohn, in *Illuminations*, p. 100.

16. Ibid., pp. 108–9.

17. Geoffrey Green, *Literary Criticism and the Structures of History: Erich Auerbach and Leo Spitzer* (Lincoln: University of Nebraska Press, 1982).

Hart, "Literature as Language"

1. Alberto Vàrvaro, *Guida alla Facoltà di Lettere e Filosofia* (Bologna: Il Mulino, 1980), p. 96. All translations are my own unless otherwise noted.

2. "Eine unveröffentlichte Korrespondenz: Erich Auerbach / Werner Krauss," *Beiträge zur romanischen Philologie* 26 (1987): 314–15.

3. "Eine unveröffentlichte Korrespondenz: Erich Auerbach / Werner Krauss," *Beiträge zur romanischen Philologie* 27 (1988): 165.

4. Auerbach, *Introduction aux études de philologie romane* (Frankfurt am Main: Vittorio Klostermann, 1949), p. 9. Guy Daniels's translation, *Introduction to Romance Languages and Literature* (New York: Capricorn Books, 1961), omits the introductory section, "La philologie et ses différentes formes," from which my quotations are taken. Further page references to *Philologie romane* appear in the text.

5. I discuss Spitzer and Jakobson in a review essay on *Representative Essays* and *Language in Literature, Comparative Literature* 41 (1989): 170–76. On Auerbach, see my "Insight and Method: Erich Auerbach," in *Literary Theory and Criticism: Festschrift Presented to René Wellek in Honor of His Eightieth Birthday*, ed. Joseph P. Strelka, 2 vols. (Bern: Peter Lang, 1984), 1:249–65.

6. Roman Jakobson, "Langue and Parole: Code and Message," in his *On Language*, eds. Linda R. Waugh and Monique Monville-Burston (Cambridge, Mass.: Harvard University Press, 1990), pp. 80–109; see especially pp. 104–6.

7. Jakobson, "Problems in the Study of Language and Literature," in his *Language in Literature*, eds. Krystyna Pomorska and Stephen Rudy (Cambridge, Mass.: The Belknap Press of Harvard University Press, 1987), p. 48. Further page references to *Language in Literature* appear in the text.

8. Leo Spitzer, *Representative Essays*, eds. Alban K. Forcione, Herbert Lindenberger, and Madeline Sutherland (Stanford, Calif.: Stanford University Press, 1988), p. 446. Further page references to this work appear in the text.

9. Auerbach, *Literary Language and Its Public in Late Latin Antiquity and in the Middle Ages*, trans. Ralph Manheim, Bollingen Series 74 (New York: Pantheon Books, 1965), p. 20. Further page references to *Literary Language* appear in the text.

10. I am grateful to Professor Gumbrecht for making available to me a copy of his paper "Erich Auerbach's Everydays," presented at the Stanford

Auerbach Symposium in October, 1992, together with photocopies of much of the material on which his paper is based.

11. Karlheinz Baeck, "Fünf Briefe Erich Auerbachs an Walter Benjamin in Paris," *Zeitschrift für Germanistik* 6 (1988): 691.

12. Ibid., p. 692.

13. In *Weltliteratur: Festgabe für Fritz Strich* (Bern: A. Francke, 1952).

14. See Spitzer, *Representative Essays*, pp. 329–56; Jakobson, *Language in Literature*, p. 70.

15. René Wellek, *A History of Modern Criticism, 1750–1950*, vol. 7, *German, Russian and East European Criticism, 1900–1950* (New Haven, Conn.: Yale University Press, 1991), pp. 119, 122. For the equation of literature with works of fiction, see René Wellek and Austin Warren, *Theory of Literature* (New York: Harcourt, Brace, 1949), p. 16.

16. Auerbach, *Zur Technik der Frührenaissancenovelle in Italien und Frankreich* (Heidelberg: Carl Winter, 1921).

17. Wellek, *A History of Modern Criticism, 1750–1950*, vol. 8, *French, Italian and Spanish Criticism 1900–1950* (New Haven, Conn.: Yale University Press, 1993), p. 123.

18. Quoted in English in Lionel Gossman, *Between History and Literature* (Cambridge, Mass.: Harvard University Press, 1990), p. 278.

19. Roman Jakobson and Krystyna Pomorska, *Dialogues* (Cambridge, Mass.: MIT Press, 1983).

20. Auerbach, *Mimesis: The Representation of Reality in Western Literature*, trans. Willard R. Trask (Princeton, N.J.: Princeton University Press, 1953), p. 298. Further page references to *Mimesis* appear in the text.

21. Louis O. Mink, *Historical Understanding*, eds. Brian Fay, Eugene O. Golob, and Richard T. Vann (Ithaca, N.Y.: Cornell University Press, 1987), pp. 11–13.

22. Robert Alter, *Partial Magic: The Novel as a Self-conscious Genre* (Berkeley: University of California Press, 1975), p. ix.

23. Auerbach, "Epilegomena zu *Mimesis*," *Romanische Forschungen* 65 (1953): 16.

24. I discuss Spitzer's interpretation in "¿Cervantes perspectivista?" *Nueva revista de filología hispánica* 40 (1992): 293–303.

25. Montaigne, "Of the Inconsistency of Our Actions," in *The Complete Works*, trans. Donald Frame (Stanford, Calif.: Stanford University Press, 1958), pp. 239–40.

26. Wellek, *History of Modern Criticism*, 8:173.

27. "The Aesthetic Dignity of the *Fleurs du mal*," *Scenes from the Drama of European Literature* (Minneapolis: University of Minnesota Press, 1984), pp. 201–26. The essay first appeared in German in 1951.

28. Brownlee, "The Ideology of Periodization," p. 158.

29. *Gesammelte Aufsätze zur romanischen Philologie* (Bern: A. Francke, 1967), p. 303. I thank my colleague Steven F. Rendall for a careful reading of this essay and suggestions for its improvement.

Index

In this index an "f" after a number indicates a separate reference on the next page, and an "ff" indicates separate references on the next two pages. A continuous discussion over two or more pages is indicated by a span of page numbers, e.g., "57–58." *Passim* is used for a cluster of references in close but not consecutive sequence.

Library of Congress Cataloging-in-Publication Data

Literary history and the challenge of philology : the legacy of Erich
    Auerbach / edited by Seth Lerer.
        p.   cm. — (Figurae)
    Includes index.
    ISBN 0-8047-2545-4 (alk. paper)
    1. Auerbach, Erich, 1892–1957.   2. Philology.   3. Literature—
History and criticism—Theory, etc.   4. Language and history.
5. Literature and history.   I. Lerer, Seth, 1955–   .   II. Series:
Figurae (Stanford, Calif.)
P85.A87L58   1996
809'.912–dc20   95-10992
                                                                      CIP
                                                                      REV

∞ This book is printed on acid-free, recycled paper.

Original printing 1996
Last figure below indicates year of this printing:
05   04   03   02   01   00   99   98   97   96